ALSO BY JOSHUA DUBLER

Bang! Thud: World Spirit from a
Texas School Book Depository (with Andrea Sun-Mee Jones)

DOWN IN THE CHAPEL

DOWN IN THE CHAPEL

RELIGIOUS LIFE IN
AN AMERICAN PRISON

•

JOSHUA DUBLER

FARRAR, STRAUS AND GIROUX   NEW YORK

Farrar, Straus and Giroux
18 West 18th Street, New York 10011

Copyright © 2013 by Joshua Dubler
Map copyright © 2013 by Jeffrey L. Ward
All rights reserved
Printed in the United States of America
First edition, 2013

Grateful acknowledgment is made to the Pennsylvania Department of Corrections
for permission to reprint the Sermon of "Reverend Baumgartner" on pages 319–325.

Library of Congress Cataloging-in-Publication Data
Dubler, Joshua.
   Down in the chapel : religious life in an American prison / Joshua
Dubler. — First edition.
      pages   cm
   Includes bibliographical references and index.
   ISBN 978-0-374-12070-2 (alk. paper)
   1. Prisoners—Religious life—Pennsylvania—Graterford.   2. Graterford
State Correctional Institution.   I. Title.

BV4595 .D83 2013
200.9748'12—dc23

2012048079

Designed by Jonathan D. Lippincott

Farrar, Straus and Giroux books may be purchased for educational, business, or
promotional use. For information on bulk purchases, please contact the Macmillan
Corporate and Premium Sales Department at 1-800-221-7945, extension 5442, or
write to specialmarkets@macmillan.com.

www.fsgbooks.com
www.twitter.com/fsgbooks • www.facebook.com/fsgbooks

1   3   5   7   9   10   8   6   4   2

Author's note: This is a true account, though some
names and details have been changed.

To the lifers

The judge sentenced me to this institution, but I've chosen to follow the Quaker path . . . and live in the penitentiary.   —Teddy

We have brothers who struggle because they're still carrying the dead man on their back. Back when we came into the love of God and the relationship grows, the things God doesn't like are dismissed. That's how we don't do the things that we used to do.   —Al

The Creator made the world and said: *Have at it, fellas.*   —Baraka

CONTENTS

Preface   xi

Map   xv

Approved Activities Schedule   xvi

The Men of Graterford's Chapel   xix

MONDAY   3

TUESDAY   43

WEDNESDAY   97

THURSDAY   157

FRIDAY   205

SATURDAY   267

SUNDAY   309

Notes   327

Acknowledgments   357

Index   359

PREFACE
THURSDAY, FEBRUARY 16, 2006

Baraka warned me against talking to Al about such things. And yet, only weeks later, I arrive in the office to find the two old friends warring over God's Word and how we come to know it. Al's enormous frame is hunched behind his desk, disquietingly still. Baraka sits opposite him, riding the desk still referred to as Sayyid's, though by now everyone pretty much accepts that Sayyid isn't coming back. Teddy is reclining in his desk chair by the window, exuding impishness. I grab an empty seat and catch myself up.[1]

In Al's perspective, because God is a loving God, He wants to be understood and so grants man unmediated access to His Word. For Baraka, by contrast, God's mind is knowable only via a tenuous chain of custody, one that stretches from the prophets, to the scribes, to the compilers who endowed certain accounts with the seal of authority. For Baraka, then, placing faith in Scripture means trusting other men. For Al, faith requires circumventing man's machinations and trusting only in God.

To find Baraka and Al at opposite ends of a religious dispute should come as little surprise, but not simply because Baraka is a Muslim and Al is a Christian. In the chapel, as it turns out, such boundaries are far less decisive than I had initially assumed. Rather, if this morning's clash reveals a chasm between the two men, it is less a matter of creed than of temperament. Baraka is intellectually playful, a lover of ideas and debate, and a great believer in the power of the mind. Nothing riles Baraka like genuflection before orthodoxy, whatever its standard. As one of the politically minded graybeards who came of age in the Nation of Islam before the movement collectively converted to Sunni

Islam in 1975, Baraka sees in the Qur'an and the Bible not so much rigid formulae for serving God as catalogs of time-tested strategies for individual and collective improvement. It's an approach that, in Al's judgment, can't possibly yield anything good. For Al, because the human is rotten to the core, the intellect can only lead him astray. Through God's abundant love, however, the Holy Spirit delivers the truth of the Word directly to the believer's heart and elevates him to a moral plateau he couldn't possibly achieve on his own. Mulish in his convictions, and not only in matters of ultimate concern, Al is alternatively capable of unnerving fury and disarming love—a fury that hints at the monster Al says he used to be, and a love I'm tempted to call Christian, though Al would not, since if Jesus wanted His followers to call themselves "Christians," He would have told them so himself.

Baraka holds up a softbound New Testament that he must have pulled off the bookshelf. "Who put this book together?" he asks Al.

"Man did!" Teddy barks. "I know, because my sister works in a bookshop!"

"The Holy Ghost," Al says, accustomed to tuning out the noise.

"And what about the Council of Nicaea?" Baraka asks. "What about the process of canonization?"

"That's what *they* did," Al says. The *they* here is the Roman Catholic Church—a manmade entity, which, for Al, has little overlap with the transhistorical band of Jesus' true followers he calls "the body of Christ."

"But didn't *they* put it together?" Baraka presses.

"No, not the body of Christ."

Baraka elevates an eyebrow. "Then where do you get this information from?" He points to the Bible.

"The Holy Ghost," Al says, still unmoved.

Never one to feign understanding, Baraka doesn't get it now, either. "So let me get this straight. You recite stuff that's in *their* book, but—"

Al cuts him off. "That's *them*. I know what the Holy Ghost said."

"And how do you know?"

"I know because of the Holy Spirit."

With prosecutorial coyness, Baraka cocks his head to the side. "And yet you read the exact same book."

"Look. I'm not part of that there. That's the birth of something else."

"But you recite verbatim what *they* wrote!"

"It's not about what they *wrote*. It's inspiration."

Baraka tries a different tack. "And what about the books that didn't make it into the canon. They real?"

"No."

"And how do you know?

"Because the Holy Spirit shows it to me."

"The Holy Spirit shows you the whole truth?"

"Yes. The whole truth of the Word."

Teddy sits up, suddenly earnest. "Look," he explains. "We don't know everything about God. But we know what the sixty-six books say."

"But you've got it all in English!" Baraka objects.

"I don't know what language He talks to *you* in," Al snaps.

Springing himself off Sayyid's desk, Baraka crosses the cramped room in two steps, flips open the Bible, turns it over, and places it in front of Al. He points to a line. "What does *that* say?"

Al reads from what I will later determine to be Isaiah's vision of Zion's destruction: "*Your country lies desolate, your cities are burned with fire; in your very presence aliens devour your land; it is desolate, as overthrown by foreigners.*"[2]

"Thank you," Baraka says. He snatches back the Bible and crisply returns to Sayyid's desk. "Now, what language is *that*?"

Staring down his old friend, Al answers a different question. "But *why* does the country lie desolate? Because of man's disobedience." That is to say, I take it, because of arrogant inquiries of precisely this sort. At which point, feeling that Al's indictment is directed as much at me as at Baraka, I break my silence and jump in.

Baraka, Al, and Teddy—these are not their real names, but over time they have come to suit them fine. Each works in the chapel at Pennsylvania's Graterford Prison: Baraka as a clerk, Al as an audio-video technician and Teddy as a janitor. Baraka is a Muslim, and Al and Teddy are Christians. Each grew up in South Philadelphia, and each was convicted of homicide. Baraka and Al are in their early fifties, while Teddy is a decade their junior. Teddy has been at Graterford since the nineties, Al since the eighties, and Baraka since the seventies. As is true of roughly two-thirds of Graterford's 3,500 residents, all three men are black.[3] Like a quarter, the three men are lifers, which in Pennsylvania means just that.[4] Barring a change in the law, a revision to administrative procedure, or a legal miracle, all three will die in prison. As for me, I'm far more transient. By now more or less a secular Jew, I've been in the chapel for a year, researching my dissertation—research that, in time, will grow into this book.

This book tells the story of one week's time in Graterford's chapel. It recounts seven days during which two prison guards, five chaplains, fifteen prisoner workers, a score of outside volunteers, and hundreds of religious adherents frequent the chapel to work, pray, study, and play. Driven by characters in conversation, this book offers a mosaic of the ritual and banter through which the men at Graterford pass their time, care for their selves, foster relationships, and commune with their makers, among a variety of other activities earnest and absurdist, quotidian and momentous. Inescapably, it is also the story of what happens when an interloper, in the form of a visiting scholar of religion, is thrown into this mix with the hope of making sense of it all. As such, while this book is an exploration of doing time and doing religion in contemporary America, it is simultaneously a chronicle of the tangled process by which one comes to know things through dialogue with other people.

Within and beyond the week at hand, the book struggles with questions of faith and doubt, authority and license, freedom and fidelity, and the demands of the ethical life, whether lived with or without relation to God. Navigating this thicket with my interlocutors at Graterford also requires working through the competing reflexes by which religious prisoners are alternatively scorned as liars or pitied as casualties. By taking these reductive impulses themselves as objects of inquiry, I hope to think through and, fortune permitting, trouble prevalent assumptions about prisoners and religion both—assumptions that are caught up in a host of systemic American injustices.

Like the exchange above, the events that follow are, in their way, wholly ordinary, but no less astonishing for that. Is it not truly bizarre how unremarkable it has become that for so many Americans—black men, especially—the practice of religion takes place in spaces like these?[5]

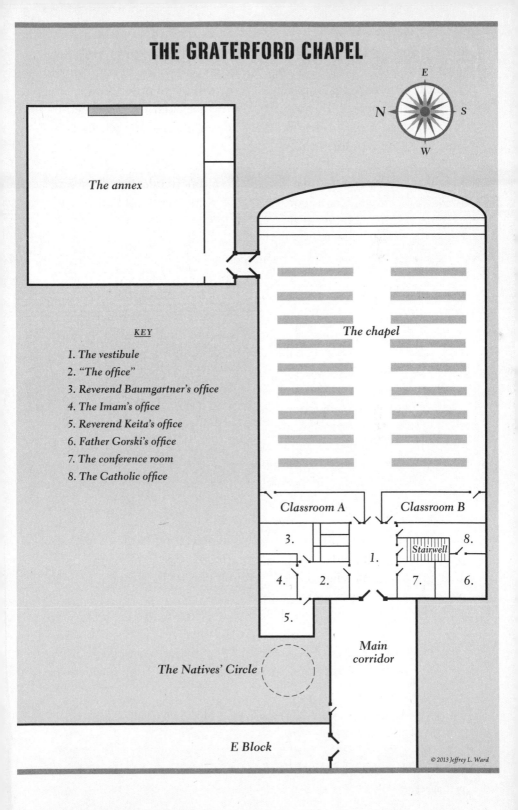

THE GRATERFORD CHAPEL

The annex

KEY

1. The vestibule
2. "The office"
3. Reverend Baumgartner's office
4. The Imam's office
5. Reverend Keita's office
6. Father Gorski's office
7. The conference room
8. The Catholic office

The chapel

Classroom A

Classroom B

3.

8.

Stairwell

1.

4. 2.

7. 6.

5.

The Natives' Circle

Main corridor

E Block

© 2013 Jeffrey L. Ward

APPROVED ACTIVITIES SCHEDULE—THE GRATERFORD CHAPEL

A House of Prayer for All Peoples

		CHAPEL	ANNEX
MONDAY	8:30		
	1:00		
	6:00		
TUESDAY	8:30	Blues Bible study	
	1:00		Talim (Muslim study)
	6:00	Yokefellows Bible study	Jewish study
WEDNESDAY	8:30	Muhammad's Temple	
	1:00	Memorial service	
	6:00		Talim (Muslim study)
THURSDAY	8:30	Nation of Islam	
	1:00		
	6:00	Spanish service	Interfaith
FRIDAY	8:30		Moorish Science Temple
	1:00		Muslim Jum'ah
	6:00	*Protestant choir*	Jewish Sabbath
SATURDAY	8:30	Spanish Bible study	Jewish Sabbath
	1:00	Seventh-Day Adventists	
	6:00	Catholic mass	
SUNDAY	8:30	Protestant service	
	1:00		
	6:00		

Italics: Musical rehearsals.

- A chaplain must be in the institution for any religious activity to meet or any religious volunteer to be admitted.
- Chapel procedures as approved and posted are to be complied with at all times.
- No group may meet without the supervision of a chaplain or approved volunteer.
- No unscheduled groups may meet without written permission of the Facilities Chaplaincy Program Director.

CLASSROOM A	CLASSROOM B	CONFERENCE ROOM
St. Dismas Episcopal	Jehovah's Witnesses	
	Catholic study	Video Ministry
		Spanish band
Education for Ministry		
	Jehovah's Witnesses	
Liberty Ministries study		
Native American service	Ushers	*Keepers of the Faith*
Baptism class		*Mighty Way*
		Gospel Messengers
Legion of Mary rosary		*Catholic choir*
Catholic Devotions		*True Vine*
		Christian Science

- No scheduled groups may change meeting location without permission of the Chaplain on duty.
- You may arrange an appointment for personal or spiritual counsel by submitting an Inmate Request to one of the chaplains. You will receive a pass for your assigned time.
- All approved Chapel programs can be attended by way of regular activity line movement when Chapel is called.

THE MEN OF GRATERFORD'S CHAPEL

THE CHAPEL WORKERS
Muslims
Baraka
Omar
Sayyid
Kazi
Mamduh
Muti

Protestants[1]
Al
Teddy
Papa
Santana

Catholics
Jack
Mike

Jews
Brian
David

An Atheist
Vic

CHAPLAINS
Reverend Baumgartner
Imam Namir
Chaplain Keita
Father Gorski
The Rabbi

CORRECTIONAL OFFICERS
Watkins
Bird

ETHNOGRAPHER
Josh

DOWN IN THE CHAPEL

MONDAY

Graterford Prison is in Pennsylvania's Montgomery County, thirty snaking miles northwest of Philadelphia's city line. The prison sits on a bucolic plateau of 1,700 acres that rises above the Perkiomen Creek. Fallow farmland runs uphill away from the creek, where, seasonally, deer and Canada geese lounge unmolested. At the top of the rise beside a small reservoir is the OSU, the Outside Service Unit, which houses the "grays," who are misconduct free and creeping up on their minimums. Past the parking lots is the prison itself, sixty-two acres enclosed behind a thirty-foot-high nine-sided wall. Atop the wall, armed sentries man turrets from which, on a sunny afternoon, they can watch the grays play handball against the outside of the wall. Past the creek and across the valley, one sees the billowing silos of the Limerick nuclear power plant. To the south, the big-box stores inch closer by the year, but even from atop the wall, there is, I imagine, little evidence of that.

Though barely, it is still country here. On a summer evening, at leaving time, when the baseball game waiting for me in the car will be in the fourth or fifth and the cobalt heavens bleed to orange over the valley, this place is not unbeautiful. But in winter, when the wind pushes up from the valley, driving rain and snow sideways into the worn concrete of the wall's outer shell, the prison feels suddenly like a refuge and the world outside apathetic and grim, a place for coyotes and bears, but not remotely suited for men.

Declared "state of the art" when it opened in 1931, Graterford is by now a relic of an era gone by: clunky, decrepit, and unconducive to orderliness.[1] Five two-tiered cellblocks, each of which houses 500 men, feed into a central corridor that runs from the front gate to the heart of the prison.[2] To the right, past the hospital and the "new side" dorms, come the shop floors, the auditorium, the school wing, and the field house. At the corridor's terminus lies the chapel.

With its fluorescent light, yellow brick walls, crushed stone floor, and acrid odor, the main corridor could well be the hallway of my high school were it not pushing a quarter of a mile long—a span broken by locked gates manned by uniformed guards with whom I exchange good-mornings as I pass. Past the security bubble at the second gate, I step to the right to avoid a correctional officer leading a train of fifty orange-clad "jumpsuits," the system's new processees.

"I've got two words for you: job security," the CO says to the gate-keeper.

"*Chugga-chugga chugga-chugga,*" chants the CO at the caboose.

The COs couldn't care less if I heard them, and I don't flatter my-self by pretending otherwise. Absent the slate-colored band on the ID clipped to my lapel, there's no telling me from any of the jail's other civilian-clothed employees, whether administrator, counselor, support staff, or vendor. Nor am I on edge. Come and go a few times and Grater-ford is not a hard place to feel invisible. Presuming, that is, that you're not a woman.

With movements already over, the odd burgundy-clad prisoner scurries this way or that, a bit late to work, to the hospital, to counseling, to someplace else. "Browns" is what, for the earthy color of their uni-forms, these general-population prisoners are called. At the entrance to A Block, I bump into Omar, who flashes me a gummy smile. He's been thinking about me, he says. When I ask him why, he says he'll come down and let me know just as soon as he gets himself some teeth.

Between B and C, I come upon Mamduh, another chapel worker, with his young companion, Nasir, at his hip. Quiet, if not soft-spoken, Mamduh, who is from North Philadelphia, has sharp eyes and a scrag-gly beard that covers most of his pockmarked face, and he looks older than the 1961 birth date claimed by the ID he once showed me to prove it. During the Tuesday-afternoon and Wednesday-night activity blocks, when the Muslims are slotted for the annex, Mamduh instructs a small group of men in Arabic language and grammar.

Mamduh encourages me to come to his Ethics of War class, to take place at 1:30 in the school. The class is an offering of Villanova's Associate's Degree Program, which the nearby Catholic university has run for over a generation. Many of the chapel workers and regulars are also college students in the Villanova Program, an overlap that contributes to the commonly shared perception of this cadre as being among the most serious men in the jail.

I won't make it to the school, I tell Mamduh, but I'll be sure to catch him later on. As Mamduh recedes, I notice him limping and wonder if something happened over the weekend or whether this isn't simply the way he walks, one more thing that in my overfamiliarity I've come to overlook.

The side yard between C and D blocks is empty at this early hour, as is the chain-link enclosure beyond E Block, where the "blues" have their yard.

The chapel door is unlocked.

Watkins, an African-American correctional officer from nearby Phoenixville, is perched at his desk, his elbows splayed and his arched hands clasped. A navy-blue PA DOC baseball cap is perched high on his forehead, its bent brim low. Weekends were good, we establish. Without apparent agenda, Watkins asks me if I've been to church as of late.

"Sure," I say, pointing downward. "Here. Almost every day."

"What about on the outside?" he asks. "Synagogue or anything?"

I signal the negative. And though I've been a thrice-a-year Jew for a decade, I add, apologetically, "These things go in cycles."

Watkins empathizes. "It *has to be* that way," he says.

While Watkins has long since stopped taking too much notice of my comings and goings, I warn him that he's likely to see a fair amount of me in the weeks ahead. For an intended chapter recounting a week in the life of the chapel, I explain that I'm going to be here all day, every day this week, instead of the three to four partial days that is my normal pattern. Watkins nods his head, squints his eyes, and asks—or suggests—in a hushed voice, if, when I'm done, I'm going to "break him off a piece." I don't understand.

He looks me in the eye and clarifies: "What's my cut for the movie going to be?"

While no small number of prisoners have me pegged in some way or another as a mark, most commonly one heaven-sent by a meddling deity as part of His plan to secure their freedom, it has been the chapel's correctional officers who have been most overt in their plays for financial remuneration for their participation in my research. Watkins's predecessor tried to solicit my bid for his notebooks documenting twenty years of salacious goings-on in the jail, but Watkins has hitched his cart to my project's movie-rights star.

I play along. "Fifty-fifty," I promise him in deadpan. "Just you and me." Apparently finding the terms favorable, Watkins purses his lips and nods.

In the opposite corner of the vestibule, the maroon-clad Jack has a bottle of Windex in his right hand, a wad of paper towel in his left, and is scrubbing the small, square window in the door to the Catholic suite. Jack, who in the past has stated his preference that the role of Jack be played by George Clooney (though Watkins, with a colder eye, suggests *Seinfeld's* Jason Alexander to be a better match), is a short, bald, bulbous-headed Irish-American in his late forties. Jack works as a chapel janitor and helps out Father Gorski in the Catholic office. As has Mamduh, Jack has been scrupulous in bringing to my attention people and things to which he thinks I should attend, once going so far as to attempt to schedule a rendezvous with an Aryan Nation guy he knows from the block. As he assured me, while the two of them get along fine, they are in no way aligned. "I wouldn't want to be a member of any master race that would have me for a member," Jack explained. Proposing that I blow him instead, the Nazi declined.

Jack looks at me with puzzlement. "There are no services on Mondays," he says. Translation: What the hell are *you* doing here?

I explain.

"So what goes on on Mondays?" I ask.

"A lot of this," he says, holding up his Windex. Jack edges over to tell me about a book he read over the weekend—a biography of the founder of the Knights of Columbus, the Catholic fraternal organization.[3] I ask Jack whose book it is. It's his, he explains, but the guys in the Catholic community will all pass it around. They do the same with the *National Review*, he adds leadingly, digging at our political differences. Affecting a mock conspiratorial air, Jack looks behind each shoulder before saying that he could slip the book to me, just as sometime back he'd lent me a right-wing radio talk-show host's political-conversion memoir. Affecting the same air, I ask him to please do just that.[4]

Jack can be alternately magnanimous or dyspeptic. He often seems hungry for exchange, but he tends to lead with a jagged edge. His rage is channeled primarily through the culture war in whose stark light I'm an America-hating, Israel-betraying, homosexual-agenda-pushing cancer on our great nation. When politics fails, Jack falls back on sports, where my New York allegiances align me, again, with the forces of evil. Jack likes to bait, and more often than not I'm happy to be baited. Together we walk from the vestibule into the chapel. He offers me some coffee, which I decline, saying that I need to be mindful because I haven't been sleeping.

"Liberal guilt!" Jack diagnoses, and walks away. The truth is that I'm jet-lagged from a trip overseas, but this I do not advertise.

Jack returns with a peace offering: "I don't know if this will help you, but you know how they say how there're no atheists in the foxhole? Well, when I was arrested, the first person I asked to talk to was a priest." After a slight hesitation, Jack says it's on his mind since he only recently learned of the priest's passing.

Following mass on Saturday night, Jack further informs me, they convened the first installment of the monthly Spanish-language Bible study. I'm pleased to hear it, I tell Jack, because I know Father Gorski has been trying to get something like that off the ground. Jack underscores the alienation the Spanish-speaking Catholics feel at the English-language mass.

"So you're losing them all to the Evangelicals?" I ask, presuming that developments at Graterford accord with wider cultural trends.[5]

Jack grimaces playfully.

There has been a lightness to Jack of late. I know he's recently doubled his dose of Prozac, which has drawn some color back into his cheeks. Meanwhile, he's also been edging toward coming out of the closet as a Christian Scientist. He has been confessing his divided allegiance to me since I first arrived at the prison, but has yet to tell his father or sister. And though it's been years since official policy restricted a prisoner to the religious services of the group with which he is administratively identified, and while to my knowledge no one is forcing him to choose, Jack is conflicted. From the time he first picked it up eighteen months earlier, he has found in Mary Baker Eddy's *Science and Health* a powerful witness that fills him with hope and makes him feel like he's finally getting some things under control. But as much as he enjoys his

Sunday studies and the visits of his spiritual advisor, Jack—a perennial altar boy—worries that he is neglecting the Virgin Mary and therefore dishonoring the memory of his mother. So he gives equal time to his Catholic observances, especially to counting the rosary, when Jack likes to focus on Mary's assumption to heaven and the grace of a happy death.

Religious boundary crossing of Jack's sort is, in the chapel, hardly unusual, but it is generally cast as a passing phase. Sure, one is free to sample and search, but ultimately, as Jack would be the first to tell you, a man must choose. And so, in pursuit of coherence as much as grace, Jack experiences his balancing act as a stopgap, a hedging of bets before he takes his money off the table and settles back into his life as a Catholic or lets it ride on the healing Jesus he's come to know through the Church of Christ, Scientist.[6]

Baraka jerks his head over his right shoulder, fixes on my eyes, registers surprise, and saunters into the chapel with his hand outstretched. "So," he asks with a cock of his head and an interrogative flick of his wrist, "what's going on?"

Save for a narrow ridge of goatee, Baraka is clean-shaven, and his tiger-print glasses frame his almond eyes. Often, as today, his browns are almost pink, an ancient vintage prized for its softer fabric, and by now worn almost to parchment. Baraka is the Imam's clerk and my most crucial interlocutor. (For different reasons, he and I both are made uneasy by the classical anthropological term *informant*.)[7] In practice, he might well be my dissertation advisor. Most crucially, Baraka is the person I commonly consult to make sense of what is real and what is not in this strange place. It is a need that Baraka alternately satisfies and thwarts. With his conviction that "things are far more simple than they appear," Baraka sells me on the importance of reading surfaces. This clarifying interpretive principle, however, is wholly at odds with a second position Baraka advocates with equal insistence: that "*everything one sees in here is real*" (and therefore dicey), the feints and dodges no less so than the brutally honest confessions.

To his question of "So what's going on?" I answer that I have insomnia. With sarcasm, he asks if I'm anxious. Confronted with the same formula last week, I'd misguidedly confessed to being preoccupied with concerns over where my paycheck was to come from come

July, in particular whether I'm going to get the job at the nearby college for which I've been shortlisted. Baraka greeted my disclosure of academic job-market anxiety with equal measures of incredulity and intolerance, berating me for being "like a cork in the ocean."

Like many of the chapel regulars, Baraka preaches the virtues of self-mastery. "If you don't have mastery over yourself, then you're just reacting," he has said. The consequences of which, in a place like Graterford, are dire, since "just reacting will get you killed." For Baraka, controlling the body begins with the regulation of one's thoughts. He has little patience for those who fixate on what they've done, what they've lost, or where they might be headed when they die. Get stuck in one of those traps, he's said, "and I'm useless to myself and to anyone else."[8]

This is the week, I tell Baraka, and reconfirm that he remains willing to be my supplementary eyes and ears. Baraka nods and asks me what I'm hoping to "catch as I slide down the slope." I don't understand what he means.

He rephrases his question: "What are you hoping to get out of it?" I shrug my shoulders and bite my lip, and Baraka nods once more.

The experiment is hardly an arbitrary one. It was geared to get at the chapel's stunning range of religious practices, a *variety*—to echo the immortal William James—for which a seven-day span of time is an apt showcase. On any given week, the chapel plays host to thirteen recognized religious groups whose members convene more than forty weekly assemblies, including worship services, textual studies, devotional groups, and musical rehearsals, activities that draw between a quarter and a third of the prison's residents. In addition to the predominant Muslims and Protestants, Catholics and Jews share time and space here, as do Episcopalians, Seventh-Day Adventists, Christian Scientists and Jehovah's Witnesses, adherents to the black nationalist religions such as the Nation of Islam, Muhammad's Temple, and the Moorish Science Temple, and practitioners of Native American spirituality. In short, in the fecund coexistence of its many ways of religious life, Graterford's chapel is, among other things, a wonder of American religious pluralism, or (as I hyperbolically italicized it in a preliminary report to my Princeton advisors): *arguably the most religiously eclectic sliver of real estate in the history of the world.*[9]

In response, one advisor suggested for a possible opening chapter a narrative retelling of one week's time in the chapel.[10] It struck me as an excellent idea. Hoping for a "normal" week, for months I waited. November and December passed, and with them the heightened intensities of Sunni Ramadan, the Nation of Islam's Ramadan, and the sentimental morass of the Christmas season. Returning last week after two away, I found the iron to be sufficiently cool.

I ask Baraka about his back, which I know has been bothering him of late, but he brushes off my inquiry. He's been working on his case, he says, and mentions a federal decision handed down on Friday that might have a favorable bearing. "You mean *Collins?*" I ask. Baraka is impressed. I explain that I'd heard Brian talking about it on Saturday. Brian, the Rabbi's clerk, is the chapel's top legal mind.

Baraka unfurls a printout of the case and begins to leaf through it, absentmindedly conceding as he does that actually it's Brian's and that he has to give it back to him in a minute, which is fine because Brian is fussy and it's easier to cater to his fussiness now than to have to hurt him later on when fuss comes to shove. Intuiting that the copy in Baraka's hands is the only one around, I say that I understand how quickly the introduction of an object of desire can lead to bloodshed. Bar looks up, flares his nostrils, scowls, and promises that he won't hurt Brian, though of course he could. This is all shtick, I have every reason to suspect. For a few minutes we sit in silence, he reading, me writing. In the rear corners of the chapel, fans whir. The lights are on, casting the wan glow of fluorescent light in a cavernous space on an overcast day.

Depending on where one is standing in the jail, "the chapel" can refer either to the entire chapel complex or, more specifically, to its centerpiece, the airy ecumenical sanctuary where Baraka and I are currently sitting. From pacing it out, I would guess it to be 110 feet long and 70 feet wide, a space filled with twenty-two rows of weathered wooden pews, conventionally cut with aisles down the center and at the margins. The brick walls are regularly broken by wooden panels, which run floor to cciling and encase a terraced array of Plexiglas boxes colored in pastels of pink, lavender, and lemon. Roughly thirty-five feet up, a lowered ceiling implies a function as much acoustic as aesthetic. In the front, an unassuming dais, carpeted in speckled red and black, rises two shallow steps from the chapel's salt-and-pepper floor. Centered at the front of the dais, a raised square is flanked with a haphazard array of chairs, amplifiers, and potted plants. In the wood veneer cradling the altar from behind, a knowing eye can detect how a rotary stage used to accommodate a week's succession of sacraments—although, for security reasons, it's been a decade since it last turned.

Teddy seems perturbed. Upon seeing me through the propped-open chapel doors, he performs pained convulsions on my behalf. Standing hands on hips, Teddy lays into me: How can I come in here and not stop by the office to say hello? He means, when exactly was I planning on stopping in to let them know I was here? He means, Sheez! He turns and walks away. Because Teddy, when he's feeling all right, is a cutup, I can't tell if his protestations of neglect are playacting or expressive of something closer to the bone. Jump-started in whichever case, I follow Teddy into what the Protestant and Muslim chapel workers know simply as "the office."

Excepting the aged, the infirm, and the mental-health cases housed on the new side, most of Graterford's browns work some sort of job, labor for which they are compensated at between nineteen and forty-two cents an hour. At twenty-five to thirty hours a week, that adds up to between $30 and $60 per month, with most of the chapel workers earning at the upper end of this spectrum. Guys with jobs on one of the Correctional Industries factory floors, where at Graterford they manufacture shirts, pants, boots, and underwear for distribution throughout the DOC system, are eligible for production-based bonuses that can boost their salaries to over $130 a month. The chapel workers make less than half that, but theirs are coveted positions, offering the opportunity of relatively easy labor in an environment commonly regarded as the most humane in the jail. Whereas other browns may come down to the chapel only for formal activities or when summoned by a chaplain's slip, the chapel workers are allowed in the chapel whenever it's open, and, once there, they are afforded the time and space to pursue their intellectual and spiritual interests. Consequently, the chapel workers tend to be religiously active long-term prisoners, men known and respected by the chaplains who have actively petitioned for their posts. Of the current roster of fifteen clerks and janitors, all but one is serving life, presumably for homicide.[11] As for religious affiliation, Reverend Baumgartner does his best to maintain something approaching denominational parity. As of now, there are six Muslims, four Protestants, a pair of Catholics, a pair of Jews, and one atheist.

While the chapel's workers were initially reserved, within a couple of months of my arrival discussions with Baraka and Al were taking up pages in my field notes. They seemingly warmed to me as one would to a quirky new colleague in an otherwise tedious job, and by now, if I judge it correctly, my presence has for them simply become part of the way things are. As for me, in spite of the radical differences of setting and circumstance that make my encounters here so compelling, by now the office's daily rhythms of integrated work and play don't feel any more unfamiliar than does killing time with my own coterie back in my office at Princeton.

Kazi and Sayyid have books open on their desks. Kazi is reading a text-book about race and the criminal justice system. Sayyid, translating a text from the Arabic, is thumbing through a dog-eared English-Arabic dictionary.

At a classificatory distance, Sayyid and Kazi could be interchange-able. Both are black South Philadelphians pushing forty. Both are chapel janitors, Villanova students, and practicing Muslims—specifically, of the legalistic variant of Islam known as Salafism, which is popular at Graterford. Like Mamduh, Sayyid and Kazi signal this allegiance by means of three prominent physical markers: their beards (Sayyid's is full, if somewhat wispy, while Kazi sports a thick gray goatee); the white cloth kufis that they wear low on their foreheads; and their pant legs, which are hemmed high at the top of the ankle in an Arabian fashion.

Size alone—Sayyid stands a stocky six feet and Kazi is half a foot shorter—could make them a comedy duo, which, in a way, they are. Sayyid is rambunctious and capable of voluminous badgering, often directed at Kazi. By contrast, Kazi is unwaveringly placid, contributing, no doubt, to his reputation for being perhaps a little too well adapted to the prison environment. In office dynamics, Sayyid and Kazi can often be counted on for a laugh, with Sayyid playing the provocateur and Kazi roped as the straight man. For weeks prior to the present one, for example, a clipped *National Geographic* photo had been taped onto the locker in the office that houses the cleaning supplies. The photo depicted an Australian mole rat—labeled as such—its sole bottom fang bared belligerently upward. In a dialogue balloon someone had pen-ciled: "My name is Big Kaz . . . and I aint going to the hole no more."

The cartoon commemorated two things, both at Kaz's expense: first, the uncanny similarity in appearance between Kazi and the Australian rodent; and second, Kaz's recent return to work following thirty days in the RHU, the Restricted Housing Unit, after getting jumped in his cell. In such incidents, the administration does not distinguish between aggressor and victim, relegating both parties to disciplinary custody and its twenty-three-hours-a-day lockdown; but because Kazi was reportedly not the one at fault, Reverend Baumgartner has allowed him to keep his job. As far as the rat prank was concerned, while opportunity, motive, and craft all pointed in Sayyid's direction, Sayyid bullishly withstood the off-and-on attempts to secure his confession, chuckling now and again at the aptness of the caricature but never wavering in his declarations of innocence.

Al lumbers through the door and plants himself in his chair. Pushing 300 pounds, Al has the mien of a bulldog, and a drawl that attests to childhood summers with his grandma in Georgia. Al handles the chapel's AV requirements and fronts a gospel group. Still capable of searing intensity in spite of his years, Al is the sort of person whose presence changes a room. The office is never more fun than when Al is playful, just as it is never as tense as when Al is brooding. As if trapped in Al's orbit, a bunch of secondary characters follow him in. Each is bearded, the majority in the same calculatedly unkempt fashion favored by Mamduh and Sayyid. Issuing *Assalamu alaikums* to the men in the room, a couple grab chairs as the others disappear into the Imam's office.

"I'm sorry," Vic says, picking up our argument from last week about language and the nature of reality, "I just don't think we're living in a dream."

Vic is a heavy, balding Caucasian from central Pennsylvania. He is in only his second week as a chapel janitor, having taken the spot vacated by Hamed, who, it is said, for the cash and for the change of scenery, opted to trade up to an underwear plant job. An unusual hire, and one that I suspect Reverend Baumgartner made with my benefit somehow in mind, Vic is an iconoclast, an intellectual, and a self-identified "heathen," which is to say an atheist—the first I've come across at Graterford.

Vic and I share a great deal of common ground philosophically, but we've quickly whittled our way down to the irreconcilable cores of our respective positions. In Vic's view, my insistence that language shapes what we collectively take to be "the world" makes me a reality-denying idealist. By contrast, Vic affirms the existence absolutely of an objective reality.[12] While this reality, according to Vic, tends to escape our perception, Vic speaks of "moments of transparency" when one may peer through "the matrix" (as, after the movies, he dubs what generally passes as reality) and into "the real."[13]

"So *what?*" Vic asks me rhetorically, and not for the first time. "The microscopic world of germs didn't exist before the advent of the microscope?"

Toeing the pragmatist philosophical line common to the Princeton Religion Department, I maintain my skepticism about making any definitive judgments, necessarily *in* language, about a realm putatively *prior to* language. Better to think of truth as itself a property of language, I argue now to Vic, than to continually be disappointed by language's inability to go *beyond* language. Vic, meanwhile, sticks by his insistence that the partiality of our own positioning as observers has zero bearing on whether or not the microscopic world existed *objectively* before the microscope. We go back and forth. Eventually, cornered into what feels to me like a petulant postmodernism, and concerned that I'm missing some better, more revealing conversation taking place elsewhere in the room, I go *ad hominem* and call Vic a mystic.[14] As a direct response, or to capture my wandering eye, Vic brings up religion.

From my point of view, religion is a property of modern discourse, a concept with a particular history that has been used to delineate and make sense of a certain sphere of human activity. While we need be self-conscious in how we apply it, religion is a conceptual tool and, as such, is ours to use as we see fit.[15] Vic's position is both more critical and less critical than that. Passing a tin of dip between his hands, Vic proceeds to distinguish between two kinds of religion. Religion in the first sense is "the matrix," or rather, a significant part thereof. Purely a social construction, this religion is a "control edifice" used by the powerful to manipulate the weak. In this regard, religion is much like psychology. As he said last week, "Both are mechanisms of social control, but while in psychology the mechanism is explicit, in religion it's obscured." As far as religion in this former sense is concerned, it's imperative that we "kill off the illusion." There is, however, a second sense of religion, Vic says now, one that stands in stark opposition to this first kind of religion.

"And what would you call that?" I ask.

"Individual humanity."

Jefferson, the embattled leader of Graterford's small community of Moorish Scientists, arrives, a white slip in hand, which he extends to Al. Al glances up, glances down, pauses, glances down, then up again before informing Jefferson that he can go in and see Reverend Baumgartner, whose door is open. Irritation past, Al returns to what he was doing: poring over his prisoner-accounts statement from the past month. Does he ever break even? I ask him. He looks at me like he's never heard a dumber question. He puts it this way: "It's hard to break even on $57.45 a month."

And men like Al are the relatively privileged ones. Most of the chapel workers get visits and some receive financial support. Al, Baraka, and Teddy even have wives (women that they committed to well after being sentenced to life in prison). Nevertheless, between commissary fare purchased to offset the high-starch, high-fat diet and the telephone monopoly under which a fifteen-minute call to Philly sets a guy back five dollars, even a shop-job paycheck is quickly gone, especially for those who, like Al, try to talk to their wives on a daily basis.

A couple of guys are talking hip-hop too new for me to know about. I've yet to hear anyone mention football—what Reverend Baumgartner has called "the *real* religion around here"—which surprises me, given that yesterday, after a year when the Eagles fell from title contention to mediocrity, the Steelers had the audacity to make it to the Super Bowl.

Omar arrives, his teeth now in place, and together we adjourn to the privacy of Chaplain Keita's office. As is common of the aging Sunni Muslims who came up in the Nation of Islam, Omar is socially conscious and engaged. Omar's energies for individual and group uplift are channeled primarily through PAR, People Against Recidivism—a nonsectarian organization Omar and others launched some twenty years ago to try to lengthen the now even odds that men released from Graterford will return to prison within three years.[16] PAR's primary tactic is its "Day One Parole Preparation Course," a sixteen-week program that seeks to inculcate the attitudes and skills necessary for one to successfully transition from the acute regimentation of prison life to the free-form day-to-day of what men here call "the street." Especially in a place where so many outsource their agency to God, PAR facilitators emphasize the need for solid practical plans. Where are you going to live? How are you going to afford to pay your rent? What else will you be able to afford on that budget? As the facilitators say: "Dreams bring us back."

Omar almost got his shot once, coming, in 1994, within a single vote of a clemency recommendation. The *Philadelphia Daily News* forecast a likely reversal in two years' time, when Omar was next eligible. With the election of Republican Tom Ridge as governor a week later, however, two years would suddenly be far too soon. Ridge revamped the clemency procedure to require that those on death row or serving life receive a unanimous, rather than a simple majority, recommendation from the Pardons Board, and mandated the inclusion of a victims' rights advocate. While under the Democratic Casey administration, which governed between 1987 and 1994, twenty-seven Pennsylvania lifers had their sentences commuted, in the decade-plus since, clemency has been granted only once.[17]

"Things are happening," Omar exuberantly declares. He is fresh off a couple of promising meetings with representatives of the Pennsylvania Prison Society that make a possible partnership seem imminent. In Omar's vision, with the Prison Society as its public face, PAR might be able to tap into the spout of federal funding earmarked by President Bush for prisoner reentry, in which case his program might become a model for programs across the country.[18]

Of late, Omar has been selling me, Father Gorski, and, it seems, anyone else who will listen on PAR's need for a piece of property to serve as its headquarters on the street and as transitional housing for newly released PAR participants. This is again his emphasis today. I engage, first eagerly, then dutifully, and then agitatedly. While I'm sympathetic to Omar's cause, I'm sometimes exhausted by the single-mindedness of his messaging. Making me additionally antsy is that I believe I've heard my name repeatedly invoked in the office. Managing to free myself, I reenter the room, and, exhibiting an overeagerness violating every unwritten rule of prudence, tact, and cool, inquire as to whether there isn't something I should know about.

Baraka looks up only long enough to assure me that if something was to go down, I would certainly be the last to know. I chuckle, thinking as I do on those rare moments when I am reminded where I am: *Note to self: room full of convicted murderers. Should probably be mindful.*

I make my rounds. The chapel is empty; the classrooms' windows offer back only my reflection, and the Catholic suite appears similarly vacant. Poised to move on, I catch the faint tinny sound of an old radio. It's playing something instrumental, countryish and peppered with fiddle. As my eyes take to the gloom, I'm startled to discover Papa sitting silently in his customary chair, his jowled cheeks drooped floorward.

While none of the chapel workers is youthful, the gray-stubbled Papa is the only one who presents as an old man. Taking Papa to be asleep, and not wanting to disturb the evocative tableau of a geriatric inmate slipping slowly into darkness, I begin to back out. Only as I reach the door do I notice that Papa's left foot is tapping to the music. The song ends, a station jingle is chimed, and a pop tune comes on—dispelling with its profanity the whisper of the holy conjured in my fantasy.[19]

Baraka trades whispers with a succession of young men who pass by, disappearing periodically with a partner into the vestibule. Returning to the office from one of these conferences, Baraka snuggles Al from behind his desk chair, encircling the larger man with two outstretched arms. His eyes are squeezed shut in what looks a whole lot like glee. Al feigns boredom.

Though not uncommon any day of the week, this horseplay makes additional sense on Monday. While men like Baraka and Vic praise the weekend as a time to catch up on projects and correspondence, others speak of the challenges. On weekends, much of the jail remains dark, and the rest is turned over to the correctional officers. For men accustomed to the weekday routine, the enforced Sabbath reportedly brings anxiety and loneliness. By today, those who don't live on the same block, or play on the same football team, or see each other at Saturday's

Catholic mass or Sunday's Protestant service, will likely not have seen each other since Friday. For Al and Baraka—chapel coworkers and intimates for more than thirty years—two days of enforced separation is a long time. In short, it seems to me, as I watch Baraka touch his old friend, that Baraka missed him. Neither are the chaplains immune to this dynamic. As Reverend Baumgartner will tell me at lunch, Mondays are infused with a general air of neediness in which a class of men familiar with sudden catastrophic change seek assurance that everything remains just as it was. Al rises from his chair, picks Baraka up in a bear hug, and swings him around.

Things quiet down. Water is boiled in the electric kettle, a tower of Styrofoam cups is pulled from a desk drawer, and coffee and tea are brewed. I'm offered one or the other, and decline. Teddy and Al take umbrage. I plead my case, arguing that I just drank tea on Friday. That was Friday, Teddy points out.

Both sides know the rules of this game. After six months of polite refusal, I finally broke down and drank chapel coffee, first with the Jews upstairs and shortly thereafter in the office. At that time, Teddy wanted to know if the chaplains had warned me not to. I explained that while I had been explicitly instructed at orientation not to accept gifts of any kind, my reluctance to accept coffee was less about conforming to the rules of the DOC and more an adherence to the doctrine of the French anthropologist Marcel Mauss, who canonically posited the gift as a seizure of power by the giver over the recipient.[20] To receive a gift is to be placed in a state of indebtedness, a disadvantage to be rectified only through charitable retaliation. While many of my theories draw blank stares here, this one made perfect sense. And since then, Teddy's generosity has only become more dogged.

Vic is drinking tea. Since he is new to the office, and white to boot, I caution him that he best use his tea bag more than once. When I first accepted tea from Teddy, shortly after I drank his coffee, I made the mistake of throwing a tea bag out after only one soaking. Teddy decreed that he was "confiscating my ghetto pass," a punitive measure—to censure me for some faux pas or other—he takes on almost a weekly basis. Teddy likes to play me both ways. On the one hand, he jumps at the opportunity to call me out for my social missteps. On the other, he often commends me for my social deftness, telling me how he tells guys on the block about "this crazy white boy" in the chapel. Normally,

Teddy tells me, it takes people a while to adapt to a new environment, but I just eased into it, which is doubly remarkable given my background. Teddy's assessment is likely too flattering by half, but he would be the one to know. Unlike Al and Baraka, who remained incognito for some time, Teddy was there from the start. Back then, Teddy frequently reminds me, he'd "throw some crazy black stuff" at me and was shocked when I took it in stride.

At present I've apparently failed to be quite so shrewd. Acerbically, Teddy schools me in the distinction I missed: as long as it's his own tea bag, Vic can do what he wants; but if he ever uses anyone else's, he'd best use it eight times.

"Until there's no tint left," Sayyid adds, laughing.

Sayyid's criminal justice textbook sits open on his desk, and he and Vic are talking shop. Vic likens the prison to the plantation of the antebellum South and to the Indian reservations of today. Sayyid concurs. I begin reporting the "job security" crack that I heard on the way in this morning. Before I can finish, though, Vic interrupts me with the prescribed rejoinder: "But job security at minimum wage!" The gag has special significance these days, since the COs, who have been working without a formal contract since July, are nervously awaiting the arbitration ruling that will set their base pay and overtime.[21]

Prompted by the criminal justice textbook, I idly ask the two men if the oft-quoted statistic of one out of three black men in the United States between the ages of eighteen and thirty-five being under the care of the criminal justice system isn't somehow cooked. No, they agree. If anything, that statistic understates the reality.[22]

Teddy is at the word processor, his sculpted hair and square plastic frames poking above the shoulder-high wooden bureau that houses the machine under lock and key. Having sensed a raw nerve and wanting to check in, I peer over the top. Without looking up, Teddy shakes his head. Lying atop the ancient machine is a letter, which I move to read without any protest on his part. Since the signature at the end of the brief two-paragraph draft belongs to Teddy's wife, Lily, it's unclear whether it is she or he that is its author. Perusing the draft, I discover what's eating at Teddy. Addressed to a Philly law firm, the letter expresses dismay that although the author has dutifully paid $2,200 with the understanding that the firm was to take on Teddy's case, to date all that he has received is a small booklet consisting of only the court filings arranged in chronological order. Surely, the letter plaintively insists, *this* cannot be the sum total of the firm's efforts on her husband's behalf.

Teddy, as I know from a request for legal assistance he showed me back in November, is serving life on a conviction of murder, burglary, and arson. Titled "The Nightmare of an Innocent Man," the request detailed how after the failure of his first marriage, and after losing his job, Teddy fell into drug addiction. While he was no stranger to the police during those years, he had no history of violence. On the night when the victim was beaten, robbed, and died of smoke inhalation, Teddy was doing drugs with a woman elsewhere in West Philly. Neither the Philly PD nor Teddy's court-appointed attorney made any attempt to contact the woman, and eventually Teddy lost contact with her. Through God's grace, however, the request concluded, Teddy has found the woman, who has cleaned up her life and has provided Teddy with an affidavit establishing his alibi.

I sit down with Teddy and help him line-edit the complaint, which is riddled with errors. After a few minutes, grammar and syntax have ceased to be a distraction, but the only thing clarified, it seems to me, is the hopelessness of the plea. By the time we finish, everyone else is gone.

Baumgartner beckons me down into the chair opposite his desk. Baumgartner is Graterford's head chaplain, or, in DOC parlance, its FCPD—its Facilities Chaplaincy Program Director—a job he's held for more than a decade. A theological liberal, Baumgartner was ordained as a Lutheran minister and has a Ph.D. in Hebrew Bible from a Jewish seminary. In his other spiritual pursuits, Baumgartner is an avid cyclist and an accomplished jazz trumpeter. Because Baumgartner was out last week, I haven't seen him since Christmas. With baggy eyes to match his saggy chin, Baumgartner seems fatigued in a postvacation way, and for the first time he speaks to me of the prospect of retirement.

Baumgartner's office walls are decorated with prisoner artwork. Two paintings depict figures I take to be Jesus. In one, He is white and bearded, while in the other, superimposed before a blue sky, He is clean-shaven and black.[23] A third painting, which bears Teddy's signature, depicts in one-point perspective a paved street claustrophobically lined with South Philly–style row houses, giving way at the vanishing point to a setting sun.

Officer Watkins pops his head in to report that the chapel is secured, and Baumgartner waves him on to lunch. I remind Baumgartner of what I'm up to this week. He tells me that I should check with him daily and that he'll let me know if something is going on—that is, he adds with a chuckle, if *he* hears about it. But by now, he says, I've seen pretty much everything there is to see.

After lunch, I successfully deflect another play by Watkins for the movie rights to my book, which he's counting on to pay down his mortgage. To counter, Watkins asks me again if I've read the Book of Jasher. "Jasher" is a book alluded to in Joshua and Second Samuel, a purported version of which Watkins found on the Internet. I confess that while a Bible scholar friend debunked whatever it was Watkins read as in all certainty a pseudepigraph of far more recent authorship, I have not, as yet, checked it out myself. Watkins is unimpressed. He chastises me: "Every man has the right to go to the source and to see for himself what to believe—not just to believe what he's supposed to believe. Why not see for yourself in your inner self?" I have no adequate response.[24]

The guys begin to filter in. When Teddy shows, Watkins catches his eye and runs his hands gloatingly along the armrests of his reclining desk chair. Watkins informs Teddy that he was fine with the inferior chair he'd found beneath his ass sometime midmorning, but that he'd decided to trade back. Teddy bursts into laughter and takes a seat, as Watkins, remembering his point, continues on about the Book of Jasher, about how it gets into all sorts of stuff the Bible is silent about, like how Jesus spent his missing years.

"We just don't know anything about that if we stick only to what we've been given," Watkins argues. Did I know, for example, that according to Jasher, Moses went to Africa for ten years?

"Was it even called Africa then?" Teddy wants to know.

"That's not the point," Watkins says. "The point is that we are under this system called 'canonized,' and we've got to be suspicious of the ones doing the choosing."

I urge Watkins on.

"For example," he continues, "suppose there was a hostage situation down here and when it was over, they came down and took Teddy out in cuffs, and then they would take you, me, Baumgartner, and the Imam somewhere to debrief us. And we would all sit there in that room and tell different stories because we would have different perspectives on what went down." Moreover, not merely do the four Gospels reflect a multiplicity of perspectives, they reflect as well a variety of interests, not all of them necessarily on the up-and-up. For, as Watkins argues, the process by which the canonizers boiled down these different perspectives to the definitive accounts we have today was by no means innocent. "Things were taken out of the Gospels to make people *do* different things," Watkins explains.

Teddy is prepared. "True," he counters, "but if you have the Holy Spirit, it doesn't matter. Because the Holy Spirit will do what?" He pauses for emphasis. "The Holy Spirit will always lead you to what God said even if man tried to do what?" Another pause. "Switch it to fit his lifestyle."

Whether critically or apologetically, Teddy and Watkins are nothing if not readers of outrageous confidence; and, still relatively fresh off my qualifying exams, I cannot but hear in their approaches to the Bible the echoes of the early-nineteenth-century religious upsurge that American religionists have long known as the Second Great Awakening. For if every man believes he has the right to read Scripture himself and forge his own judgments, neither by God nor nature is he so authorized. That authorization comes to him, rather, via the curious confluence of religious enthusiasm and democratic dispensation that in the days of the new republic was already emblematic of the emergent American character.[25] At revivals and camp meetings, men and women generated radical new denominational routes and devotional methods through which, as much via the medium as via the message, many came to feel empowered (and therefore obligated!) to read the Bible for themselves and form their own judgments. As the story is told, the gates that Luther and Calvin had cracked ajar were, amid the exploding market revolution, swung wide open. Henceforth, just as no one needed a priest for salvation, neither did one need a minister to facilitate understanding. For those with faith, the thinking went (and goes), the process is overwhelmingly visceral. Scripture isn't hard, it's easy! Simply open your heart to the Word and let the Truth flood in![26]

But in Watkins's present account, the radically accessible nature of God's truth is only part of the story. Rather, God's bountiful generosity with the Truth (and, by extension, with salvation) is a damn good thing, Watkins would say, since Jesus' message, as it's come down to us, is *not*, in all likelihood, Jesus' message as it was delivered. In so saying, Watkins betrays a secondary attitude toward Scripture, one less theological than sociological, and (the raging Dan Brown phenomenon notwithstanding) arguably indigenous less to America at large than to black America specifically.[27] Some would call it paranoia. Watkins would call it common sense. That is, if history teaches anything, it's that those with power will do whatever they can to promote and preserve their self-interest. If sin and pride will lead man away from the Truth here and now, why should we assume that the canonizers were somehow exempt?

Teddy isn't buying it.

Watkins presses him: But won't the Holy Spirit guide us the same way when we're reading the texts that were left out?

"Look," Teddy reiterates. "If you don't have God, you only have what?" Beat. "Man's words. And man is fallible."

"Hey, Watkins! You're not proselytizing again, are you?" This comes from Brian, the Rabbi's clerk, who is standing at the stairwell door. Fastidious in his appearance, with pressed browns, sculpted hair, shadowless cheeks, and, in summer, the uniformly bronze hue of an intentional tan, Brian carries himself with the harried air of a corporate professional.

Watkins shakes his head.

"You know, of course," Brian says to me with a smirk, "that Watkins is a well-known proselytizer, don't you?"

"*I* knew that," I play along, "but I didn't know it was an open secret."

"Well, it is now," Brian says.

Scowling, Watkins tells the story. It was during Friday's Jum'ah prayer a couple weeks back, and this one Muslim just kept coming and going and coming and going. Growing aggravated at the guy's blatant disregard for the rules, Watkins told him to cut it out. The Muslim got up in Watkins's face, and told him that he'd best stop discriminating against Muslims. Watkins threatened to write him up and the Muslim calmed down, but only so as to later file a grievance with the superintendent's office detailing Watkins's systematic pattern of discrimination against prisoners of a Muslim persuasion. The first Watkins hears about it is when he's called in by the day captain, admonished, and told not to proselytize anymore.

In no simple sense is Watkins a proselytizer. In uniform and out, the jail has no shortage of narrow and dogmatic religious exponents, but Watkins is not one of them. Though he is serious about his faith—a characteristic common to the COs who bid for the chapel post—he is not bullheaded. In fact, in an environment dominated by doctrinal certainties, Watkins is notably elastic. And though he's not afraid to publicly engage in Christian apologetics, it is always with a willing sparring partner. "Show it to me in your Scripture! Show it to me in your Scripture!" I once saw Watkins passionately beseech a prominent Moorish Scientist. As for Sunni Islam in particular, Watkins has repeatedly declared his solemn admiration for the intensity and humility with which they "worship the Lord."

And yet, it doesn't take too great a leap of imagination to see where Watkins's accuser might have been coming from. You're a Muslim prisoner in a Christian-majority country, and the man tasked with protecting your First Amendment right to free religious exercise—which is to say, the man who stands between you and the exercise of your constitutional rights—makes little effort to mask his Christian faith. When the gears inevitably get gummed up, it's easy to suspect that it's by design.

There is also a more systemic critique to make of the authority wielded by chapel officers. According to this perspective, even if Watkins should successfully hide away all the trappings of his faith, or even if he was swapped out for a sober secularist, his very presence in the chapel bears witness to the potentially self-defeating paradox inherent in attempts at regulating religious liberty. The U.S. Constitution protects the "free exercise" of religion and prohibits the "establishment" of religion. And yet, the protection of free religious *exercise*—in prison and out—necessarily demands someone in power to *establish* the rules by which religion is regulated.

I am not without sympathy for this critique. While the rule of law differs in substantial ways from the rule of whim, and while the chapel would be a far worse place were Watkins truly the unhinged zealot his accuser mistook him for, it is equally the case that no formula for protecting the free exercise of religion can avoid playing favorites. Even when the aspiration to religious pluralism is pursued in good faith, as, by and large, I take it here to be, overseeing "A House of Prayer for All Peoples"—as the chapel is designated on the weekly schedule of events that is taped to the vestibule bulletin board—necessarily demands drawing distinctions about what counts as legitimate prayer and what counts as a recognizable faith.[28]

In the chapel, then, defining religion is no academic matter. And if the sacred language of the Constitution furnishes the inspiration, it does so from a distance. Rather, the rules by which the free exercise of religion finds protection here are shaped up and down a hierarchy of authorities stretching from the Supreme Court to the Third Circuit Court of Appeals, to the Religious Accommodation Committee (RAC) up at DOC headquarters in Camp Hill, to Reverend Baumgartner, and, finally, in a packed vestibule on a Friday afternoon, to Officer Watkins. Even when evenly enforced, these rules are never neutral.

As scholars of religion have often observed, the nominally nonsectarian rules by which Americans regulate religion belong to a particular theological tradition: namely, liberal Protestantism.[29] What is a theological liberal? Well, if a theological conservative like Watkins or Teddy would maintain that faith in Jesus Christ is the only viable road to salvation, a liberal would be far more accommodating. There are many different religious paths, a liberal might say, of which faith in Christ is only one. And yet, in spite of his or her best efforts at inclusivity, the liberal's notion of religion often imposes Protestant presumptions that locate the essence of religion not in peoples or public works but in individuals and their private convictions—faith in God paradigmatically, or in a secularized version, the truths at the core of a person's being that are thought to drive his or her actions.[30] As the existentialist theologian Paul Tillich put it, in language that in 1965 the Supreme Court would adopt and which remains today resonant, religion is about your *"ultimate concern"—"what you take seriously without reservation."*[31] Under this standard, "real" religion is those practices and beliefs *truly* foundational to an individual's outlook on life and, consequently, to his or her being in the world. Subordinate preferences would not suffice, and scoundrels need not apply. Other than that, in theory, all creeds were to be equally entitled.

Even were it not outmoded, that ideal is impossible to actualize.[32] In practice, some peoples are welcomed to the chapel with open arms, some are tolerated, and others are excluded entirely. If Graterford's

Muslims feel scrutinized, as of now no formal space is provided for fringe religionists like Wiccans, Odinists, Satanists, Yogis, Rastafarians, or even Buddhists, who though licensed to practice their religions alone in their cells are not afforded a public platform in the chapel. Afforded no accommodation at all are the Five Percent Nation of Islam and the black naturalist sect MOVE, which, four years before the police firebombed its West Philly home, killing eleven, was deemed by the Third Circuit to be merely a social philosophy and *not* a bona fide religion meriting constitutional protection.[33]

It doesn't take a cynic to see in the regulation of religion an arbitrary exercise of state power. "Describe, in detail, your religion's basic tenets or beliefs, which you feel require that you be provided with the requested accommodation," the DOC's Inmate Religious Accommodation Request Form instructs.[34] But the resulting evaluations of religious authenticity and sincerity take place on scales tipped in favor of those whose practices are already familiar. The strange, the new, and the contentious tend to trigger the system's security alarm, which, when rung, trumps the petitioners' First Amendment rights.[35]

But for the marginalized, both in the chapel and out, even subjection unto exclusion is not necessarily without some ancillary benefit. Via a spiritual jujitsu, the affliction of state oppression can become a marker of defiance before one's captor, and of righteousness before one's maker. Consider, for example, Gaston Carlsby.

At Reverend Baumgartner's urging, Baraka would later spin me the yarn about how when they were on cooking crew together, he discovered Gaston soaking loaves of bread in the industrial vat used to catch the slaughtered cow's blood—this was back when the farm was in operation and the jail produced all its own meat and milk. Baraka learned that drinking cow's blood had something to do with Gaston's religion. Not yet prejudiced by such sensational hearsay, when I sat down with Gaston, I knew only what Mamduh had told me: that he was an interesting guy, a Satanist, and somebody I should speak to for my project's sake.

When Gaston met me in the library, he turned out to be a 350-pound African-American man with a lazy left eye, a head of unkempt braids, a wry disposition, and a low-key, mildly unnerving intensity. Gaston was not a Satanist at all, I learned, but a Wiccan. He grew up Christian but rejects Christianity for its patriarchal God, its homophobia— "I don't see why it matters who you sleep with"—and its genocidal attitude toward witches. He said: "If you want to know about a religion, go to their book and see what they say." He quoted Exodus: "Suffer not a witch to live."[36]

Careful not to speak for all Wiccans, Gaston nonetheless asserted the essence of Wicca to be the ethical imperative *Harm no one*. A decade into his practice, only last fall did Gaston discover that he was *truly* a Wiccan. That's when, after being stabbed fourteen times by a couple of guys he worked with in the underwear plant—in part, he figures, because of his religion—he felt not the slightest impulse to kill them.

Gaston wears a silver pentagram around his neck with a red stone inset. It took him two years to get it, having to work his way first through Reverend Baumgartner and then up to the RAC.[37] After he managed to finally get one, he said, the DOC made it close to impossible for anyone else. Gaston is dubious about the "silver-tongued" Baumgartner. "As someone whose job it is to be responsible to all religious groups," Gaston said coldly, "Baumgartner is a very good jazz musician." With little faith in the agents of the state to assure his First Amendment rights, Gaston marvels at the genius of his fellow pagan prisoners: how they make altars in their cells, candles out of crayons, Thor's Hammers out of cardboard. Able to turn his cell into a sacred place, Gaston has no interest in practicing his religion in the Christian chapel.[38]

As he translated it for my benefit, "Praying in the chapel would be like eating kosher in a pork factory."

In the otherwise empty chapel, Al, Papa, and a third old head are facing the dais, doing something I can only assume pertains to technical maintenance. Alone in the office, Sayyid sits at his desk, quietly reading and writing. I loiter in the vestibule.

"Do you ever think about why we're here?" Watkins asks me.

I try, and fail, to gauge where Watkins is coming from.

He looks up at me. "Have you ever felt love?"

"I guess so," I say.

"Unconditional love?"

"Sure," I say. "From my parents." This line of inquiry is making me uneasy.

"No," Watkins says, "that's not nothing." His eyes glisten and he holds out his hands, palms up. "Unconditional love," he says, "is what you feel the first time your newborn child looks at you. It just looks up at you with total love. Like it just thinks that you're perfect or something." He stares off in silence. "You have nieces or nephews?" he asks me.

"Yeah," I say.

"Well, you know how much you love them, right? Well, that's nothing compared to what you feel for your own kids."

Unequipped to respond, I try to steer the conversation into less threatening terrain. "But then, someday, they forget," I say. I'm referring to recent conversations in which Watkins has lamented his teenage daughters' mounting insolence. But Watkins isn't thinking about his vexing daughters from his first marriage; his mind is fixed on the sinless baby from his second. So, rather than launching into his stock lamentations about kids' lack of respect these days, the breakdown of families in this modern era of women's liberation, and the destruction we reap when we replace God's law with our own, he continues with his impromptu devotion to the sublime power of an infant's love.

"And when you come home at night," he says, still transported, "and it looks up at you like that—you just remember what it's all about."

Men waft into the vestibule to watch the red light over the door and wait. When the two o'clock shift-change finishes up, the red light will go off, the suspension of movement will be lifted, and guys should be able to get back to their cells. Watkins watches the bulb, too, knowing that once it goes dark, Officer Bird, his replacement, won't be too far behind. I glance back and forth between the beacon and the men and consider the monotony of prison time: tedious for these men who live here for decades on end; tedious for Graterford's employees, who, it is said, are serving "twenty-five to life, eight hours at a time"; tedious for all but the ethnographer, for whom everything is, in its way, a wonder.

Climbing the stair, I take little notice of the vibrant depictions of Muslim holy sites and calligraphic renderings of Qur'anic verses that line the right-hand wall and wrap around the landing heading toward the basement—remnants of an earlier era.

Upstairs, in the Rabbi's study, Brian and Baraka are poring over the *Collins* opinion at the lacquered wooden conference table that runs alongside the wall of books. To the left, in the nook next to the small kitchenette, a dozen chairs face an open wooden ark where a Torah is draped under a white-and-blue prayer shawl. With its well-stocked library and wall-to-wall carpeting, the Rabbi's study is easily the warmest space in the chapel.

Baraka's knotted brow is buried in the case, and Brian is lecturing. The most serious of Graterford's Jews about the observance of the biblical commandments, Brian is also a serial litigant. If before God, then, Brian presents himself as law-bound, before the state he evinces no such deference. In addition to his ongoing criminal appeal, Brian has a couple of other cases pending before the federal court, one seeking the full accommodation of his Jewish dietary observance. Brian already pushed for and won the right to a vegetarian diet, but in the current case—*Pot Roast v. Pork Chops*, as he refers to it jokingly—he's pressing for kosher meat. Brian knows that with the thousands of Muslims with similar dietary needs poised to follow suit, the DOC is unlikely to budge. As he also knows, from his other lawsuits, he is already on thin ice. If, for example, the administration catches wind of Brian having supplemented his meager allotment of fruit, raw vegetables, crackers, and nuts with unsanctioned cafeteria or commissary fare, he will lose his accommodation once and forever.

When Brian is being argumentative, which is most of the time, he lectures in the formal language of a legal complaint, filling his speech with all sorts of cumbersome locutions along the lines of "as I submit to you," "I maintain that," and "my contention is." After spending the greater part of the day digesting the *Collins* opinion, this is how Brian is talking at Baraka now. From what I can surmise, the case bears on prisoners seeking relief on the basis of an ineffective assistance of counsel (IAC) claim. The animating disagreement between the two men is *Collins's* reach. Baraka wants *Collins* to say that if your IAC claim was not dismissed expressly on its merits, then *Collins* authorizes you to get back into court. For Brian the opinion is a much narrower holding.

Making me arbiter, each presents his respective position. Without having read the case (so that, as Watkins or Al might say, my inner self might decide for itself), I rely on experience and instinct, which, based on the authority of its source and the pessimism of its content, point to Brian's position. Baraka appeals my decision, but I defer to Brian, who is preaching a tough love seemingly befitting the situation. There's nothing *he* can do for him, Brian tells Baraka. Baraka must simply go to the law library and do the necessary legwork to see how *Collins* might or might not apply to *his* case. Baraka makes a sour expression.

"Can't you have a shorty do it for you?" I tease Baraka. Meaning, can't he send some youngster to do it on his behalf? This sets Brian on a riff I've never heard before but which, as my joke betrayed, I am less than shocked to hear. Apparently, Brian mirthfully reports, Baraka has no shortage of "support" from within the Muslim community.

"Did you know, for example," Brian asks me, "that a member of the Muslim community cleans Baraka's cell? Did you know that when Bar goes for a visit, someone is already there saving a prime seat for him, and should he or the missus find themselves in the mood for a snack of some kind, there is an underling on hand ready to heat it up for them?" Bar cackles, his head disappearing, turtle-like, into his shoulders. In his voice of incredulity, the one Baraka plays an octave higher than his normal speaking voice, he stammers out his defense.

"This is impossible," he pleads. "How am I going to pull this kind of weight around here when I'm so diminutive?"

"Who do you believe?" Brian asks me, palms upraised. Again I'm to be the judge.

Reassuming his posture of baroque efficiency, Brian says that while he'd like to stay and play all day, he needs to get cracking. Asking us gentlemen to make sure we turn off the lights and close the door when we leave, Brian glibly issues each of us a "Good day, gentlemen," and takes off.

Seemingly weary of wearing the dunce cap, Baraka quickly makes it my turn for school. Sitting catty-corner at the end of the conference table, he cradles my pad inside the crook of his elbow, grabs my pen, and begins to write something. Upside down, I read:

Chapter—1 data—
Religion and Inmates: Reality or Tool?

I ask Baraka what he's getting at. The distinction he's trying to draw, he says, "is whether what somebody practices is what they're *really* about, or are they merely wearing the requisite clothing demanded by the fashion judges on the parole board." Go on, I say, despite my misgivings about what I presume is going to be an attack on the religious sincerity of some of his fellow prisoners, specifically, I suspect, the Salafi.

It is not a move that I am predisposed to tolerate. To the degree that I came to this project with any sort of ax to grind, it was against the kneejerk assumption that prisoners' religion is fundamentally insincere.[39] Popular culture is rife with riffs on the manifest fakery that is jailhouse religion, which is thought to fall just shy of "real religion." Jailhouse religion is, at the benign end, a ruse perpetrated for protection, or for meager material privilege. At its more malignant—as "jailhouse Islam" most commonly—it is a smokescreen for gangsterism or for seditious politics.[40]

Such a characterization is less wrong than it is wholly inevitable. It is a consequence of what happens when a narrow conceptualization of religion intersects with the reductive way we think about prisoners. For, if in order to be authentic, religion must be measured against the presumed fixed core of a man's soul, the reviled prisoner finds himself procedurally barred. As a figure, the prisoner is closely akin to the one that for Hegel stood in for the problem with abstraction as such. "This is abstract thinking," the German philosopher wrote, "to see nothing in the murderer except the abstract fact that he is a murderer, and to annul all other human essence in him with this simple quality."[41] And so it is, in our own day and age, for the prisoner. Predominantly, the prisoner is little more than the personification of the crime for which he was convicted. Add religion and the outcome is clear. A prisoner's *performance* of piety may be presumed as a given. How else, after all, is a villain to present himself? But performance here is *mere performance*. Until he overcomes the burden of our doubt, the religious prisoner is to be presumed a wolf in sheep's vestments. Reduced down to an anthropological fact, the religious prisoner is to be shrewdly regarded as one trying to get by, or trying to get over, and rarely if ever as trying to commune sincerely with his maker—as in suitable conformity, that is, with the theological litmus test he (or she, but mostly he) has been set up to fail. For this essentially "bad man," dissimulation is thought to be tantamount to vocation, and religious conversion is thought to be just another version of the con.[42]

Given the attendant material and personal benefits, the sincerity of anyone's religious practice could be called into question. Would that, as an interpretive device, this "bad man of religion" were so indiscriminately deployed. But church bingo players and synagogue presidents are not its targets. Rather, the bad man of religion is found only—and circularly—among classes of people already deemed suspect. Through the bad-man framing, Omar's activism is efficiently converted into a low-level power play, and Brian's litigiousness plainly becomes little more than a gadfly's gambit. Indeed, for the desirability of their posts alone, all but the most scrupulous and pious chapel workers can be felled by the bad-man presumption. Although in the end, for the presumed exquisiteness of their artifice, they, too, may be laid low.

As should have come as little surprise, the bad man of religion is no stranger to the chapel. Sincerity matters a lot here. Not by the fervor of his prayers, however, is an inmate's religious sincerity validated. In this fishbowl, rather, the truth of a man's professed faith is measured by how he conducts himself on the block, in the showers, on the chow line. Does he act with dignity and humanity, or does he lumber naked to the shower, screw other men, and in summer, when it's precious, hoard more than his share of ice? If in such adverse conditions a man manages to somehow act like a man, then his religion might well be real. But if he doesn't—and most fail this test—then religiously he is a fraud, and perhaps, considering what else he's seen doing, he's a hustler, a huckster, or a gangster too.

Were Brian still here, the case for fraud would be open and shut. As he ceaselessly argues, what I observe in the chapel has nothing to do with real religion. For his fellow prisoners, religion is a game, nothing more. According to Brian, men here are "a bunch of animals," and "nothing that happens in this trash can matters." Reverend Keita reads Brian's categorical rejection of the reality of his world as an attempt to distance himself from the brutalities he's endured, and that may well be. But in Brian's opinion, I'm wasting my time studying such nonsense, and nonsense is all I get since everybody is just bullshitting me anyway. The Muslims especially see me as a white boy and a Jew, and I can be sure that anything I say to one will be quickly transmitted to all the others.

Gaston Carlsby was even more concise. "First," he said, "people will tell you what you want to hear. Second, they will tell you whatever will do them the most good. Third—and this is only if you pay very close attention—you will encounter the core of excrement that is there."

Baraka is not quite so discouraging. When guys speak with me—he says he assumes—same as when they speak with God, they're generally speaking the truth at least as far as they know it from their experiences. When it comes to the Salafi, however, Baraka is not always so charitable. While he's careful not to single out anyone in particular, certainly not Salafi office workers like Sayyid and Kazi, he's said that many Salafi "wear their religion as a cloak." I once pressed Baraka on the apparent inconsistency of his two positions, arguing to him that he can't assert that people mean what they say while excepting those he disagrees with. In his typically frustrating fashion, Baraka curtly countered: "In *your* world maybe you can't do that. In *my* world I can."

Given this history of exchange, I'm expecting Baraka to detail how his own cohort—the so-called Warith Deen guys—are on the up-and-up and how the Salafi are merely faking it. Surprisingly, however, he takes precisely the opposite tack. For him, Baraka confesses, revelation is something of a far-fetched notion. He roots his skepticism in his years in the Nation of Islam, where, while wholeheartedly embracing the Nation's ethos of personal discipline, practical politics, and economic uplift, he could never quite get with all the talk about dragons, angels, the mother plane, and the like.[43] For Baraka, religious metaphysics remains somewhat beside the point. What is essential in religion is to "have faith in one God and to do unto others" what one would have others do to you. Everything else is up for grabs. For him, he concludes now, Islam is a lifestyle, his adherence largely instrumental. In Islam, Baraka says, espousing the Nation's self-help ethos, the bottom line is not submission but self-improvement, the highest value being that of education. For the Salafi, by contrast, it's way more than that.

Primed to defend the Salafi from the charge that they don't really mean their religion, I suddenly find myself in the funny position of having to defend these sometimes obdurate men from *meaning* it perhaps a little bit too much. In defense of this suddenly suspect true believer, I ask Baraka to picture a kid who "falls"—as going to prison is called—at twenty, a kid who lived by the code of the streets, and, having just gotten hit with a long prison bid, comes to the realization that the game he'd been playing was way too hard, its stakes too steep. To compound matters, this newly disillusioned young man must process his belated revelation in a lonely and hostile environment. In such an instance, I argue, could Baraka not see the appeal of a time-tested tradition that claims to lay out for you—you, who suddenly and for good reason find your own judgment lacking—a comprehensive rule book for navigating your life choices? On top of which, it is promised to him—he, who may have done something terrible—that should he obey, he will one day receive the ultimate reward. Can't Baraka see the sincere appeal of that?

Baraka sees the appeal, but he rejects fundamentalism in *all* of its forms. Fundamentalism, he says, is precisely about perpetuating incarceration indefinitely. Fundamentalism is all about keeping him infantile, dependent, and, as such, in full conformity with the mindless behaviorism promoted by the prison system. As Baraka once caustically wondered aloud about his fellow prisoners: "What would happen if everyone woke up and the building wasn't there? Would they still stand for count?"

I ask Baraka if what he's saying applies equally to Christian fundamentalism.

"Christian fundamentalists are bigger frauds," he says. "At least Salafism is an old thing. Christian fundamentalism is a new thing, an American thing." His face betrays the unpleasantness of being forced to share cramped quarters with what he deems to be idiotic.

While I don't interrupt him, I only partially share Baraka's judgment. As I see it, Salafism is no less modern than Protestant fundamentalism. And, while scholars of religion rightly tend to bristle at the category of "Muslim fundamentalism" and its shoddy transposition of a category belonging to American Protestantism to a very different milieu, the two movements do share more than a passing resemblance.[44] Fundamentalism emerged at the turn of the twentieth century as part of what is known as the Third Great Awakening, a religious surge that saw the emergence of a slew of mass movements, ranging from Pentecostalism to the Social Gospel. Taking its name from the twelve-volume set of tracts *The Fundamentals*, which was published in Los Angeles beginning in 1910, the movement was an effort to get back to the basics of Jesus Christ's message. If, theologically, fundamentalism's goal was to recover the lost truths of the past, the spur in its flank was forged in the Industrial Age. In stark contradistinction to fin de siècle liberal Protestants, who embraced Darwinism and biblical criticism and built bridges to other religious denominations, fundamentalists reasserted the absolute centrality of Jesus Christ as plainly recorded in the inerrant Word of God that is the Bible.[45]

Salafism is similar. While traced back by insiders and critics to the eighteenth-century Arabian legal scholar Muhammad Ibn Abd-al-Wahhab, Salafism only became a mass movement in the twentieth century. Like Protestant fundamentalists, the progenitors of modern Salafism sought to get back to an unadulterated truth—in their case, the practices of the Salaf, the pious predecessors of Islam's first three generations. Rejecting in principle the authority of the medieval schools of jurisprudence on which Sunni Muslims traditionally rely, Salafi jurists turned directly to the Qur'an and the hadith (the sayings by and about the Prophet) to divine how Muhammad and his companions lived their lives.[46]

From a secularist perspective, Protestant fundamentalism and Salafism each represent a refusal to adapt to modern life. It is a characterization fundamentalists and Salafists would happily accept, with the proviso that the innovations of modernity mark not the march of progress but a further deviation from God's Truth. As I see it, both accounts—the traditionalist story and the progressive one—are stories of self-authorization. Whereas the traditionalist draws authority from the purported truths of the past, the progressive draws his from the presumed advances of the present. The identification of fundamentalism and Salafism as somehow premodern buttresses the conceits of progressives and traditionalists alike. As mass movements, however, Salafism and fundamentalism are inescapably modern. In spite of their best intentions, their textual innovations and the neotraditionalist lifestyles they promote belong to the modern worlds in which they have flourished. Analogous to constitutional originalism in the American legal context, fundamentalists and Salafists engineer new and uniquely modern forms of religious practice, driving forward even as they take themselves as mere recoverers of past truths lost.[47]

For Baraka, fundamentalism's intellectual shortcomings pale in comparison to its de facto social ends. The system *wants* to breed fundamentalists, he says, so that guys will bring it back outside to the street. "They're breeding it in this place, so it'll grow all over, so that guys will be incarcerated forever, regardless of whether they're behind bars or not."

"But not Salafism!" I object. Certainly the system isn't trying to promote a Middle Eastern form of Islam.

He shakes his head: "The Salafi believe in stasis. They want you to live as if we're in the seventh century. You find yourself in an impossible position in which you're defying the rules of your religion every time you pick up an ink pen. But it's an impossibility," he says. "You can't make your arguments from the seventh century, because you're not there. You make your arguments from what is available now in the twenty-first century."

I nod. "And the Warith Deen brand of Islam?" I ask of Baraka's own

Muslim subculture, whose members identify with and look for guidance to Warith Deen Muhammad, the son of Nation of Islam leader Elijah Muhammad. "What about you all?"

"We believe in progress," he says. "That what happened back then happened, but that we're *here* now."

Trying to close the remaining philosophical distance between the two of us, I ask, "Would you call yourselves pragmatists?"

Baraka signs on to that description but then reconsiders. Most of the Warith Deen guys aren't like him either. By and large, they're literalists too. In his views about religion, he concedes, he doesn't have too much company.

As we tidy up, I idly inquire whether Baraka ever talks to Al about stuff like this.

"No, no, no, no," he cautions, "that wouldn't be such a good idea."

On the stair, I ask Baraka about this morning's whisperings. Baraka explains that as a resident of A Block, he likes to check in on Mondays with guys from the other blocks to make sure that everything is cool. Plus, he uses the opportunity "to teach them about the history of *our community*," he says, referring, I can only presume, to the Warith Deen community.

"And about honor?" I ask, alluding to Baraka's cardinal virtue.

"Yes," he says, "that lesson cannot be taught enough. It's so alien to guys in here that you can't just do whatever you want whenever you want it."

Back on a summer afternoon, Baraka offered the following criteria for honorable action.

HONOR IS:

1. Conformity of one's actions to statements about one's intentions:
2. that these actions be courageous in kind;
3. that these actions be undertaken consistently;
4. that the actor possesses a sense of heightened self-worth such that he feels that in order to fulfill his mission on the planet, he has a little more to do than the average guy.

More than in integrity, consistency, and courage, it is in the "little more" where the demands of honor begin. Because one's social world generally allows a man to get away with so much less, Baraka's honorable man must resist playing the game merely according to the rules as they are presented. The given rules surely delineate the safe course of action, and they might even represent the *moral* one, but to achieve the character that is his special obligation, the honorable man must go further.

The clock in the vestibule tells me that in another half hour this short day is finished. Officer Bird is at the desk. Cooler-headed than Watkins, Bird is also black and is also a believing Christian. Confirming that the chapel is indeed closed on Monday evenings, I ask Bird what he'll be doing after 3:30.

"Maybe try to find a place to hide out the rest of the day," Bird says, straight-faced. "I won't lie to you."

Save for Al and another lifer who are hunched in caucus on a rearward pew, the chapel is bare, its yellow brick walls graying in the afternoon light. The classrooms and Catholic suite are dark, and the office, though still lit, is empty. In his office, Baumgartner is speaking with mounting volume and decreasing patience to a woman on the phone who, from what I can surmise, has repeatedly failed to get a parcel through to her son, while in the adjacent office, the Imam, Sayyid, and Kazi are praying, their haunches raised up and foreheads pressed to the floor.

The Imam's door opens and Sayyid and Kazi emerge. Sayyid is glad to see me, he says. He has the papers he promised me last week that he wrote for Sister Barkley, the lively but astringent octogenarian Villanova professor who proudly goes by "Attila the Nun," and who—in a manner that made me appreciate the luxury of doing fieldwork on a population barred from calling or writing to me—has repeatedly excoriated me for the amorphousness of my scholarly methodology. Sayyid says he got an A-plus. Kazi alleges to no one in particular that Sayyid and the sister "had something going on," and, with that, takes off.

Sayyid returns to his Arabic textbook and dictionary. Sitting at Kaz's desk, I leaf through Sayyid's midterm paper, which uses the Trinity to demonstrate what the comparativist of religion Ninian Smart calls the "doctrinal dimension" of religion.[48] Sayyid extols doctrine as the force that endows order not only upon God's revelation, but the entire world. Whether they be religious or secular, "without doctrines," Sayyid concludes, "the world would be in a complete state of chaos."[49]

Indeed, by his own accounting, Sayyid is nothing if not doctrinaire. After he shared with me a number of Salafi tracts espousing a range of prohibitions, from smoking and drinking alcohol to singing and listening to music, I asked if he could identify any purported prohibition that upon further examination proved inauthentic.[50] He could not. Pointing me once to a verse in the Qur'an, he recited, "It is not for a believer, man or woman, when Allah has decided a matter, to have any option in their decision."[51] Nor is Sayyid's purported abnegation of open-ended inquiry limited to the sphere of Muslim learning. Identifying himself as part of the "ninety-seven percent" of Graterford prisoners who find the theory of evolution absurd, Sayyid complained, "Why is man so arrogant? Why does he try to know more than what God tells him?"

And yet Sayyid is not so easily pigeonholed. He has a quick, playful mind that makes him temperamentally unsuited to stop at faith. His claims to lockjaw epistemological modesty are belied by his exuberance in his Villanova classes, where he seems readily lost to the delights of learning for its own sake. At least in such secular spheres, Sayyid is hardly deferential.[52]

I glance up at Sayyid and find that he is still translating away.

Having secured the rest of the chapel, Bird shambles into the office and drops down into Al's chair. Sayyid looks up at him and bursts into laughter.

"You're a little bored, ain't you?" he asks.

Bird points up at the clock, which though a bit fast, now reads a couple of minutes past 3:30.

"Man," Sayyid says, stuffing his books and papers into his yellow mesh commissary bag, "I got to get out of here. I was sitting here and I got caught up!" He jokes: "It's your fault, Josh." I apologize and offer to walk him out. Okay, he says, but first he needs to quickly go into the Imam's office and confirm the meaning of a couple of words he can't figure out.

The main corridor is almost empty. At D Block, Sayyid holds up his commissary bag, and, after a couple of grunted biceps curls to dramatize its heft, hands the bag to the CO manning the metal detector. Once through, he points at me with both index fingers.

"No road rage," Sayyid says, and turns and disappears onto the cell-block.

On Monday evenings, the chapel is officially unused. And through the night as well, until roughly 8:00 the next morning, when staff and prisoners will return for another bout, it will remain dark. In the interim, what goes on is anyone's guess. Reverend Keita, for one, presumes the dirtiest.

"Things happen in this chapel at night," he said. More than once he has told me of arriving in the morning to find used condoms here. "Wash your hands carefully when you leave here," he counseled. "You don't want to bring hepatitis home to your family."

Who's having sex in here—staff, prisoners? I asked. Who knows? he said. Someone is. Couldn't I sense it? The way the place pulses with sex and power? Hadn't I seen the line for medication after noon count? Most of those men are HIV positive and many of them contracted the virus here, after they were raped.

"They'll rape you over nothing," he said. "Over cigarettes."

I asked, "And if I said that it used to be like that before the raid but not anymore I would be being dangerously naïve?"

"Yes," he said, his delivery languid, his pallid eyes earnest.

In his ministry, Keita can be alarmingly unyielding. My first exposure was in his baptism preparation class, where a young man described a recent failed parole in which he'd tried in vain to make peace with the brother of the man he'd killed. The brother had wanted nothing of it and pledged to kill the storyteller at the first viable opportunity. So now, facing a second chance at "going home," as it's called, the young man was struggling with how to deal with this impending dilemma. When he makes his choices out there, Keita told him, he ought to keep the model of Jesus Christ in mind. He quoted Paul, who instructed one to live "as if the night is almost gone."[53]

When the men had left, I sought to deflect the sick feeling in my stomach. What, I challenged Keita, could a cliché like *What would Jesus do?* possibly mean, given the realities presented? I mean, what if emulating Jesus is going to get this guy killed? Without raising his voice in emphasis, Keita said, "If what he must do is die, then that is what he must do."

Like so many whose lives have brought them to Graterford, Keita has not come by his moral sensibilities idly. Twice in his life, in his telling, he found himself in territory that renders this dark and strange place cozy by comparison. Born in Sierra Leone, he belonged to a terrorist group in the final days of colonialism, and he later returned to serve in a guerrilla army in the civil war there. He lived in the bush and toted a submachine gun. Atrocity happened in every which way. In Keita's telling, there was little discernible moral logic to any of it. He saw men he respected descend to beastliness, and he saw men he disdained risk everything for the vulnerable. The first was far more common. "People prefer darkness over light," Keita said matter-of-factly. In the notoriously unexceptional evil of Arendt's Eichmann, Keita sees the general order of things.[54] As he said at a recent Wednesday-afternoon memorial marking the passage of a week at Graterford with two suicides: "There are no good people. There are no bad people. There are only circumstances."

"This is a house of men fallen from grace," Keita once said. "For a Christian or a Muslim in this place, the game is not faithfulness or spirituality. What comes first in the mind of prisoners is survival." He compared the prisoner's lot to the exile's, for whom all available means must be in play. "External morality doesn't work here," he said. "If you're too moral, you won't survive. If you're too weak, they'll kill you. Building muscle means accepting certain things as part of me. Instead of healing, the prisoners have turned the prison into a world of their own. What goes on at night . . . what goes on is horrible. If you are a snitch, they'll kill you brutally."

It was late in my fieldwork when Keita said these words to me. In the darkened chapel, I asked him about those men I know well. All he has is rumors, Keita said, and passed the rumors on to me. Illicit sex was a common feature. And while for a socially conservative African like Keita, for whom consensual sodomy and rape are both abominations, insinuations here bent decidedly toward the latter.

When I reported back this destabilizing conversation, Baumgartner dismissed Keita's depiction as hopelessly outdated. But pressed for his own estimation of the frequency of sexual assault in the jail, he didn't dare hazard a guess.[55] Where the two long-term DOC employees agree is that with respect to life on the blocks, the unincarcerated can only be agnostic. The guys have a world of their own, Keita conceded, with its own language and rules, a world inaccessible to outsiders.

Just as there is pleasure to be drawn from the congeniality on the chapel's surface, there is consolation to be found in the silence that shrouds what happens below. But the comforts drawn from such elision are surely unwarranted. What goes on at night? I have little idea. Keita and Baumgartner, shrewd men who know Graterford as well as they know anything, have their intuitions about what they can't see, intuitions that experience has clotted into what feels to them like knowledge but might just as well be fantasy. To dig deeper would be impossible— and might also place the digger at risk of finding out what's down there. And so, graciously excluded from the abyss where men may be forced to confront whether, as Keita says, "good will vanquish evil or evil will vanquish good," the ghost stories Keita whispered about the world that comes to life when we're not around can only be left in the murky realm of the maybe, no more credible—from my sheltered perch—than the equally emphatic assertions to the contrary that such ghost stories are *merely* ghost stories and needn't keep me up at night.

TUESDAY

Years from now, at a critical stage in this book's realization, I will cull from this manuscript ten theses about religious life at Graterford Prison. Here's the first.

THESIS 1

Not only in our prisons are Americans crazy for God. We are a people who talk to God and to whom God frequently talks back. God talks to us through Scripture and through our waking thoughts and dreams. In our judgments about God, we are a remarkably confident people. We are generally confident that God exists, that He is personally invested in our lives, and that He reveals to us signs for discerning His will.[1] When and where it sprouts, our disbelief in God tends to reflect this very same self-assurance.[2]

Religion at Graterford Prison exudes the confidence and creativity that has dominated American religion and spirituality for the last 200 years. Somewhat curiously, confidence often yields claustrophobia. At the shimmering shell of this phenotype, one finds the chaotic genius of confident men like Joseph Smith and Elijah Muhammad, iconoclastic visionaries unafraid to approach God without intermediary.[3] At the hardened kernel lies the hermetic regimentation of the Nation of Islam and the Mormon Church. In America (and arguably in religion as such), innovation and authoritarianism go hand in glove.[4] Religions at Graterford participate in this contradiction. Through the impulsive religious judgments of each man, idiosyncratic religious forms are emphatically embraced as but the recovery of ancient truths. No sooner are such judgments made, however, than the putatively self-evident character of the resulting truths is marshaled to preclude the sorts of spontaneous discernment through which the individual came by them in the first place.

Their many differences notwithstanding, Graterford's predominant religious discourses—Salafi Islam and Protestant fundamentalism—share in this regard, too, a family resemblance. If, as a collective, the Salafi keep the Qur'an and hadith at the center of the recovery enterprise and the scholars bury their noses in the text, the rank and file seem contented with predigested doctrine. Ignorance of the tradition need be no obstacle to religious certitude. Similarly, with an interventionist Holy Spirit at work in a Bible believer's heart, the Bible itself can become more or less redundant. Interiority is endowed with divine authority; common sense becomes law and personal experience its jurisprudence. And, indeed, with so many of one's former friends and adversaries long since returned to dust, proof of His miracles is as plain as my next breath. As it is said: *Because by all rights I should be dead ten times over, I know that God has a special plan for me.*[5]

In the waiting room, a busload of black women, many draped in voluminous black fabric that covers all but their eyes, clutch their shyer children on their laps while throwing the occasional arm or rebuke in the direction of the more rambunctious ones.

Three steel doors and a long corridor away, meanwhile, the fifteen men gathered for St. Dismas Episcopal services are discussing what it takes to be a man. The brown-clad men fill most of the molded plastic chairs—colored tan, burgundy, and Pepto-Bismol pink—that line Classroom A's wainscoted perimeter.

At the far end of the cramped classroom, the chalkboard reads as follows:

"To Relinquish Possession or Control to Another—to Give Oneself Up to an Emotion"

V			yielding	D
I	succeeding			E
C			submitting	F
T	overcoming	v.		E
O			obeying	A
R	conquering			T
Y			surrendering	

From the conversation under way, it is clear that contrary to conventional thinking of the vertical characterizations, the rightward column is where the praiseworthy behaviors lie.

Oscar is talking. Oscar is a flat-nosed, dreadlocked lifer, thirty years into his sentence for a homicide committed when he was fifteen. In the free-form exchanges at St. Dismas that precede the homily, in which few who talk come off as reticent, Oscar stands out for his candor.[6] In his nasal but commanding voice, and favoring arresting hypotheticals along the lines of "Let's say I kill *you*," Oscar offers savvy testimony to the ways that a guy "gets caught up doing time."[7] With an emphasis on the everyday, Oscar stresses the inured passivity this place breeds; how via fear and prudence a man learns to shoulder petty humiliations and turn a blind eye to brutality.

"Yeah, we've got to surrender, like it says in Romans 8:36–39, but at the same time, like it says in Ephesians 6:11–13, we've got to be victorious against the devil. We've got to go like sheep. We need to die daily for Christ. We need to give ourselves up the way *God* wants us to give, not how *we* want to give it. I've been in the penitentiary almost thirty years, but it's not for me to say that I want to be free. It depends on what God wants for me. But, you know, this is the thing that's hardest for us to accept." Leaning forward, he gestures at the other seated men. "We're all warriors in here. I mean, why are the streets all full of women? Because the alpha males are all locked up in Gratersford"—as the old heads tend to, Oscar inserts a gratuitous "s" in the prison's name. He points at the board. "You see the 'V'? Well, that's us: stuck right there in the middle. Trying to be victorious in the way that *we* want to be victorious. But it's not about what *we* want. Cause when you surrender to *Him*, that's *real* victory."

Waving a rolled-up devotional pamphlet, another regular picks up the thread.[8] "*Surrendering* means surrendering our desires just as He surrendered himself on the cross. You see, what we need is the daily sellout." Consistent with the inversion of values being extolled, "selling out" here means not *capitulation*, as used to be said of hip-hop artists who crossed over to pop, but *conviction*. "Selling out" is the total commitment of self to a particular way of being in the world.

"That's right," pipes in the slim brown at the chalkboard. "We need to make an effort moment by moment. Like the moment I told you about earlier. It was eating me up. So I had to surrender, to apologize. I wouldn't have done that in the past. But now I'm free of it."

"Submission isn't just a onetime thing," a fourth man adds. "We're going to be tried *daily*, and we need to *deny* ourselves daily."

Paul's demand to the Corinthians that they need die daily, that they redirect their will and desire away from the ephemera of the world and onto the Lord, carries additional resonance here, where, as Baraka says, serving impulse's whim will get a guy sent to the hospital, to the hole, or to the morgue. In this light, Paul's prescription in Romans— "For thy sake we are being killed all day long; we are regarded as sheep to be slaughtered"—flips the "code of the streets" and furnishes for the men in this room a practical formula for surviving the abuses and humiliations of prison life. Whereas out on the street, to endure affronts without retaliation marked one as less than a man, here, in Christ, suffering is ennobled and self-sacrifice becomes self-mastery. Not merely a strategy for self-preservation, surrendering is the warrior's way in the cosmological struggle between God and Satan.

"And the more we struggle," says the brown at the board, "the more we're *tested by the fire*—as it says in First Peter, Seven—the more we honor God. I used to think: 'Lord, I gave myself to you, so why aren't things any better?' But it's not like that! We must be led like lambs to the slaughter every day. Prosperity isn't here on earth like they say in some of the churches. It's waiting for us in heaven. But as long as we're here, our relationship is between one another. We've got to learn to treat one another right. Despite all the nonsense we've done, God blesses us and watches over us and that's how we're still here. That's by God's grace. A lot of guys say, 'I'm saved.' But saved *for what*? You've got to be saved every day of your life!"

When the conversation dissipates, I trade discreet nonsense with

Neil, who is seated to my right. Despite his thinning mess of cornrows, the wispy ends of which overhang his cloudy eyes, at thirty-five, Neil presents as, in effect, a boy. And so he is treated, by St. Dismas's minister, Marcus Madison, at least, who frequently arrives with overbearing reports of e-mail exchanges with Neil's mother. Neil, who speaks with the Pittsburgher's Appalachian twang that never fails to exhaust the Philly guys' ridicule, is St. Dismas's worship coordinator—a position that consists largely of distributing prayer books and providing two of the four hands necessary for carrying in the table for Communion. When not in the chapel, Neil kills his time mostly among the small Dungeons and Dragons subculture on C Block.

Marcus Madison barges through the back door. Madison primarily ministers to St. Dismas's sister congregation, St. Mary's, an ailing brick structure in South Philly. Between gigs, Madison—a self-proclaimed bullshitter, so don't try to bullshit him—drives around in a fir-green Acura with tinted windows and a bumper sticker that reads: REAL MEN LOVE JESUS. As though the topic is already on the table, Madison launches in on the subject of Christmas gifts. It is a selling point for St. Dismas that all congregants and their children receive something for Christmas.

First off, Madison says, he wants to apologize to those who didn't get their packages.

"I thought that my family forgot me," says the brown at the board, "but then I found out that the institution just didn't deliver it." He looks relieved.

In the future, Madison instructs the men, they need to make sure to print their names rather than writing in cursive. They also need to make clear to their families what is permitted and what is not. The institution simply will not allow in anything decorated with tape, stickers, or glitter.

A triumphalist-sounding tape-recorded organ track emanates from Classroom B, where the Jehovah's Witnesses are meeting.[9]

Standing in the narrow passage between the two classrooms, I peer through the gap in the drawn curtains, but don't consider joining the half dozen worshippers on the other side of the glass. While men who worship are free to come and go as the spirit moves them, once the door to Classroom B shuts at 9:00 sharp on Tuesday and Thursday mornings, it does not generally reopen until the service is done.

Suddenly, Jack, the Catholic Christian Scientist, is at my shoulder. "Remember what I told you about the Jehovah's Witnesses?" he asks.

A month ago, in the course of his custodial duties, Jack took me aside and told me in the most serious of tones that something "you need to note in your report" was that in contrast to every other denomination, the Jehovah's Witnesses were punctilious about cleaning up after themselves.

"Rest easy," I assure him, "I'll be sure to indicate that they *always* clean up after themselves. Not like these . . ." I wave my hand around the chapel in search of the appropriate term of derision. Jack beats me to it.

"Protestants!" he barks.

The chapel is bright. Color pours in through the stained glass flanking the altar, projecting watercolor splotches of orange, green, blue, and purple onto the crushed-stone floor. In the front-right corner, where small groups congregate, a blue is preaching the Word.

Known for their navy pants and periwinkle shirts, the "blues" are the twenty percent of Graterford's population that are here for violating their parole. As classified but conceivably misplaced men, who, upon arrival, might or might not be in substance withdrawal or be nursing an old beef with another Graterford resident, the blues live sequestered on E Block; they don't work jobs. Until recently, they were barred from all chapel activities too, but after successful lobbying by Baumgartner, they were welcomed to the most popular worship services—the Thursday-night Spanish service, Jum'ah, Catholic mass, and the Sunday Protestant service—venues that furnish their only sanctioned contact with the browns. After further petitioning, the institution also okayed a Bible study, which last month was moved off of E Block and into the chapel.

The preaching blue is young, by chapel standards, soft-spoken, and, like everyone else clustered in the corner of the chapel, black.

"The devil is trying to take away from us, all day long. We need to stand with the bell of truth. Satan fights with lies."

Behind the blue, a second chalkboard offers another set of clues:

Phil 4:13
John 15:4–5

Luke 17:32
Hebrews 11:25
Ephesians 6:3–17
Phil 4:13
Subject: Ten ways to go into 2006 under God's supervision

A list of proof texts for some contention left undeclared. Were I among the initiated, I would be able to extract the thrust of these selections just as an avid baseball fan might reconstruct from this morning's box score the ins and outs of last night's game. On a snowy night under a desk lamp in my basement apartment, I will crack the code. Philippians 4:13 is the key.

I can do all things through Christ which strengthens me. It is a declaration that creates—or aspires to create—the new man it describes.[10] For those who, in John's language, have been "regrafted to the true vine," who, as Paul put it to the Ephesians, have "donned the armor of God," the affirmation divides one's life into two very unequal parts. There were all the moments prior to one's rebirth when failure was assured, and there are all the moments from here on out when success is achievable, so long as one keeps his focus on the here and now. Outfitted with the sword of the Spirit, the new man may be confident that he is up to the task.

This, as it is generally called, is "transformation." Transformation, as many in the chapel will tell you, is the opposite of "rehabilitation." For whereas state-sponsored rehabilitation can only change a man's external behavior, transformation—which comes from a man's own will or via the will of God within him—is said to fundamentally and irrevocably alter a man's character.[11] Arguably the dominant metaphor of evangelical prison ministry, transformation at Graterford comes foremost in a more secular iteration.[12] Men like Oscar who repeatedly complete Monday night's End Violence Program employ the language most influentially and ecumenically.[13] And so, while the traditions of Abraham, the Apostle Paul, and the Caliph Omar each furnish an array of men radically reordered, here it is the prisoner Malcolm X, who, for the inner-directedness of his self-refashioning, is transformation's patron saint.[14]

At the aisle's source, John, one of two prominent Protestants deputized to supervise the study, moves in from the rolling cart of Bibles on which he's been leaning and gestures toward the blue who has been preaching. "How are we looking at him right now?" John leadingly asks the assembled men.

"Like he's stepping out on faith," someone says.

"But how would the parole board look at him?"

With suspicion, says the silence. I know from Keita that the last time John was denied parole—it was his ninth rejection, for a sex crime of some sort—he left with the impression that his earnest testimony to the power of the Lord had roundly alienated the board members.

John continues: "But he's got to see himself as *God* looks at him. Because God loves us. Because where is truth?"

Silence.

"Where is truth?" John repeats.

"In the Word?" the preacher responds tentatively.

"No," John corrects him. "It's in the pudding. The proof is in the pudding." That is, to one day convince the suspicious, words are only the first step. Actions are what count. Among the oft-cited good news, however, is this: If a guy can live righteously in this crazy place, then he'll surely be able to do it back on the street.

John commends the guys for coming out this morning and begs them not to give up on their fellow prisoners. He says, "You might hear 'That's the white man's religion!' or 'That's what my *grandmother* used to tell me!' But remember for yourself, and remind them as well that 'God has a purpose for *you*.'"

Jack, Papa, Mike Callahan, and Father Gorski are seated in the bowl of the ladle-shaped Catholic office. Like Omar, Papa commonly hangs out over here, making me think of the Catholic office as, among other things, the place where, once they can no longer keep up, the elderly black chapel workers are put out to pasture. Mike is the other Catholic office worker. Rarely venturing outside the Catholic office, Mike sits at his desk with his *Daily News*, listening to public radio and goading his colleague Jack into states of increasing agitation. Father Gorski is the Catholic chaplain. Mustached and soul-patched, as well as collared, the early-forties Gorski lives in a parish house in nearby Pottstown, his hometown. The youngest of the chaplains, and the most sardonic, Gorski is also the only political conservative among them.

Jack begs me over with a wave.

I congratulate him on yesterday's confirmation of Samuel Alito to the Supreme Court. In spite of the direct and, one has to assume, unfavorable history many here have with that former Third Circuit judge, I figure a political conservative like Jack should be enthused.

"Oh," Jack says with a despondent wave of the hand, "it doesn't make much of a difference as long as the court's still full of wacko liberals."

Jack hands me the book he mentioned yesterday and directs my attention to his right where today's *Daily News* is opened to a photo of the Philly district attorney Lynne Abraham.

"Look how manly she is," Jack instructs me. "That reminds me," he perks up. "I've been meaning to ask you: How come Democratic women are so manly-looking?"

"Who else?" I ask.

"Well, Janet Reno," Father Gorski pipes in. This I concede.

"You know," Jack says, pursuing his hypothesis, "as a general rule, Democrats are *uglier* than Republicans. I mean, look at Ted Kennedy."

The resort to absurdist vitriol suggests that Jack is too lazy to play today for real. Largely, I have only myself to blame for the pattern of shoddy discourse I solicit from the Catholic side. One day, a few months in, I responded to a run-of-the-mill expression of revulsion about gay marriage with an impassioned defense of gay rights as a species of civil rights. The analogy proved little match for the "God made Adam and Eve, not Adam and Steve" party line, and set an excruciatingly static agenda for weeks to come. While we eventually got over that ideological hump, the news cycle is always good for another.

Sayyid has his head buried in his translation. Kazi is reading his textbook for this afternoon's class. A peppering of nosy pokes reveals that Keita, Baumgartner, and the Imam are each engaged in one-on-one counsel in their respective offices. The only office conversation to speak of consists of Brian explaining the implications of *Collins* to Teddy, though the term *conversation* is something of a stretch. Engaged with the case's finer points, Brian is breathlessly coming at Teddy, who, for his part, is listening intently, in search of anything that might possibly be interpreted along the lines of "and so therefore a reversal is in the bag" or "so tell your lady that you'll be home soon"—sentiments for which Brian finds little precedent in the case law, as he submits to you. When Brian finally takes a breath, Teddy asks him if he's got an extra copy for him. Brian says he's on it.

I ask Sayyid what precisely *he's* working on. "A *tafsir* of Al-Asur," he says. "Al-Asur?" I ask. "Yeah," he says, "it's about time." I perk up, eager to explore the resonances of a Qur'anic commentary *on time* for one *doing time*. More than willing to humor me, Sayyid explains that the author Sa'di is emphasizing the indispensable nature of four things to a Muslim. They are: (1) belief in Allah; (2) knowledge; (3) righteous action . . . at which point I begin to fall behind. I ask Sayyid to slow down, and he starts again, but the list is distractingly full of nuance, and the third and fourth elements each boast a number of dependent clauses that somehow refer back to the first two principles. Finding it too complicated for a quick fix, I tell Sayyid to forget it and let him get back to his work. With a good-natured titter, he promises to break it down for me this afternoon. For now, he needs to get the translation done so he can get the book back to Mubdi—an old Warith Deen head—who's been grumbling about wanting it back.

In spite of their doctrinal differences ideologically, Sayyid is the star pupil in Mubdi's Wednesday-night Arabic class.[15]

Across the hall, in the ten-square-foot box known as the "conference room," which is used primarily as a rehearsal space by the chapel's musical groups, four musicians—Al, Oscar, Santana, and a fourth guy—are discussing the challenges of trying to make it on the street following a lengthy prison sentence. A South Philly black Puerto Rican in his late fifties, Santana works in the chapel, directs the Sunday Choir, and, in Baumgartner's schooled estimation, possesses the chapel's most beautiful singing voice. When at the Veterans Day service I finally got to hear him do "Love Lift Us Up Where We Belong," Baumgartner sidled over to me and said, "I've left express instructions for Santana to sing this at my funeral."[16]

A gentle-seeming soul, Santana has been, since his return from the hole at summer's end, irritable and weary. As hearsay has it, the trip to the hole and subsequent foul mood both stem from Santana's mounting debts, which sent him away for his own protection and forced him to kick his drug habit cold turkey. In flusher days, Santana would offer me insights. "I've been told no so many times it just rolls off me like water. I know that if I stop trying, I'll die." Sometimes perseverance finds its mark. "*This* is what you should be writing about!" he shouted in my direction one day from the back of the chapel, waving a wrist-watch from his outstretched hand that an erstwhile Catholic regular had just given him, presumably to offset a debt. Santana is of the school that prison is little more than a microcosm of society at large. Just as Mamduh often quotes Dostoyevsky as saying, "The degree of civiliza-tion in a society can be judged by entering its prisons," Santana ob-serves that "anything you want to know about what's going on in this jail, just look at your society. You'll see it. You can't miss it. The only thing missing is the physical building."[17]

From behind the drum kit, the fourth guy, whom I know only by sight, is recalling a time from his childhood when a friend of his mother's got out of prison and was struggling to make it. From what he remembers, the guy had quite a hard go of it.

Oscar feels what the drummer is talking about. Sometimes, it's the little things that freak guys out, he says, like seeing dogs and cats.

Santana scoffs at this ridiculous empathy. He's sorry, he says. While he's happy to acknowledge the difficulties that go with the territory, he hasn't got any time for the bellyaching. "Of course it's hard," he snaps. "But what I wouldn't give for a shot! And the guys who do get the shot? They just wanna come back and complain about how hard it is! I mean, *please*."

"Yeah, that's true," Al says. "But it's like my lady tells me. It ain't nothing like how it used to be on the street. It's a different world out there now than the one we used to know, she say. And worse. Meaner. People won't even cross the street to piss on you if you on fire. And then you supposed to make it out there after being shut in for so long?" After a pause, Al continues. "That's why you need a real system of halfway houses, whether a guy is getting out on parole or maxing out . . . to help a guy adjust. It's like back on the outside when I used to buy fish. When you go to buy a fish at the fish store, they give it to you in a bag of water from out of the tank where *it* was living. And when you get home, you take the fish in the bag and put the bag in your fish tank. And then the water inside the bag adjusts to the new temperature, *gradual-like*, and then only after it's been in there for a while do you open up the bag and let him out into the tank. That gives the fish the chance to adjust to its new environment. If you just open the bag as soon as you get home and drop the fish in, it would die of shock."

A St. Dismas regular pokes his head in the door to let Al know it's time for Communion. Al hauls himself up out of his chair and follows the guy across the hall. I stand outside the open classroom door and listen to the song that accompanies the receipt of the sacrament. Few of the voices are particularly refined, or even in key, for that matter. Nonetheless, the song never fails to make the back of my neck tingle.

> *Let us break bread together on our knees*
> *Let us break bread together on our knees*
> *When I fall down on my knees*
> *With my face to the rising sun*
> *O Lord have mercy on me*

I listen in together with an obese Latino dwarf who lives on the new side, floats between various chapel rituals, and who explains, when I ask him why he's not inside, that he's not prepared to take Communion yet. Saying that I probably wonder why I haven't seen him around lately, he explains that he's fresh from two months in the hole.

"Seems like a long time," I say.

"No, that ain't nothing," he says. Once he spent eleven months in the hole. That was back when he first fell, though. And it had been for his own good, 'cause when he first fell he'd been hearing voices that told him what to do. He'd even gotten to thinking that he was God, if I can believe that.

> *Let us drink wine together on our knees*
> *Let us drink wine together on our knees*
> *When I fall down on my knees*
> *With my face to the rising sun*
> *O Lord have mercy on me*

But they got him on the right meds now.

"That's good," I say. As I know from experience, I tell him, meds can save your life.

He hates taking them, he says. This is no surprise. While fifteen percent of Graterford's prisoners are prescribed psychotropic medication, pharmacology is commonly disparaged as mind control.[18] So he just takes little bits of them, to sleep, he explains. You know, if he took everything they prescribed him he'd be a zombie. Plus, he saw in the media how they cause diabetes.

I encourage him to stay with it, that life is hard enough as it is. He knows, he says, and he will. But, he adds, it's not the meds that saved him. What saved him was *this*—he pats his Bible.

Let us praise God together on our knees
Let us praise God together on our knees
When I fall down on my knees
With my face to the rising sun
O Lord have mercy on me[19]

"Can I ask you a question?"

I look up from my notes to find a man whose unkempt appearance and coarse manner suggest shaky mental health.

"Sure," I say. "But first tell me, who are you?" He gives me his name, explains that he's been back inside for six months and has been a St. Dismas regular since then. He saw me in there this morning and he's been dying to ask me a question. Outside, he worked for a caterer. They worked a lot of Jewish functions and he's been trying to figure something out.

"Shoot," I say.

"Why is it that Jews drink so much at weddings and bar mitzvahs?"

"Because they find it difficult to deal with their families when they're sober?" I suggest with the pop-psychoanalytic common sense common to where I'm from. Not translating, he gives me back empty eyes. "How could you tell I was Jewish?"

"I can just tell," he says, and waits for a better answer.

I shrug off the failure of my first effort and give it another shot, delivering a clipped series of non sequiturs on how there is no prohibition against drinking in Judaism, how there are even certain holidays, Passover, for example, and Purim, on which you read the Book of Esther— he nods in recognition—when one is *obligated* to drink. His stare remains vacant. I fire off a few overintellectualized nuggets about how Jews aren't traditionally prone to alcoholism and some nonsense about how "drinking levels are cultural"—whatever the hell *that* means. Still no register.

Out of tricks, I go Socratic. "Are these bars cash bars or open bars?"

"Open bars," he says.

"Okay," I say. "And how do you act when there's an open bar?"

"I drink," he says.

"Do you drink a lot?" I ask.

"You bet," he says with a blustering exhale.

"Well, there you go!" I say, and turn back to my notes.[20]

In the back of the chapel, Sal is shelving the Jehovah's Witnesses' songbooks on their cart, flattening their tops and pressing their spines flush. I ask him how it went this morning. "Always beautiful," he says. With his characteristic combination of aggression and concern, Sal makes a crack about how tough it must be for me out on the street. I play along, complaining about what a drag freedom is. Good-naturedly, he pantomimes slitting my throat. I explain what I'm up to this week.

Sal reiterates what he told me one long summer evening in Baumgartner's office. In jail, he says, there just aren't too many things a man can choose for himself. So in those few realms where one has *any* freedom, exercising that freedom becomes very, very important.

Apologizing for my nonattendance this morning, I ask Sal if he'd be willing to detail for me what they did. They did a *Watchtower* Bible study, he says, and they learned about the workings of the Jehovah's Witness organization. He says he'll write me up an outline.

As promised, tomorrow Jack will hand me a sealed envelope, in which I will find a copy of the current *Watchtower* and a double-sided handwritten page. On the top it will read: "Joshua, Hope this helps. Sal."

At the heart of the itemized account, Sal will detail how the Witnesses read a *Watchtower* study article, "Now Is the Time for Decisive Action," whose title comes from First Kings and which takes as its theme Elijah's challenge to the Nation of Israel: "How long will you be limping upon two different opinions?"[21]

Sal's meticulous précis will capture the tenor of the Witnesses' meetings, the bureaucratic flavor of their biblical urgency, their catechistic regimentation. *Watchtower* essays read like grammar school exams in reading comprehension. Every question has a correct answer, which the reader must locate in the article, which has been peppered with scriptural proof. As examples:

Question: "What great apostasy did the Bible foretell, and how has that prophecy been fulfilled?"

Answer: Just as in biblical times, the worshippers of Baal were eradicated, so too will the "false religion" practiced by most Christians today be wiped out in the great tribulation fast approaching.

"What must we do to survive God's day of judgment?"

We must get off the fence and "act decisively now"! We must "take decisive action and zealously work toward the goal of becoming dedicated, baptized worshippers of Jehovah."

Back in the summer, I pressed Sal on this brand of scriptural certitude. Don't biblical passages at times possess multiple possible interpretations? I asked. No, he said, there are multiple translations of the Bible, which reflect the multitude of vantage points born of people's varied experiences, but there is only one interpretation because interpretation belongs to God. "Let the Bible do it itself," he counseled. "We cannot interpret God's Word, because he already did it for us." And those who believe Scripture to say something different? "They ignore the proof," Sal said. "They hear what they want to hear."

It is for me a challenging position. As I was taught back in Jewish day school, those texts that merit studying—the *sacred* ones, if you like—drive irrepressibly in the direction of openness. The Torah may be the perfect Word of God, but its verbal economy demands earnest interpretive labors. As was true in the Garden then, where man gave names to all the animals, also in the realm of Scripture are humans tasked with completing creation. Which, given the depth ascribed to these texts by the rabbinical tradition, means the obligation to never cease discussion.[22] In addition to the vital pleasures afforded, this attitude toward scriptural interpretation yields—I tend to think—at least one crucial ethical principle, that being: Thou shalt presume no monopoly over the Truth.

Which is all well and good, Sal might say, were not the final judgment soon at hand and the fate of humankind teetering in the balance. With such stakes, dillydallying in the wondrousness of the text is a luxury easily sacrificed. Quite simply, an erroneous interpretation will land you on the wrong side of eternity. One must act decisively now.

"Acting decisively now" means spreading the true religion to those who otherwise will be consumed in the fire. It means going cell to cell and passing out literature, even though such proselytizing is a violation of the rules and could, in theory, land you in the hole. It means bearing witness to every soul you come across, a Jewish skeptic no less so than anyone else. It means giving this skeptic, shortly after first making his acquaintance, a seven-page single-spaced letter that you'd sent to all but three of your graduating high school classmates in response to a print of the twenty-fifth-reunion picture that one of them anonymously sent you—a letter in which you apologize for your history of violence, an ugly character trait of which some of them were undoubtedly on the receiving end, and which culminated in your murder of an off-duty cop. But true to the cliché that there are no atheists in foxholes, you will say that in prison you have found a way to live other than selfishly, and though you have little hope of ever getting out, you believe with all your heart that a wonderful future awaits you. But in the meantime, you will say, oversight from God does not come without cost. It involves, rather, the tremendous responsibility of letting each and every one know about the coming Armageddon and reminding them of how in the Sermon on the Mount as it appears in Matthew, Jesus speaks of the broad road and the narrow road, and how on the broad road walk the spiritually indifferent, the misled, and those who do not know Jehovah, and that that broad road leads to everlasting destruction. But there is another road, a narrow road, on which walk only a few. These, you will explain, are the Jehovah's Witnesses. And you will say how it doesn't matter who you are or what you have done, for like the prostitute who cries at Jesus' feet, in the might of Jesus and Jehovah even the greatest of sinners may also find forgiveness.

Baraka is discussing the ethics of war with Vic the heathen. Yesterday, the professor, a moral philosopher whom they generally speak of with reverence, outed himself as a pacifist. To these two veterans, it is an asinine position. Baraka says something vague about "just blowing them all up." Then, staring at me for effect, he adds, "Just kidding."

"What?" I ask. "You think I'm going to submit an unsolicited note to the Clemency Board?"

"Be careful," Vic cautions. "We're both lifers"—he nods at Baraka—"both former Marines. It doesn't get closer than that."

"But what about our shared whiteness?" I appeal to Vic. "Doesn't that mean anything anymore?"

"Maybe fifty years ago, when we were wearing sheets," Vic says, laughing. "Now, not so much."

A call for Baraka comes from the Imam's office, and Baraka follows after. Vic points at me, stopping as if trying to remember something he had wanted to tell me. "Oh yeah," he says, "Princeton came up in class yesterday."

"Why?" I ask. "Walzer?" I figure that if they're talking about the ethics of war, they're probably talking about the political philosopher Michael Walzer, who is at the Institute for Advanced Study, Einstein's old haunt.

"Yeah, that's it," he says.

I explain the difference between the university and the Institute, how the folks at the Institute get paid simply for being who they are and don't have to do anything for it.

"Like you," Vic says, "getting paid for nothing." Vic is referring back to my explanation of how in my department, funding is not dependent on teaching.

"No, better than me," I say. "They're not beholden to anyone." Back from the Imam's office, Baraka flips out in my general direction.

"No, they're not *beholden* to anyone," he says, cocking his forehead to the right. "They're just called up now and again by the NSA to produce white papers, which they dutifully provide without having to be asked twice. They're all patriots, after all."

At "patriots," Vic issues forth an impromptu *Sieg Heil!* We argue about this a while. I say that while I appreciate Baraka's point about the various levels of beholdenness, if there exists a single bastion of freethinking in this country—where knowledge, though not produced in an ideological vacuum, is, at the very least, produced with minimal procedural fetter—it would be a place like the Institute. Baraka rolls his eyes as if I'm saying that our great nation is a place where everyone is born free and equal and rises and falls solely on the basis of merit. He takes his pad out of his breast pocket and jots something down.

Soon he and Teddy head for the blocks. "Look, all I want to say," Baraka says, continuing a conversation that I missed, "is that, contrary to what many guys around here say, death is *not* life, death is death."

"No," Teddy objects with equal vehemence. "Death *is* life because to live you must die every day."

"No," Baraka repeats. "Death is the opposite of life. Death is death, and it's final."

After lunch, Father Gorski brings Keita back a couple of staff dining hall apples and the Imam and I follow along. Though Keita's office, following lunch, is usually a sleepy venue, today things get absurd fast. Gorski berates Keita for having bided his time until his wife, Martha, left for her annual Africa trip before springing into action and putting her cat to sleep. Keita squeals coincidence, but Gorski knows better.

Behind Keita's desk, a colored-pencil drawing of eighties TV puppet and camp icon Alf spits forth a dialogue box reading "Got cat?"— a reference, if I recall correctly, to the idiosyncratic alien's preferred cuisine.

I ask Keita whether the cat killers let him take the carcass home so he could eat it.

"Maybe in Africa," Keita says, "but not here among the white man. Here it is, unfortunately, against the law."

Passing my eyes to the far wall, I notice that a full year past its expiration date, Keita's single-paneled *Shrek* wall calendar has finally been taken down. "What happened to Shrek?" I ask about the animated ogre.

"Yes," Keita solemnly says, "it was time to retire him." He will always love Shrek, though, he says, mostly for how he cooks mice rotisserie style. It reminds him of how back in Africa he would eat cave bats in the same way. Adopting a wistful air, Keita recounts how when he was little they would rise before dawn, climb into the hills, and watch the sunrise from the mouth of a big cave. There they would wait. Eventually, the bats would appear, fat from a night out preying on mosquitoes, and the hunters would crack their whips and smack them from the air. Then they would roast them on spits, just like in *Shrek*.

The Imam is horrified. No, he groans. In his native Nigeria they eat pigeons, but never bats.

Feigning incredulity at such prudishness, Keita reminds the Imam that back when they were wandering in the desert, the Hebrews ate bats as well. He points at me: "Your grandparents, or great-grandparents, or great-great-grandparents—they were bat-eaters too."

"Says us. But *my* people only converted with the Khazars." I'm playing with the trope common among the Black Nationalist religions that the biblical Israelites have no genealogical connection to today's Jews. "The true Israelites were Africans."[23]

Still chewing on the winged rodents' culinary potential, Gorski muses that bat wings must be light and crispy, an assumption that Keita confirms.

Baumgartner arrives with a stack of mail in hand, which he distributes, piece by piece. Baumgartner points out that he, Keita, and Gorski each received an identically worded communiqué from a freshly blued parole violator, pleading with them to please do something to stop his wife from divorcing him. Their collective response is a cross between bemusement and scorn. They've seen it too many times before, and this blue they don't even know. All they can do is laugh mirthlessly, substituting for their inefficacy the consolation of shared frustration.

The chaplains are in a bind. Because they are trained in a caring profession, they are predisposed to distinguish themselves from the administration's custody-based approach, in which prisoners alternatively appear as dangerous criminals or as tedious babies, requiring, in either case, the identical regimen of callous discipline. While the chaplain's aspiration to treat the prisoners as men is generally quite practicable, a conspiracy of factors nonetheless reinforces the prison's dehumanizing operating logic. From above, they must placate the custody hierarchy for whom accommodation spells weakness and empathy is a slippery slope. From below, they must fend off a population squeezed between infantilization and deprivation, and prone to crisis. In a facility of 3,500, this means a constant flow of tugging, cajoling, game-playing. Exacerbating matters, the chaplains are one of only two classes of employee in the prisoners' wings of the jail with direct phone lines to the outside, resulting in a parade of men pleading, on account of a family crisis, to please place a call for them, just this one time.[24] Periodically burned and, before long, burned out, the chaplains come to deflect, to indulge in gallows humor, and to adopt as a default condition a posture of sardonic remove, which in a roundabout way brings them into proper alignment with—as Father Gorski puts it—"the World of No!" in which the prisoners live, a world antithetical in ethos to the affirmative mode to which the chaplains consider themselves vocationally attuned. But such is the job.

As they commiserate over the letter, the Imam relates a story about a guy who came into his office last week frantic to get married before his child is born. He laughs. From a Muslim perspective, he complains, the child will be considered as born out of wedlock regardless, and anyway, he doesn't even perform marriages!

The Imam's anecdote returns Keita to Africa, calling to mind how his brother had so many girlfriends that in their village today, there are dozens of kids running around who look just like him.

"That's what you tell Martha, anyway," Baumgartner says.

Keita explains to me that his brother, as the village imam, gets up before dawn to make prayer, and when that's taken care of, he stops by his girlfriend's house.

"No!" the Imam hollers.

Surely, I suggest, the predawn tryst can only be a Muslim contribution to illicit sexuality, since without having to get up before the sun to pray, a Jewish or Christian man would surely rather stay in bed.

I excuse myself for Baumgartner's bathroom. When I emerge the prisoners are back, but Baumgartner pulls me aside.

"There is general concern that when you write your dissertation you're going to say that the chaplains just sit around and talk about sex."

I take up my spot in the back of the chapel and wait for the action to come to me, which it does presently in the form of Gabril, or, as most everybody calls him, Sugar. Gabril is stylish, and not just because of his Italian glasses and the sharp beard that he has pulled to a point with a razor blade. Rather, Gabril's whole way of being in the world is stylish, a manner heightened since his picture recently appeared in the *New York Times* in an article about middleweight champion Bernard Hopkins. Hopkins spent half his twenties in Graterford, where, per the old Hollywood formula, Gabril taught him to fight—this back when the jail had a traveling boxing team. According to the new formula, there's now talk of a movie, a project which, according to Gabril, Hopkins has vowed to postpone until his old mentor is free. Like Oscar, Gabril is serving life for a crime committed as a juvenile.

Gabril peppers his conversation with various sayings of the Prophet, in English mostly. His favorite, which he repeats like a mantra, instructs the Muslim to "Take care of these five before you take care of the other five: health before sickness, youth before old age, wealth before poverty, work before leisure, and living before death."[25] Of late, Gabril has been brokering conversations with some of the more influential yet lower-profile Muslims from the Salafi side.

"What's up?" Gabril says.

"Same old," I say.

Gabril is decked out in his browns' winter wear, featuring a burgundy corduroy coat and an even purpler knit hat, both of which fit as if tailor-made. I compliment him on the coat.

"Yeah, these," he says, dragging the backs of his fingertips along the wales. "This ain't nothing compared to what I would wear on the outside. I'd be wearing a *fine* coat, you can be sure of that, with my car keys in this pocket right here." He pats his breast. He seems preoccupied and turns to go, but then reconsiders.

Gabril looks at me with his milky fighter's eyes. "Have you heard the rumor?" he asks.

"What rumor?" I bite.

"Well, not the rumor," he corrects himself, "but the hearsay. Seventy-five percent of which, in my experience, turns out to be true."

"What?"

"Sayyid is in detention."

"What?" I stammer. "What's going on?"

"Unclear, unclear," he says. "I was hoping to come down here and find out."

"Well, let me know what you turn up," I say. He will, he says, though we both know that for want of opportunity or motive he probably won't. With an *Assalamu alaikum*, Gabril leaves me with this troubling revelation.

If Sayyid is in detention, then he is likely headed to what is known to all but the administration as "the hole." Though men in the chapel can emphasize the hole's positive aspects, speaking of it as a time apart where one can hone his spiritual discipline, refine his focus, and re-emerge recharged, being locked up in a two-man cell for twenty-three hours a day is a profoundly upsetting and arduous undertaking. Depending on what Sayyid is accused of, he could be looking at weeks or even months there. If found guilty of a violation, he could lose his job and his place in the Villanova Program. If things break bad, he could easily find himself shipped to another institution.

Even as I worry about Sayyid's welfare, I can't help but feel in Gabril's probing presence the excitement that accompanies the periodic eruptions of violence here—whether that violence be spontaneous and hot like last winter's, when a misprocessed new prisoner sent a guard to the hospital via medivac, or brutally clinical like today's.[26]

Teddy bursts in to find Baraka staring down the typewriter from over his lowered lenses.

"I just can't believe that you don't believe in the afterlife," he grumbles.

"Death is death," Baraka says, his scrunched brow unlifted.

Vic, who was inventorying bottles in the cleaning-supply locker, is thumbing his way through an old *New Yorker*. He says he's got a question for me. I tell him I've got a question for him.

"You first," he says.

"Okay," I say, trying to be an asshole. "Shouldn't you be cleaning?"

Vic gives me a cock-headed furrow. "No," he says. "I cleaned up this morning before you even came in." On his turn, Vic asks me about "the deal with Zionism," so I deliver a spiel about the movement's ideological drift from nineteenth-century socialism to twenty-first-century ultraorthodoxy.[27]

Scowling, Teddy announces that he's "bringing you both up on charges."

"For being white?" I say, fighting absurdity with absurdity. "If so, I'm innocent."

"No, not for being white—that's not your fault. But for invading the ghetto. Y'all gonna drive the prices up and pretty soon me and Kaz and Al ain't even gonna be able to afford to sit in here!"

And with that, Teddy leaves.

Below the chapel floor, pressure slowly builds as an ancient boiler turns water back to steam and pushes it through the closed loop that runs, when it runs, to every last corner of the jail. Absent the hum and clack of this hidden machinery, the chapel is silent. The winter sun casts long shadows from the pews' leftward edges, and shines on Al, who, alone in the chapel, is priming the PA system for tonight.

In the darkened conference room, meanwhile, four black men are watching a video of celebrity preacher T. D. Jakes.[28] Quiet for now, they will periodically erupt with "Yes, sir!" and "Amen," and when prompted they will lay their hands on one another. I'm looking for Charles, who's been missing since I've been back.

Unlike most of my interlocutors, Charles is slightly my junior. In addition to video ministry, the religiously eclectic Charles is a regular at the Sunday service, a student in Wednesday morning's Education for Ministry class, and even an occasional presence at the Native American smudging ceremony. Largely unschooled, Charles has a penetrating if not somewhat perverse intellect and does not shy away from provocative positions. He has openly condemned as "delusional" the sort of prayer that enables a guy to sit back and wait for God to intervene. He spoke too of "'these dudes' syndrome": how guys are always talking shit about *other* people, saying how crazy or pathetic "*these dudes*" are, whoever *these dudes* happen to be. But, as Charles sees it, "*We* are these dudes," and as such, "failures at life."

"I don't want to disillusion you," Charles said to me once, "but a lot of these dudes just come to the chapel for something to do." I was in no way disillusioned. For an anthropologist of religion for whom religious ritual, at root, is human activity, Charles's insight made all the sense in the world. Put simply, a Graterford prisoner who is looking to grow intellectually or spiritually may read in his cell, go to the school, or go to the chapel. The Graterford prisoner who wants to hang out with others may loiter on the block, try the yard, or come down to the chapel. Of course "these dudes" come to the chapel "for something to do." For Charles's peers, however, for whom religious sincerity is paramount, observations of this sort can only be taken personally. Consequently, the same live mind that commonly thrills me seems to render Charles a chapel pariah.

If varied, Charles's attendance in the chapel is also sporadic. As an out-of-state lifer, Charles is doing his time alone, and sometimes—I get the impression—he can't quite cope. Which is why, peering through the conference room window, I'm disappointed but not entirely surprised to discover that Charles is nowhere to be found.

Officer Bird's glasses are still tinted from the outdoor light.

"What's up with your hair?" he asks me. I pat it down. Solely by virtue of neglect, my frizzy head has grown into something of a spectacle.

I marvel with Bird at the madness of last night's ice storm, which left my Philly neighborhood a fairy tale and the highway a disaster.

"It's a sign of the times," Bird says.

A few minutes past 2:00, Al and Santana pass through the vestibule on their way back to the blocks. Apropos of the weather, I ask Santana if he's been outside today.

"You crazy?" he snipes at me. "Why don't *you* go out there?"

Baraka passes through and I pose for him the same question. He shakes his head. "Nah, nah. It's cold," he says. He then adds matter-of-factly, "*We* don't *go* outside."

"When's the last time you went outside?" I ask.

Another shoulder shrug ends the exchange. I don't think to ask Baraka who "we" is.

Half in search of the skinny on Sayyid, I venture back to the annex to check out who's shown up for Talim class, as it is designated on the weekly activities schedule but by no one else. In practice, Talim (*talim* is Arabic for "learning") is little more than unstructured time during which Muslims are allowed to congregate in the annex.

By the chest-high partition of flowered terra-cotta blocks that cordons off the shoe area from the rest of the annex, Mamduh is leading his small Arabic class. Behind these four, along the annex's eastern wall, two old men sit with books in their laps. Otherwise, the austere cinder-block cube is empty.

Early in my fieldwork, Tuesday afternoon's sparse attendance posed the chapel's most manifest mystery: Why, in a 3,500-man facility where a quarter identify as Muslims, does one find, during one of the two weekly windows when they are allowed unstructured time in the chapel, only a handful of men exercising the privilege?

Like today, Mamduh was usually one of the few Muslims around. He had a lot of questions for me back then, about where I'd been, what I'd read, who I knew, and how I knew my Arabic. He wanted my editorial help, too, on a manuscript he was completing for a correspondence degree in Islamic learning, a comprehensive guide to the "customs of nature" (*sunan al-fitra*) through which the devout Muslim's body may be restored to the state of purity in which it was created. Expressive of both his puritanical disposition and his encyclopedic scholarly style, the manuscript consisted of three-to-four-page chapters on subjects such as bathing, hair care, beard trimming, cuticle maintenance, and tooth care, findings resourcefully culled from a hodgepodge of sources ranging from medieval commentaries and modern religious tracts to commercial promotional material. A tract for insiders, each chapter concluded with a definitive prescription, or in cases where disputes resisted ironing out, with the humble acknowledgment that Allah knows best.[29]

In return, what Mamduh had for me was information, clues that pointed me toward the missing Muslims, which in turn helped me piece together Graterford's history more generally. Mamduh spoke with the affect of discretion—huddling close over the partition, dropping, at critical moments, his hoarse voice to a near whisper—but as time went on, he ceased to mask his partisanships and resentments. Mostly Mamduh was frustrated, frustrated with the intellectual lifelessness of his community, how unserious people had become, and how little support his community received from the Imam—a man whose observance of Islam he saw as deviating wildly from that of the Prophet. While I bristled against Mamduh's religious absolutism and came to understand his reputation among the chaplains as a malcontent, his facts tended to check out. His general air of lamentation didn't seem far off, either. For while I'm attuned to the fact that one of the moods that religion tends to foster is the preemptive mourning of its own passing, I took at face value the cataclysmic communal loss Mamduh described, and sensed that his bitterness, though partially misdirected, was in no way disproportionate to the devastation wrought by "the raid."

As recently as the summer of 1995, the chapel was awash in Muslim activities, which took place mostly in the basement. The jail had no fewer than ten Muslim-identified sects back then, but the two most prominent were Masjid Warith Deen Muhammad and Masjid Sajdah.[30] Both of these downstairs mosques—the more progressive Warith Deen and the more traditionalist Sajdah—were vibrant community centers. Each mosque convened daily for three of the five prayers and for a variety of self-administered programs. The two masajid had expansive libraries, too, where, in an era of residual openness, Graterford residents were allowed, with few restrictions. On Fridays, each mosque's Jum'ah service would draw hundreds of men, who, for the occasion, were allowed to dress in civilian clothes and invite in family and friends. Intellectually, spiritually, and socially it was a good time to be a Graterford Muslim.

Not all, however, was so wholesome. I'd been in the prison only a couple of weeks when I began to hear tell of a mythic figure—one more out of *The Arabian Nights* than HBO's *Oz*—a giant with humongous hands who used to run the show downstairs back when the Muslims were down there. It was said that his viziers would bring him trays of food, that he had his own phone line with outside access through which he ran his criminal enterprises—prostitutes on the inside, drugs on the outside—and how nobody had a goddamn clue.

Reverend Baumgartner also told me about the former leader of Masjid Warith Deen Muhammad, Ameen Jabaar. Relating a legend that also made it to the news, he described how one day a group of guards had come downstairs to announce an evacuation drill. Everyone was instructed to leave. One hundred men refused to move. The COs cajoled, but the men stood firm. The COs didn't generally go down there, and they didn't know what to do. Eventually, Ameen was sent for. In the *Philadelphia Inquirer*'s version, Ameen is a genie. "He came over and waved his hand, and it was done."[31]

Back then the administration's reliance on prisoner leadership for the maintenance of social order was undisguised. But a decade into the crack epidemic, violent crime was up, conservative social theorists warned of a new generation of super-predators, and even Democratic politicians couldn't be tough enough on crime.[32]

Corrections was the new master category, and control its linchpin. In institutions across the country, prisoners' movements were restricted and surveillance was heightened. Educational and psychological resources were gutted. The nominal purpose of incarceration ceased to be about rehabilitating prisoners. Prisons were now for punishment.[33]

Meanwhile, as American industry rusted, "the prison industrial complex," as activist Angela Davis dubbed it, boomed.[34] During the 1980s, the Commonwealth of Pennsylvania doubled its number of prisons, from five to ten, and in the nineties added eleven more.[35] Like the spike in traffic that often follows new highway construction, Pennsylvania's prison population skyrocketed as legislation and administrative adjustments raised mandatory minimums and restricted parole.[36] At Graterford, the new-side cellblocks were constructed.[37] A facility that in 1981 had a population of 1,900 men had nearly doubled in size.[38]

On January 17, 1995, Republican Tom Ridge was sworn in as Pennsylvania's governor. Responding to a moral panic over the exploding crime rate, Ridge had run a law-and-order campaign, promising as governor tough new policies, like a three-strikes-you're-out law and a streamlined death penalty process.[39] As promised, changes were instituted system-wide and at Graterford in particular: newly sentenced prisoners were shipped as far from home as possible, forced to earn their way closer to their families with good time; and the lifers, some of whom had lived in the Outside Services Unit for a generation, were brought back inside the walls. Neither was the chapel exempt. On February 3, a policy in place since the mid-seventies guaranteeing the right of prisoners to convene their own religious services was revoked.[40] Henceforth, no service or instruction would take place without a supervising chaplain or volunteer. And these were merely the tremors.

In his subsequent report to Pennsylvania's Senate Judiciary Committee, Governor Ridge's new secretary of corrections, Martin Horn, described the anarchy he had inherited. He explained how, at Graterford in particular, the liberal and humanitarian innovations of the 1970s, left unchecked for a quarter of a century, had festered. And Horn had taken it as his express mission to "sanitize this facility."[41]

Yunus, a former Imam of Masjid Sajdah, remembers what happened next. It was a warm night for late October and he was lying in his cell, the 99-cell, which sits at the top step in the front of B Block. It was after the regular 9:00 p.m. lockdown and his window was open. From the main corridor, the sound of hollering, of a commotion, roused him from his bed. And then: "Police is here!" "Raid!"

State troopers and COs from across the system stormed into the jail, 650 men in all. Over the next seventy-two hours, each of the prison's 3,490 inmates was strip-searched, and each of its 2,750 cells was ransacked.[42] When the swarm finally receded, prisoners' possessions were reportedly piled shoulder-high the full length of the cellblock. Casualties ran low and high. Nine employees were fired on the spot, and twenty-one prisoners, most of them community leaders and power players, were transferred, some across the state, and some, through a measure allowing states to trade their most dangerous, across the country. Among those shipped was Ameen, who, according to legend (and Baraka insists it is only that), was paraded away in nothing but handcuffs and underwear.[43]

The press trumpeted the size of this game. In its coverage on day two of the raid, the *Daily News* ran a feature on Ameen, entitled "Inmate Throne for a Loss; Prisoners' 'Kingdom' Toppled." Drawing no distinctions between Graterford's various Muslim groups, the piece described how "the Iman [sic], or religious head of Graterford's Muslim population," and his battalion used religion as a cover for criminal activity. "As the religious services were going on in one room, a brothel was being run in another."[44]

The Muslims' sway was eminent. "'If you don't want no trouble, become a Muslim,'" the *Daily News* reported a Graterford-bound prisoner being told on the bus. "They'll protect you 'cause the Muslims run the jail. That's how come a lot of guys get religion when they go to prison.'" The article concluded on an up note: "But he remained a Christian."[45]

When lockdown ended and the Muslims returned to the chapel for Jum'ah, they found the mosques ransacked. Soon thereafter they were informed that their days downstairs were numbered. A new era had dawned. Family and friends were banned, and civilian clothing was prohibited. For nine months following the raid, no volunteers were allowed in the jail. Graterford's chaplains oversaw the larger services, and the gatherings of the smaller groups were suspended. The Muslims continued to meet downstairs, now under the supervision of the COs and Graterford's first Muslim chaplain, who was hired on a contract basis.[46]

Of the two masajid, the traditionalist Masjid Sajdah was the more obstreperous. A lawsuit was filed. Avowing a decentralized democratic sensibility indigenous to American religion and Islam both, Sajdah opposed the DOC's new concentration of religious authority. "O you who believe!" the Sajdah brief quoted the Qur'an. "Obey God and obey the Apostle, and those charged with authority among you."[47] For Sajdah, "among you" was proof that a DOC appointed imam would not suffice *Islamically*. Further support for this principle of local autonomy was found in a hadith, a saying of the Prophet: "No man must lead another in prayer where the latter has authority, or sit in his place of honor in his house, without prior permission."[48]

The Sajdah plaintiffs made a strong case, but the climate was not what it once was. Relying on the guidelines laid out by the 1993 Religious Freedom Restoration Act (RFRA), the DOC trumped Sajdah's expansive reading of religious autonomy with an appeal to security. Making explicit mention of the mosques' raised floors and drop ceilings, the DOC argued that these spaces were "conducive to hiding contraband, which can include weapons, money, and illegal drugs." The DOC made no explicit claim about criminality on Sajdah's part. Indeed, it acknowledged the masjid's two-decade track record of clean behavior. However, because the equal protection clause requires that all groups be treated the same, this record was immaterial. Similarly, because allowing an inmate to occupy a leadership position affords him "a power base" from which to incite violence or conduct illegal activity, such positions were also, for security reasons, to be eliminated.

It is easy to imagine the forked resentment with which members of Masjid Sajdah greeted the DOC's response brief and the resounding defeat it foretold. As it could only seem to them, the Warith Deen guys stepped out of line, the DOC retaliated, and Sajdah got caught in the crossfire.

Such was the poisonous environment into which the mild-mannered Nigerian émigré Namir Kaduna was thrown. To exacerbate matters, before becoming Graterford's imam, Namir had provided the DOC an affidavit stating his understanding that there is no prohibition in Islam against being led in prayer by a government chaplain. Inevitably, the hostility only grew once Namir was on the ground. As Mamduh said, "When a chaplain threatens to give you a write-up"—a measure that could mean two additional years come parole time—"you know where he stands."

While Baumgartner now sees "the Imam"—as most call him—as his "right-hand man," he too initially presumed Namir to be a plant from the secretary's office. Three candidates had been up for the job— the current contract chaplain, a second African-American, and Namir. When Baumgartner showed up for the interviews, the assistant secretary of corrections, Jeffrey Beard, pointed to Namir and told Baumgartner, "That's our guy."

The conspiracy, as it turned out, was somewhat different. As Baumgartner and other Pennsylvania prison chaplains figure it in retrospect, Namir's hire was plainly a part of a DOC effort to replace the first wave of African-American contract Muslim chaplains with full-time ones from the Middle East and Africa. Thought of as being both apolitical and devoid of compromising ties to the neighborhood, the foreign chaplains were seen as less dangerous than their African-American counterparts, who, a generation later, still carried the revolutionary odor of Malcolm X. Still years away, of course, was 9/11.

Namir's marching orders were to take Graterford's divided Muslim community and make it one. It was a directive Namir wholeheartedly believed in. Why should Muslims who pray to the same God pray separately under the same roof? "Do you believe in Allah?" Namir asks would-be schismatics. "Do you believe in *rasul Allah?*"—that is, in the messenger of Allah, the Prophet Muhammad? If the answer to both questions is yes, then you are a Muslim and you can pray with all other Muslims the same as they do in Mecca. Or so the Imam continues to insist.

Not all have been equally obstinate. The Warith Deen elders, who tend to be politically savvier than their more absolutist counterparts, knew not to look a gift horse in the mouth. And so, opting for graciousness over contempt, it was Baraka, then a chapel janitor, who ended up the Imam's clerk, with use of a desk in his office and access to his ear.

Ten years past, the raid is still an object of great passion and frequent discussion. In the ritualized recollections of prisoners as well as staff, it is generally derided as having been a wasteful and capricious exercise. Even the military-styled career DOC employee who began his new staff orientation with a half-hour retelling of the raid attested to the fact that the cache of drugs and knives paraded before the media consisted entirely of items seized beforehand.

Baumgartner isn't over the raid, either. The chapel's criminal excesses were a humiliating revelation; the DOC's brutal response was destabilizing, as intended; and Baumgartner remains equal parts wary and resentful. Nonetheless, if pushed to say one way or another, Baumgartner figures that in aggregate, the net effect of the raid in the chapel has been a positive one, with the increased security and oversight leading to "more authentic" forms of worship.

In Graterford's institutional memory, the raid is the pivot point between two periods: Before the Raid and After the Raid. Albeit belatedly and imperfectly, the raid yanked Graterford into the era of carceral control. In the ascendant regime of diminished opportunities and heightened restrictions, not all of the new measures seem excessive.[49] Whereas prior to the raid, prisoner movements at Graterford consisted of simply throwing open the cellblock doors and flooding the prisoners into the main corridor, nowadays, work lines, activities, and yard are each moved in deliberate sequence. So whereas before the raid, drug deals and contract killings would take place right in the main corridor, such occurrences are now almost unthinkable. In 1995, Graterford had 102 reported inmate assaults, but by 1998 that number had fallen to thirty-two—though the vast majority of assaults still go unreported, just as they did before.[50] And while prisoners, staff, and administrators all assert that anything one can get out on the street a guy can also find at Graterford, drugs are allegedly much harder to come by.

Meanwhile, the bygone era, characterized by Mamduh's protégé, Nasir, as "TVish" for the grotesqueries of its purported realism, has become an object of considerable nostalgia. As one longtime female CO compared the present to those *realer* days: "Yeah, it's safer now. More boring, but safer." It was harder then, it is commonly said, but better. The new era is worse, not in spite of the increased safety, but precisely *because of it*. Doing time has gotten *too* easy, many older heads say. As Baraka put it, these days there's "too much breathing room," which keeps the young guys from committing themselves wholeheartedly to anything. "Back then," he said, "there was no gap between what you said and what you did."

"Then we had men here. We just have children in here now," Santana said, complaining that the young guys treat their time like a vacation, just lying in their cells and watching TV. In the old days, it is said, the prisoners had a sense of unity, one that they would channel into strikes for better food and health care, but such actions could never take place now. By stick and carrot, the prison population has been broken down and atomized. Whereas once there was a system of block representatives and prisoners would employ the tools of organized labor as a counterweight to the administration, nowadays, according to the youthful president of the Graterford Branch NAACP, "if you try to stand together, they treat you with Thorazine." Or, more likely, would-be agitators are simply shipped out, losing in the process the few privileges they enjoyed—their jobs, their activities, their stuff, and proximity to their downstate friends and family. Since, as Al put it, "He don't know me and I don't know him," one has little trust his fellow prisoner won't snitch. Unlike back in the day, now everyone just looks after himself.[51]

In such an environment, is it any wonder that the religiously inward Salafi Islam common to the former Masjid Sajdah crew has ascended while the activist Warith Deen brand of Islam has increasingly acquired the dull face of a historical artifact?

What was lost in the raid remains palpable in its absence. In Mamduh's accounting, whereas Jum'ah downstairs used to draw in aggregate between 700 and 1,000 people, it's now half that. Some guys study on the blocks, but if they try to do so in groups larger than six, the COs are supposed to break them up. According to Mamduh, many of the former Sajdah guys actively boycott the chapel. Everyone comes to Jum'ah because according to the Sunnah it's obligatory, but that is all the legitimacy they are willing to lend to the man mistakenly honored, in their view, with the title of Imam. Others tell it differently. Chapel attendance is down, they say, not just for the Muslims but for everyone. Before the raid, the chapel provided a precious haven from the insanity common to the rest of the jail. Nowadays, increased security makes the need for a sanctuary somewhat less pressing.

For whatever reason, on Tuesday afternoon, with Talim on the program, I'm not at all surprised to find only five men in the annex. And so, in search of details about Sayyid's detention, the annex seems unlikely to bare any secrets.

Teddy ambles up the center aisle and drops down in the front row of pews. I'm standing at the lectern at the foot of the altar, where I've been scribbling in the formerly empty chapel. It's all I can do not to ask about Sayyid.

"You know," Teddy says to me, "usually when someone starts at a new job, it takes them a while to figure things out, but you come in here, and right away . . ." Teddy trails off, his flattery unfinished. "What you doing, *lurking* back there?" he growls past me. I turn and find Baraka, who has materialized on the rear of the stage. He is helicoptering his arms in the widening circles that make up the concluding reps of his daily stretches. Teddy hops to his feet and closes in on Baraka. They trade a few words out of earshot and then wander over in my direction. As they come back into range I make out something about Sayyid being on L Block.

"How do you know?" I ask to blank stares. Thinking the problem to be an unidentified antecedent, I repeat: "How do you know Sayyid is on L?" Again, no answer. "How do you know?" I ask again as Teddy approaches me. Teddy leans into the mic stand at the foot of the stage, amps up his voice, and echoes, "Know? Know? Know?" With evident impatience, he cocks his head toward the security camera.

Baraka adds, "You forget that we are living in a police state here."

"Shit," I say. "Oops." Silence.

Baraka smiles. "You never know if we're joking, do you?"

"No," I say, "but"—I echo his words back to him—"I proceed as if *everything* in here is *real*, or at the very least it better be treated that way." Apparently, Teddy is not the only suck-up around here.

Teddy takes off. Meanwhile, as the next phase of his exercise regimen, Baraka starts walking a determined circuit between two rows of pews to my left. He thinks out loud about some projects he might undertake under the auspices of the newly launched Graterford chapter of the Villanova Alumni Association: a video to be shown on the in-house Graterford network, about domestic violence; a facilitation program for kids with incarcerated parents; a resource bulletin to be distributed in the visiting room that will inform family members of their rights. Having recently met a woman who's offered to help, Baraka asks which option sounds appealing.

I say that she'll likely be game for whichever. "Given your prominence," I add, recalling Brian's teasing from yesterday.

"What are you talking about? I'm not anybody," Baraka says in the high-pitched tone that might just be his tell.

"That's not what I hear," I counter. "I hear that when you go down to the visiting room, four shorties carry you in a litter while a fifth walks alongside, feeding you chocolates." Baraka indulges me with a wheeze. He continues to walk. I continue to write.

Baraka brings up his case. Last year, he tells me, his wife and daughter found previously undisclosed statements made by the state's key witness, none of which makes any mention of him.

"So you're claiming innocence?" I ask him. This I didn't know.

"Innocence and *Brady*," he says, referring to *Brady v. Maryland*, the 1963 Supreme Court case that established a prosecutor's willful failure to turn over potentially exculpatory evidence as reversible error.[52]

In a direct disclosure atypical enough to make me wonder about his motivation, Baraka continues, filling in a number of details I hadn't known. His 1974 conviction was based on eyewitness testimony alleging *not* that he was the shooter but only that he participated in a conspiracy to commit murder. And for this, life? It strikes me as odd, but I hold tight to my confusion. "Unfortunately," Baraka says, "the guy with the hardest time proving his innocence is the guy who doesn't know anything about the crime." The first he saw of any of his alleged coconspirators was at his trial.

"Hmm," I start, "so as easy as it is to *allege* conspiracy . . ."

"Is how difficult it is to unprove it," Baraka finishes.

"So why you, Bar?" I ask. "Why did they put the frame on you?"

"Because a few weeks earlier I shot a cop," he says. He adds derisively, "That is, according to them, I did." This Baraka has told me before. As Baraka explains it, the charges were later dropped for lack of evidence. Nevertheless, I am momentarily curious enough to make another social misstep.

I ask: "So am I to believe that despite all your talk about *putting something in somebody's head*"—Baraka's preferred term for retaliatory assassination—"you never put anything in anybody's head?"

Baraka's laugh this time is not high-pitched. "You know, there are some things I will not answer."

Clumsily I cover. "Well, you know, there are some things I won't ask seriously." We each let it drop.

Two older Muslims emerge from the annex. Baraka hails them in Arabic and they respond in kind. They turn and slowly edge their way toward the back of the chapel.

Baraka turns to me. "When you're done here," he says with assurance, "you can say that you met certain people."

I don't understand. "Isn't that Abdullah Shah?" I ask, referring to a man who though a widely respected Warith Deen elder, is—as far as I'm aware—no more famous than that.

"Nah," Baraka says, "that's Rafiq."

"Rafiq? Who's that?"

"Rafiq?" he repeats. Nothing is triggered. He tries a Christian name, first and last. The name rings only the vaguest of bells. Baraka looks at me incredulously. Then it clicks. It's the name of one of the men featured in a recent book that a couple of the younger guys turned me on to, which chronicles the rise and fall of Philadelphia's Black Mafia. This guy was one of the ringleaders.[53]

Baraka jumps to a subsequent conclusion. He instructs me: "You have an obligation based on what you've seen to tell folks out there that some people are not what they are said to be."

We watch the two hunched men slowly recede. "You know, those guys were both my lieutenants back in the FOI," he says, referring to the Fruit of Islam, the Nation of Islam's paramilitary order. With a look of pride and protectiveness, Baraka watches over the trudging old men as they leave the chapel behind.

From the volume of the quiet, we intuit that it's time for Baraka to head out, too.

Teddy is in the process of leaving the chapel. Jutting out of his mesh commissary bag is an ostentatious brick of candy. The candy is surplus stock from Christmastime when the Brotherhood Jaycees, a youth service organization, distributed the sweets in the visiting room as part of their annual fundraiser. Now a month past, Teddy, the Jaycees' secretary, is in the process of removing the remainder from its storage place in Keita's office.[54]

Teddy and Bird are stepping at each other, with Bird making phantom peaks into Teddy's stash. Teddy pushes him away. Bird thrusts. Teddy parries. Why this is only a game I have no idea.

Once the prisoners are gone, I ask Bird about why Sayyid is on L.

Bird corrects me. He's not on L yet. They have him in detention on the block.

"What does that mean?" I ask.

"Could mean lots of things," he says. "Could mean that there's a new guy in jail that's scared of Sayyid, somebody that knew him fifteen years ago. Could be extortion, could be any number of complicated things they're trying to piece together."

"Contraband?" I ask.

"Nah. If it were contraband, he would've had it or not, and he would be in the hole already."

"What's gonna happen?"

"Too early to say," Bird answers. "At a minimum, he'll get ten days for suspicion."

"Do you think he did anything?"

"Who knows?" Bird shrugs.

"Of course," I say, push-polling. "From what I can see, though, that guy is super-diligent. Always down here, working on his translations."

"Who knows?" Bird repeats. "Whatever he might or might not be doing, that doesn't make his religious activities insincere or anything."

The Rabbi shuffles in, carrying a stack of books in one hand and dragging with the other a tote bag with this month's *Graterfriends*, the newsletter of the Pennsylvania Prison Society. Retired for the better part of a decade from the pulpit of a Reform New Jersey congregation, the Rabbi works a ten-hour-a-week contract. Refusing my offer of a hand, the Rabbi invites me upstairs, and I follow.

Upstairs, he asks me about my research, and I tell him what I'm up to. Why the experiment? he wants to know. I explain that detailing a week in its entirety should allow me to showcase the chapel's amazing religious diversity and explore what ecumenism looks like in practice. After all, I add leadingly, its brand of ecumenism is itself a liberal Protestant vision.

The Rabbi puts his palms on the table. What I need to recognize, he says, is how truly extraordinary the chaplaincy staff at Graterford is. "Where else," he asks, "can you find a Lutheran minister with a Ph.D. from Dropsie, a Jewish institution"—where Baumgartner received his doctorate in Hebrew Bible—"and a rabbi with his Ph.D. from Drew, a Methodist school?"

It's not that I disagree with the Rabbi's claim on behalf of the chapel's ecumenism. It's just that as I see it, a mode of religious pluralism that aspires to treat all descriptions of God as equally valid does not burden all religionists evenly. It asks much more of a man who believes that Christ's death on the cross changed *everything* than it does of someone like me or the Rabbi, for whom what happened on Sinai is one factor among many. Theologically, socially, and politically, the Rabbi is very much a liberal, which often lands him to the left of his small group of parishioners. He is outspoken in his criticism of Israel's imperial expansion and regards religious orthodoxy as but one of many forms Judaism assumes. He and Brian recently went at it over the 613 commandments (or *mitzvot*), which Brian passionately framed as *the* defining obligations of Judaism—whether Jews choose to follow them or not—and which the equally animated Rabbi played down as at root a rabbinic mnemonic.[55]

On judgments of others' Jewish observances, the Rabbi throws up his hands. "I'm in sales, not management," he says, though as goes with the territory, manage he must. So as to protect, for example, against his community being overrun by black nationalist Black Israelites as has happened elsewhere, the Rabbi enforces a rule that to participate in Jewish services one must have at least one Jewish parent. Jailhouse converts need not apply. Or, for the stated reason that incarceration excludes the necessary autonomy, the Rabbi categorically rejects jailhouse conversions to Judaism.

Perhaps sensing some hesitation on my part, the Rabbi states, "Ours is not a shallow ecumenism."

"How would you typify how Graterford is different from other jails in this regard?" I ask the Rabbi.

"At other jails, religion is undoubtedly framed in more emotional, less intellectual terms," he says. "Plus, at Graterford we find a true commitment—not a lip service—to the attitude that *my religion is the best religion for me*, and not necessarily the best religion absolutely.

"You've heard of Ramirez, the former Spanish chaplain?"

I nod. "What about him?"

"Well, he needed more. He needed not only that his religion was the best for *him*, but that his religion was the best, period."

"And how did that play out in practice?"

"Well," the Rabbi says with his usual discretion, "let's just say that he did not regard Islam as a religious equal." Others have been more pointed. According to David, a Jewish chapel worker, Ramirez had no compunction in declaring Islam to be the devil's religion and telling the Jews to their faces that they were all going to hell. When he was around, I'm told, the chapel was an exceedingly tense place to be. "If a guy like him were in charge," Al said to me, putting a flat hand across his chest, "the blood would be flowing up to here in here."

The Rabbi excuses himself to go make his rounds of J and L blocks, to see the men in the hole and on death row.[56] Filling the Rabbi in on the day's news, I ask him to keep a lookout for Sayyid. The Rabbi apologizes, saying that he's not so good with names. I say that he'll know him by sight. We descend the stairs and part ways in the vestibule.

In the office, Gorski and Keita are waiting for the Imam to finish up whatever he's doing so they can all walk out together. Pressing me for precision, Keita asks me to identify the distinct smell of the white man. I can't name it, I say, but when he smells ripe, it means that he's ready to be eaten.

"Mmm," Keita says. "You smell ready. I think I will eat you."

Deadpan, Gorski asks Keita, "Albert, when you first saw a white man, did you think he was a god?"

"How could he have?" I say. "What kind of god sits in a big cast-iron pot?"

Which again reminds Keita of his rotisserie-cooked bats. "You eat them with pepper," he says, smacking his lips. "They are tasty, juicy, and as big as pigeons."

Teddy rouses me with a caustic *tsk*.

"Sleeping in a jail?" he asks. "What are you . . . crazy?"

I'm twisted in Al's chair, my feet up on his desk, my head pressed against the wall. Teddy steps around me and falls into his chair. Behind him, glare from the fluorescent lights shines back against the window, beyond which is night. Rolling his desk chair back and forth, Teddy talks about how little sleep he's been getting. It's been shallower even than the usual dreamless, one-eye-open stuff Teddy says is the only sleep a prisoner can afford.

"You know," Teddy says, "guys get so desperate, so pathetic about this law stuff." He shakes his head side to side. "It makes them lose their cool, you know?" He pauses and looks me down. "Me, I'm stepping out on faith. Because, you know, I can want something with all my heart, but if God doesn't want it, then it's not going to happen. But if God is good and everything happens for a reason, then I just need to wait and *He'll* take care of it. Because with the courts and with my case and this whole incarceration thing . . ." He trails off for a time. "It's like when God hardened Pharaoh's heart in order to punish the people. But eventually, even Pharaoh had to let His people go. And if Pharaoh was no match for God, then what chance does the Pennsylvania DOC got? Know what I'm saying?" Taking cover in my post-slumber fog, I merely nod.

The door opens and the Rabbi enters. "I saw him on L," he announces, before seizing up when he notices Teddy in the corner.

"Who did you see?" I ask.

"Sayyid?" Teddy adds excitedly.

Realizing that he's gone too far to retreat, the Rabbi says, "Yes, I saw Sayyid." Bird leans in the door as the Rabbi continues with his accidental report. He saw Sayyid on L in the riotproof glass wedge that doubles as visiting room and holding pen. Sayyid told the Rabbi that they have him there while they investigate a possible infraction; what, he has no idea.

"Did he seem okay?" I ask.

"Unnerved," the Rabbi says, "but none the worse for wear."

Teddy asks if Sayyid sent any special word. "No," the Rabbi says, "just that I should tell the guys that he's okay." The Rabbi quickly checks his mail, which sits sorted on top of the filing cabinet in front of Baumgartner's door, and then heads upstairs.

"Thanks for reporting," Teddy says.

"I didn't mean to," the Rabbi says, punctuated by a Yiddish shrug of his shoulders.

Bird props the door open with a chair and lingers in the threshold. Having seemingly overheard Teddy's sleep talk, he says he's been fighting with his bed since he changed his habits—started drinking less, stopped taking some dietary supplements. A ringing phone in the vestibule pulls Bird away.

Gesturing at the door, Teddy says, "It's beautiful, he's about to testify."

I look at him without understanding.

"About to reveal something personal," Teddy clarifies. "We didn't ask him for it, but he was about to tell us something personal about himself. It's a beautiful thing."

Not thinking of Bird as particularly reserved, I listen for some note of irony but don't catch any.

When Bird returns, Teddy cautions him against taking supplements. "God made us beautifully, in His own image," Teddy says. "You don't need to try to improve on what He's given us. Not that you shouldn't go to the doctor like some guys say, just that He's made us how we ought to be already."

I ask, "So some guys say that going to the doctor messes with God's plan?"

"Yeah," Teddy says, "but they're fools. God doesn't want you to be stupid. You've got to be careful with your body, especially in this place, with the stress and all."

"And the food," I say, throwing in a common theme.

Teddy exhales. "If you're a fool enough to eat the food," he says.

"You don't eat it at all?" I ask.

"Nah. You see these dudes that work in the kitchen?" he asks incredulously. "Some of them don't even wash."

Bird leaves and Papa takes his place. With sagging jowls and an expression to match, the elderly chapel worker gazes toward the garbage can by the bookcase. "Man," he says, shaking his head, "I purposely didn't clear that wastebasket to see if anybody on this side would do it. And nobody did. The new guy has got to learn about his responsibilities." I'd seen Vic engaged in custodial activities this afternoon, I vouch.

Khalifa slips into the office and sits down at Al's desk. Though not a chapel worker, the prematurely bald and fully bearded Khalifa kills a fair amount of time down here.

"Did you get your visit?" Papa asks him.

"Yeah," Khalifa answers, pulling on his beard, "it was good." He adds, "My mother sends her love, of course." I'm surprised that Papa, a Christian in his seventies, and Khalifa, a Muslim in his thirties, would have people in common.

"Hold up," I say, "you two knew each other on the outside?" I'm confused.

"Sure," Papa says. "I know 'Lifa's mom real good. We grew up together."

I register my surprise.

"Why you surprised?" Papa asks. "Don't you know that *all* us chapel guys knew one another on the outside?"

"You're from South Philly, too?" I ask Papa.

"Sure," Papa says. "All of us is."

This I hadn't realized.

I've been living in Philly for a year now but I want to make sure: "When you say South Philly, where exactly are you talking about? What are its borders?"

"Pretty much from river to river," Khalifa says, "and from South Street on south."

"So you're all from the same neighborhood," I press. "That doesn't automatically mean that you all know each other."

"Everybody knows each other in South Philly," Khalifa explains, South Philly being comparatively small.

"Everybody?" I ask.

"Yeah, everybody," Khalifa says.

"Regardless of race, even?"

"Regardless of race," Khalifa says.

"Black, Italian, whoever," Papa adds.

Teddy returns and I press him for confirmation. He looks me over before speaking. "This is not the first time you're asking about this." I forgot that the last time we talked neighborhood, Teddy chastised me, explaining that along with politics, religion, and family, people's backgrounds are "places that you don't want to go" because "it makes people feel challenged."

"Why are you so curious about South Philly all of a sudden?" he asks.

"My bosses at the FBI want to know," I say.

Dead stares.

"Not really," I say, "but it's only recently that I've started to figure out the importance of neighborhood, and I'm trying to catch up." This explanation seems not to do much. "You know," I add, "there's a lot of stuff going on around here that I don't see."

Teddy seems to take offense. "Whaddaya mean?" he shouts. "You see how conversation stops when the cops come in, but we're real with you. You know that."

"I'm not saying that you're not real with me," I say, "though I'd be a fool to think that you're real all the time."

Teddy looks hurt. "Why would you say that?" he says.

"Nobody's real all the time," I say. "I know *I'm* not." I feel their eyes on me. "But more important than real or fake is how what we say is shaped in part by who we're talking to. Meaning, I don't assume that the *you* I see is the same *you* the guys on the block see."

"That's because I don't show those guys nothing," Teddy says. It's hard for me to reconcile the boisterous Teddy I know from the chapel with the buttoned-up character he describes from the block, but so he consistently claims.

"Maybe you do, maybe you don't. I have no way of knowing," I say. "But that's not my point. All I'm saying is that sometimes y'all will say something to one another, and I don't understand because I'm not from where you're from."

"Yeah, that's true," Khalifa says.

"Especially when it comes to things that you all take for granted," I say. "Things that no one will have ever taken the time to clue me in to. Like with this neighborhood thing. It's all totally obvious to you, so why would you ever suspect that I wouldn't get it?"

This stokes their incredulity. "Whaddaya mean?" Khalifa says. "Of course neighborhood is important! All of us from South Philly know the same people in common, and we share the same experience and values. Of course that's gonna mean something."

"Ah," I say. "But that's a slightly different claim than the one you've been making. What you're saying now is that people naturally gravitate toward people they know in common and with whom they share experience. That sounds right to me. Thinking like an anthropologist, I would say that based on our shared experiences and values, we form something like tribes. But neighborhood is only one possible criterion for such tribes. Why should I assume that the key dividing line is North Philly versus South Philly and not Christian versus Muslim?"

"Because," Khalifa says with growing impatience, "you see us Muslims hanging with Christians every day and you can see that it's no thing." Abstracting from this particular case a general rule, Khalifa continues: "But what religion you are is *clearly* not as important as what your neighborhood is. You know, when I see a couple of dudes acting close, nobody has to tell me that they have a connection that extends beyond these walls. You just don't get close like that in here. Even with a guy I've known for years and years in here, if I never knew him on the outside, I'm never going to drop my guard completely."

As if to demonstrate Khalifa's point, the door swings open and in comes Qasim. A wiry man with a wispy gray beard, Qasim was the imam of Masjid Sajdah when the raid came down, and remains, for many, Graterford's foremost religious authority.

"What's up with Crocket?" he asks, referring to Sayyid.

"Still don't know nothing," Teddy says flatly.

Qasim remains by the door, shifting his weight from foot to foot.

Unable to stomach the silence, I add that while there are rumors that Sayyid's on L, according to Bird he's still in detention in his cell. Qasim trades some words with Khalifa. After a few more awkward moments, with his left hand wrapped in his overhung sleeve to ward off the doorknob's germs, Qasim opens the door and leaves.

The door closes without comment. "You shouldn't get the wrong idea," Teddy says. Even though the guys down here tend to be from South Philly, the chapel isn't some sort of South Philly thing.

I ask Teddy what he means.

He says, "'Cause, you know, these dudes be talking about how the chapel is a South Philly thing and that stuff be going on down here and that's not true." Teddy harps on my obliviousness. "Of course, neighborhood is important," he says. "It's so natural."

"But not every neighborhood is like South Philly," I say. I mention my father, who grew up on Brighton Seventh Street in Brooklyn and how in high school I had a friend whose father was from Brighton Sixth. Since the two men were born a year apart, we each excitedly inquired if they knew one another. Not only was each ignorant of the other, as I recall, but both men found the suggestion that they might have known one another completely absurd.

Khalifa argues: "That's because your father and your friend's father were busy taking care of their families. Not just hanging out on the street." That is, the relevant difference was not geographical but vocational.

Our rhythm is once again broken when the door swings open and Eugene, a Jewish prisoner, arrives with an open dictionary in hand. Eugene navigates the jagged teeth of desks and places the open book in front of my face. He's pointing to the word *bit*. He skips down to the third definition: "a small bit of time." This is to settle a dispute we had on Friday. He was using the word *bit* to refer to a jail term. I said that I'd thought the term was *bid*.

"That's cool," I say to Eugene. "I was just basing it on a Nas lyric—'*What up kid / I know shit is rough doin' your bid*'—but that might be a New York thing."[57] I catch Teddy's amused eye. "I don't know."

"But guys here say *bit*," Eugene says, spitting the "t."

The second the door closes behind Eugene, Teddy says, "Yeah, some guys say *bid*."

Adds Khalifa, "It depends on where you're from."

"Thanks for getting my back while Eugene was here," I say, mildly incredulous.

Teddy snorts through his nose.

"So tell me," I say, reclaiming our focus, "after Ridge comes in and guys get scattered throughout the system, neighborhood starts to matter less, right?"

"No," says Khalifa, who spent eleven years in Pittsburgh. "It matters more, the Philly part, anyway."

Teddy muses: "Maybe it *is* more a tribal-type thing than a neighborhood-type thing. You see it in here. When Brian comes down here, where does he go? He goes right into Baumgartner's office. Why? Because he's more *comfortable* in there."

"That's because they're both Europeans," Khalifa says.

"That's why Brian carries himself like he's better than us," Teddy says. "And, you know," he adds, his voice deepening, "that's an attitude that don't play well in here. A guy'll get *victimized* for acting that way."

"Maybe he *was* victimized," I say, "and his standoffishness is his way of protecting himself."

"Yeah, he *was!*" Teddy says. "But that was a different era back then. Get over it."

Shit, I think.

"I mean, *sheez*," Teddy continues, "even David sits in here with us more than Brian does. And David is down *now*, but you know that before he was in prison he was just like the rest of them." Teddy starts in on how exceptional I am for a European, for a Jew, with my hip-hop-lyric-spitting, black-person-fraternizing ways.

"You don't understand," I explain. "Where I come from, there were millions of kids just like me, who listened to hip-hop, who wanted to be down, and who probably would have done stupid and dangerous things at an impressionable age if they'd only been *real* enough to have been given half a chance. Plus," I shift from confession into lecture, "for somebody like me who grew up identifying with the *Exodus* narrative as a key episode in his cultural memory, it was impossible not to see the African-American freedom struggle as *the* critical story of American history, past *and* present. That's why among Jews you find such a strong sense of identification with blacks."

"What?" Teddy objects. "I don't know what Jewish people *you're* talking about."

In a flash, I see the Jew as Teddy and Khalifa must see him: not as the corny wannabe freedom rider but as the greedy and contemptuous shopkeeper. This is the portrait Teddy now paints, of how the Jews he knew were racists and were all about sucking money out of the ghetto. Khalifa picks up where Teddy leaves off, saying how when the Jews left the ghetto, they made sure to sell their businesses to non-blacks so that black people would remain in poverty.

I concede that while race undoubtedly played an active role in determining which groups had the resources available to buy those businesses, I doubt there was any kind of conscious conspiracy between Jews, Asians, and Latinos to keep the black man down.

"Of course *you* wouldn't think so," Khalifa says.

The figure of the Jew comes up not infrequently, with Teddy and Khalifa especially. Whereas for the African-American men Baraka's age, the Jew was a neighborhood fixture, for the youngest guys, the bygone Jew—like Shylock for the Elizabethans—is an almost mythological type. For guys like Teddy and Khalifa, in the middle generation, I'm not always certain what exactly a "Jew" is. When, for example, I recently made an empirical objection to Khalifa's assertion that Jews run the country, Teddy explained to me: "When guys say 'Jews,' they mean Caucasians." Might it be, I wondered, that these men haven't any notion that WASP blue-bloods even exist?

Despite the murkiness of their ethnic categories, Teddy and Khalifa have, in exchanges like tonight's, made a series of highly idiosyncratic and yet stunningly apt observations about my background. For example, when they read my affiliation with Princeton as evidence of my wealth and I argued for a demographic distinction between Princeton undergraduates and graduate students, Khalifa was having none of it. He knows I'm rich, he said, because I'm interested in things that rich people are interested in, weird things like *religion*—which is to say, religion as a matter of scholarly attention.

Not too long ago we had a similarly illuminating exchange about my status as a rich Jew. While, as a point of fact, I did grow up without want on the Upper West Side of Manhattan and consider myself the bearer of all the privilege the world has to offer, I was trying to dislodge Teddy and Khalifa's tendency to historically overestimate Jewish wealth and power in America. From their perspective, the Jews have always been on top, and their present status is but an expression of that structural constant. My grandfather was an orphan from the Ukraine, I explained, who came to New York by himself at the age of thirteen and eventually opened a furniture store with his brothers. If I was trying to brandish my middle-class cred, Khalifa drew a different conclusion. He responded: "Your grandfather had a furniture store? Oh, so you're *old* money"—which, in their world, I suppose I am.

"Man," Teddy recently declared in frustration when I wasn't understanding how a guy can break up a pack of cigarettes and sell it for nine times the value. "You must be one rich Jew, because you don't know shit about money!"

"You know what you need to write about, though?" Teddy says now. "What?" I ask.

"About how we all need to have them conjugal visits. It's inhuman to deny us the way they do." A hug at the beginning of a visit and a hug at the end is all that is allowed.

"Plus, it's just plain stupid," Khalifa adds. "It would make administration much easier if we had conjugal visits."

"As a privilege that could be taken away?"

"Yeah," he says, "that, but also 'cause there would be much less tension in here, less fussing and fighting if a guy could just go see his lady once in a while."

"So why don't they allow it?" I ask. "Just mean-spiritedness?"

"Yeah," Teddy says. "It's just hate. Plus, the *system* wants to turn us all into faggots."

In Teddy's view, which seems commonly shared, homosexuality is a result of sexual trauma. These days, it is said, lots of men enter the system ready and willing to play the passive sexual role—a far cry from the old days when men had to be raped into it. But that the system is actively trying to turn Graterford's prisoners into faggots? This I have not heard before.

My face apparently betrays my skepticism. "Come on, it's obvious," Teddy says. "If you get caught kissing your wife in the visiting area, you get ninety days in the hole and no visits for six months. But get caught getting dirty with another dude on the block? Nothing happens. You see? The system is promoting fornication."

Khalifa says, "They want to stop our procreation."

And presumably their salvation, too. Still, the conspiracy doesn't quite make sense. "I don't get it," I say. "Do you mean that they need black bodies to fill this place?" That the system would need an ever-expanding crop of black men to fill its prisons, and that the most effective way to get at the sons is to first remove the fathers, would seem to me the paranoia to have were I in their shoes. But Khalifa is saying the opposite.

"Man," Khalifa says, "do you know how many babies I could have made in the last eleven years?" I get it now.

"You don't have any children?" I ask.

"Nah, I have four," he says. "But I could have had so many more, don't you see?"

Looking at Khalifa's shiny pate, I do the math. Khalifa is thirty-three and has been in jail for at least thirteen years. Teddy, I know, has seven kids—four boys and three girls—and he fell at twenty-six.

We've reached another dead end. For me, the dead end resides in

Teddy and Khalifa's refusal to differentiate between conspiracy and hegemony, between people's *explicit* intentions to do evil (as they maintain about the *system's* nefarious operators) and the absentminded process by which injustice remakes itself in the interests of some and at the expense of others. In one form or another, this is the argument I ritually have with Vic, Baraka, and Teddy. While we all aver the existence of unjust social structures that prey on certain vulnerable classes, in my view the harmful acts enabled by these structures do not require explicitly malevolent intentions. Wealth is hoarded by the few, and men are placed in inhuman conditions. While there are surely sadists out there, immense harm may also be inflicted with the most virtuous of intentions (to serve God or country, or to protect one's family), with baser intentions (to earn a paycheck) or without much of any intention at all (because whatever it is, is simply what one *does*).

To choose a common concern, consider drug-related street crime. As I see it, these eruptions of violence—which often result in the loss of life—commonly take place at the tail end of a host of social and political choices collectively taken and not taken that make violent crimes statistically inevitable. Individuals make terrible choices that destroy worlds, it is true. And because our thinking, talking, and legislating about wrongdoing make a fetish of individual bad actors, relegating those people to places like Graterford comes to seem like a sound strategy for safe streets. With endemic poverty, broken families, underfunded schools, and the circulation of handguns making the corner drug trade what it is, however, the scourge of street crime in cities like Philadelphia requires a legion of malevolently intentioned, irredeemably bad men no more than gross and perpetual income inequality requires a cabal of gleefully racist Shylocks. Malice and avarice certainly play their part. As do fear, desperation, ambition, loyalty, and stupidity. Given the world as we find it, each aggregate outcome foremost requires only enough men unimaginative enough to accept and play the game according to the received rules.[58]

This is not to reject the importance of personal responsibility. On the contrary. Because it is as much through mindlessness as through calculation that we collectively nurture the civic enterprise that an agitprop poster above my desk (appropriating the language of Catholic worker and cultural icon Dorothy Day) dubs "this filthy rotten system," it behooves each of us to acknowledge the many roles we play in its maintenance.[59] Far from being an omnipotent machine that merely processes those who live under it, without the avid and idle hands of each of us invested with the task of its reproduction, the system is nothing.[60] And because the system is little more than our collective agency and inertia, critical dialogue becomes a viable strategy for social repair. By coming together and figuring out what we're trying to do and what we're actually getting done, we foster opportunities to generate alternative practices, which, if actualized, might better serve our collective interests.

If such democratic faith is, in Princeton's Department of Religion, standard orthodoxy, in Graterford's chapel it comes across as terribly naïve.[61] As many here see it, there's no point discussing any of this as anything more than a pleasant diversion. Malevolent outcomes are never unintended. From the designers on high to the low-level profiteers, the operators knowingly operate the *system* to do precisely what it does.[62]

Having had this argument many times, I decide to let it drop, and Teddy and Khalifa seem to have reached the same conclusion. Especially in such close quarters, they are used to holding their tongues. Better to afford me my ignorance than poison the well by insisting on the obvious facts that prison administrators are fiends and the Jews who bled the ghetto knew precisely what they were doing.[63]

After the raid, the compromise was that the resident rabbi could keep the upstairs as his study, but that Jewish services would take place in the new annex. When the Rabbi is willing, however, the Jews remain upstairs. And while *davening*—praying—has been known to happen, more commonly when they gather, the Jews do what the five men upstairs are doing now: drinking coffee from plastic cups and talking loudly, frequently about something derived from the traditions of Judaism.

David is reading aloud from a biography of Maimonides. A chapel janitor with an angular face, a long white beard, and searing eyes, David is the rare regular who wears his rage on his sleeve. David told me the details of his criminal case the first time I met him, about how—as he tells it—his ex-wife's new husband was molesting his daughter, and when it became clear that neither the police on the Jersey side nor those on the Philly side gave a fuck, he did what he had to.[64] He left it to others to supply the critical detail that when he shot up the guy's car, his wife and daughter were inside it. When, on Passover, the other Jews recite the liturgically inscribed hope that next year they will all be in Jerusalem, David loudly proclaims his aspiration for this year to be his last. Dying isn't such a big deal, according to David, since as prisoners they're already dead. "This isn't life," he's said to me, "it's mere existence."[65] To put it mildly, David's wallowing does not ingratiate him with his peers.

If David's mind is a torture chamber, its torments do not inhibit his appetite as a reader. Literature, history, philosophy, politics, Judaica (about the Holocaust and Kabbalah, in particular): David churns through volume after volume, stockpiling knowledge, which he deftly reproduces on command. So while he is quick to shrillness, he is exceedingly shrewd, and when things get heated upstairs, I'm forever surprised to find myself in David's corner.

If as a Jew David is animated primarily by the tradition's intellectual resources, Lenny, who sits across the table from him, finds inspiration in its ethics. As a middle-class kid in the late seventies, Lenny became a drug addict. One evening he murdered his girlfriend. At the appropriate time, Lenny told me this story so as to help me make sense of the obligation he feels to give something back. Indeed, if one canvassed the jail for a poster child for rehabilitation, one could do far worse than Lenny Berkowitz. Searches through the Philly papers cough up Lenny's name every other year or so, always for a different accomplishment. Here's Lenny running marathons in the yard for charity. Here he is setting records for selling Girl Scout cookies. Here he is graduating summa cum laude from Villanova—a feat that briefly made him a culture-war piñata to be batted at by no less than Rush Limbaugh, for whom Lenny was Exhibit A in how killers are growing fat on your dime. Lenny is one of the busiest people I know: he clerks in the school and is active in the Villanova Program; the Mural Arts Program, through which Graterford residents contribute to public arts in Philadelphia; and in the Inside-Out Program, through which prisoners and college students explore criminal justice alternatives. While Lenny derives no small amount of pleasure from his many activities, they also provide his primary vehicle for *tikkun olam*—repair of the world—the ethical principle that according to Lenny "is what Judaism is all about."

Arriving for his weekly Hebrew language session with the Rabbi is Peter. A round-faced, sandy-haired Catholic intellectual, Peter is also exceedingly active both in the chapel and out. Peter fronts the trio that accompanies mass, is a few credits shy of his Villanova degree, and, along with Brian (who tonight is elsewhere), is one of ten opening-round volunteers in Graterford's hospice pilot program.

As the Rabbi continues with an extended interjection about the social position of both doctors and Jews in medieval Europe and North Africa, David offers Peter and me each a cup of coffee.

Downstairs, an adolescent citron tree grows beside a second potted plant at the foot of the dais. David grew it from the seeds of last year's *etrog*, one of the four species, which along with a palm branch and sprigs of myrtle and willow, are ritually shaken and paraded around by Jews during the fall harvest holiday of Sukkoth. The belle of the desert, the *etrog* is the object of considerable rabbinic fuss. As a fruit of beautiful taste and scent both, it stands in—I learned in seventh grade—for those Jews possessing both a knowledge of Torah and the practice of good deeds.[66]

Clustered to the right of the tree, thirty men of color have assembled for Yokefellows, a ministry serving prisoners in Pennsylvania's county, state, and federal facilities. I'm five rows behind everyone, save for Oscar, who's in the row behind me.

A brown is reading from a double-sided handout titled "The Will of God: His Plan for You." The handout, which declares that "every believer should desire to know the will of God in their life," details seven purported biblical principles, most accompanied by biblical proof texts, for ascertaining His will. The men have already read and affirmed how God will not hide His desires; how He will use several methods to make His will known; how He will provide inner peace concerning His will; and how to know His will you must avoid selfishness, fear, and doubt, and have a personal relationship with Jesus Christ.

The brown recites the sixth principle: that to know God's will you must live in obedience to Him. Prompted by the volunteers—a husband-and-wife team of prosperity gospellers—to offer testimony affirming the principle's truth, the brown talks about the challenges of living with a cellmate who was not God conscious. Frustrated in moments to the brink of violence, through obedience to God he came to realize that what his cellie really needed was love, and that if he could love him in accordance with God's will, then maybe not today or tomorrow, but someday, that love might one day lead him to Christ.

As I transcribe this testimony, I'm increasingly aware of Oscar's eyes on my back.

Oscar's unnerving candor is not limited to the struggles of faith and the humiliations of incarceration. He is also one of the very few men here who voiced reservations about projects like mine where researchers "come in to profit off of our misery." By the time he told me that, six months into my research, he'd changed his mind about me. The difference with me, he said, was that I *participate*. Which is why my uncharacteristically ostentatious note taking makes me uneasy now.[67] Without provocation, I turn and explain to Oscar what I'm doing this week. He nods. Seeing me without a copy of the handout, he insists on giving me his. These folks, he explains, indicating the visiting couple, are from the North Philly church he grew up at. Although Yokefellows is nondenominational, he explains, their church is Pentecostal. I nod and turn back to the service. After a time, he leans into my ear and asks, "You gonna be here Saturday and Sunday as well?" When I grunt the affirmative, he lays his hand on my shoulder and whispers, "God bless you."

When the men have finished the final principle, they circle up to pray. I hesitate, uncertain of whether or not to go. Perhaps contrary to Oscar's impression, while my demeanor in ritual settings is hardly aloof, I'm fairly determined to not try to pass for something I am not. But when Oscar passes me on his way toward the altar, I follow along. The circle is full of familiar faces—Santana, Daffy Ball, Matthew, Young Mike, and Rafael and José. Once again I'm the only white person. I hang my head and close my eyes. With his raspy voice, Daffy Ball prays:

"Thank you, Heavenly Father, for thinking of us. Heavenly Father, thank you for caring for us, for protecting, for comforting us. Heavenly Father, thank you for thinking of, caring and comforting the guys that are in the hole. Thank you, Heavenly Father, for thinking of, and caring and looking out for guys who are in the hospital. Thank you, Heavenly Father, for watching over those of us in the hospice program, patients, staff, and administrators. Heavenly Father, thank you for looking out for guys on death row. Thank you, Heavenly Father, for loving and caring for those guys who did their crime and for those guys who didn't do their crime. Heavenly Father, thank you for watching over and ensuring the safe passage of our present guests. Heavenly Father, thank you for watching over and protecting the staff here at Gratersford, the COs, and the administers of this here system."

There are many things to be thankful for, and Daffy does his best not to let a single one pass by unacknowledged. Nor do the assembled men, who respond with calls of *"Amen!"* *"Thank you, Jesus!"* and *"In the name of Jesus!"* at each recognition of the Heavenly Father's bountifulness.

Toward the conclusion of Daffy's prayer, having stood with my eyes closed for quite a while, I am gripped by what I've long thought of as the evil Shema impulse. As I was taught as a boy, the Shema prayer—"Hear O Israel, the Lord is our Lord, the Lord is One"—is to be recited with one's eyes covered by a tightly pressed right hand. As I recall, no holy spectacle was alleged from which my eyes required protection, and no divine wrath was promised for peeking. Nonetheless, as happens, custom came to acquire the unspoken suggestion of something more.

In what I sometimes regard as my earliest steps away from the practice of religion in the direction of its study, I was often seized by the impulse to look, a transgression for which I lacked the courage. For, as I somehow even in my yeshiva days intuited, when one *does* look, one runs a far greater risk than seeing *something*. Rather, one runs the risk of seeing *nothing*. One risks seeing not the irruption of God's presence, but only the dull thud of God's absence. For if God's presence is *is*, and seeing is believing, then the act of looking risks rendering the *is isn't*, or at least the *maybe not*, which slopes off in the same direction. So I never looked. It was only later, as a man, when the *not being* of God became for me fully manifest, with God reduced not merely to *was*, but to *never was*, that I finally surrendered to the temptation to peek—to peek not at God (faith in whom would preclude such sacrilege) but only at my shut-eyed cocongregants, whose clasped lids testified to their sacred fidelity to a Being who for me had become a thundering null set. Nonetheless, even as I've traded down from hermeneutics to anthropology, moved with emphatic ambivalence from the practice of religion to the study of other people's practices, and followed the *religious* path (as one former day school classmate put it) of "Those who can't do . . . teach," I don't think I've mustered the courage to peek on more than two or three occasions. In the name of empiricist rigor, perhaps, I yield to the urge to do so now. Hyperaware of others' hands in mine, I lift up a chin and eke open an eye.

Heads are slouched low. Some men are still. Some shake from side to side. Some mouth, "Thank you, Jesus." Many are crying.

Feeling suddenly scrutinized, I gaze across the circle and find myself caught in the stare of a sunken-cheeked old head whose honest eyes are fixed squarely on mine. I shut my eyes and drop my head, momentarily deafened by my pounding heart.

When the circle breaks up, I find myself face-to-face with a striking, shaven-headed blue I'm fairly sure I've seen before.

"I'm Christopher," he says, "though everybody calls me Prophet to remind me of my Lord and Savior, Jesus Christ." His vibe is manic.

"Prophet with a 'ph' or an 'f'?" I ask, angling for small talk.

"'Ph,'" he confirms. "So you're Jewish, right?"

"Yeah, that's right."

"Well," he says, "I read something interesting the other day and it said that Jesus was a Jew, and I just wanted to apologize to you because the other day I saw you and I was vilifying you, because I've got problems with Jews, but I was thinking that if Jesus was a Jew, then Jews can't be all bad, so the problem is with me. So, I just wanted to apologize, because there you were, just doing your thing, and there I was, vilifying you."

I try to be gracious. "We all struggle to see the humanity of others," I say, "whether that other is a Jew, a prisoner, or whatever he or she is said to be." I ask him where he's from.

He's a technical PV—meaning a parole violator who has merely broken the terms of his parole, rather than having been charged with a new crime. This time, he says, it's for the last time. He's got 132 days and a wake-up left, and until then, he's gonna be in the chapel every day.

I'll be sure to see him around, then, I say cheerily, and head for the vestibule.

When the clock reads 8:25, I tell Bird that I'll see him tomorrow. Despite the slightness of my company, Bird seems crestfallen.

He sighs. "Man, I'm bored."

"Yeah?"

"Yeah. Usually I'd be looking at the *Daily News* now 'cause Sayyid gives me his when he's done with it. But with Sayyid in the hole, I ain't got jack to read."

WEDNESDAY

In America, a man is not a man without his confidence. And a man cannot have his confidence without someplace to put his certitude. As Protestant theology stretched to its pluralist, pop-existentialist extreme, the mandate of American religion is quite simple: *Thou shalt believe. Believe in one thing, whatever that thing may be.*[1] This pluralization of legitimate creeds functions as the cornerstone of American religious freedom and, as a derivative, as an engine of tribalism.

Similar to the Land of Canaan, then, and its menu of religious cults, American religion is henotheistic: there are many Gods but you must choose one. In principle, as long as a guy is what chapel regulars call "God conscious," his belief in some other God needn't be a threat to me. Far from being a "conversation-stopper," then, our mutually reinforcing religious certainties offer up endless fodder for dialogue.[2]

But good fences make good neighbors, and so a hedge is erected. To avoid fraying nerves, "religion," it is often said, is a topic to avoid. Because across denominational lines, many practice this restraint, religious conversations become largely an intramural pastime. And so, in the fecund field of religious plenty, enclaves sprout. If, from a crane shot, there are at Graterford many religious paths, from the position a man comes to occupy on the ground there is, more often than not, conventionally only one. This path is a narrow path, and error encroaches from all sides.

As a hotbed of religious diversity and personal transformation, if any environment was to be supportive of religious in-between-ness, one might figure that the chapel would be it. But this presumption would be wrong. Religious seeking here is encouraged only if one proves himself willing to find what he is looking for. Indeed, the conviction that one has conclusively *found it* conventionally becomes a core facet in one's presentation of self.

There is reason to distrust the force of chapel certitudes. It doesn't take a psychoanalyst to turn the theological confidence of confessedly convicted wrongdoers into a proclamation of spiritual insecurity. Or, to chip away on another façade: If the Lord demanded that I produce from Graterford ten undogmatic souls to keep Him from reducing the place to smoke and ashes, I have zero doubt about my ability to do so.

It was at St. Dismas on one of my first days at Graterford. Exacerbated by the close confines of Classroom A, I was still quite self-conscious, as much from the discomfort of watching as from being watched. Communion commenced. The men offered me grape juice from dosage-sized plastic cups, which I politely refused. I remained unsure of what to do with my body or my eyes. Following the liturgy, the singing, the eating and drinking, everyone traded hugs. At the crescendo of my discomfort, I received an embrace from the enormous man who had joined the group only for Communion. Beyond the man's sheer size, there was something grounding in his touch that made my anxiety dissipate. I made a note of him. Gradually, over the coming weeks and months, this large man would crystallize into Al.

Now, almost a year later, Al is my primary source for making sense of Graterford's Christian practices, and is my sparring partner in some of the most thrilling arguments.

By his own lights, Al is an unyielding Biblicist. Everything that happened after Jesus' death and resurrection—the Church fathers, the Catholic Church, the Protestant Reformation—that's man's history. This historical, manmade stuff—*that's* religion. Religion is a wrong turn. What matters is one's relationship with Jesus Christ. For it is through Jesus, and not via any church, that we come to the truth of His Word. In explaining this, Al pointed me to John 14:26, where Jesus assures His followers that His imminent disappearance will prove no obstacle to their ongoing understanding of His Word. As Jesus said: "But the Counselor, the Holy Spirit, whom the Father will send in my name, will teach you all things and will remind you of everything I have said to you." While Al frequently cites chapter and verse, he also talks about "my Bible"—the highly subjective yet nonetheless objective Truth that the Holy Ghost renders on his behalf transparent. "I don't need this book," Al said to me, pointing to his Bible. "It's only when I'm talking to a nonbeliever that I need this book. Do you think that when we talk amongst ourselves we use this book? Why would we?"

Keita places Al's anti-intellectualism in cultural context. In their blindness to history and textual complexity, men like Al turn Jesus into a boorish American: jealous, judgmental, individualistic, and not remotely demanding enough of righteous action beyond faith.[3] Action, moreover, when it is called for, is rendered by this literalism somewhat perverse—to reconcile after a row, Al and Teddy wash each other's feet.

Al is unswayed by such criticism. For Al, the Holy Ghost is the ultimate democrat, speaking directly to the heart of the Christian, Jew, or Muslim, the saved or unsaved, the learned or unschooled. In his populist skepticism, Al grants as much credence to Keita's ministerial appraisals as he gives to the dismissive judgments of the prison psychiatrists. "According to them, I'm ignorant. A psychiatrist says that I have a third-grade education. That's what *they* say. That's why I don't go by what they say."

Truly a gigantic presence, Al is magnanimous, charismatic, and, in moments, residually terrifying. In a way unique among the chapel workers, Al remains a dangerous man. At least that's how he tells it. "Oh, you wouldn't like Al," Al responded to my onetime inquiry into how I might square the man before me with the man Al once was. "Al is an animal. The Al you know and like is the Al that loves Jesus."

"When I was a child I did childish things," Al cites Corinthians.[4] Among the childish things Al did was inflict tremendous cruelty. Now and again, gruesome details bubble up in the office: snatches of breathtaking violence, sometimes lethal, mostly wanton, coldly reported without rationalization or apology. Still more revealing has been Al's testimony, a genre that favors the prideful recollection by the saved of the consummate sinner he used to be and the still worse sinner he would have been had not God been looking out for him, especially back in his time of overwhelming ignorance.

If through his relationship with Jesus Christ Al overcomes his natural proclivities, and submits instead to what God wants for him, he still struggles. While his years in the hole are long behind him, he struggles with his temper, as he does with overeating, and with the smut mags he recently threw out when he realized that he was hauling them around like a spare tire. Like Baraka, Al cautions against the dangers of having too much latitude, especially in a place like Graterford. He likened man to "a frog on a lily pad in a pot of water. Turn up the heat. The frog will survive. That's the danger of being in here. A man can adapt to anything."

As a first-year student in the Education for Ministry program, Al is working on a spiritual biography, which he is preparing to deliver orally. Over the year I've picked up some of the defining moments: how as a kid in Macon, Georgia, Al was a Baptist, but how in prison he converted to Islam. Since it was 1970, that meant the Nation, and so from 1975 to 1983 he was a Warith Deen Muhammad Sunni and attended a mosque in West Philly. Back then he was called by his Arabic name, Mumit—the Angel of Death—and he "took care of problems in the mosque." He thought he was doing right, that he was "eliminating heresies," but one day in 1983, after he'd dealt with a couple of guys, he was told that he'd just taken out a couple of rival drug dealers. Having thought that he was doing God's work, Al was shocked to learn that he was just murdering people for criminal gain. Shortly thereafter, Al was on his way to another job when God stopped him dead in his tracks. He was up at Broad and Allegheny, in North Philadelphia, and suddenly he found that he just couldn't go on. He called his wife, sobbing. She came down and met him and took him straight to Greater Ebenezer Church, where he joined "the right hand of fellowship," getting involved at once in a range of church activities, including Bible studies and musical groups.

While I doubt I know personally another man as directly responsible for as much physical suffering as Al, the Al I have come to know can be disarmingly loving. One morning he pulled me into the conference room, where a group of guys were concluding the meeting of a self-appointed committee dedicated to "moving the members of the body of Christ at Graterford in the direction that God wants it to go." He was offering the concluding prayer: "Lord," Al said in a way that didn't feel the least bit overbearing, "You plan for everything in such good ways, and Brother Josh came here to learn, but as you've seen, he's also here to teach." Another time, after noticing that I was walking funny, Al asked me what was wrong. I'd screwed up my back, I told him. "Does it hurt there?" he asked, touching the spot to the right of my spine just above the waist. That was the spot. "Yeah," he said, "back when I trained fighters they used to get that, too." In the sort of presumptiveness from which intimacy is fashioned, he instructed me to lie on the floor, where, holding my left shoulder down, he pushed my right knee across my body until something popped, cracking my back into place.

Al can be hilarious, too. On Christmas Day, a day that is, in Al's view, a pagan holiday, no more special than any other, Al waddled up to me. The choir was singing "Joy to the World." He said: "When I was a kid, I thought they was saying, '*And never let a nigger sing.*'" In his flat bass, he sang along with the carol, laughing from his belly.

And never let a nigger sing
And never let a nigger sing
And ne-e-ever let a nigger sing.

At other times, I've glimpsed the hazardous edge to Al's attentiveness. One morning, a week after I'd drunk a couple cups of his coffee and casually promised to bring him in a replacement bag, he greeted me with a firm handshake. "Where's my mud at?" he said. I didn't understand. "My coffee," he explained, still shaking my hand. I told him I would bring it in the next time. With a silent smile, he nodded his affirmation, but refused for an uncomfortable duration to release my hand from his grip. Even as the joke I presumed it to be, I took the incident as not unrevealing of Al's modus operandi, and it was scary.

Back over the summer, after a teenage mugger "fishhooked" me (the term, as I learned in the office, for dragging somebody down from behind by the inside of his mouth) and I showed up with scrapes, cuts, and the story of what had happened, Al and Baraka both were quite unimpressed. Some punk put his fingers in my mouth and walked away with all ten digits still attached? What the hell was wrong with me? Slipping into character, I asked them if they would train me, just as Peter Sellers's Inspector Clouseau asks his Chinese houseboy, Cato, to jump out and attack him when he least expects it. After sharing a good laugh, I promptly forgot about the joke. A couple of weeks later, though, as a portentous thunderstorm gathered to the north, blackening the sky, Al called me into the Imam's office. Pointing toward the window, he asked, "Have you seen what's-her-face?" Not catching what he said, I followed him into the dimly lit office, only to find myself locked in a smothering chokehold. With Al's forearm pressed against my larynx, I met Baraka's eyes with inquisitive shock. Three interminable seconds later, Al released me, laughing as he did. Soon I laughed, too. But into the next day, my mortality remained lodged in my throat like the ghost of a fishbone.

But these were moments of play. Where I've truly managed to awaken the devil in Al is in arguments about God. One August night, Al and Teddy were pressing me about the strange attitude articulated by the Rabbi and Brian both that God is not an active presence in shaping their day-to-day lives. I owned up to the fact that this, too, was my position. Speaking frankly of a distant God, the only one afforded by my feeble theology, I testified that as I see it, God doesn't care who wins wars or who scores touchdowns or what exactly I do with my brief time on earth. I explained that after I learned about the Holocaust at age nine or so, I figured that either God doesn't pay too much attention to what's going on down here or that he has some serious explaining to do.

"You're giving God the case!" Teddy yelled at me. That is, I was blaming God for man's crimes.

Al was less charitable. His face trembling, he tore into me. "Over here we have a worthless piece of mud, a lifeless piece of dirt, a piece of garbage," he said, and gestured as if shaping clay with his humongous hands, like in Genesis God made man. "And over here, we have the Creator of all that ever was and is! Now, this piece of mud is gonna talk to the creator like HE got some explaining to do?"

Filled with holy rage, Al slipped into testimony. Here he was, on the lam, bare-assed in the South, being dragged out by a bunch of cops with loaded guns after he'd taken a shot at one of them, and they're about to kill him. And then this one cop, a guy a hundred pounds smaller than Al, grabs him in a bear hug and drags him away from the other cops who are ready to shoot him dead. God saved him that night. He doesn't know why God saved him. What he knows is that God *did* save him as part of some plan that God has for him. "*Why do you let me see these things?*" Al quoted Scripture.[5] He doesn't claim to *know* the reason why. But in his heart he knows that there *is* a reason.

By what was at the very least a curious twist of fate, an hour and five miles down the road later, I walked away from a head-on collision that saw both cars totaled. When Al saw me next, again black and blue but this time only half as glib, I met his questioning eyes with: "Now, about that divine plan for me . . ."

In time, Al will come to hold me personally responsible for his EFM frustrations. "There is no Holy Spirit in there," he will say, condemning the program. But that time is still a ways off.

Education for Ministry is unique among the chapel's Bible studies.[6] While most of them consist of spontaneous scriptural selections and exchanges of personal testimony, EFM adds critical and historical readings of Scripture, Church history, and Christian ethics. The mixture can be volatile. So while chapel Bible studies are generally conducive to fellowship, on Wednesday mornings Classroom A is prone to acrimony.

Only last week, Al got into a knock-down, drag-out with Charles, the youthful provocateur for whom yesterday I searched in vain. With misty eyes, Charles had confessed feelings of regret and of loss, and the dawning realization that as a young man facing life in prison, the best days of his life were most certainly behind him. He spoke longingly about the summer of '99, which he spent with his girlfriend and his baby boy. Nothing would ever be that sweet again. It didn't seem fair. If not for the fact that he hasn't gotten to be a father to his children, he wouldn't mind dying and going to heaven right now.

Rather than greeting Charles's candid confessions with sympathy, the rest of the group berated him for wallowing in the past and cowering before the challenges of the present—for being, as Al put it, *a baby in a man.* "I think somebody needs a hug," Al said bitingly. As a rule, the older lifers exhibit little patience for such things. For them, nostalgia is an indulgence to be refused. Al had told Charles to buck up, to stop being a child.

Having offered of his vulnerability, Charles received nothing in return.

I ask Daffy Ball how he's feeling. After months of asking guys how they're *doing,* only to be asked back how I'm *feeling,* I seem to have finally assimilated the appropriate idiom.

"You know better than to ask me that," Daffy says. "I'm blessed as always." And though it was initially a challenge, in time, I've come to believe him without hesitation. Literally and figuratively, Daffy Ball is a piece of work, a caricature of what can happen when a fervent temperament turns to spiritual discipline and an exemplar of how some men manage not merely to grow old here, but to grow old with grace. Daffy stands five foot five and weighs a hundred and ten pounds soaking wet, maintaining now, a year shy of sixty, the welterweight's body he fought with forty years ago. His daily exercise regimen consists largely of jumping jacks, up to 11,500 at a time, with 5,000 of them coming religiously between lunch and count. Daffy eats once a day, a whole step toward moderation from his death row days, when for nine years he would reportedly engage in regular forty-day water fasts and eat only once a week. "Fasting is the hardest thing," he once told me. "If you can do that, you can do anything."

Daffy has been a lot of things—a juvenile delinquent, a boxer, a junkie, a Fruit of Islam, a notorious gangster, a multiple killer, and a long-term resident of death row. It was on death row, in 1987, that Daffy became a new man. Back on the street he'd done a lot of things— "things that only me and God knew about"—and once on death row he was overtaken by suicidal thoughts. After three years of that, he whittled his choices down to "death or *this*," at which point he accepted responsibility for what he'd done and embraced Jesus Christ as his personal Lord and Savior. As he sees it now, the only reason for *not* giving one's pain over to Christ in exchange for salvation is "if you like pain." As the seeming expression of the Holy Spirit that has taken up abode in his *Peanuts*-character body, Daffy doesn't walk, he bounces, bearing buoyant witness with each step to the redemptive power of Jesus Christ. These days, in addition to EFM, Daffy serves as the vice president of the Sunday service Usher Board, and is another of the hospice volunteers.

While unflinchingly optimistic, Daffy can still bare his teeth. Charles is especially adept at getting him to bite. Once, Charles was arguing that Daffy's rhetorical reliance on his own experience of Christ served him poorly in bringing others to the Lord: "You're beyond reality!" Charles asserted. "If all you've got is faith, then you've got nothing."

"I know how you like to stir it up," Daffy snickered. "You're lucky I'm older. It wasn't so long ago that I would've come across this table and broken your jaw."

The question of freedom is another flashpoint. As far as his life arc goes, Charles flirts retrospectively with a fatalism that renders him little more than idle passenger. He talks about "being stereotyped and then blamed for what we are," and about the consequent feeling of being trapped in the wrong self. "It's not my fault that I'm here," he said, "I was raised to be this." Daffy couldn't disagree more. As Daffy tells it, he had eleven siblings. His seven sisters all went to college and his four brothers "all did good" (although one of them is currently a blue). The *system* didn't turn Daffy into a criminal: "I'm here 'cause of the choices I made." Even more important are one's choices here and now.

For a model of how to survive in this place, men like Daffy, Al, and Oscar point to Paul's self-description (to the Philippians) of how he learned to find contentment whatever his circumstances.[7] Contentment means living life productively regardless of where one happens to find oneself. Contentment entails not the denial of the thorniness of one's predicament but, rather, the adamant refusal to allow one's state of mind to be determined by it. Contentment allows one to find peace, and even freedom, in spite of one's material conditions. Consequently, it is not unusual for men like Daffy to claim they possess a greater freedom than that enjoyed by their counterparts out on the street—the coveters and the addicts as well as the garden-variety sleepwalkers. As Santana, the chapel worker, put it, "People out on the street, they're not in prison, but mentally they are. A lot of guys in here, they've been saved by Jesus Christ, and they're free."

There is a fine line, however, between the freedom of Pauline contentment and what the chapel's Christian lifers call "acceptance." Acceptance is the grubby, vicious habituation born of the total surrender of one's will and desire to the cultural logic of incarceration. To be "fully institutionalized" in this way is to be dead even as one lives. Resistance to such behaviorist debasement begins with God-given positive thinking and must be enacted daily through practice. To find the sweet spot of contentment, one must read the Bible and cultivate Christian fellowship. More defensively, one must erect barriers before those whose actions might, if one isn't careful, drag one down: people like Charles, actions like wallowing.

Perhaps more than anything, the dynamic between the older lifers and Charles is a drama of generational struggle, a snapshot of the frictional, glacial process of acculturation to Graterford Prison. Charles is in his twenties; Daffy and Al are in their fifties. Presumably, they, too, were once like him: tormented by anger, regret, and self-loathing; spiritually unmoored. Now, with the zeal of the convert, which is to say the zeal of the cured, they respond to Charles's undisciplined emotionalism with tough love, if that. In their seasoned perspective, Charles's denial of responsibility for his past actions and present reality is a tacit embrace of the dependency the *system* pushes on him, a bad-faith refusal to accept the autonomy naturally afforded him as a child of God. Not merely unmanly, Charles's willingness to stage a "pity party" is also destructive—a down payment on his own future suffering, and corrosive to those around him, and as such, an abnegation of the ethical demands of the Christlike walk.

As for Charles, it seems to me that he longs for nothing more than the comfort and contentment exhibited by the saved lifers. However, much like Nietzsche's man gazing upon the untroubled and unpained cows in the field, he wants what they have, but not in the way that they have it.[8] For now, he seems too angry and prideful to sell out as they have, at least not yet. Also, he is too intellectually curious, too skeptical by temperament, too insistent on calling the obdurate reality of his world by its proper name.

Some months back, talk had turned to crime and punishment. Richard Kipling—the aging Episcopalian minister who teaches EFM—and I were trying to own the advantages that had made the two of us significantly less likely than the six black men in the room to descend the chute of incarceration. Richard used the phrase "white privilege," but Daffy objected. To the intimation that he was somehow *not* privileged, Daffy gently but uncompromisingly demurred. *He* is the privileged one, he argued. He was on death row and now he has life. And God has shown him so many things! And he praises God every morning for opening his eyes for yet another beautiful day. He doesn't worry about things that are beyond his control now that he has come to know the world for the illusion that it is. Men kill one another over gold, tits and ass, but when you come to know those things as the illusions they really are, they become less important. *He* is the privileged one, he said, privileged because he suffered so much and now lives with knowledge of self and peace in his heart.

Daffy's speech threw me into sudden awareness of the unthought haughtiness of my secular materialist prejudices. It shamed me to think that my commitment to economic justice bound me somehow into a relationship of condescension toward someone like Daffy for the presumed pity of his existence: a life rendered as little more than social consequence. Charles, however, didn't miss a beat. After a perfectly timed silence, he responded, "That's funny. I can't imagine back in slave days a slave saying, *Oh massah! I's is just so privileged to be a slave!*"

If exceptionally pointed, in the chapel Charles's sentiment is hardly unique. Perhaps a mite too unfailing in its enthusiasm, Daffy's demeanor places him, for some critics, in the realm of the "religiously drunk," a designation applied to men whose depth and consistency of religious zeal is credited neither to will nor grace, but rather to the addict's exploitation of religious practice as a substitute narcotic. Most commonly subjected to the charge of religious drunkenness are those thought to have been broken by years on death row, whose "elevators," it is said, "don't go all the way to the top floor." In the eyes of some of the younger guys, as a class, the lifers are not far behind. "If you've lived here so long," Teddy has said, making no effort to exclude his friends from his judgment, "there's got to be something wrong in your head."

In Charles's dig at Daffy's faith we find showcased the second reductive impulse for cutting down prisoners' religion. As opposed to, but oddly complementary to, the nefariously dishonest *bad man of religion* is this: the abject *poor man of religion*. As a poor man, the religious prisoner is cast in the role of victim, most foundationally as a person (usually a man) with the bad fortune of being born to the wrong social condition (poverty) and in the wrong skin (usually black or brown). Before he was a prisoner and contorted by overwhelming state oppression, he was already the passive object of social neglect, and enlisted through the paltry options made available to him in the process of his own criminalization. Placed in the total and brutal institution of the prison, the prisoner inevitably gets religion.[9] He gets religion because, for the sake of his mind, body, and soul, he desperately needs *something*, and religion is the only thing left for him to get. If the *bad man* is forged where prisonerness meets the virtue of sincerity, the *poor man* is manufactured where prisonerness crosses the problem of autonomy.

If bad men *can't possibly mean* their avowed religious truth, as poor men, religious prisoners are presumed to *mean it*, but only in a pathetic, false-consciousness sort of way. Perhaps, that is to say, they *mean* it, but they probably *oughtn't*. So while the bad-man construct negates prisoners' religion with contempt, the poor man undoes prisoners' religion with pity.

For Charles, Daffy can deny the fact of his enslavement all he wants, but that won't make him a free man. It will only make him a slave who is also a fool.

Only a few years Charles's senior, Ephraim gives every impression of being farther along the path to spiritual contentment.

Last Wednesday, Ephraim recited his testimony, which, like Al, he's documenting in the form of a spiritual autobiography. (Unlike Al, Ephraim is writing his down.) As Ephraim told it, he was the product of a rape. His mom tried to abort him, so it was a miracle that he ever got to live at all, and that's why to this day he has so much sympathy for the unborn. Later, after the evil that was his father's legacy had vanquished the good he inherited from his mom, he had his neck sliced halfway off when, on the run from the police, he and his brother wrecked their car. Though he was pronounced dead on the scene, by another miracle, he survived. His presence before us today, he said, is a testament to the fact that miracles are real.

Richard Kipling compliments Ephraim on his bright smile. "I always smiles, that's my thing," Ephraim says. With a guileless shrug he adds, "I don't know why."

"I don't want to put a nigga up," Daffy scratches at his junior from between crow's-feet of his own, "but sometimes a man will use a smile as a defense mechanism."

"That's the truth," Al says, his head decisively cocked. Ephraim's smile doesn't quiver. The rest of us are sitting in Classroom A's plastic chairs, whose backs buckle with the slightest pressure, but Al is in the cushioned desk chair he wheels in from the office. Charles is not yet here, and we proceed without him.

Ephraim reports back on what he read—the story of the golden calf. Awkwardly mixing in some newly acquired details about Near Eastern historical anthropology, Ephraim retells the familiar story of Moses' ascent to Mount Sinai, Aaron's fashioning of the golden calf, and Israel's consequent abandonment of God for the idols at hand.

"You can hear the echoes of the Eden story," Richard says. "How God can disappear for only a second or two before the people will abandon Him."

Slowly, quietly, assuredly, Al begins to speak. "Yes," Al says. "With Aaron—just like with Adam—we see how short memory is. I experienced it myself. Finding myself locked up and making a deal with God with sincerity in my heart. But then when I get out," he chuckles, "I forget *all* about my sincereness and now I'm doin' my own thing. So God took 'em out of Egypt, and He said to write it down for their children's children. And then they quickly forget. Forget their hardship in Egypt. Forget their redemption. And then they go and make a calf. So you can see, the stage they were at with the Lord, they was young. They was childlike"—he drawls the word out into three syllables: chi-ild-like—"but maybe when they grew in their faith with the Lord they wouldn't so quickly forget as they did when they was immature in the faith. They wouldn't cry out and soon forget, and if they did turn their backs, they would take responsibility, not make excuses. That's why a generation had to die off before they could enter the promise land." Al finishes to a silence that feels like collective agreement.

Officer Watkins wanders through the open door and stands along the wall.

"The problem is," Ephraim says, "we tend to look for people to follow. You know, leaders, activists, people like that."

Al disagrees. "Even back then," he says with a measured tone and regular meter, "you had strong people and you had weak people. The strong people initiate things and the weak people follow. That's the same conditions you see in this here jail. In '95 they took away the leaders. And then they brought in new people. And now"—he gestures across the table at me—"we can't have no communication between us because he don't know me and I don't know him. And now people just wanna lie around in their pain." He lowers his fist. "So that's the most beautiful thing about the forty days that Moses and Jesus went through." He pauses. "The transformation. The looking forward. The not looking back. And that's how it's got to be in the forty days of each of our lives right here."

Watkins exits, nodding.

•

An hour into it—and with Charles still a no-show—Richard brings the conversation around to the topic of leadership. Richard regards EFM as an opportunity to produce for Graterford's Christian community a leadership class of self-critical men willing to move, in Baumgartner's words, "beyond the black and white and into the grays."

"What can we learn about healthy leadership from this?" Richard asks. We are still discussing Sinai and Aaron's wayward leadership of the Israelites into idolatry. "What exactly is the difference between Aaron and Moses? What allows the good leaders to do it—to not step over that line?"

Al answers. "Everyone who fails fails because they lose focus on the big picture. They lose focus because they see the hardship ahead and they don't want to go through it."

Richard nods. "That's because they focus on themselves," he says. "They forget *who* they are and they forget *whose* they are."

Ephraim bobs his chin. "Moses even tried to run," he says, "because *he* was wanted for murder, too!"

"Yes, that's right," Richard agrees about Moses. "There's something different about the sheepherder who sees the burning bush and the man we find later, the man who went through the ten plagues, the forty days on Sinai. Something happens in his evolution. He becomes something he previously was not."

Al objects. "But he had it in him from the beginning. Being raised in Pharaoh's house, he knew something about responsibility, about follow-through."

"Right," Richard says. "You must be true to your roots. You cannot try to be something you're not."

A pluralist objection has been burning a hole on my tongue, and I try to spit it out: "But isn't this all a bit easy?" I ask. "To have been an Israelite during those forty days at Sinai—maybe like when somebody finds himself here—he might not yet *know* who he is and whose he is. We here in the present, we don't have the luxury of knowing how the story turns out. And in our own experiences, as was the case for the Israelites, we are *always* somewhere in the middle of the story. And being in the middle, we don't necessarily *know* which path represents loyalty and which path represents betrayal. And"—I say, adding a spoonful of heartfelt flattery to help my objection go down—"I've learned so much from all of you on this point, because if I found myself in your place, I doubt I would have the courage to make it through."

Al responds. "What matters back then *and* in our own day and time is that a man *has to be dissatisfied* with his condition in order to change. Like me," he growls. "Instead of coming back into this place, I'd rather live like a bum. I'd rather live like a rat in a sewer than to come back for this here three meals and a cot. They lost focus, the Israelites. In life you're gonna go through changes, you're gonna go through trials and tribulations, and periods when you can't even see your hand in front of your face. Just like when people leave here if they're stickup men. That's what they know, so that's what they go back to. But if they're in here and make changes, they're gonna get tested. They're gonna have to decide. Is they gonna go to their *old* strength or their *new* strength?"

My mouth still smoldering, I try again: "But what if"—in making the golden calf—"Aaron *is* trying to lead them forward? What if it's not about betraying a truth that is already known? What if they just don't know who God is yet, or who they are yet?"

Al's not having it. "Look," he says. "Let me give you an example. Let's say you and I plan to break out of this here jail. Right? You tell me we're gonna break out of prison, and it's on. You and me, okay? And we makes it out of the blocks and go to the wall, and then our leader say, '*Wait here*.' Now, you tellin' me you gonna go back to your cell and lie down?"

"No," I object. "That's not a fair analogy. The golden calf isn't equivalent to going back to your cell. For the prison-break analogy to fit"—as with Moses and Aaron—"we would have to have two leaders. One goes on up ahead to scout it out, but once he's gone, the other comes back and says, '*Psssst . . . it's this way*.' Now, you don't know which is the right way out. What do you do?"

This is by no means a new argument between Al and me. Al's intransigence in discriminating between God's truth and the falsehoods of men is to me astounding. Not that I take him in this regard to be too far outside the norm. Skepticism of the sort that is to me second nature, which belongs to a particular Enlightenment strain stretching from Descartes to Kierkegaard, in no way represents the human animal's default setting.[10] More often than not, it would seem, whether in Graterford's chapel, Princeton, New Jersey, or Jesus' Judaea, people seem to know what they know about the world without too much inner conflict. As I figure it, any slate of truths worth its salt, whether designating who God is or what justice looks like, belongs to a web of other beliefs and practices that enables an adherent to process new experiences in ways that verify his or her preexisting take on the world. For someone like me, then, who was raised to see texts as open and pliant entities, Al's putatively surface reading of the Bible can't exclude alternative interpretations, though I simultaneously understand how someone with different expectations of text, reason, and faith would be in no way vexed by any sort of inherent elasticity in the meaning of the Word.

What amazes me more about men like Al and Teddy is their faith's ability to endure its own verification standard, where to *feel* is to *know*. Nothing, in my experience, is more fickle than feeling. In short order a young man who demands from his feelings the proof of his love will soon find that love, for its fluctuations, desperately wanting. As I'm beginning to accept, the heart is a time-share in which covetousness and apathy have their percentages. And yet, by all appearances, the hearts of men like Daffy and Al are constituted differently. "No. I'm all sold out," Al once said with a chuckle when I asked if he ever experiences doubt. In response to the same query, Daffy went didactic: "The one who doubts," he said, paraphrasing the Apostle James, "is like one getting tossed on the waves."

Baumgartner chalks up doubt as yet another indulgence that these men can ill afford. Keita attributes its absence to the men's steely resolve to believe, their silent bluster of doubtlessness being but the negative expression of their deep-seated guilt and fear of God's final judgment. While I can't peer into psyches, what is certain is that to the extent chapel regulars struggle with doubt at all, it is rarely breathed in public. Moreover, the certitude in their convictions and the accompanying gratitude for the salvation that is theirs doesn't merely define the present and assure the future. Certitude also expunges from the past whatever uncertainty might once have been. When reminiscing about their wicked pasts, it is a common trope that in one's heart, one *always knew* who God was and that what one was doing was wrong. While in the arrogance of youth they denied it, in their hearts—or, in the case of Daffy Ball, who, out on his first caper, was gripped by an acute need to take a shit, his gut—they never had any doubt. God has always been who He says He is.

Teddy and Al think me a sophist when I argue that judgments about the true and the good sometimes entail not only the separation of the true from the false but also the discrimination between competing truths, a determination almost always made with partial information and uncertainty as to outcome.[11] My position that truth itself might as yet reside in a process of becoming, and that coming to know it might require as much invention as discovery—this they dismiss as the senseless ramblings of the overeducated. As for the uncertainty I profess toward who or what God may be, here Al and Teddy quickly leap from contestation to pastoral care. Of course the ultimate Truth still evades me, they contend with loving condescension. Certainty of that kind will be delivered to my heart only when I take that final step and accept Jesus Christ. They are serious, surely, and as such, both concerned and generous. Given the nature of our relationships, however, they are also joking. As Teddy likes to say, "Converting a Jew counts for two."

"Look," Al says, "if you're a follower and you follow someone wholeheartedly or halfheartedly, it don't matter. You got to know what are your *reasons* for following. Do you *believe* or are you just trying to get out of a situation? If we're going to do a robbery, and somebody gets killed, you *not* going to roll on me, is you?"

"Don't matter if you do," Daffy says. "They gonna hit you with a conspiracy count either way."

"Right," Al says. "If you gonna get a bullet in his head, you gonna get a bullet in his head." Given the stakes, that is, there's no reason to half-step.

What is it, Richard presses the men, that allows people not to veer from the path?

In his raspy, lilting way, Daffy begins to speak. "I was talking about this with Moose, right? So, what's the definition of *exodus*? It means 'coming out.' And we was talking about the hospice program. And he has diabetes and he said, 'I almost died from diabetes, and they were giving me insulin.' But now he was going to try to do it without medication, just with diet and exercise. And you know what? My man hasn't taken an insulin shot in years. He did it by faith alone, and he was successful. Leading is like that. Leaders are those who can endure. We experience lots of things in our own personal Exodus. I was in the dark, you know? I was on death row. But I had faith that I could make it through."

If for Daffy the essence of leadership is steeliness, Richard sees it in the willingness to be democratic. "Jesus says, 'Let this cup pass from me.' You see?" Richard asks. "He doesn't want it. He's not after the power. He says not *my* will' but rather, 'let *your* will be done.' In Jesus we see a willingness to trust in a radical way."

"And a willingness to forsake all," Al adds, fast-forwarding to Calvary.

"That's right," Richard says. "Now, to say, 'I sacrifice my own wants and desires and submit my life to your will.' Now, that might sound easy *in theory*, but to do it in the dark, to do it in this state of incarceration . . ."

Al picks it up. "I thank God that Christ Jesus saw the bigger picture, and said not '*my* will' but '*your* will be done.' That's why He died on the cross. That's why He denied hisself. But that's the thing about following. If you're gonna follow, you're gonna have to go all the way. In a robbery, other things might happen in that robbery. And you're making a choice right now: Is you in or is you out?"

"Not just in a robbery," Richard says, "but in any adventure."

Again, I feel compelled to go for it. "I fear that this is all too easy," I say. "In my experience—and, mind you, I don't know Jesus Christ—it's not always a matter of being loyal to the Truth versus betraying it. More often than not, it's a matter of choosing from *multiple* truths, competing truths. Like, for example, let's take someone who finds himself in this jail. And he doesn't know God. And he could choose Christianity, and he could choose Islam. Now, I never want to be in a position that says that there's only one righteous loyal path, because, in my experience, the righteous path is always, coincidentally, *our* path and the unrighteous path is always *yours*, or *his*. I mean, what's faithful depends on your perspective. If I was having this conversation back in the community I grew up in, say, it would be the *Jews* who stayed true to God's word and the *Christians* who followed the golden calf." The fire on my tongue is out.

"Look," Al says impassively. "It don't matter. Just believe *something*. Sell out to it. Have your conviction. Whatever it is."

"But what about Paul on the road to Damascus?" I ask. "Can't there be virtue in changing one's mind?"

"Look here," Al says. "What matters is my relationship to God. I don't get caught up in this or that doctrine. You've got to have a made-up mind. And then, once your mind is made up you've got to continue to make the choice to be obedient, continue to make the choice to be faithful, continue to make the choice to be trustworthy. It doesn't seem to be in the human being to deny hisself for another, to deny hisself for a cause. But to me, it ain't hard to do that if you see the bigger picture."

Daffy says, "When you go back and look at the lives that a lot of us have lived, it almost looks ironic that we're saying what we're saying. But the thing that binds us all together is love. In the hospital, I saw an old Muslim brother I used to know back from my Muslim days, and he was dying. And he says, 'Rahim, is that you? Daffy from Twenty-third? I hear you's a Christian now.' So I says, 'Yeah, that's right.' And it's Tito, and Tito and I used to be Muslims together. And Tito says, 'You know, back when we were going through that whole nationalistic thing, I never judged a person based on whether he believed this or he believed that. I just trusted that he believed whatever he said he believed in.' And *that's* how Tito stayed free all these years. And so that's why I say that if you're a Buddhist, and he's a Jew, and he's a Christian"—he points sequentially around the table—"it don't matter. We have to leave all that up to God for later and just love one another while we're here.

"I was back on the block the other day," Daffy says, pivoting to another recent encounter, "and this guy, he's leaning over and he's smelling the lock on his cell, and when he looks up and sees me, he says, 'It smells like steel.' And you know how I am, right? I was going to exploit this to spread the Word. So I says to him, 'Isn't it funny that it's been here all these years and it never lost its smell?' You know, things remain the same from the past. Me and Al—we'se old heads, and these young bucks, they think we can't relate, but if you show 'em that the old spirit is the same one that lives today, they see that all we gotta do to be good leaders is to follow what those in the past did. But, look, I'm a good defensive fighter, tall for a welterweight, longer reach. So if I see a good fighter, I'm not going to make him fight like me. His body type might be different. His style might be different. In training him to fight, I'm going to let him use *his* strengths."

"That's exactly right!" Richard proclaims. "A good leader doesn't try to make clones. A controlling person is always a destructive person. The difference between a healthy leader and a dangerous leader comes down to an issue of control. A dangerous leader emphasizes what separates us. A healthy leader sees that there is something beyond our difference that bonds us all. And that thing is love."

Ephraim says, "The only leader we should have is God, because any human or man will let us down."

Richard agrees. "The story of the Israelites would have turned out different had they not looked to Moses as their intercessor, if they had had a direct relationship with God. Followers need to understand that they, too, have a direct relationship with God, and that a leader's job is to facilitate that relationship."

"But one can be a conscientious follower," Daffy says.

"That's also true," Richard acknowledges. "Being a conscientious follower doesn't mean that you have to give over your own responsibilities. Quite the opposite."

Al speaks: "Like Jesus said, if you want to be a leader, you must be a servant to all. But those in the community, they have an extra responsibility, too. I see a lot of brothers who profess Jesus Christ as their personal Lord and Savior, and I can't look into their heart, but they don't live it out in their actions, even when they're down here in the chapel. They don't live with the gifts. They act like *guests*. They don't act like *family*." Al drives his head down into his shoulders and juts his bulldog brow toward Ephraim.

Ephraim responds. "But how can you say they're not using it if you don't know what God gave them? Your gift is music, but maybe they're a teacher. You can't tell them what the proper expression of their gifts is! That's like Protestants who say you've got to speak in tongues. But I gave my life to God on December 11th, 1991, and I ain't never spoke in tongues yet!"

"Yes," Richard says, "some do and some don't. But Al's point still stands: being a healthy member of the community entails being an *active member* of the community."

Ephraim's already plaintive voice rises in pitch. "Look, there're only three times in the service you gets to be active." He counts them on his fingers. "One, when Daffy tells you to say something to your neighbor; two, when you read the Word. And the rest is everybody telling you to stand up and sit down. That's it. So really it's just two times.

"We be talking about being active on a deeper level," Al says.

"That's right," Richard says. "Do you know what *worship* means? It's old English for 'to give worth to.' The most essential act of worship is not to read the Scripture or be in the choir. It's to give *to God* that worth, and it needn't be shown in any other way. That's what *liturgy* means; it's from the Greek for 'the work of the people.'"

An unfamiliar African-American CO comes to the door of the classroom and holds up five fingers. Meeting his eyes, Richard nods in acknowledgment.

"That's what I'm talking about," Al says. "Our community is bigger than what happens down here on Sundays. We got Bible studies and counseling on every block. Guys minister on their blocks, in their jobs, everywhere. Your gifts, once you come into the community, it's just like walking. I'm not talking about who claps their hands on Sundays. They might not show it physically but the inward part is rejoicing. But who am I to say what one is praising?"

"That's my point exactly!" cries Ephraim.

"No, no, you're not getting me," Al says. "Like with music, African-American guys be more expressive. But some will sit there silently during the service, but afterward they'll come up to me and tell me how they enjoyed themselves and repeat every word back to me. On the other hand, some of the African-American people, they'll be on the beat"—he snaps his sausage-like fingers—"but then, later, when I ask them, they can't repeat a word of what I said."

"Look," Ephraim says, "some guys, you might not see them participating in counseling or Bible study on the block, but they know who I follow. Like you know, I'm a coach, but if there's a football game on Sunday, Ephraim won't be there."

"And what do your actions show?" Al asks.

"Love," Ephraim says. "They show that Ephraim gives everything. I be tutoring guys." Ephraim works in the school as a literacy tutor. "I be teaching them to read, teaching them to write, and teaching them to count."

Unmoved by Ephraim's secular contributions, Al flatly asks, "Look, Jesus is your personal savior, right?"

"Yeah," Ephraim interrupts, "and Jesus was a teacher like I am. Look, I'm *active* in the activities I'm in."

"And what are you doing in the body of Christ?"

"Everyone knows I'm a Christian!" Ephraim whines.

"And *how* do they know?"

"They know 'cause I'm in church on Sunday."

Al looks at me. "They know he's a Christian on Sundays," he says.

Perhaps coming to realize that he's been backing the wrong dog in this fight, Richard asks Al: "Al, what point are you trying to make?"

"My point is," Al says, driving his chin up and then slicing it downward, "what is Ephraim doing in the body of the Christ—in the community—to edify the body?"

"I'm changing hearts!" Ephraim says. "Changing minds. I'm doing it with action!"

Rhetorically, Al asks Richard, "Then maybe *he* might not be aware of the resources that are needed on the block?"

"I'm secretary of the NAACP!" Ephraim pleads.

As time runs out, Daffy seeks to smooth over Al and Ephraim's dispute about Christian duty. "Ultimately," Daffy says, "it's not really about what we *do*. We ask who's worshipping when they're down here, but look, if we're touched by the Holy Spirit, then we have the power of discernment. So we know what we are. You don't have to set yourself apart or anything like that. Because when it comes down to it, it's not what we *do*, it's *whhhhhhh, whhhhhhh*"—he blows twice through a hollow fist—"it's what we *are*. And this, *whhhhhhh*"—he breathes slowly into his unfurling palm—"*this* is what we are."

Spirit is what we are.

"Al is something else," I say. We're in the vestibule, waiting on Richard's escort out.

Richard says that people on the outside refuse to believe the sort of spiritual maturity guys in here have.

Some of this, I propose, is a tribute to him.

"No," Richard says. "The guys who end up with it already have it when they come in." Shooting for humility, Richard's words clank fatalistic.

"It's too bad that Charles wasn't here," I say, giving voice to a feeling I've had for the past two hours.

Richard sobers up. "Charles is going through something very, very hard. He's so angry. But at the same time he's so open about his anger, about his disappointments, about the horrors of his past. And it makes him incredibly vulnerable."

I ask Richard if he knows anyone else with Charles's combination of skepticism and biblical literalism.

Richard shakes his head. That's why he's so impressed that Charles sticks with it, Richard says, and why he regrets it so profoundly when Charles is a no-show.

Still hawking my pluralist wares, I identify Charles as one who strikes me as standing between competing goods.

"And surrounded by dangers," Richard adds, "within and without."

He's going to have to figure out his *own* way, I assert.

We share what feels like a weighty silence.

Together we wax paternalistic about the burdens the prisoners carry. Richard firmly believes, he says, that everyone here was a victim before he became an offender. I think back to a story Daffy once told of how he felt, one Christmas morning, when there were presents under the tree for all of his brothers and sisters but nothing for him. Though told with a smile, the story sounded a rare dissonant note in Daffy's refusal of victimhood.

"When I hear about their childhoods," Richard says, "I'm struck by the chaos, how the gang was in many cases their first experience of order."

"And the terrible irony," I say, "is that many of the guys have more structure, support, and opportunities in here than they ever would have had on the outside."

Richard says, "To have the poverty and despair that we have in this country, this unbelievably wealthy country. That's the real crime."

"Quite literally a disgrace," I say.

He shakes his head. "And those who support these punitive policies are ninety-seven percent God-fearing people."

On his morning rounds Baumgartner saw Sayyid. I ask about his spirits.

"He's Sayyid," Baumgartner says, meaning that he gave every appearance of optimism. Baumgartner is sitting at Sayyid's desk and I'm at Al's.

"What does he know about his charge?"

Baumgartner raises an eyebrow and flops his jowl. "That he's 'under investigation for violations of the rules and regulations of the institution,' meaning not a hell of a lot." Baumgartner jokes: "I told Sayyid that Kazi set him up because he wants his job." While the motive is plausible, that Sayyid's childhood friend would be the culprit is patently absurd. We slide into a discussion of Kaz.

"The chillest, most even-keeled guy," I say.

"The most *institutionalized*," Baumgartner adds, lodging the piteous condemnation. "Just minds his little store"—when Kazi was busted and taken to the hole last spring, the chaplains learned that he was selling commissary goods out of his cell—"essentially content with the fact that he's going to spend the rest of his life here. Though of course," Baumgartner observes, "Kaz likely doesn't know this about himself. That's why he was so freaked out when he got jumped. More than anything else, it signaled a rupture in his routine."

Lazily, our office gossip turns to Teddy, who, Baumgartner says, is forever poking and probing and gaming and scheming, doing by tongue and wit in this place what he used to do on the street with polished steel and foot speed. As is common knowledge in the chapel, Teddy was a stickup kid—someone who robbed drug dealers for their drugs and money. "He just loves the chase," Baumgartner says, "the fact that he can rob you and then outrun you. For him, religion is just another game to be played just like that." While Teddy likes to play games at least as much as I do, I would hardly characterize Teddy's religious disposition this way. Neither, I assume, if pressed, would Baumgartner. Still, for the sake of passing the time, the image of Teddy as some sort of religious sportsman makes for a satisfying caricature.

I report in on EFM. The two of us laud Richard Kipling's efforts in the trenches to forge an appreciation for theological nuance. Baumgartner laments the shallowness of Graterford's predominant fundamentalism, its "spiritual immaturity" and its insistence on obedience to a very narrow, conservative and, in his view, *un-Christian* slate of propositions.

After repeatedly failing to make any dent, I've stopped voicing my objection to the rhetoric of "immaturity" favored by Baumgartner, Kipling, and others, in which the reputedly judgmental fundamentalists are regarded as spiritually stunted and we, the open-minded liberals, are cast as the grown-ups. While I share many of Baumgartner's sympathies, any developmental model that presumes *us* as being further along than *them* strikes me as inherently suspect. While Christian conservatives do a version of this, too, the liberal version bothers me more. It gets my hackles up because it's a bigotry common among my intimates, and because when deployed unselfconsciously it gives the lie to liberal pluralism. Indeed, all else being equal, I don't presume that liberals—whether theological, social, or political—are necessarily any less doctrinaire than our conservative counterparts. Moreover, as I tell Baumgartner now, my deep suspicion is that our preference for our way of reading texts is at root an aesthetic judgment more than an ethical one: as worshippers of the text, we think the text is due respect for its intricacies, and we reject as insufficiently adulatory the restriction of Scripture to the flat, putatively commonsense readings that fundamentalists afford it.

Baumgartner disagrees. His objection, he says, is different. His problem is theological. In his view, the fundamentalists get Jesus totally wrong. Jesus is about loving everyone, your friend as well as your enemy, not about erecting a barrier between the ones inside who are saved and those outside who are damned.

I relate a bit of Al's argument with Ephraim. Despite my intuitive sympathies with Ephraim's position, I look to defend Al's more restrictive sense of where one's ethical energies ought to be directed. "There are always going to be in-groups and out-groups," I say, "and, like in a family, folks *do*—and *ought to*—have a greater responsibility to those within their own group than they do to those that lie outside."[12] And for men like Al and Daffy, they do genuinely seem to be motivated by a sense of obligation to others.

Again, Baumgartner is more skeptical than I am. "But what form does that take?" he asks. "For a fundamentalist, there's only one way—and that's through Jesus Christ."

I readily concede Baumgartner's criticism of conservative Protestantism. Nonetheless, I simultaneously wonder if there isn't some sort of universal sociological fact about the necessary discriminations of love that Al accepts but a humanist like Baumgartner refuses to concede. Baumgartner might plead universalism, but his universalism can't help but define itself against its other, in this case the Jesus-betraying proponents of the Pauline doctrine that there is but one way to salvation and that way is through Jesus Christ.[13]

We get to talking about Baumgartner time at Dropsie, the defunct Jewish seminary where he got his Ph.D.

"Wasn't it alienating to be a sole Lutheran in a sea of Jews?"

"No," Baumgartner says impishly, "I enjoyed it."

He relates an anecdote. They were discussing the passage in Exodus where Moses is fighting the Amalekites. One of the more outspoken and talented exegetes in class was arguing vehemently for a most abstruse and far-fetched midrashic position—Baumgartner can't remember the specifics, exactly—as to why Moses' raised arms succeeded in keeping the sun from going down. One by one, other classmates proposed alternative interpretations, and one by one, the virtuoso shot them down, sticking to the guns he'd mounted on what, in Baumgartner's judgment, was a rather rickety hermeneutic garrison.

Baumgartner finally chimed in: "You know what *we* say, right?" There was no need to identify who the *we* was. "*We* say that Moses was able to orchestrate this miracle because he was standing in the shadow of the true cross." Baumgartner was greeted by silence, but to me his point is clear and true. From his Christian perspective, the execution of a brilliant rabbinic maneuver appeared as arbitrary and unconvincing as a prefigurative Christian reading would appear to a roomful of Jews. Reading Scripture takes place within a wide range of social practices, and there is no Archimedean point from which to distinguish the true readings from the false ones. While from the outside we may discern the contours of a text designated "Scripture," if it is the text's *meaning* that we are after, then we must nudge closer to a particular community that posits it so. Even and especially when such truths are alleged as self-evident, it is within a given tradition of interpretation and debate that a group of religious actors render a purported true. Without these received and defended rules of engagement, there are no truths to live by, just a bunch of words on a page.[14]

If every set of social norms operates according to rules whose power stems largely from the fact that they go without saying, the conservative Christianity of men like Al strikes me as especially averse to interrogation.[15] It is a mode of religious observance that pledges (or aspires to pledge) absolute fealty, and demands the same of one's fellows. In its rigidness no less so than its bullishness, Al's religiosity seems curiously well suited to this environment, where strong-arming is law, and the single-minded may thrive while the swayable flounder. And so the old heads preach it to their juniors—though a skeptic could argue that it is not on behalf of their juniors' spiritual security, but for their own, that they campaign. Thus the Wednesday-morning drama: wise old heads like Al and Daffy schooling undisciplined young bucks like Charles and Ephraim on how to properly be in Christ. As meanwhile, these as-yet-unbroken youngsters defiantly demonstrate to their long-since sold-out elders that, just maybe, there is more than one way for a Christian to live.

Sitting at his desk, Keita works his thumbs over the dining hall orange in search of a seam. We're waiting on Baumgartner, who, following lunch, broke ranks for the deputy's complex in search of information on Sayyid.

Seemingly driven by boredom and opportunity more than desire, Gorski unlocks the filing cabinet on which I'm leaning, and we filch a miniature Nestlé Crunch and York Peppermint Pattie apiece from Teddy's stash. It's well past 1:00 p.m. and the office remains empty.

Eventually Baumgartner makes his entrance. Without looking, I can sense his eagerness to report in. He lifts the plastic sheeting off the chair by the door and piles it on top of the filing cabinets. He shuts the door and slowly takes his seat. The door cracks open. He gets up, shuts it again, and sits back down with a pronounced exhale.

Facing away from the door, Gorski theatrically turns his head toward Baumgartner, as if, in the language of Baumgartner's silent melodrama, to say: *Well?*

"Well," Baumgartner says with puffed cheeks, "they laughed at me." The other chaplains remain silent. "Simpson likes to pretend that he holds all the cards, and that you are an idiot, especially if *you* are a chaplain." Hard-nosed in countenance and attitude, Simpson—the security captain—is known for the paranoid pessimism that one would expect of a man of his station. "Simpson says that Sayyid is heavy into contraband trafficking and that we need to find a new clerk. When I spoke to Sayyid this morning, I told him that we'd hold his job for him until that time if and when he gets written up for an infraction. I don't think Simpson has anything, or else he would have rubbed my nose in it. What I wish is that they would just charge Sayyid or let him go. In the interim, though, responsibilities will have to be redistributed."

Keita speaks. "Whenever something is going on, the jail automatically assumes that it's got to be coming from the chapel."

"Why is that?" I ask.

"Because of the history," Keita responds.

"Well, it *is* a porous site," Baumgartner concedes, "with lots of volunteers still coming and going." Somewhere in the ballpark of seventy volunteers come and go from the chapel every month. Though that's only a fraction of the pre-raid count, in the new era, the chapel's relative permeability is hard to miss.

"But volunteers and staff," Keita objects, "we *all* have to go through the metal detector. Sometimes they search us. Sometimes they search our cars. Never do we have anything on us. So what exactly are we bringing in, and how? Please . . . they *know* that it's the COs who are bringing the contraband in." It is the consensus of prisoner, staff, and administrator alike that the lion's share of smuggling is done by staff.

"When we talk about contraband," I inquire, "what exactly are we talking about?"

"It could be anything," Baumgartner says, "from drugs to cell phones at the upper end down to something as simple as too much food from commissary. In this case, Simpson implied that Sayyid's got his fingers in oil."

No one is surprised. While oils and perfumes are banned in the jail, prohibited for their ability to mask other smells, they are permitted in the chapel—an accommodation won long ago by members of the Nation for the purpose of pre-prayer purification. The jugs of scented oil, which the groups pay for themselves, are kept under lock and key in Baumgartner's closet. Prior to Jum'ah and each of the black nationalist Muslim services, an authorized representative transfers, under Baumgartner's watchful eye, a small amount from the group's jug to a sample-sized plastic bottle. The deputized congregant, which in the case of the Sunni Muslims happens to be Sayyid, stands by the door and issues each arrival a splash or two. As the Imam and Keita attest, however, what little surplus remains after he has parsimoniously divvied up squirts among the hundreds of men who've come to make prayer, Sayyid painstakingly rubs into the community's blue carpets so that when they are unrolled the next week, they will retain the vague scent of perfume. Nonetheless, from the chapel or from elsewhere, scented oils—the sorts sold on 125th Street in Harlem or on Fifty-second Street in West Philadelphia—find their way to the blocks, where they are sold at a hefty markup to those seeking to smooth their skin or to smell like something other than imprisoned men on those days when their mother, daughter, or sweetheart is visiting.

"Maybe Sayyid *is* doing something," Gorski suggests. "I mean, none of us had any idea that Kazi was running a little store out of his cell until he was busted."

"Of course, anything's possible," Baumgartner says, shaking his head. "But I don't see how Sayyid would even have the time to run contraband when he spends every free second he has doing either his Villanova work or studying the Qur'an." Baumgartner doesn't even mention Mubdi's Wednesday-night Arabic or the time Sayyid spends trading letters in Arabic with Mohammed, another of Mubdi's students. But to Simpson, these signs of Sayyid's diligence can only read differently.

"Simpson likes nothing better than to get in my face," Baumgartner says, "and show me letters or play me phone conversations. But I am *not* an idiot." Baumgartner is especially affronted by Simpson's condescension today, he says, when "just last week I turned the——over to him on a platter"—Baumgartner drops the name of a famous prison gang.[16] This is the first I've heard of anything like this. Baumgartner continues: "So the fact that Simpson treats me like a bleeding-heart idiot who has no clue that actual criminal activities are going on here is a real slap in the face."

Gorski asks, "Is there some way that Crocket's pickup"—in a move atypical of the chaplains, Gorski refers to Sayyid by his last name—"might be related to Hamed's transfer to a new job? It's no secret that there was no love lost between the two of them."

Once or twice I'd witnessed Sayyid and Hamed, Vic's predecessor, carp at one another, but hadn't made much of it. Had Hamed wanted to bring Sayyid trouble, it would require only an anonymous slip to the authorities alleging that Sayyid was in possession of oil, or drugs, or commissary fare in surplus of fifty dollars' value—any one of which would be sufficient cause for detention. As for motive, as the Muslim's oilman and the vice president of the Brotherhood Jaycees, Sayyid's removal could stand to benefit any of a number of would-be rivals.

From the din behind me I can tell the prisoners are back. I turn and through the window in Keita's door see Vic, who is staring back in my direction. I catch his eye in mine and turn away, embarrassed.

Baumgartner says, "When the prisoners go back at three-thirty we should search through Sayyid's desk. If anything is to be found down here, it most certainly should be found by us." The Imam nods. "Oil . . ." Baumgartner moans. "But none of the chapel oil is missing! Sure, Mac Swan claimed that somebody stole some of the Moors' oil, but Simpson knows they orchestrated that job themselves." (Not coincidentally, Mac Swan, a former death row prisoner and Moorish Science Temple heavy, perennially has a breast pocket full of comically thick pens in which, the chaplains assume, he smuggles oil back to the block.) It is commonly alleged, Baumgartner concedes, that Sayyid is an able lock picker, but again, none of the Muslims' oil is missing, so that's a red herring. Baumgartner is thinking aloud now, and floundering to make sense. Not merely as a jolt from routine does Sayyid's detention upset the chaplains. Albeit one of an unusual sort, he is their coworker, after all, and their concern for his welfare is unforced. Simultaneously, Sayyid's detention sparks an unwelcome resurgence of the sorts of doubts that in Simpson's mind *ought* to plague the chaplains the rest of the time, too—doubts that if kept perpetually in mind would make Sayyid much more of a criminal than a man and render the chaplains' jobs, both as bosses and pastors, impossible. When forced to think about it, though, the chaplains know they would be fools to place even the most trusted worker above suspicion. We talk on.

"I'll tell the guys only that Sayyid is being held on suspicion and that that's it," Baumgartner says. "They'll surely learn more than that, but the chaplains should not be the vehicles of that knowledge. What's crucial," he concludes, looking at each of us in succession, "is that we keep our own ethics aboveboard and make sure that we ourselves are above reproach. If they decide to crack down back here, it'll make all of our jobs that much harder."

Baumgartner's statement is conclusive, but the five of us seem reluctant to leave these four walls. The conversation turns to miscellanea. Unable to stop myself, I report in on the discrimination grievance that had been filed against Watkins.

"I could see that," Baumgartner says with a blank stare.

"For proselytizing, perhaps, but for discrimination? I doubt it," I say, mounting Watkins's defense as if someone else had brought it up. "I assumed you'd all heard." Apparently not. Keita is talking to the Imam about how he has to send money to Africa for animals to sacrifice. Gorski and the Imam commiserate about the additional challenges of grieving at a distance. I have no referent here. We linger on.

In the back of the chapel, I write:

1. The administrative beauty of having two codes of conduct—
    the official code of conduct (the formalist) and the code
    people live by (the realist) is that at any time the administra-
    tion can bust anyone for anything . . .

2. I have marveled in the past how oddly loose it feels here compared to what one would expect for a maximum-security prison. But it is precisely in this gap, in the play between the rules (1) and the rules (2) that terror as usual is manufactured—an aperture to be snapped shut at any moment depending on the needs, will, desire, and whimsy of the controllers.[17]

3. I never felt so not-a-prisoner as when I left that room. Teddy called me over to sit down and I raced on by. The guys in the office all knew that I was privy to something solely by virtue of being free, and that I wasn't going to tell them solely because they are not.

Under a cover of clouds, the chapel has dimmed. Baumgartner passes me by. Trying to make sense of what Keita and the Imam were talking about, I ask him who died.

"Keita's brother," Baumgartner answers. Suddenly I understand all of Keita's Africa wistfulness over the past couple of days.

Baumgartner leaves me to my notes.

The Wednesday-afternoon activity block is left deliberately vacant, reserved for memorial services to honor prisoners who died during the previous week. For now, a service happens every third week or so. As Graterford's population ages, that frequency will increase.[18] Some of these events are more solemn than others. For popular prisoners, such as a prominent Catholic lifer who died last spring, the occasion was a festive one. The Sunday choir and the Catholic band played, eulogies were recited, reminiscences shared, jokes cracked, and good cheer shared. The memorials for the anonymous prisoners, which are attended by only a handful of new-side regulars and are over in five minutes, are much more upsetting.

On memorial-service Wednesdays, the chapel air is more tetchy than usual. The workers do their jobs, study, conduct their private business, and play around as usual, but in somewhat muted tones. No doubt their quiet shows respect for the dead. Almost as surely, their disquiet betrays the lifers' knowledge, difficult on memorial Wednesdays to repress, that someday the DOC processing photo taped to the poster board beside the conference room will be theirs.

And yet, in the chapel, men like David the Jewish janitor, who are demonstrably wrapped up in their own mortality, are the exceptions.

Like those of us out on the street who joke and love and worry ourselves with nonsense in spite of the fact that someday soon we will be dust, the lifers don't seem too preoccupied with the fact that they will die here. Inasmuch as the acceptance of this cold fact is the sine qua non of acceptance, the raised white flag declaring that a man's holy contentedness has turned cancerous and rotted his soul, the taboo guarding this awareness is also cultivated in practice. Teddy has called it "lifers' disease," this enabling dementia that allows a man to teeter on the tightrope for decades, as if he doesn't know how the story ends.

But since nobody died last week, such concerns are, today, no more manifest or latent than usual.

Finding Al in the vestibule, I ask him what he was talking about when he referred to the "counseling" that takes place on the blocks.

Years back, Al explains, he and some other guys asked Baumgartner about providing resources for guys who answer the altar call at the Sunday service to learn "the ABC's of the faith" rather than simply coming up again and again, week after week. Saying that there were no more slots available for Bible studies, Baumgartner instructed the community to take care of the need itself. So they formed an auxiliary board to the Sunday service that schedules ABC Bible studies, advanced Bible studies, and counseling. When someone comes up to the altar on a Sunday, he fills out a slip with his block and cell number, and after the service, that slip is given to the representative from that guy's block. Later that day, the block rep stops by the guy's cell and together they agree on a time when they can get together to study the ABC's. In addition, each block has a weekly advanced Bible study, and counseling is scheduled as the need arises.

Religious life on the blocks remains to me largely a mystery. When in February 2005 the Graterford Psych Department counselor who doubles as the institution's research supervisor took me for the first time to the chapel and told me that I'd been granted access to the entire prison, I was flabbergasted.[19] If I was unfettered in theory, however, in practice the blocks revealed themselves to be more or less out of bounds. No one told me so expressly. Rather, as part of the acculturation process, I imbibed the chaplains' attitude—one shared by staff more generally—that unless one has explicit business on the blocks, one doesn't go there. For the chaplains, it is a place well beyond their comfort zone, a scary, vulgar realm of sweat and stink, catcalls and pinups. More than that, to visit the blocks is to render prisoners wholly visible, to see men through bars where they sleep and where they shit, surrounded by what little they have. It's an embarrassing encounter for both parties—for the man made a master as well as for the man made a slave.[20] Predisposed to stop short of such discomfiting voyeurism (if it wasn't too late already), I embraced the undeclared rules of engagement.

Modest pushback came from below. When, early on, I would press men at Graterford on what I should write about, a compelling few insisted that I needed to go to the blocks, that that's where the real story of the jail takes place, and that I had a unique opportunity to bring it to light. From these exhortations, a mixed picture emerged. Some, like Teddy and Sayyid, complained that whatever religious fellowship takes place down here stops at the chapel door. From Al and many others, however, the alternatively regulated religious landscape of the blocks came off as even more vibrant than the chapel itself. By the spring, I was pressing Baumgartner on whether I could go—to the blues' Bible study specifically, which was meeting on E Block. Baumgartner was vaguely affirmative but deliberately deferring. When subsequent requests were similarly deflected, I understood that if block visits were to happen, I would have to push, which I found myself reluctant to do. Most of the time, backing off as I did strikes me as having been the wise course of action.

"And what exactly is your beef with Ephraim?" I ask Al, blowing on the embers of this morning's dispute.

"My beef is that Ephraim doesn't give anything to the community."

"What about his tutoring, though? Isn't that giving?"

"Of course that's giving, but what's he doing for the body of Christ?" As if anticipating my objection, Al explains that the Bible makes only one defense of prejudice—he can't remember exactly where right now—and that's where it says: "Do good to all men but especially to those in the household of faith."[21] "And Ephraim should know that," he says, "but he don't. Look, how long has Ephraim been saved?"

I confess that I don't remember.

"Since 1991," Al says, stone-faced. "That's fifteen years. In fifteen years he should know his ABC's, but he don't."

"But he's in EFM," I say. "Surely he knows a thing or two."

"He should, but he don't. That's the problem. The studies down here, they all advanced studies. You gotta already know your ABC's to participate in them. But Ephraim thinks he above that, and now he's too prideful to go back and learn them."

"Is it not possible that he knows a *different* set of ABC's?" I ask.

"No."

"Well, what exactly do you mean by ABC's?" I ask.

"To know the ABC's," Al says, "you gotta know the ABC's of the birth, life, death, and resurrection of Jesus Christ."

"And Ephraim doesn't know those things?"

"No."

I offer no counter. I suspect Al for reading as Ephraim's "ignorance" what are, in fact, profound differences between the two men over what Jesus Christ's death on the cross means for how a man is to get to heaven and for how he is to live in the interim. And while I'm not afraid to push back harder, for the moment I find myself driven strangely inward by the force of Al's certainty. Faced with such a concrete formula—and the ways of feeling, doing, and knowing that follow upon Al's religious program[22]—my own hodgepodge of convictions and commitments that circle loosely around a humanist's sense of kindness and a liberal's ideal of fairness feels suddenly desiccated, secured to the stem of my being, perhaps, but only so long as the breeze doesn't pick up.

Baraka is pacing his exercise loops through two adjacent rows of pews to the left of the lectern, where I am standing. His vibe is peppy, "chipper," as Baraka himself might call it, using the sort of white-person talk that riles Teddy. Baraka is singing opera in a scratchy baritone, no longer powerful but still true.

"What is that?" I ask.

"You don't *know*?" he asks coyly.

"It's familiar," I say, "but I couldn't name it."

"It's Verdi," he says. "*La Traviata.*" If amplified sound in the chapel is often dissonant, Baraka's undoctored voice resonates warmly. I wonder if this impromptu concert is for my benefit.

As if answering my thoughts, Baraka explains, "I've been singing it since sixth grade, when I sang it in choir." He watches me raise an eyebrow. "I'm showing you a little something just to give you a sense that I'm not such a bad guy. People think that we're all dark and dangerous villains," he says, "but a good quarter of us in here could be in anybody's community and you'd never hear a peep out of us."

"That's precisely what worries folks," I say, with a wink.

Reverend Baumgartner comes two-thirds of the way down the center aisle and catches Baraka at the extremity of his orbit. Baraka falls out, and the two men drift together toward the rear of the chapel. When they're done, Baraka resumes his circuit, and his song.

"So," he says like we've just been talking about it, "tell me—what exactly is theater?"

"I don't know," I say.

"No, tell me."

"I don't know," I repeat. I don't feel up to this.

"Are you telling me," he says, "that with all your fancy education, you can't tell me what theater is?"

I comply. "I suppose that we might say that theater is a bourgeois art form, a tradition that takes off in the early modern period but that traces itself back to the Greeks."

Baraka hums along.

"How's that?" I ask.

"Go on," he says.

"That's not enough for you?"

"Twenty years of education, right?" he goads me. "Go on."

"I don't know," I say, "I guess, in the broadest possible terms, we might say that theater is one of the sites where we late capitalists go to squander our surplus." Baraka is in the waning part of his revolution, with his back to me, but I needn't see his face to know that he is unimpressed. "In this context," I continue, "we might consider it alongside sports, celebrity culture, war, and even incarceration as ways that, as a society, we choose to spend down our excess resources, and in the process entertain ourselves and bring meaning to our lives."

Baraka gives me a cockeyed look as I continue by rote to channel Georges Bataille's theory of "the general economy." According to Bataille, human cultures are a series of exercises in targeted wasting. It is an account expansive enough to accommodate phenomena as wide-ranging as human sacrifice, asceticism, and consumer capitalism. As a critical apparatus, Bataille's is a hammer, one that bludgeons all variety of phenomena down to the same damn thing. That's why, in spite of its resonances with religion and mass incarceration both, I'm not too tempted to apply the theory of the general economy to the chapel. As I see it, a domineering theory like Bataille's renders the empirical encounter more or less redundant. I mean, if every thing is one thing, then why suffer the traffic only to prove it so? Nonetheless, Bataille is scrumptious food for thought—food that I continue to serve up to Baraka.[23]

I can't tell what Baraka makes of my lecture. While I know that he has no taste for Freud, finding it absurd how "a European who studies only privileged Europeans could think that his observations apply to everyone," I don't know if this disfavor extends to theory as such. For my part, I'm aware that I'm clumsily evading a question to which I have no good answer. Or, rather, I'm perpetrating that classic academic sleight of hand of forcing the untamed phenomenon into a well-worn theoretical framework, a framework perhaps more notable for its self-authorizing stylishness than its responsiveness to the phenomenon at hand. Coming to this conclusion, I say to Baraka: *"The sage points at the moon, the fool looks at the fingertip.*[24] Well, that's me," I say, "the fool. I haven't the first clue as to how to answer your question, but I will happily rehearse for you the words of some of those who have failed before me."

"Do you ever *go* to the theater?" Baraka asks, keeping his eyes on the prize.

"Not too often," I confess. He chides me on how often he'd go to the theater if he were on the outside, and that I should really take advantage of the cultural opportunities available to me.

"Thing is," I say, "for the time being, my standards for drama are really high. I get far more than my recommended daily quotient in here, you see."

"Try again," he says, turning the screw. "So what is theater?"

Worn down by the past few days, I don't think to turn the question around. I try again, this time ratcheting it down a notch with a short Aristotle's *Poetics* primer. I talk about the *catharsis*, the feeling of emptying experienced by the audience member when witnessing the tragic hero's undoing. After getting waylaid in a couple of associative cul-de-sacs, I circle back to critique Aristotle for artificially delineating dramatic performance from other modes of human practice. Inasmuch as our lives are always already shaped by the narratives that we have imbibed from the theater and its many modern-day counterparts, I can't reasonably point to the place where theater ends and life begins.

Baraka emits a Holmesian "Aha!" Whatever it is that pleases him, however, he keeps to himself. Again staid, Baraka asks: "So what goes on in theater?"

"I don't know," I say.

"Come on," he coaxes.

"Fine," I say. "People play parts."

"Right. And how do they do that?"

"In costume," I say.

"Exactly!" He seems authentically pleased. "That's your answer," he says. "Theater is a masquerade."

After all my heavy lifting, the conclusion strikes me as arbitrary. "But life is a masquerade!" I complain.

"Aha!" Baraka claps his hands. "And that is precisely my point." Dropping the Socratic pretense, Baraka goes didactic. "Look," he says, "a man is himself only when he wakes up and when he performs his constitution. But as soon as he steps out, he is no longer himself. That's where the masquerade starts. And it never stops. Most people are like this because they don't know themselves, or they know but don't want to know. And so they try by any means available to hide from themselves."

"Why do they _do_ that?" I ask.

"Because they don't want to have to be responsible to themselves," he says. "To make the decisions they would be obligated to make if they were truly cognizant of who they are."[25]

"But what does it mean, 'who they are'?" I ask. "I can only speak for myself, but inasmuch as I'm a being in time, I'm always changing. And even if I stayed the same, inasmuch as the _know thyself_ directive is necessary at all, it's because we're largely oblivious to ourselves."

This is well-trod terrain for Baraka and me. If my theology makes me an oddball around here, my conception of what it is to be a self isn't much more intelligible. Informed by psychoanalysis and Continental philosophy, I regard myself as a mushy and amorphous entity, one that takes different shapes across time and in it, depending passively on the mood I find myself in, or, strategically, on what the situation calls for.[26] To me, this permeable and dynamic version of the self better captures the uneven, sometimes inscrutable behaviors of those I know intimately, myself included. As well, from a political standpoint, this version of the self provides the conceptual leverage to push back against some of the more violent ways we tend to slot people as essentially and incorrigibly this or that. In the chapel, by contrast, the self is insistently described as fixed and unchanging. Or, to the extent that it does change, as was the case for Daffy or Al, it does so once and inalterably.

Baraka vehemently rejects my characterization of the pliable self. As he sees it, there *is* an essential unchanging self. This essence, moreover, is eminently knowable if one merely takes the time to look. To the degree that a man fails to know himself, he remains incapable of shouldering a man's responsibility. As Baraka often counsels me (and, surely, others): "Know yourself and let the world figure you out." Or, as he repudiated the conceit of "criminal rehabilitation": "People don't need to change: they need to stay true to themselves." A man commits a crime not because the man is bad but because he is ignorant of who he is. Educate the man about himself and he won't do the things he otherwise would've done. Self-uplift through self-knowledge: thirty years later, the values Baraka acquired in the Nation remain foundational to his senses of self and duty.

In the way that, in time, one partially embraces the fantasies of those one holds dear, I've come to accept—in spite of my philosophical misgivings—Baraka's image of himself. As best I can tell, Baraka *is* a fixed, unchanging individual, not merely because he is older than I am but because of his temperamental disposition toward resolve and constancy.

Splitting the difference between nature and nurture, Baraka attributes a man's unchanging self to the character forged in one's early experiences of "being born through a family." A psychoanalytically apt phrase that seems to nail the relevant shaping force, coming out of Baraka's mouth it nonetheless sends the amateur analyst in me on the hunt for precipitating traumata. There is no shortage of candidates. There was, of course, the decades spent in prison back when even a moderate bout of inconstancy could have gotten him killed. There was his experience, his first time in jail, of weeks in the pitch-black hole, where, after watching his buddy lose his mind, Baraka decided that rather than try to hold on, he had to "release himself into the darkness." Before prison was Vietnam, and earlier still, in a childhood painted as not wholly devoid of material privilege, there was the "sex" he had with his babysitter between the ages of five and eleven. Which (if any) of these facts is relevant to the purported fixity of Baraka's self, I'm uncertain. Baraka, for one, refuses any such examination. "You can't go *there* if you want to go home," Baraka said, referring to the psychologist's office: come parole or commutation time, a guy doesn't want to look like a mental health case. But there is another reason for Baraka's refusal. As with Al, that which to Baraka appears a virtue—in this case, his resoluteness—in the counselor's office reads like psychopathology. As he has said, "The power not to be affected by stuff—that's what scares the bejesus out of psychologists."

"I believe you," I tell Baraka now, "and I understand that the continuity you see in yourself, and that the self-knowledge you describe, are true to your experience. But you must also believe me—they are not true to mine. And furthermore, my gut impulse is that in this case it is *you* and not me that is the outlier."

Baraka objects. "So if everyone is forever changing, then how can we hold anyone responsible for their actions?"

"Because it is both socially expedient and necessary," I say. "However, just because it is expedient and necessary doesn't make it philosophically or psychologically apt." Baraka chews on that for a second or two and doesn't say anything back.

"So, tell me," I say, "if you are essentially *something*, what exactly *are* you?"

"Frustrated," Baraka says.

"Why?"

"Because I expect more of people than they are willing to give. I want them to use their potential, but that seems to be simply too much to ask." He laments how rarely people use common sense. I laugh. "What?" he asks.

I tell him that in the presumed obviousness of their referents, "actualizing potential" and "using common sense" strike me as exceedingly male standards. Now it's his turn to laugh.

"Do you hear that from your lady?" I ask him.

"No," he says. "From her I hear much, much worse. What you just said I hear from Brian."

Sensing an opening, I say, "So might we agree that there might be more than one way to live responsibly?" And then, as if to defend the integrity of my dithering nature, I confess: "Look, I'm not a person for whom being alone with his thoughts is easy. If you are correct and one's true self is the self that one encounters in isolation, then I must conclude that my essential nature is profound discomfort. That being the case, I would prefer to think instead that the individual is social, existing not in isolation but in relation with others, and that I am authentic not necessarily in the discomforts of solitude but in the joyful self-forgetting of social exchange. It is precisely in doing *this*"—I point back and forth between the two of us—"where rather than knowing myself, I forget myself. And it is in such moments, I suspect, that I maximize my own becoming."

"That's because you are essentially an emotional creature," Baraka says cuttingly.

"And you are an intellectual?" I half ask, half state. I nod in agreement, even though I know on which side of the scale the finger is pressed. "So how is it we get on so well?" I ask.

Baraka explains that I'm "sticky," by which he means something like infectious. He is rather oblique on the point, and it is precariously personal enough that I'm not inclined to make him define his terms. What I get from him is that I approach encounters with a willingness to be affected and to affect others. Ordinarily, he says, he stays away from such people, but in my case he doesn't because the payoff is generally quite good.

Again acknowledging Baraka's self-description, I press at the sources and function of his alleged immobility. I ask him how much his insistence on fixity is an adaptation to prison.

Baraka nods. Some guys, he says, allow themselves to be affected by their experiences. "Like Al. Al is essentially emotional. And he's always been that way, even way back when we were on the street, on opposite sides, with me growing up on Fifth Street, and Al growing up on Taylor, over south of Washington. Most guys in here won't let themselves be affected by others because they're scared of being close. That's not true in Al's case. He's scared of far-off things. Close things make him feel comforted."

When he's not singing his friend's praises, Baraka likes to insist that Al is the scary one, and that while he might have a soul, Al has no conscience. Al maintains the opposite. Recently I watched Al check Baraka's pulse, touch Baraka's forehead, and shake his head in a display of concern before pronouncing, "The head is hot but the heart is cold."

Not for many years have Baraka and Al shared a cell. By preference and privilege, each lives alone now, as the old heads tend to. Whereas the young guys prefer a cellie around as a buffer against loneliness, the old guys would sooner stomach the gnawing silence than the clamor and rancor of having to share with another grown man what is basically a bathroom. Al wasn't the easiest man to live with, either. Now the stuff of jokes, he had rules his cellies were forced to observe, principal among them being that if one needed to use the toilet, he'd best do it during waking hours.

Not long ago, where we're currently standing in the front of the chapel, Baraka told me the story of how he first met Al. As the best storytellers do, when Baraka tells a story about the past, he dissociates just a little bit, as if during the span of his yarn he's once again *there*. There was South Philly, 1969, a setting that down here is the misty landscape of legends. Baraka was returning to where he'd fought a guy the day before. He'd forgotten something and had to go back. Being in another gang's territory, he was watching his step, scrutinizing his surroundings. Approaching the schoolyard at Twenty-fourth and Christian, he discovered a giant of a man fighting an entire basketball game, ten guys, all by himself. Baraka watched as the ogre took the guys down, one after another. When the basketball players were all on the ground, the brute lumbered off the court. More than a little bit curious, Baraka approached him and introduced himself. The brute was Al, who had just gotten out of jail and had returned to avenge the murder of one of his homies. In short order generative fascination gave way to friendship.

Al wasn't afraid of dying? I asked. Back then, as Baraka understands it, death, for Al, was simply out of the question. In fact, it's that Al *felt* invulnerable that made him so dangerous. The moral of Baraka's story? "It's precisely because of the individual that Al used to be that makes his religious conversion so extraordinary."

I ask Baraka, "So how did Al get that way?"—meaning emotional, unafraid of intimacy.

"Don't know," he says. "Just always has been. So there's no reason for him to hide. That's what's different about me. I'm always present because I don't care what other people think. Never have."

"You don't care, huh?" I say. "Then it's pure coincidence that I like you so much?"

Baraka looks me in the eye. He's happy to be misunderstood, he says. Like when people take him to be not as smart as he is. He's fine with that. Either they figure it out or they don't. And if they don't, then the advantage is his.

"Like Kaiser Söze," I say, referring to the diminutive criminal mastermind from the film *The Usual Suspects*, who in the end turns out to be everything he appeared incapable of being.[27]

"Exactly."

According to Baraka, his advantage accrues not in how he is perceived but in his own ability to perceive—and therefore move. In a recent riff, Baraka affirmatively spun what the onetime sociologist of Philadelphia black folk W.E.B. Du Bois called "double consciousness." If for Du Bois the Negro's experience of being forced to move between two radically uneven worlds meant "always looking at one's self through the eyes of others, of measuring one's soul by the tape of a world that looks on in amused contempt and pity," in Baraka's view, that which engenders alienation also endows cunning.[28] In making this claim, Baraka extended his index fingers and pantomimed a dance of electricity between them. Folks like himself, he said, in a barrage of mixed metaphor, can "move between the boxes." They "can drop in" and participate in a "tea and crumpet session" on one side "but then swing way over here."

I make one final attempt to tie Baraka down. "Philosophically," I say, "my one issue is with your claim that all acts are masquerades but one. Why stop there? Why not say that *all* of them are? *Perhaps* one isn't—who knows? Maybe in thinking that we know which one it is, we're just masquerading again. Ultimately, it doesn't matter. Ultimately, as you say, it's just '*have at it, fellas.*' Meaning, a guy has got to commit himself to a particular masquerade and go with it."

The two of us are not going to agree, but our variance feels in no way acrimonious. Baraka realizes that it's almost 3:30 and that he'd better be off. Walking out, he reasserts his lack of fear in being present and real. Like the other day when he was walking the pews and this guy he doesn't know comes in and asks him what he's doing. Without thinking twice, Baraka tells him he likes to walk the pews twenty minutes a day for exercise. Kazi, who'd been sitting silently in the chapel, observed the exchange and was duly impressed. "I wouldn't have told him nothin'," Kaz told Baraka. "I would've said 'Nunya.'"

"Nunya?" I ask.

"Yeah," Baraka says. "Nunya business."

I laugh. If anything, I know from experience, Baraka welcomes the scrutiny.

The invitation to scrutinize was issued most directly to me back in September at the close of a long, riveting, and upsetting day on which I'd pushed Baraka too far. Earlier in the afternoon, in an office crowded with the regular cast, Al and Teddy among them, Baraka had spoken puzzlingly and extensively about a "subject" of his, a figure he would dub in prose years later "the deliberately self-created nebulous man." Identifying his "subject" as a guy from the block, Baraka described him as a "true natural actor," a man wholly unselfconscious but simultaneously socially graceful. As Baraka said, oracularly: "This guy doesn't come up to the surface gasping for the air of why." Baraka described his subject as extremely talented—what most chapel guys attribute to God, Baraka attributes to "talent"—and self-evidently so.

What, I asked him, made his subject's talent manifest?

He said: "Because he hasn't gotten killed yet."

Baraka continued to describe his "interrogation" of the subject and the man's strange propensity to disappear into states of psychosis during which he goes someplace else entirely. Neither during nor after does the subject have any awareness of these events; he knows of them only secondhand via the reports of others. Because of his immense talent, however, even in this hypnotic state, the subject retains complete self-control. Baraka speculated these episodes to be "triggered" by certain words.

I hadn't the flimsiest idea of what Baraka was up to. Who precisely was this *subject*? Did the man exist? Was Baraka's clinical report a burlesque of my research? What was going on here? I was provoked.

Without the care befitting such opaque terrain, I steamrolled Baraka on the sources of his subject's condition, badgering him on whether, in accounting for these spells, talent alone was a sufficient cause. Laying out what I acknowledged to be a Freudian caricature, I described how in looking for the roots of such a curious condition, a psychologist would likely look to the past. For clarity's sake, I offered the example of someone who was sexually abused as a child and therefore had difficulty with intimacy later on.[29] Mid-example I was thrown into an awareness of where I was. Keita had explained to me the men's disgust for sex criminals as partially rooted in the fact that many were themselves victims. I knew about Baraka's premature sexual initiation. To whom else in the room, I wondered too late, might this "caricature" be only too real?

Seizing my momentum, Al began to hem Baraka in. Whether the man's condition was in his blood or from his experiences, either way, Al insisted, the family must have known about it.

Sticking to his story, Baraka continued to emphasize his subject's immense talent. He stressed the premeditated character of his subject's actions, and the subject's access to the same social repertoire available to so-called normal people. He said other things, too, that made increasingly less sense to me.

Coldly, Al said that he knew who the individual was and why he goes through what he goes through.

Why? I pressed on, somehow already knowing the answer.

The man disappears, Al said, because disappearing is his last defense. When he blacks out, he doesn't give a damn anymore, and when he comes back he has no idea what took place. Al concluded: And the person that we're talking about is Baraka.

Never before or after have I experienced the office so tense. Shortly thereafter, Baraka was called into the Imam's office. While he was gone, Al recounted—much in the terms that Baraka would later describe Al—how he saw it once: Baraka taking a battery of punches, kicks, and bruises without slowing down. "It doesn't matter, he just moves." It's fear that drives him into this other state, Al diagnosed. Not fear for himself but fear for the other guy. "He's gone because he's not willing to deal with or accept the reality that's taking place."

Feeling largely responsible for Baraka's unmasking, I sought, upon his return to the office, to help Baraka save face. Baraka wasn't having it. His speech got cryptic and his laughter turned to cackles. "Four and back again," he kept repeating as if in a riddle. Was this the precipitating trauma? I wondered. Something that happened at age four?

Baraka issued me a caution. "If you watch one train coming from this way," he said, "you may get hit on the back of the head by a train headed in the other direction." This, I realized, had been my trespass: the denial to the man of the compartmentalization Baraka saw as his inalienable right.

Teddy validated my fear that the fuck-up had been all mine. On his way out, Teddy mirthfully rubbed his hands together and announced his intention to "get here bright and early tomorrow . . . in time for court." Plainly, it was I that was to be on trial.

I was thoroughly unnerved. Dependent as I am on Baraka to be my decoder, the episode was doubly distressing, both for how it threw our bond into doubt and for how his bizarre behavior seemed to call his sanity into question.

That evening, upon finding Baraka in the chapel, I sought to restore our conventional roles. Redirecting the afternoon's exchange, I asked him to compare guys' attitudes toward religious practice to their attitudes toward psychiatry. In his experience, I asked, do people ever frame religion, like they do meds and psychiatry, as a mechanism for control? Slipping easily back into mastery, Baraka reflected on the young guys' lack of discipline and unconscious anger. "Disinherited" is how he described them. From observing the Muslims and Christians around them, in religion they see "a way out for me—not out of the environment but out of this frame of mind." But, he said, religion and psychopharmacology are opposites. In religion a man is trying to elevate himself, whereas through medication a man is trying to lose himself.

We wandered into other topics. For me, content was secondary to form, and I was increasingly lulled by the familiarity of our rhythms. Late in our exchange, I expressed regret for having earlier "used some very dangerous words." To demonstrate that his tutelage was not entirely wasted on me, I was uncharacteristically oblique in referring to my careless talk of sexual abuse.

His authority reaffirmed, Baraka again had the room to temper his pedagogical rigor with a modicum of playfulness. "When you decipher, at the end of the day, your encounters," he said, "I know that the advantage lay with me, because you're confused, but I am myself. What you're getting from me is the real me. Most people can't give you that, because they don't know what 'the real me' is."

Through silence, I affirmed Baraka's judgment. Then, as we split, Baraka offered a final tweak, this one without any patina of menace: "I want you to understand first and foremost that what you see is what I am. Now the question for you becomes: *What am I?*"

•

I tell Keita I'm sorry to hear about his brother, that I hadn't realized that he had died. He thanks me. Was this the early-morning Casanova? I ask. No, he says, that is a younger brother. This brother was four years older, and he taught Keita everything he knows.

Keita's family, which was polygamous, was also religiously diverse. His father, the patriarch of a clan of 30,000, was a Muslim. According to Keita, Christianity arrived via an ancestor who participated in the *Amistad* rebellion and accepted Jesus Christ in a Boston jail. Others followed what Keita calls "traditional religion." Keita disparages the category of "animism" as a lie Europeans tell to make Africans look like stupid children—"We don't pray to trees or rocks or rivers."[30] After struggling in a Qur'anic school, Keita was sent to a Wesleyan missionary school, which started him on a path toward ordination as a Methodist minister.

I ask Keita about the sacrifices. He says he's going to send money to provide for the animals that have to be slaughtered on the seventh and fortieth days of mourning. And he can't go? No, not now. Maybe in a couple of years, after he retires with a pension and disability. A few years after that, Social Security kicks in, too. Between it all, he'll be pulling down like $3,000 a month. In Africa he could live like a king on that much, he says, and he can snap all of the bats out of the air that he wants.

What about the kidnappings? I ask. A rich man like him would be a real prize. Oh, he says, that's no problem. He would pay people to guard him. But not when he's hunting for bats. That's private time.

Keita declares his intention to leave his children with nothing. He gave them an education, an American life, and that's more than enough. What else do they need? He came to this country with $80 in his pocket, and he's lived from paycheck to paycheck ever since. I say that while my own background was cushier, I fear I'm headed in that general direction.

"But you're a rich Jew!" he says, dumbfounded.

We discuss the Jews who run the world.

"Ed Rendell is a Jew, no?" he asks of Pennsylvania's governor. Brian pokes his head through Keita's open door to confirm that, yes, Rendell is indeed a Jew, but a nonpracticing one.

"Oh, and what does *that* matter?" Keita says. As if proper observation of the Mosaic Law would be a prerequisite for the advantages of membership in what Keita calls the "super race."

Keita brings us back to Africa, and how nice it'll be when he's an old man. Playing the rube, I ask if there are monkeys there. Of course, he says. He grew up with them. They would eat out of the same plate. And you could ask them questions, and they would nod their heads. And when he was a boy they would bite one another.

"And no one would get AIDS?" I ask.

"No," he says. "Of course not. The United States hadn't invented it yet!" I can't tell whether or not he's kidding. There is a short silence.

"Where do you think the AIDS virus is from?" I ask him. Of all the accounts Keita's read, the most convincing credits a failed U.S. biological-weapons program in Haiti. There's a secret UN document about it, he says.

"What about you?" he asks. I say that AIDS being a product of U.S. imperial malfeasance strikes me as about as plausible as its stemming from Africans doing something or other revolting with monkeys. At the very least, I say, each presumed source is a reasonable projection of how each locale is configured in the myths of the other.[31] Again, *always the fingertip, never the moon*, I think to myself, which gives me an idea.

"Perhaps the Jews made it," I suggest.

Keita shakes his head. "No, not enough money in it."

I fill the kettle from the Imam's bathroom sink, snag some coffee crystals and a couple of sugar packets from Al's desk, make a cup of pale coffee, and write.

Back from dinner, the Imam sits down at Sayyid's desk. Idle conversation turns to Sayyid.

I can't help myself. Has he searched the desk? I ask him.

Oh, yes, he remembers. He disappears into his office and re-emerges, his keys in hand. He tries one, and then another. With his third key the padlock pops open. He lifts it off, swings open the metal bar that runs down the desk's right edge, and opens the top drawer. Out come coffee, granola bars, sugar packets, papers. Finding nothing out of the ordinary, he returns them to the drawer. Turning to the side drawer, the Imam repeats the process to reveal books, more books, a folded prayer rug, a couple of packets of ramen noodles. Again—to my eyes—nothing.

At a little shy of 6:00 the men return.

"You know," Teddy says, reclining back in his chair, "it's like Ecclesiastes says: 'It's better to cry than to laugh.'" His mood seems lighter than it's been all week.

"How's that?" I ask. Teddy takes a letter out of his breast pocket, unfolds it, and tosses it onto my notes. It's from the woman whose name he has tattooed from shoulder to shoulder. Typed in a large font, the letter runs a short two pages. In it, Lily reports on her conversation with the attorneys, who confirmed that the $2,200 they'd paid was for the report, which concluded the firm's contractual obligation.

I shake my head demonstrably.

"I'm just so mad at the lawyers," Teddy says.

"It's messed up," I say.

"Not just them," he says. "I'm mad at *lawyers*. All of them."

"They're scoundrels," I agree, "thieves."

"They'll get theirs from God," Teddy says. He lightens. "But God has a way of testing those he loves. That's what Ecclesiastes is saying when he says it's better to cry than to laugh."

Upon hearing this, Bird, who is passing through the office, says, "Yeah, Ecclesiastes . . . There you go, giving your opinion again," and walks out. In my quick read, Bird's sucker punch is part of some ongoing argument with Teddy about what it is to read the Bible, with Teddy professing disinterested literalism and Bird calling attention to the ways that Teddy is shaping his interpretation. But that could be miles off.

Teddy waves away Bird's comment, but the interjection was enough to break his chain of thought. Then: "Oh yeah. About yesterday, notice that when what's-his-face came down, I didn't say nothing, right?"

I'd been awaiting praise for my complicity in yesterday's minor conspiracy depriving Qasim of seemingly innocuous information as to Sayyid's whereabouts, and figure that now is my time. But Teddy is done.

"And," I say. "What about me?"

He scowls. "Yeah, you *added* something."

"No I didn't!" I plead. "I didn't add anything. All I said was that *all we've got is rumors.*"

I shouldn't be surprised. I've been told about "dry snitching," the social sin of confirming through silence an allegation made about an absent third party. Admittedly, my contribution last night was irrefutably more substantive than that.

"Yeah, that guy talks . . ." Teddy says, trailing off. "But you know, when I was back in my cell last night, I was thinking over it, about what we was talking about yesterday, how you was saying that you can't see everything that's going on in here, right? So when I was thinking over it, it clicked in, what you'd been saying. On stuff like that, there *is* a lot going on that you don't understand."

"Exactly," I say. "I'm not saying that you guys are bullshitting me. It's just that I would be a fool to say that I'm getting everything that goes on." We give one another a pound. It's not the recognition I thought I had coming, but more gratifying at that.

Papa, who's been listening in, adds, "Well, you should know, Josh, because we talked about this. You know we're much realer with you. You know you see things that most people don't see"—most *free* people, he means.

"You know how much I appreciate that," I say, genuinely touched. "This project wouldn't have been possible without your openness. And, truly, I wouldn't have been at all surprised if it had been the opposite. I don't begrudge *anyone* in here who greets me with suspicion. I mean, who the hell am I? And as I've said"—and I have, most earnestly at the office Christmas party—"there is a sense of debt that I take seriously, and I will try to repay it through what I write, and by how I choose to live my life from this point onward."

"Yeah, about that debt . . ." Teddy says, puncturing the cloud of sentimentality.

"No," I say, shaking my head, "all proceeds are going to Watkins."

"And what does that leave for us?" Teddy asks.

"Alas," I say with open palms.

"You know, Josh," Teddy says, "when you're out of here soon and then the next time any of us hear anything about you, you're on TV, you know how that's gonna be?"

It's not going to be like that, I promise.

Vic moves in, talking again about the Ethics of War. He's pissed off about the professor's bullshit pacifism. I ask Vic whether any recent American wars have been justified. Dismissively, Vic concedes only one, and it is yet unfought: "A war against the United States government!"

"Don't take this the wrong way," he says, "but academic arguments are just so . . . well . . . academic."

"Meaning what?" I ask.

"Fucking useless," he says. "War is war. People should shut up and fight." And if you're an academic opposed to war, then you should "pick up your big fucking textbook and go beat the war hawks on the head with it."

I'm of two minds, I say. On the one hand, I want my side to fight as dirty as the other side. On the other, I'm sympathetic to the idea that by sinking to their level we've already lost.

"Ah, fuck 'em all," Vic says.

"Fuck who?" I ask.

"All of 'em," he says. "But in this case academics especially."

What's really bothering him, Vic goes on to explain, isn't Villanova, but the Inside-Out Program, which stages dialogues between prisoners and outside college students. Tiring of all the hypocrisy, Vic recently dropped out. "According to the mission statement," he says, "the point is supposed to be to create sustained personal dialogue between insiders and outsiders so as to change perceptions out there about prisoners, one person at a time. But then Katie"—the program's director—"says that you're not allowed to have any outside contact with the students who come in. So what's the point?" He pauses. "I'll tell you, it's all about institutional reproduction, that's it. Changing society? Screw it. We've got a program to protect!"

As it can only be, I concur. Reproducing itself is *always* the first agenda of any institution.

Apparently, there was recently a young woman in the group, and she and Vic hit it off. They'd both wanted to correspond but were prohibited from doing so.

"It's just bullshit, plain and simple," he says and continues on about the fucking hypocrisy. Meanwhile, through the door's wired-glass window three kufied heads bobble chapel-ward, catching my eye.

Even when the cinder-block annex isn't freezing cold like tonight, Wednesday evenings—like Tuesday afternoons—only draw a handful of Muslims. On the eastern wall, Mamduh and Nasir huddle together, talking and giggling, while in the shoe area by the door, four coatless men study the Arabic language around a table. The only one not fully bearded and kufied—which is to say, not Salafi—is Mubdi.

Raised in nearby Norristown, Mubdi was brought up on murder charges in the weeks prior to Martin Luther King's assassination. Having taken his Shahadah (declaration of faith) in the Montgomery County Jail in 1969, Mubdi arrived at Graterford a lifer. Once here, he quickly became prominent in the Nation of Islam. While never formally the community's minister—or, after the group's 1975 mass conversion to Sunnism, its imam—Mubdi's steady manner and mastery of the Arabic language, among other traits, made him a natural leader of the Warith Deen Muhammad community, and according to many its moral compass. In the days of the downstairs masjid, he taught classes on economics and politics, as well as on Islamic practice, and would frequently deliver the Friday *khutbah* (sermon), just as, at the Imam's behest, he does so once a season to this day.

At sixty-five, the freckle-faced Mubdi still works on a maintenance crew. Many refuse such work, not wishing to maintain the institutional infrastructure of their imprisonment, but Mubdi doesn't mind, especially because when they're working on the roof he's able to see over the wall. Mubdi's calling is language. In recent years, he's taught himself Spanish, working his way through Borges and Márquez just as decades ago he plodded his way through Naguib Mahfouz. To help others along, he still keeps up his weekly Arabic class, participation in which, I suspect, would be higher were it not for his dubious allegiance to Warith Deen Muhammad and his ongoing advocacy for Warith Deen's outdated religious program of social uplift. Mubdi will soon describe to me the frustrating recent experience of trying to coax a young Salafi guy into taking a vocational class. "I was encouraging a guy to learn a trade, but he went on a rampage, asked me when I was going to shut up and speak on *din*"—religion. "He only wanted to hear about religion!"

While I'm drawn to Mubdi's seasoned materialist ethos and awed by his autodidact's discipline, I'm most enamored of his temperament. In a place where rigid orthodoxies are the norm, Mubdi stands out for his reluctance to declare himself to be on the side of the righteous. Yes, he laments the apolitical vibe currently predominant in the jail, not merely among the Salafi but among the vast majority of young guys on the block who just kill time without a thought of productive expenditure. It was different in the old days. Back then there was unity, and people were willing to risk something for a cause. Now they just want to lift weights, or, more likely, just lie in their cells, watching TV. "But maybe I'm not any different," he'll say to me with a shrug. "Me lying in my cell, just reading my books."

It is this quality—Mubdi's willingness to entertain the possibility that he might be as full of shit as the next guy, not superlatively sinful, just vaguely ineffectual, and as such thoroughly complicit with the rottenness of the stinking system—that makes him a candidate, in my eyes, for righteousness. For to prevail over its hazards, piety, whether to God or otherwise, is strongly served by a willingness to subject even its most vehement commitments to such self-critical irony.[32] Rare under any conditions, Mubdi's capacity for irony is especially remarkable in this place of do-or-die certitude, where men tend to bind themselves to the masts of their convictions and tenaciously hold on to those revolutionary moments in time when they first became what they continue to resolutely become.

On February 25, 1975, the Honorable Elijah Muhammad, who for forty years had led the Nation of Islam, died.[33]

The next day was Saviour's Day, commemorating God's incarnation in the body of Master Wallace Fard Muhammad, the Nation's mysterious founder.[34] In front of 25,000 men and women, Elijah's son Wallace—Fard's namesake—became the Nation's Supreme Minister. In the months to follow, Wallace would begin to speak of the advent of a new dispensation. If his father's revelations had constituted for black men and women a *First Resurrection* out of the false consciousness of slavery and into self-knowledge as a people, then beginning on that day was the *Second Resurrection*, in which black men and women would transcend racial sectarianism and embrace true Islam. With his father now passed, so, too, Wallace declared, was his doctrine.[35] The men in the Nation of Islam were now Sunni Muslims.

For some members of the Nation at Graterford, conversion to Sunni Islam required a fundamental reorientation of self. For others, the shift was experienced as merely a new set of marching orders. Because the Nation of Islam's organizational structure was more powerful than whatever theological spirit happened to animate it at any given time, the corporate transition was fairly seamless. Many knew Wallace from his two stints as minister at Temple Twelve—the Nation's Philadelphia division—and felt loyal to him personally. It was Wallace, for example, who had bestowed upon Baraka his Arabic name.

Also named by Wallace was the dignified Warith Deen elder Abdullah Shah. For Abdullah Shah, the shift from the Nation of Islam to Sunni Islam couldn't have been smoother or more welcome. By age eighteen, when Abdullah Shah joined the Nation, much of his West Philly family were already Orthodox Muslims. From them Abdullah Shah had learned elements of the Sunnah, which he passed on to others. According to Shah, even before 1975, nobody in the Nation gave him any problems for teaching guys Arabic or instructing them in how to properly make prayer.

"The religious aspects were very narrow," Abdullah Shah says of the Nation, "but the social aspects were great." The Nation instilled morality, unity, love, and trust, and taught its members "not to smoke, not to drink, not to fornicate"—much of which later proved to be in concordance with Islam. "We were already doing a lot of the Sunnah and didn't even realize it," he said. In some cases, they were even going further. Under the Nation, men at Graterford would fast Friday through Sunday, going seventy-two hours without food or water. "After that," he said, "Ramadan is a breeze."

In a half step between black nationalism and Sunni universalism, Wallace Muhammad's followers took to calling themselves "Bilalians" in honor of Bilal ibn Rabah, an ethnically Ethiopian companion to the Prophet and, by tradition, Islam's first muezzin (caller to prayer).[36] Deeming it no longer appropriate as Muslims to pray in the Christian chapel, Graterford's Bilalians petitioned the superintendent for an alternative space, and were granted the field house.

On August 7, 1976, Graterford's Bilalians threw their first banquet. Among the hordes of friends and family, the community was joined by one very special guest—Wallace Muhammad, or, as he in the new era would eventually be known, Warith Deen Muhammad. At the banquet it was announced that the Bilalians had been authorized to commence construction on a new basement masjid.

Before they could build the mosque, they would first have to tame the space. To evade the small river that ran through the basement even in the mildest of rains, they would raise the floor. Walls would then be erected from cinder blocks and a ceiling dropped on top. According to a bundle of archival papers that Baraka gave me, by the time they broke ground on April 12, 1977, they'd gathered from their fellow inmates seed money in excess of $30,000.

Some years later, Baraka, the community's Minister of Information, in a script for an intended video documentary, wrote the first draft of the epic project's history. The script details how the men worked morning and night, and how, with the support of the "All-knowing and Most Merciful, Allah," "the best of planners," and assisted by the chaplains and their fellow prisoners—"Christian, Jew, Bilalian (Black), Caucasian, Puerto Rican" as well as "the other Brotherhood of Muslims"— they triumphed over Satan, who had sought to sabotage their efforts with heavy rains, burst pipes, and a cadre of reprobate correctional officers.

While Baraka's narrative voice is not to me wholly unrecognizable, his providential emphasis is surprising, reading more like an affectation than a reflex. Perhaps he was merely aping the new party line. Or maybe the God of Baraka's youth was a more active presence in men's lives than He would later become. As Baraka notes to himself in his own marginalia: "Reason for Masjid in the first Place: Glorification for Allah."

On August 12, 1977, construction was completed. The floor was carpeted in green, and the walls were covered with vibrantly colored murals depicting the holy sites of Islam. Printed alongside them in spare but elegant Arabic calligraphy were some of the foundational passages from the Qur'an. In his video script, Baraka has talking points for a public tour: "Explain wall . . . (vestibule area) . . . explain offices . . . explain flags . . . explain purpose of the shoe room . . . explain the name: MWDM."

For so the former members of the Nation had decided to call their new mosque and, by extension, themselves: Masjid Wallace (later Warith) Deen Muhammad.

Twelve short months after his initial visit, in a ceremony in the newly completed masjid, Wallace Deen Muhammad spoke to the congregation that now bore his name. Wallace thanked Allah for His multitudinous bounty, which in addition to the Scriptures and the prophets also included his father, Elijah Muhammad, who employed symbolism and mysticism to bring them to the threshold of al-Islam. Now, in al-Islam, they had a real identity, an affirmative identity, and they could stand up to the many challenges of being black in America.

"So we thank Allah for blessing us, so much, with all of His Truth, Unity, Understanding, and Love between ourselves. We thank Allah for today the mental burden, the psychological burdens, are not so great on earth that we can't handle them, and make ourselves productive people in the communities of the great cities of the United States. The burden is not too great anymore, because our identity is real now. We are not looking for false identities. We are Muslims! We are human beings! We are Americans! We are Bilalians!"

In the transcript Baraka gave me, Wallace stressed that all thanks and gratitude were due to Allah. But he also showered immodest praise onto the assembled men, men whose epic actions he placed alongside the great accomplishments of Scripture and history: "We are grateful today, and I'm also grateful that I've been blessed to come here and visit Graterford Prison, and seen what Muslims . . . inmates, have been able to do. . . . I believe if this had been done three thousand years ago . . . they would go down in Holy Scripture, and the people that followed them would come up and have a new tradition. They would have to visit this Graterford Prison at least once in a lifetime, or once a year, and see what these great men have done."

Not everyone was quite so bullish. Chief among the detractors were the members of Masjid Sajdah. Sunni Muslims from their inception, the Sajdah guys remained, back then, a minority group, though, suddenly, it was not black nationalist sectarians, but other Sunnis who outnumbered them. As Yunus, who was, in those days, Masjid Sajdah's imam, told me: "We were asked to become one group, but I rejected it. We feared that we would simply be absorbed. We didn't want to be subject to their majority. We thought they should follow us because we had been doing it all longer, but there were more of them. . . . Their power structure was already laid out. They just put a new cloak on it."

If not reconfigured quite so tectonically, neither was Masjid Sajdah static. Shortly after the Bilalians were bequeathed space for their basement mosque, Sajdah was granted the space across the hall. Downstairs, the growing ranks of Masjid Sajdah—the vast majority of whom were also relatively new to the faith—continued to hammer out what Islam entailed.[37]

With Sajdah under Yunus's leadership, and Warith Deen led by Ameen Jabbar—already infamous for being a ranking member of the Temple Twelve hierarchy, his past as Elijah Muhammad's bodyguard, and his conviction for the infamous 1971 Dubrow furniture store murder-arson—Islamic practice at Graterford flourished. Hardly incidental to this blossoming was the era's laissez faire administrative mood in which prisoners were afforded unprecedented freedoms of movement and opportunity. Above and beyond the mere fact of their existences, the downstairs masajid were allowed to remain open from 8:30 in the morning till 8:30 at night. Each group was allowed to conduct its own religious services, and to convene banquets with family and outside guests. During Ramadan, Sajdah was even allowed to prepare its own meals and eat on its own. "The only caveat was that we had to clean the kitchen," Yunus said, "but the institution loved it because we would clean it from top to bottom."

Dissatisfaction with existing policy gurgled up only at the margin. In 1983, the Bureau of Corrections settled a long-standing suit filed by Sajdah and stipulated a new set of rights—rights soon enshrined in the new "Religious Activities in the Bureau of Corrections Handbook." Henceforth men were allowed to wear kufis anywhere in the jail; a shower room on each cellblock was kept open throughout Friday morning to allow washing before Jum'ah; every effort was made to provide an alternative protein source when pork was on the menu; and each Muslim community was henceforth entitled to two *Eid* feasts annually— one on Eid ul-Fitr, the holiday marking the conclusion of Ramadan, and one on Eid al-Adha, the holiday commemorating Ibrahim's aborted sacrifice of Ismael—which replaced the "banquets." As Yunus explained, "We didn't want to call it what it isn't."

The two Muslim communities also generated a slew of classes and programs. "Ameen was a good organizer," Yunus said of his counterpart across the hall, "and he didn't think young brothers should have any idle time." Masjid Warith Deen Muhammad ran a range of secular programs geared to engender the tools necessary for economic and social uplift, among them a GED program that cycled through twenty-five new students every six months, and a Stop-the-Violence program run in partnership with the LIFERS organization and the NAACP. Across the hall, meanwhile, on six evenings out of the week, Masjid Sajdah sponsored programs of its own. These programs were, in character, exclusively religious. Offerings included classes in Arabic language, Muslim history, Qur'an recitation, and Adab (Muslim etiquette). Drawing on its extensive library, Sajdah also facilitated advanced study into the Sunnah and Fiqh (Muslim jurisprudence). Crucial in the development of these curricula was Qasim, who in 1986 was elected Sajdah's new—and as it would prove, final—imam.

Sajdah would continue to evolve, with local shifts of ideology and practice registering global movements. With the integration of Asian and African immigrants into the landscape of American Islam, a vanguard of black American Sunni Muslims were inspired to track the traditions back to their geographic source. Some went to Saudi Arabia. Taking the particular practices they encountered there to be the authoritative ones, these men embraced the mission of spreading this true Islam to their home communities. These men authored translations of influential Salafi scholars—such as the eighteenth-century Arabian Muhammad ibn Abd al-Wahhab and the twentieth-century Albanian, Muhammad Nasiruddin al-Albani—and authored treatises of their own. Originating from a flagship mosque in East Orange, New Jersey, by the early nineties, Salafi mosques were popping up throughout the mid-Atlantic region. One of these, Masjid An-Nabawiyyah, was founded in the northwest Philly neighborhood of Germantown.[38] Through the pipeline connecting Germantown and Masjid Sajdah, Salafi literature began to enter the prison. Inspired by these authoritatively rendered missives, Masjid Sajdah drifted to the right. By the time the raid came down, many in Sajdah would identify as Salafi.[39]

For the two decades before everything came to an end, a range of dignitaries visited Graterford from far and wide—just as Warith Deen Muhammad had predicted—*to see what these men had done.*[40] Among the visitors were Afghani mujahideen who'd been brought to Philly for treatment at the Crozer Burn Center. When, over the course of the visit, the Graterford Muslims learned that in order to keep up the fight what these cold war heroes needed more than anything was sneakers, they gladly surrendered theirs. The mujahideen left with hundreds of pairs of Reeboks and Nikes, and members of Warith Deen and Sajdah gladly returned to their cells in only their socks.

When Mubdi has finished correcting his students' translations, the four men open their textbooks. The book is the third installment (of four) on Arabic grammar authored by Dr. Jochanan Kapliwatsky, formerly of Berlin, published in Jerusalem in 1945, and made affordably available by Halalco, a Muslim superstore in Virginia. By lesson twelve of the third volume, which has taken the current group two years' worth of Wednesdays to reach, each lesson consists of a five-paragraph vignette on some feature of life in the Arabian Peninsula. This week's selection is about women.[41]

At Mubdi's urging, Mohammed leads us through the first long paragraph. At thirty-five, the preternaturally gracious Mohammed is, excluding myself, the youngest man at the table by a decade. Mohammed's reading is slow and self-conscious—a far cry from the confidence that Sayyid ordinarily brings to the task. Mubdi prods an older student to help, but he proves to be of little assistance. The subject of the first sentence is proving particularly elusive.

"*Al-akil?*" Mohammed tries.

"No, not *al-akil*," Mubdi sings.

"*Adad?*" Mohammed tries again.

"No, not *adad*," Mubdi coos back at him.

Mubdi urges Mohammed on. "You know," he says, "you don't have to read every word, translate every word. You need to go with the *flow* of it."

Drawing on my never expert, now rusted, Arabic, I give the translation a shot, but am also in error. Mubdi points out a typographical error in the first sentence and explains that if we swap out a *kasra* for a *dumma*—one diacritical mark for another—we should be able to figure it out. With that in mind, I provide the correct translation, much to Mubdi's affirmation.

By fits and starts, we navigate our way through the passage, which speaks to the formality, chastity, and modesty with which courtship and eventually marriage are regulated in the Arabian Peninsula.

When we read about how men and women are married off young, everyone sees the inherent wisdom. Saves you at both ends, they concur. Keeps you from getting in trouble with sex when you're young, and locks you into lifelong partnership when you still have the energy for such a taxing undertaking. We read on, learning about how aside from a little bit of Qur'an reading, the women of the landed Bedouin receive little to no education, are prized principally for their housework, and, how aside from occasional visits to relatives or to the sick, are rendered, behind thick veils and household walls, almost entirely invisible.

My Arabic is not strong enough to gather a solid sense of how precisely Kapliwatsky feels about these women's lot; whether he is unselfconsciously celebrating the authentic folkways of a proud people, or whether he is subtly railing against the backwardness of this alien way of life. Nonetheless, acting as the interpretive machine I have been engineered to be, I try to get at the question by commenting (with rather paltry evidence) on Kapliwatsky's apparent antiurban bias. My cry of orientalism, however, goes nowhere. Evidencing zero interest in Kapliwatsky's agenda, Mubdi's students receive his text as an unclouded window into the utopia where the Sunnah finds its organic, authentic expression. As romantic primitivists themselves, these men find in the Arabia presented a sensible, pastoral world, a world of ultimate significance and local coherence—in short, a world diametrically opposite to that of their own experience. Despite my modest provocations, in Kapliwatsky's portrait they find nothing but beauty, a world narrowly circumscribed, yet within which is nestled a people so very, very free.[42]

Mohammed exhales deeply. "So is this how it is among the Bedouin today?" he asks, his eyes wide in wonder and deference. "Is it still just like it was in the days of the Prophet?"

When we are done, Mohammed, forever humble, laments his dawdling progress. As he'll explain to me on our way out, to date he's learned his Arabic solely by listening to and memorizing tapes of Qur'anic recitation, and while he did pick up a bit of colloquial speech from an Egyptian guy on his block, and a bit of grammar from a Villanova class, this is the first time he's doing grammar for real.

Mubdi tells Mohammed, just as he counsels all his students, that the first time he reads anything, he's got to write it out. "You've got to go with the flow," Mubdi says. "The first time you write it out, does it make sense to you? If not, then you have to go with the flow. Don't get caught up in each individual word. Try to feel what it's getting at altogether." Mubdi also encourages his students to read Arabic visually. If they can get in the habit of assembling the phrases into pictures, he promises, then the seemingly distant world conjured by the text will eventually come into focus.

In the gathering snowfall of the parking lot, I decide that rather than brave the highway I will crash at a local motel. After driving around for a while, calling a number scored from the Internet, getting no answer, and driving around some more, I finally pull up to the place. With no streetlamps to offset them, my headlights are all glare as I turn off into a gravelly cul-de-sac. The motel is dingy and dark. I turn the engine off, but nothing more. A place like this, I know from the movies, and from experience, can offer me only one of two things: death by psycho or a long, sleepless night in anticipation of same. I turn the key. The engine growls and I head for home.

Only a few miles down the road, the silence of the falling snow is unstilled by grumbles of thunder.

THURSDAY

THESIS 3

As such things go, places like Graterford do not foster an affinity for nuance. The dictates and rhythms of incarceration enable men to come to know their religious truths with a remarkable fixity of conviction. This economy of certainty is driven by the chaos endemic to the cramped and hostile quarters of the cellblock and to the encaged mind. Cloistered charisma also plays its part. Many sellers (themselves former buyers) push religion not as *an* ameliorative to the problem of chaos but as *the* solution, and, as such, one demanding utter fealty. Far from setting off alarm bells, however, this epistemic closure is a reward unto itself. From available evidence, after all, the convict has not to date been judicious in directing his will and desire. The code of the streets, consumer culture, secularism—these have all proven to be false gods, their yields too meager and their sacrifices too exacting. Moreover, one's bad choices were symptomatic of the problem of choice itself. From the vantage point of fallen men, autonomy has been none but a license for error. Better to surrender all to God, whose exhaustive prescriptions will give shape to the chaos.

This is classic stuff. Fathers of the discipline of religious studies, both Emile Durkheim and Mircea Eliade extol religion for precisely this capacity: how it takes primordial amorphousness—the *tohu v'vohu* of Genesis 1:2—and delineates darkness and light, water and earth, taxonomies of nature and culture.[1] It is unsurprising that in the definitively modern institution of the prison the scholar of religion should find accentuated the romantic solution to the ostensible challenges of modernity. So goes the generative fantasy of the anthropology of religion: unlike us moderns who, socially and metaphysically dislocated, know not what they are for: *Who am I? What is this place? What am I for?* The primitive man, for whom the world discloses itself seamlessly, suffers from no such insecurity. Which is why the modern man's anguish begs for old-time religion as its answer.

African-Americans' uniquely excruciating experience of modernity foments for many Graterford prisoners an additional but no less foundational query: *Who are we?* What we might call "black religions" are all attempts at answering this question.[2]

In the chapel, the response to the chaos is often as vehement as the prompt: materialism, debauchery, and lawlessness become asceticism, puritanism, and originalism. And on this ramrod spine, the self, the group, and the cosmos are strung in concentric succession.

And yet, while the controlling will-to-order midwifes an army of narrowly focused hedgehogs, the chapel simultaneously breeds a subculture of men characterized by stunning breadth and catholic curiosity, men with the time and discipline to follow rabbit after rabbit down the hole of intellectual and spiritual inquiry.[3] The incarcerated lifer and the tenured professor aside, not too many people in our day and age are built to take advantage of this uncommon latitude.

One of Father Gorski's former altar boys from the street—a real snot-nosed punk if you take the Father's word for it—is apparently now a professor at the University of Virginia. Gorski is beside himself at the revelation, beside himself enough to call me into Baumgartner's office to help him decipher an e-mail he just got. Sitting before Baumgartner's computer, Gorski wants to know what exactly can be gleaned about the kid's status from his sign-off. A "visiting professor" could mean a number of things, I say, but in all likelihood, if he's just finished up his Ph.D., then on the spectrum of privilege and security, he's likely closer to alienated labor than tenured fat cat. I explain to Gorski the buyer's market that is the academic marketplace, and how recently minted Ph.D.s must supplicate themselves for whatever employment they can scare up.

Gorski appears relieved and, for whatever ugly reason, I feel the same.

•

A flurry of major chords glorifying Jehovah emanates from Classroom B, while in the customary corner of the chapel, fifteen men gather for the Nation of Islam. Halfway down the center aisle, Jihad, a chiseled-bodied and stone-faced Fruit of Islam, faces sideways at attention.

This morning's meager turnout is no aberration. Contrary to the impression given by the deftness of the Nation of Islam leader Louis Farrakhan at remaining in the public eye, these days the Nation accounts for only a tiny fraction of African-American Muslims, both inside and outside the prison system. While on far-flung Philadelphia street corners one may still buy from a black-suited and bow-tied man a copy of the *Final Call* newspaper or, in season, bean pies, the once-dead and only modestly resurrected Nation of Islam is thirty years past its time.

Despite its diminished size and influence, the Nation still draws its special scrutiny. At a chaplaincy conference in central Pennsylvania, I heard the DOC's diffident chaplaincy director describe his unease when paying a supervisory visit to Nation of Islam services at Grater-ford. Of course, in striking the militant poses of their predecessors, the latter-day remnants are hardly, in this performance, a passive prop. The originators cut their style for precisely such an intimidating effect.

For the old heads, inquiries into the beginnings of Islam at Graterford take them back to a place closer to home. They speak of Holmesburg, a stone spider of a prison that sits nestled along the train tracks in the city of Philadelphia's northeastern corner. Holmesburg was—and remained, until its closure in 1996—the city's largest and most fabled jail, housing criminal defendants through the disposition of their court proceed-ings.[4] In the early 1970s the ranks of this class exploded as a generation of young men, the majority of them black, got caught in a vise of crime and punishment, pressed between the tantalizing coercion of the emer-gent street-gang culture and the policing procedures of a city admin-istration struggling to dam the bleeding of white wealth into the adjoining suburbs.[5] Overseeing this operation was former police chief and law-and-order crusader Mayor Frank Rizzo, whose cops were not above employing the means of terror for the preservation of peace.[6] Guys at Graterford tell of getting picked up on a pretext, being driven around, and, when they failed to give the cops the information they were after, being dropped off in another gang's territory. Innocent, guilty, and in-between, they all ended up in Holmesburg's bottleneck. By 1973, a facility built to hold 700 men now housed what was deemed to be an unconstitutionally crowded 1,200.[7]

In stories, Holmesburg comes across as harrowingly TV-ish. Early on in our relationship, Baraka spoke of his shock upon first entering the place, the dearth of light and the glut of sound, the rattling and screaming, the discomfort of eyes on his body. He had already been cautioned to say nothing to anyone, especially not his real name. Then and now, you don't know who's a rat, or worse; and if somebody's gone out of his way to engage you, chances are he has other than your best interests in mind. In recalling his early days at Holmesburg, Baraka's delivery is short on words and long on cackles. And Baraka was no babe either— only twenty, perhaps, but with a couple of years of enterprising on the street and a year's tour in Vietnam already behind him. "I woke up every morning surprised to be alive," Baraka said, his cat eyes wide.

Sooner rather than later Baraka found his way to cellblock D, the prison's maximum-security tier and home to the vast majority of its Fruit of Islam. In their close-order drills and karate instruction, the FOI displayed to themselves and to others that, as one forlorn CO would put it, "They are calling the shots up there."[8] Already a member of Temple Twelve from the street, Baraka found comradeship on cellblock D, comradeship that made the experience not merely survivable, but—as one can still hear in the wistfulness in his voice—conducive to the intensities and pleasures that one finds in such chaos-encircled enclaves. At Holmesburg, a guy in the Nation was relatively safe, so long as he didn't step out of line.

By the early seventies, the NOI's Temple Twelve had become mired in what is euphemistically referred to as "corruption." According to sources then and now, the Temple Twelve authority structure had become inextricable from a criminal syndicate called the Black Mafia.[9] At Temple Twelve, the Nation's hallmark discipline was redeployed by some from uplift to grift, and petit-bourgeois aspirations traded down for protection rackets, numbers running, and, eventually, the emerging dope trade. These markets were faster and more lucrative than hair salons and grocery stores, and were lumpenproletariat to the core regardless of what the suits and bow ties might have signified. Of all the Nation's strongholds, Temple Twelve—the "Top of the Clock," as it was sometimes known—was the most infamous. As one observer writing a hundred miles up the New Jersey Turnpike noted, Temple Twelve was "one temple where the rehabilitation of Muslim converts seems to have failed miserably. Philadelphia gang members, long considered the most vicious gang-bangers in the country, have put an X behind their names and have hidden behind the shield of the Nation while pursuing their former trades."[10]

If racketeering was Temple Twelve's daily bread, its High Mass was Holy War. For in 1973, its most notorious hour, members of Temple Twelve murdered seven Orthodox Hanafi Muslims, five of them children, at the Washington, D.C., home of NOI dissident Hamaas Abdul Khaalis, which had been purchased on his behalf by NBA superstar and Hanafi adherent Kareem Abdul-Jabbar. "I teach Islam is for everyone, not just for blacks," Khaalis explained.[11] A year before the massacre, in a polemic posted to fifty-seven NOI temples around the country, Khaalis denounced Elijah Muhammad as a "false prophet," a "lying deceiver," who by placing the Nation's founder Fard Muhammad on par with God, was guilty of the cardinal sin of *shirk* (idolatry). While seven men from Temple Twelve were arrested for the murders, no connection was successfully made to the temple hierarchy. Nor was the hand of leadership soiled when a suspect turned government witness was found hanging in his cell on Holmesburg's D Block.

When asked tentatively about Temple Twelve's darker side, Baraka sighed, "Nobody understood us."[12]

Graterford's institutional memory doesn't stretch back far enough to recall the beginnings of Islam in Philadelphia. Some remember the original NOI crew as having hailed from South Philly. This would have been back in the forties, sometime before 1954, when in founding Temple Twelve, a fiery minister named Malcolm X formally institutionalized in the City of Brotherly Love "the natural religion for the black man."[13]

And so for many black Philadelphia men did Malcolm's version of Islam resonate. By ingeniously rereading ancient texts, and by drafting reams of new Scriptures when the old ones failed to adequately address their present-day concerns, Elijah Muhammad and his followers made of Islam all they knew it and wished it to be. Painting the world as black and white as their collective experience, the Nation's Islam, as the quintessential black religion, would proclaim to their oppressors the truth about American racism, and would abrogate their own heretofore internalized white mores with a vociferous *NO!*[14]

Whereas the white man's religion had been a tool used to enslave them in body and in mind, Islam was to bring about their liberation. Slave names would be exchanged for X's, and the company store for small-business ownership. If, in his deluded consciousness, the Negro's greatest aspiration was to live high on the hog, then, as Muslims, they would forgo swine. If Christians read the biblical curse of Ham to justify slavery, they would find in the story of Jacob's engineering of Laban's livestock the seedling of a tale of how an evil scientist invented the white devil.[15] And if the Baptist churches of their youths foretold the coming Armageddon, then the Nation of Islam would, too, albeit one painted starkly in black and white.[16]

The Nation's relationship to the traditions of Islam consisted principally of appropriation, but elsewhere at the fringes of black culture, a more substantive bond was being forged. In 1920, a representative of the Ahmadiyya sect, a nineteenth-century Indian messianic movement, had debarked in Philadelphia. Continuing on to the Midwest, this South Asian missionary seeded the first traditionalist African-American Muslim communities. Having left little mark the first time, by the 1940s, black cosmopolitans started bringing the Ahmadiyya version of Islam back around. It was in this way—via Ahmadiyya jazzmen like Yusef Lateef and Art Blakey—that what was to be called "Orthodox" Islam first came to the city of Philadelphia.[17]

Calling themselves Moslems, the Ahmadiyya vanguard donned beards, kufis, and jalabiyas. People called them beatniks.

"Yeah," a former Nation old head said with a constricted throat and an invisible joint pinched between his fingertips, "Ahmadiyya—that was some *street din*" (religion). "They could drop *din* on you but you could peep them because they were like you." If the Ahmadi's West Philly mosque was, in the early fifties, Philadelphia's only outpost of Muslim Orthodoxy, by the end of the decade to follow Orthodox mosques— both Ahmadiyya and not—were popping up across the city's north and west.[18]

Some time prior to 1970, a group of these Moslems began meeting at Holmesburg. Calling themselves Saffat ("the rangers"), after a Qur'anic surah (chapter) of the same name, they solicited volunteers from a North Philly masjid to come instruct them in the tenets and practices of the faith. Holmesburg's entrenched FOI did not look favorably upon this Orthodox emergence. Violence was traded, more frequently in the currency of fists than that of knives. Without the numbers and influence of their counterparts, the Orthodox nonetheless gave as well as they got. Notably, it was a couple of Orthodox Moslems who scored the most decisive blow when on May 30, 1973, they stabbed to death Holmesburg's warden and deputy warden at a meeting they requested to protest the administration's shortening of their Friday prayers. The North Philly imam who instructed Saffat acknowledged the two men's attendance in his previous week's class but said they had given no indication of their intentions. Meanwhile, two leaders at a West Philly Muslim center sent a joint telegram to Mayor Rizzo in which they declared unequivocally: "The Quran (Koran) condemns all such as they who use religion as a covering for their misdeeds."[19]

Going on a half century later, recollections of Sunni Islam's birth pangs in Philadelphia are decidedly mixed. As former Nation member Mubdi diagnoses it, the problem was that "the street culture was all mixed up with the religious culture." Yunus, the West Philadelphian former imam of Masjid Sajdah, has a slightly different take. It wasn't so much the street culture but the utopian aspirations that brought forth carnage *in the guise* of Islam. "A lot of this had roots in the black liberation struggle," Yunus explained. "Everybody was trying to find their way. Christianity wasn't helping because Christianity says that we ought to be in the position that we are. We were all looking for something socially acceptable to license us to go forward. A lot of us were revolutionaries. We had no religion or anything." Of the era's swirling mix of politics, spirituality, and style, Gabril, who, like Yunus, took his Shahadah as a member of Saffat in 1971, said, "The world was *alive back then*."[20]

At Graterford, meanwhile, a new day was dawning. As a part of the Great Society upsurge, scholars and policy makers had begun to address racism and poverty as roots of criminality and to promote rehabilitation as an institutional goal. Changes occurred at every level.[21] Under Robert Johnson, the state's first black prison superintendent, rigid procedures were relaxed. Twenty-three-hour-a-day lockdown was all but abolished and prisoners were granted unprecedented freedom of movement and association. Having been freed of their stripes a decade earlier, prisoners were now allowed civilian clothing and afforded other improvements to conditions and to quality of life. Lower-risk inmates were allowed to work and sleep outside the walls and to take furloughs home. Programs promoting education and citizenship were instituted to supplement the men's vocational obligations on the factory floors and out on the farm. As part of an effort to reintegrate prisoners back into the community, volunteers were brought in to teach, train, and otherwise engage the prisoners socially and intellectually, making Graterford a cradle for artistic experimentation, cultural production, and religious diversity.[22]

Not by state largesse alone did this vibrant milieu come into being. More often than not, rights were seized rather than bequeathed, through tactics ranging from organizing to litigating to rioting.[23] For religious rights in particular, the Black Muslims were pivotal.[24] At Graterford, four members of the Nation spent over four hundred days in the hole following an altercation in the yard. While there, they took to throwing the meals that featured pork or (suspecting the guards of malevolence) that they surmised did. When they returned to the general population, they filed the lawsuit that would culminate in 1969 with the district court decision in *Knuckles v. Prasse*. Prior to *Knuckles*, Muslim prisoners at Graterford were barred from congregating and were not allowed to correspond with or bring in outside ministers. Elijah Muhammad's books and *Muhammad Speaks*, the Nation's weekly, were contraband, as was any version of the Qur'an that contained Arabic. In their mail, all allusions to Islam were blacked out. The court order in *Knuckles* rejected such blanket proscriptions. And while the somewhat wary court awarded the *Knuckles* plaintiffs only a fraction of what they had asked for, it did require Pennsylvania prison officials across the state to establish Muslim worship services that were "substantially similar" to those convened for Protestants, Catholics, and Jews. At Graterford, that meant time slots in the recently constructed chapel.

First Amendment protection was the round hole through which the Nation successfully drove a square peg. Matter-of-fact as always, Mubdi put it as follows: "We, the Nation of Islam, we was all about the practical. I did not get into the Nation because of religion. . . . The theological stuff was wacky, but the social stuff was real." When Mubdi first came to Graterford, the NOI consisted of purely "first-class individuals," men who were clean, disciplined, and focused on uplifting the race. "In '70 we had a pure concept, a righteousness, a *halo*, but after '71 it became gangsterish" and "a fad." As the Nation's integrity waned, its numbers grew. "I always opposed the corruption, and stood out for that reason. They thought I was 'spooky,'" he says, evoking the Nation's association of otherworldly piety with the fictitious "spook" God that slavery had lied into existence.[25]

In recalling these boom years, credit falls on one Clarence Fowler, or as he would come to be called at Graterford, Shamsud-din Ali.[26] Following a conviction for homicide in 1973, the charismatic Shamsud-din, who on the street had been a Temple Twelve captain, immediately became the leader of Graterford's NOI. For their regular Tuesday and Thursday chapel assemblies, where Shamsud-din delivered political sermons and the FOI ran drills, the Nation would draw between 200 and 300 men. At its peak, former adherents and detractors alike estimate, more than half of the jail's 1,500 residents were affiliated.

For those yearning for something with more of a spiritual aspect, Orthodox Islam was also becoming an option. Within a year of *Knuckles*, an early adopter at Graterford sent word to the Ahmadi mosque in West Philly, asking the imam if he would be willing to come out. The imam was indeed willing, and after overcoming considerable pushback from Graterford's administration—"Islam is not a religion," he remembers being told—the Ahmadi imam became a chapel regular. Under the imam's tutelage, men at Graterford studied the Qur'an and the Sunnah, the pillars of the faith, and learned of the Mujaddid (the Renewer) and Mahdi (the Promised Messiah) Mirza Ghulam Ahmad, Peace Be Upon Him, who a century before had come to earth. Within a couple of years, the Orthodox had doubled in size to thirty men.

In 1972, hoping to purify their Muslim practices of the Ahmadi elements they'd come to regard as heretical (the affirmation, most determinatively, of a prophet subsequent to the Prophet Muhammad), a handful of Orthodox men broke off and formed their own group. To signal their allegiance to the true Islam, these men called themselves Masjid Sajdah—the Mosque of Prostration.

Yunus arrived from Holmesburg a few months later. "Before it became apparent to the authorities that we were sincere . . . we would make *salat*"—prayer—"right outside the chapel door, or on the blocks," the onetime imam recalled. With the support of Father Galleo—the fondly remembered Croatian priest who was Baumgartner's predecessor—they were eventually allotted a space in the basement. Because they weren't allowed to meet without an outside volunteer, and the distance to Graterford made one hard to get, Sajdah "took matters into their own hands. By hook or by crook," as Yunus explained. "We'd come at eleven and slip downstairs. Then the chapel would be shut and we would sit in the dark. When Galleo would come back down at twelve-thirty, we would already be done with Jum'ah. When we could get a volunteer, we would just come down at one. But we spent a number of Fridays locked down there in the dark."

As guys filtered up from Holmesburg in twos and threes, Sajdah's ranks grew to thirty-five. With numbers came power, and before long the institution was making unprecedented accommodations—first for Jum'ah, and then for Ramadan. Describing the beginnings of practices that continue to this day, Yunus said, "We were responsible for *suhoor*, the predawn Ramadan meal. We asked them if we could buy Iraqi dates. Bought 500 pounds of them and issued each Muslim a four-pound bag. The institution let a couple of guys on each block go knock on cells, wake folks up. This was back when the Nation was still in the Nation—they weren't fasting yet. The deputy superintendent asked if we wanted anything else. That's how we got the *suhoor* bag. They put a little fruit in there, cereal. Also, we insisted that we eat together for *iftar*"—the nightly break of the fast. "So they allowed us to make a little dinner bag and all the fasters went and picked it up."

How, I asked Yunus, in the era of the Nation's predominance, were the Sajdah guys able to recognize Sunni Islam as the authentic one? "We knew it through the literature," which came up from the Islamic Center in D.C. and down from a New York City bookstore. "We had men that relished reading, researching." In response to the same question, Yunus's successor, Qasim, drew heavily on tropes from within the tradition. "I always knew it in my heart," he said. "I naturally believed in God" and "always had a penchant for Qur'an and hadith." Qasim spoke of *fitra*, the God-given state of purity into which man is born and thanks to which he is able to move toward the truth; and of *tawfiq*, the guidance God provides in helping one along. As he also explained, while his innate nature was pulling him toward true Islam, his fellow man was repelling him in the same direction. "The NOI were drug pushers, gangsters," he said. With so few members, Orthodox Islam attracted only "hard-core quality believers." Or, as Gabril put it: "When I came to the jail, I didn't want to be in a gang so I had no interest in joining the Nation."

And how did the two groups get along? "Everybody pretty much stayed to themselves." According to Yunus, men in Sajdah would refer to the Nation as "muck mucks." In return, Qasim says, the Nation would call the men in Sajdah "camel-riders and spirit-worshippers." Though no one told me about it, on at least one occasion blood was shed.[27]

Is it true that the NOI ran the jail? I asked Yunus. "They had the numbers," he laughed. "And if you have the bigger crowd you get to make the most noise." As of 1975, the Nation at Graterford had 700 adherents and Sajdah only 150. But that ratio would eventually flip.

With Elijah Muhammad's death and the advent of the Second Resurrection, all at once the Nation of Islam ceased to exist. It was not until several years later that Louis Farrakhan would break away from Wallace Muhammad's Sunni followers and fashion a new organization under the old name.[28]

With the traffic of bodies across the system, by the mid-eighties the revived Nation of Islam returned to Graterford. If the Warith Deen minority are these days a residual force, the Nation of Islam is a marginal player, a group, as Reverend Baumgartner puts it, "with many allies but few adherents." In addition to the Nation's services, an overlapping cast of characters also participates in the weekly meetings of Muhammad's Temple, an NOI splinter sect that rejects Farrakhan's authority, and which won recognition at Graterford (and at Graterford alone) via a 1994 federal court decision.[29] During its Ramadan break fasts—for the NOI, Ramadan takes place in December—the Nation pulls upwards of sixty men, among them a surprising number of corn-rowed late adolescents. Because cornrows—a rare style at Graterford— are said to be a Pittsburgh thing, I've come to suspect that perhaps more than anything, today's Nation of Islam provides a chapel toehold for out-of-towners and other nonaligned sorts.

Hulking over the lectern, Mason, the Nation's six-foot-four prisoner minister, speaks downhill to the assembled men. Behind him on the altar, the Nation's white-on-red crescent-and-star is flanked by four photographs: Elijah Muhammad and Farrakhan on one side, Master Fard Muhammad and Malcolm X on the other.

"Our destination," Mason is saying, "is to be a free people. That's why you've got to take care of your brother, help him be the best he can be. Everyone is different, and we can't be nobody other than who we is. That's what he's talking about when he says that *you've got to know thyself.* And how are you gonna judge another man when you don't even know yourself? You gonna be judging him but . . . but what about you?" He surveys the assembled men from behind his softly tinted glasses. "You in the penitentiary just like the rest of us!"

At the beginning of my fieldwork, when Al and Baraka were still lying low, Mason was front and center. On each visit he would receive me with a firm handshake, an offer of a cup of water, and a declaration of how sincerely invested he was in my project, since folks on the outside need to learn what it's *really* like in here. Insistent that all I needed to do was to tell the truth, he would pair me with a preselected member of his community (having, on occasion, to shoo away an unauthorized would-be interlocutor) and usher us into Classroom A. When I told Baumgartner of Mason's information management, he laughed. Apparently, when sociologist of religion C. Eric Lincoln was researching what would become his landmark *Black Muslims in America*, Malcolm X would do him the very same way.[30]

Mason's choreographed conversations were the first exchanges I had that resembled "interviews"—a method I had not envisaged. Hand-picked for their intellect and discipline, Mason's men recited catechisms, detailed month-long fasts, and explained how the system never changed anyone because only you can change yourself. Scripturally heterogeneous, Mason's men confidently cited as proof texts not only passages from the works and sermons of Elijah Muhammad, but also verses from the Qur'an and the New Testament, even as they uniformly maintained that our versions of these Scriptures have been doctored. When I asked the prisoner minister of Muhammad's Temple how he distinguished the clear Word of God from man's mischievous editing, he said: "Because reality speaks out."

These men also recited facts and figures about the earth and sun and otherwise exhibited the goofy pseudoscientism that is one of the Nation's hallmarks. Beyond the bounds of doctrine, they also clued me in to a universe of things that as a newcomer to Graterford I couldn't have hoped to anticipate. They taught me about the draconian policies of the Ridge/Horn era and, as a consequence, of their time "in the mountains" of central Pennsylvania. Among other conspiracies, they spoke of the high-starch diet laced with saltpeter that *they* engineered to vanquish libido and engender docility.[31] They spoke of enduring long stretches in the hole and how, away from the din and racket, they came to know themselves for the first time. They spoke of the strategies of self-mastery they adopted during those periods—fasting especially—and how when they returned to population, they would find themselves equipped with an extrasensory cognizance of the rhythms of the jail, its at-once chaotic but simultaneously repeating patterns, such that they could intuit with certainty what was going to happen before it took place.

Politically and religiously, these cherry-picked informants evidenced the Nation's deep-seated conservatism. Not revolutionaries like Nat Turner, or even progressives like W.E.B. Du Bois, these men were the ideological descendants of black incrementalists like Booker T. Washington. They had no utopian illusions, no dreams of radical social reordering, and expected nothing from the government; they merely wanted their fair piece of the American dream.[32] They regarded the Nation as a "religion" only to the extent that doing so rendered it sensible within the constitutional rules of the game. For them it was a spiritual discipline, a way of life, whose endgame was as *this-*worldly as could be, inasmuch as *this* world is all that there is. Such, in their view, is the mortal misstep of Sunni Islam, whose pie-in-the-sky afterlife and expectation of divine judgment is just an updated version of the white man's Christianity, which for four hundred years was used to counsel humility and endurance in the name of posthumous reward. Distinguishing themselves further from the Warith Deen guys who once carried their flag, they maintained the homegrown tenets revealed by Elijah Muhammad to represent an Islam *authentic* to the experience of black people in America. By contrast, the Sunnis' appropriation of Arabian Islam, a form of Islam appropriate not for here and now but for *back then* and *over there*, is symptomatic of the ignorance-of-self forged in the cultural erasure of slavery. To become who they need to become, black people need to remake themselves according to their experience, not according to what others tell them to be. Muhammad's Temple leader, himself a Mason-approved interlocutor, quoted

Malcolm X: "Even if a kitten is born in an oven—that does not make it a biscuit."

From behind the lectern, Mason says: "We can't go forward if we be backbiting one another. Sure, you a jailhouse Muslim now"—he invokes the moniker like an honorific—"but what did you do *before* you entered the Nation of Islam? What we need is love. We need to end the hate toward one another. We've got to move away from here, from this hate, from this place." Amid the standard themes—the need for unity, choosing love over hate, knowledge of self as a prerequisite for liberation—I detect in Mason's oratory this morning the coiled posture of a man defending his good name.

"There are folks in the Arab world who study their whole lives and who are still in the library, and you gonna judge a man about how little *he* knows and how much *you* know? Don't focus on your brother. Focus on God."

Mason acknowledges a brown in the second row, who gets up and says that in the twenty-one years he's been here, he's never heard anybody talking about Mason behind his back.

Mason nods.

Rising from the second row, a New Yorker named Nashawn obliquely describes an incident of conflict from last week on the block. Nashawn, whose fancy glasses and watch suggest him to be of some means, and whose new-side address and appetite for unpolished provocation imply a mind run amok, was one of the guys that Mason shooed away from me in my early days. One Sunday morning at the Protestant service, he caught up with me nonetheless. As Al's band played a funky instrumental arrangement of "Wade in the Water," Nashawn turned around and explained that back in the day, the slaves used music as a vehicle to sneak messages past the slave masters, but over time, the subversive element was drowned out, so by now music like the sort Al was playing is little more than entertainment. Nashawn always has a point to make, whether he's calling out Education for Ministry as little more than "Hucksterism 101," critiquing my "Jewish shoes," or explaining how exactly he knows that Baraka is a dope fiend.

The short of it, Nashawn breaks it down now, was that he stepped to somebody simply because it had to be done. End of story. That is, he's man enough to deal with conflict directly—in contrast, it would appear, with Mason.

"Look," Mason redirects. "If somebody wrongs me, I'm gonna speak on it publicly. That's my job. My job is *not* to call nobody out. Look at me, I'm not pointing out nobody. I ain't tryin' to be the *big guy*. I'm talking about the big picture. I'm in this for *us*. I ain't in this for me. We're all in the *Nation* here.

"If we don't die, we'll never live again. We've got to continue to die, to move on, even with our defects, even with our faults. I'm true to Allah, and that means treating you all like real people."

A chorus of "That's right!" . . . "Um-hmm" . . . "That's right!" greets Mason's assertion.

Jihad, the imposing FOI who has been standing at attention throughout, steps forward and hands Mason a cup of water from which Mason drinks. In the chapel, if somebody hands you a Styrofoam cup of water, then you're somebody, and if you're the one doing the hand-ing, then someday you might be somebody, too.

Mason continues: "If you carry yourself right with proper conduct, then people know what you're about before you even open your mouth. It's about the day-to-day. *That's* where you gotta prove yourself. You prove yourself by *not* fighting on the block. We gotta start by being brothers to one *another*, by respecting each other. Whatever is it that's keeping us from respecting one another? Let's figure out what it is and stop it! We've got to love one another."

"Yes sir!" . . . "Respect!" . . . "Yes sir!"

Mason surveys his flock. "I love you all!" he shouts, and the men applaud.

Malik, Mason's deputy, marches up to the lectern and executes a ninety-degree turn. The two leaders salute one another, grab each other's right hand and pull each other close for what might be mistaken for a pair of opposite-cheek kisses.

"Hello, Brothers!" Malik shouts, and the men echo him back.

"The Messenger said that we must be brothers first. Uniting is the key to our salvation." Malik holds up a book in front of his intelligent horn-rimmed face. "*This* is the key to our salvation. These are instruc-tions, and we should be disappointed with ourselves because we're not following the instructions. We are constantly developing ourselves, but at the same time we are disrespecting these teachings, each and every one of us. The Most Honorable Elijah Muhammad didn't instruct us to hate each other. He taught us to love each other. It's a battle of minds.

That's the War of Armageddon: a war of minds. And we've got God on our side, and the devil is on the other. Fard Muhammad told us that we had God within ourselves, that the black man *is* God. But when are we going to start living like it? When are we going to start talking like it? When are we going to start acting like it?"

Over on the Catholic side, Mike Callahan, Father Gorski's clerk, is fingering a 2006 calendar, still wrapped in plastic.

"Are you going to open that?" Santana, the downtrodden chapel worker, inquires.

"Why do you want to know if I'm going to open it?" Mike asks.

"I just want to know if you're going to open that."

"Why do you want to know?" Mike fingers the seam on the plastic. This goes back and forth for a while, to Santana's increasing agitation.

Eventually Santana explains. "I just want the cardboard so I can make a card for a correspondent."

Mike rips open the plastic and hands the cardboard to Santana. The calendar freed, Mike holds up its gridded pages to let the panoramic landscapes on the reverse side dangle free. As he examines each image in succession, Mike lazily harasses Jack, his officemate, about the red, puffy head he got from shaving it this morning without cream. His head looks like a strawberry, Mike says.

Father Gorski attributes the problem to Jack's tiny hands, one of which he holds up for collective examination. Indeed, they are rather small, I acknowledge.

Jack starts in on how evil liberals are.

"And don't forget ugly," I say.

Jack considers this. "Yes, and ugly, too."

Save for Teddy and Baraka, the office is empty, and a sour vibe hangs palpably in the air. From his uncharacteristic silence, I suspect Teddy to be the source. "So . . . what's going on?" I ask.

"I didn't sleep," Teddy mutters. "This legal stuff . . ." He trails off. "I'm just so"—he grunts in lieu of swearing—"just so angry at the lawyers," he says. "All lawyers."

Baraka and I feel his pain. "Snakes, devils, scoundrels," Baraka says.

"Gold diggers," I say.

"No!" Baraka corrects me. "That's if you're lucky. If a guy is doing something for money, then I *know* he'll do a good job. But when it's for some kind of *cause*, that's when you *really* gotta watch out." Commiseration drains into silence.

Making conversation, I ask Baraka whether a certain guy I saw this morning is a Muslim.

"He's not," Baraka says.

"He must be a Christian, then," I say to no one in particular.

"Why do you say he's a Christian?" Teddy snaps.

"My bad," I say, "he's probably a Jew. We all chill together upstairs on Friday night."

"You know," Teddy says, "just 'cause a guy comes down here on Sunday morning don't make him a Christian."

"Fair enough," I say. "I'm not weighing in on the truth inscribed in his heart, I just mean in terms of how he probably identifies himself."

"Even that you can't be certain," Teddy says. "Lots of guys ain't Christian. Like Al," Teddy says. "He don't call hisself a Christian."

"I know," I say. Al identifies as "a member of the body of Christ," or as a "saint."

As if summoned, this very saint marches through the door, a fishing tackle–sized box in hand.

"Lord have mercy," Teddy starts in. "I do *not* want to know what's in that box. Please, please, please, please don't tell me that you've got your horn in there."

Baraka runs with Teddy's riff. "Now there'll be no peace and quiet in here with all that foul-sounding squawking you're gonna be making."

Unfazed by the advance reviews, Al begins to assemble his sax.

Turning to Baraka, he gently says what to my ears sounds like "What that, Baraga"—Al pronounces the "k" like a "g," leading me to months of uncertainty as to whether Baraka's name was Baraka or Baraga—"are you *saw?*" Baraka looks back at Al with a confused look.

"What's that?" Baraka asks.

Looking to me with a raised brow, Al says, "Oh, Josh, didn't you put him down?" Now it's my turn to be confused.

"What do you mean, 'put him down'?" I ask.

No answer.

"Like, did I *dis* him?" I ask.

"No," Al repeats, "did you put him down?"

I apologize, explaining that I don't understand.

Baraka loses it. "How can you not know what *'put him down'* means?" he berates me. "How can you be here eleven months already and *still* not understand half of what is being said? Understanding entails goodwill, and if you don't understand *even half* of what's being said, then a guy must begin to *strongly* suspect that you're here for something else. And you should never forget that we could easily turn you over before anyone gets down here!"

It's a novel threat and a novel tirade. Certainly feeling more confused than imperiled, I argue my case. "But, Bar, I'm the one who perpetually insists that things are more complicated than they appear and that, as a result, I'm surely missing most of what's going on. *You're* the one that says that everything is *more* simple, not less, than it appears." And while I certainly think that "missing half of what goes on" is an exaggeration, to prove a point, I plead guilty to his charge. "Learning a language is hard," I say.

"No," Baraka says, "learning a language is easy. It's learning the *nuance* that's hard." With that distinction, I reach for my folder and pad. "Go ahead," he instructs, "write it down," which I do, though I suddenly feel like Baraka's performance is premeditated, to say the least. He repeats himself, "Not the language itself, but the nuances." Apparently, we are in dictation mode.

"The key thing with learning a language," he says, "is chimneying." I look up at him skeptically.

"Chimneying?" I ask. He gets stern again. "Man, if a guy can't understand what *chimneying* is *I'm* certainly not going to be the one to tell him."

Baumgartner's door swings open and out walks Ruth Carter, along with an unfamiliar brown who departs the office without acknowledgment. A transplanted New Yorker, Ruth has been at Graterford in various capacities for decades, since the time when she woke up (despicably late in life, if you ask her) to the systemic outrageousness of the criminal justice system. Among her many hats, Ruth is an official visitor for the Pennsylvania Prison Society, in which capacity she meets with prisoners in Keita's office, or in their cells if they're in detention, to field grievances.[33]

On Ruth's green-barred badge, instead of identifying her as a volunteer, tutor, or official visitor, it reads: "Lifer." Silver-haired, effortlessly brash, and unsentimental, Ruth's presence in the office is always a welcome treat.

Ruth sits down on Sayyid's desk. "Thank God you're here," I say. "Look, I'm clueless, so forgive me for enlisting you, but you've been here for years upon years, yes?"

"Yes, years upon years," she says.

"Okay," I say. "So tell me, what does 'put down' mean in the following sentence: 'Josh, didn't you put Baraka down?'"

"You mean, like, *to dis*?" the white lady asks.

"Yes, precisely," the white guy responds, "*to dis*. But no, that's not it. And not only is that not it, but anyone who *thinks* that that's it is apparently here under false pretenses." Al and Baraka seem entertained. Ruth is confused.

I recount how we came to this point, beginning with Al's still opaque query as to whether Baraka "saw."

"No, not *saw*," Al says. "*Saw*."

"Right," I say, "*saw*."

"No, not *saw*," he says, "*saw*. You know? *Saw!*"

"Right," I say, "*saw*."

"No!" Al says, exasperated. "*Saw!* Like *King Saw*."

"Oh!" I say, suddenly getting it. "*Saul!*"

Al scrunches up his eyes. "You telling me you been here eleven months and you *still* don't understand me?" He delivers the line in his best Baraka.

Once I've collected myself, I ask Al, "But why Saul?"

"Because David had to play music to soothe him," Al says.

Whatever misgivings I may have about *how* Al reads the Bible, he is indisputably better versed in it than is this scholar of religion.

At least one mystery solved, the conversation floats. Ruth returns to Baumgartner's office with another brown at her heels. Brian pops through and quickly returns upstairs. I jot some things down. Over my shoulder, Baraka reads my first scratches detailing our recent squabble.

"Oh, I bet you won't like that!" Baraka says, referring to how idiotic I must look in my notes, and, by extension, how stupid I'll appear in the resulting manuscript.

"On the contrary," I say, "I want the reader to entertain the possibility that I'm totally clueless. Opening that possibility up frees me to make critical reads of you people."

Baraka switches modes. No longer the quick-handed sparring partner, he's now the sage corner man. Putting a hand on my shoulder, he pulls up a seat next to mine. I continue to scribble without looking up.

"Look," he says, "the reason that I'm doing this is that a guy needs to be able to *read* his surroundings so that when he's got to get out, he can get out before it's too late. You see, if a bunch of guys can talk about him while he's there and he doesn't understand that those guys are talking about him, he will quickly come to harm. So you gotta keep on *reading*," he says, "and when it's time to be out, you've got to be out. You can't risk getting *stuck* on things."

Listening in on my training session, Al decides to cut Baraka down to size. "I know why you like Josh," Al says, and Baraka doesn't pay him any mind. "Look at you," Al says. "You with your multiple brain orgasms. That's why you like Josh, because he gives you so many brain orgasms." Al turns back to his saxophone, which recommences the earlier game of cat-and-mouse.

"Oh Gawd, put it away!" Teddy wails.

Caressing his instrument, Al speaks faux-dissociatively about how he must clean it, polish it, and get it just right before he can use it. Baraka rubs his head in anticipatory agony.

Keita waddles into the office. As with Ruth's arrival, the new blood feels like a reprieve.

"Keita," I say, "I think that the devil is waiting to see you, because he's been in this room for the past half hour."

"If that's true," Keita shouts back, "then the devil is *you*, because the devil is a white man!" As Gorski will note, Keita often gets fired up after supervising the Nation of Islam.

When the men are gone I turn to note-taking, but I'm soon interrupted by Father Gorski, who, propping himself up on Sayyid's desk, boisterously solicits my diversion.

"Uhh," I whine, "I'm falling behind."

He asks me, "Have you heard the one about the butcher that backed into his meat grinder?"

"Yeah," I say, responding by rote to the Borscht Belt gag that my father taught me as a boy. "He got a little behind in his work."

It pleases Gorski that I know the routine. Gorski explains that he gets all his jokes from an elderly Jewish guy who works at the same summer camp that he does. The guy's greatest hit, Gorski says, was when one morning he told Gorski that he'd eaten so much fiber that he'd defecated a wicker chair.

Gorski points at me: "Make sure you put *that* in your notes."

"How is Sayyid holding up?" I ask the Imam, who since returning from his weekly rounds of the Restricted Housing Units (RHU) has been quietly working at his desk.

"He can't sleep," Namir answers. "He's anxious about his status." For such an active guy like Sayyid, we agree, the hole must be especially maddening.

"Does he have any books, at least?"

"Not yet," Namir says. To avoid raising additional suspicion, so long as Sayyid is under investigation, Namir doesn't want to bring him any, either.

Might Sayyid have been into something? I ask. Namir shrugs. He has no way of knowing, but guys have such little room to maneuver that when they do get a chance to step out, they often step *way* out. "But guys can be shipped just like *that*," he adds, opening his hands like he's releasing a dove. On Ramadan, for example, he got a call from Albion—a facility out near Pittsburgh—to see if one of his guys had paid to participate in the Eid feast back here. That was the first Namir had heard that the guy had gotten into trouble, let alone that he'd been shipped. They could just as easily decide to do that to Sayyid, and then he'd be gone, his studies would be over, and he wouldn't see his family anymore.

Does his family know yet? I ask. Namir says that Kazi sent word to Sayyid's mom to warn her off visiting.

"No visit?" I ask. "Shouldn't she see him soon in case he gets shipped?"

"The policy is no visits as long as you're under investigation," the Imam explains.

"As if the bureaucratic limbo isn't punishment enough," I say, but of course that provision is to be expected.

Namir talks about this morning's rounds, how he goes straight for the person he needs to see and that's it.

"Hassled too many times?" I ask.

"No," he explains. "I don't like to look in guys' cells on account of the Qur'an's prohibition against spying. And it's very awkward." Namir holds his hand up in front of his eyes, miming how he tries to avert his gaze.

Pointing to the books on his desk, I ask the Imam if he's working on his *khutbah*—the Friday sermon. No, he says. In response to a request, he's providing citations for last week's *khutbah*, in which he stressed the need for one to take responsibility for his actions.

"The guys like to blame Shaytan [Satan]," he says, "as if their evil actions have nothing to do with them." Namir notes this same evasion in guys' propensity to take on Arabic names. "Do you know what Caliph Umar's name was in *jahaliyya*?" he says, referring to the period of ignorance that preceded Islam. "Umar. Do you know what Caliph Abu Bakr's name was in *jahaliyya*? Abu Bakr." Meaning, if *those* radically transformed men didn't change their names, why do men here feel the need to? "It says it in the Qur'an: 'Call them by their father's name.' The question is: What have you done with the name your father gave you that you can no longer use it?"

The practice of shucking one's birth name is hardly limited to the Muslims—Al dropped his the first time he ran afoul of the law—but between this Graterford norm and the Imam is a chasm of cultural difference. "In Nigeria," Namir has explained, "your birth name is sacred. It connects you to your father, and his father before him. Your name lets people know where you are from and who you are." Which is why the rampant name changing is, to him, so jarring—it reflects that strange American penchant for reinvention, and, simultaneously, the rootlessness and, often, the fatherlessness, that makes such reinvention thinkable, possible, and, eventually, as the Imam correctly observes, for many here, compulsory.

Watkins's baseball cap rides low on his brow.

A rapping on steel elicits a grouse, but nothing more. The knocking continues. Abandoning his dreams of a nap, Watkins hauls himself up, extracts a key, and cracks the door.

"What do you need?" he asks the offender, a light-skinned twenty-something brown with a tattooed tear under his left eye and a sheet of paper in his hand.

"Just a signature and a blessing," the brown reports breathlessly, waving the "green sheet," which, once inked by the requisite officials, will secure his passage home. Watkins waves the guy in and points him toward the office. When the brown leaves, no more than a minute later, others have taken his place, Baraka among them.

Placing a hand on my shoulder, Baraka takes a supercilious survey of my notes, which licenses me to read back to him, in decreasing volume as others arrive, my account of his tirade from this morning.

Baraka howls.

Keita calls my name. He's in his office with Wendell, a chapel regular who stops by this time every week for a sit-down prior to the Liberty Ministries Bible Study. When Keita calls my name again, I come.

With a gap where his upper incisors used to be and a week's worth of gray scruff blanketing his face and sagging neck, Wendell is on the ragged end of the chapel spectrum. Today, to accentuate the effect, his left thumb is wrapped in white plaster and fixed at a ninety-degree angle to his hand. As he explains, when I ask, this morning in the shop he cut it bad.

They've called me in to help search for a word, the word that identifies the feeling Wendell had last night when he met a kid on the block who, they pieced together, was the son of a long lost friend. When the kid called his mom last night, Wendell got on the phone. She was someone Wendell had come up with from the time they were just little kids, but they hadn't spoken in nineteen years. He felt euphoria, Wendell says, but he also felt this other thing—this thing he doesn't quite have a name for.

"What was this thing like?" I ask.

"Like I was euphoric but I was also checking myself."

"So you're looking for the word for this thing that went along with the euphoria?"

"Right," he says, "because I felt so blessed to talk to her, euphoric even—that's the word that comes to mind—but at the same time I also felt this . . . thing . . ." Wendell squints in search of the word.

"Hesitation?" I ask.

"No, not quite that."

"How about apprehension?"

"Nah." Another squint. "That's kinda it, but at the same time not it. Like, I was checking myself."

I'm out of ideas.

"Like I was euphoric," he says, "but I also knew that something was gonna happen."

"Oh," I say, "like you had a premonition?"

"Yeah, that's it," Wendell says, seemingly satisfied, though I can't tell whether I nailed the feeling or whether I'd simply swung and missed for the third time. Wendell is going to see her the next time she comes up. As far as I know, Wendell is not married.

"It's a beautiful thing," Wendell says, edging toward the door. From the book shelf by Keita's door Wendell grabs a stack of a dozen red hymnals, which he wedges under his gray stubbled chin.

I ask Wendell if it's cool for me to join him.

"Of course, Josh," Wendell says. "You know you're always welcome with us."

In Classroom A, where the seated men must shimmy in their chairs to let us pass, the end-to-end tables are mounded in the middle with sundry publications.[34] At the perimeter are Bibles, which lie open to reveal dog-eared, skin-slicked pages. In some cases, the exposed text is more highlighted and underlined than not.

Before the Bibles sit eight browns, all but one black and all but one from B Block, which is Wendell's block. The residential outlier is Prophet, the PV who on Tuesday apologized for vilifying me for being a Jew. At the far end of the table, with his thready hair and plaid shirt, is Jay, one of two evangelical Mennonites who trade off teaching Thursday-afternoon Bible studies for Liberty Ministries. Based in the neighboring town of Skippack, Liberty also runs a thrift store and Bible-based halfway house.[35] In his far-away manner, the somewhat dwindling Jay, who after thirty-three years at Graterford last spring was honored as Volunteer of the Year, is recounting a recent Martin Luther King Day trip to Philly where halfway-house residents fed the homeless and spread the word.[36]

The men are peppering Jay for locations, whose coordinates I fail to catch.

Did you hit such-and-such a place?
Oh, there? Yeah, I know that spot!
Oh, and out so-and-so?
What about X Street?
Oh yeah, yeah, yeah, that's where they all live all right!
And the park over by Y?
Whoa! I crashed there myself one time. That place is rough!
And how about under Z Bridge? Did you hit there?
No? Next time you gotta make it there.

When the locations have all been reminisced, we turn to the hymnals.[37]

Wendell asks me to propose one. I suggest "Praise to the Lord," but am reminded that they save that one for the finale. I flip the oily pages, searching, but come to nothing. Someone suggests "What a Friend We Have in Jesus," so we do that. Then "Down at the Cross Where My Savior Died." Loud enough to be polite but not loud enough to give the impression that my soul is in play, I sing along.

"It's good to have you around," Wendell says to me when we finish. "It's been a while."

"Yeah," I shake my head, "I've been backsliding," which draws encouraging laughter. We then belt out a couple more nineteenth-century classics: "Blessed Assurance, Jesus Is Mine," and, after that, "Holy, Holy, Holy: Lord God Almighty."

Prophet asks me whether I'm a singer. "Only in the shower," I say, cringing at my own corniness. Invariably, the guys at Liberty try to get me involved, and I'm eager to comply, though not—I can't help but feel—in the way they might wish. Unsure of how to navigate these invitations, I often end up stuck in between, failing at impromptu prompts and making penance with stock clichés. While Wendell and his crew are unmistakably warmhearted, to me Classroom A never feels quite so constrictive as on Thursday afternoons.

"All right," young Steve says, gesturing in my direction.

"Oh? Is it my time to shine?" I stupidly ask. And we sing:

Praise to the Lord, who o'er all things so wondrously reigneth
Shelters thee under His wings, yea, so gently sustaineth
Hast thou not seen
How thy desires have been
Granted in what He ordaineth?

Praise to the Lord, who doth prosper thy work and defend thee
Surely His goodness and mercy daily sustain thee
Ponder anew
What the almighty can do
If with His love he befriend Thee

Praise to the Lord! O let all that is in me adore Him!
All that hath life and breath, come now with praises before
    Him!
Let the Amen
Sound from His people again
Gladly for aye we adore Him.

Chanted gruffly, the song is nonetheless rousing. Especially follow-ing the wordy jumble of each stanza's first two lines, the final three pop with emotion, which, as guided by the lyrics, feels in my belly a lot like gratitude.

When I fail to furnish an Old Testament reading, an elderly brown suggests Genesis 1.

"You know," Jay says, when the brown is done, "I just don't see how anyone could believe in evolution like they *say* they do when verse twenty-six is so plainly clear." Twenty-six is where God makes man in his image.

"*Right*," someone says derisively. "Like we came from a bunch of monkeys."

Steve wonders if the animals in the garden were all tame and be-came wild only after the Fall. Yes, this is how it was, the men agree.

"And it's going to be like that again once Jesus comes," Wendell says. He mentions Isaiah 11:6, the wolf lying down with the lamb. Squinting his eyes, he flips through his Bible in search of the passage. The men tease Wendell about his diminishing vision. Yeah, Wendell admits, by now he's pretty much blind, but he's not gonna do it—get glasses, that is. Eventually he finds the passage and reads aloud about how the wolf will dwell with the lamb, the leopard will lie down with the kid, the calf with the young lion, and a little child shall lead them.[38]

It's going to be a beautiful thing, they all agree.

From the New Testament, Steve selects and reads from John 4, which details Jesus' encounter with the Samaritan woman.

No discussion follows. Like most of the Bible studies here, Liberty's method is less textual than associative, with the selected passage inspiring personal reflection on the miraculous workings of the Holy Spirit in one's life.[39] Between these unscripted solos, conversation will occasionally give way to argument—say, over the metaphysical condition of the dead in this period before Christ's return or whether a man's relationship with God impacts his finances. While not a prosperity gospeller per se, Wendell, for one, places no limits on God's power. "Maybe *your* God can't give you a car or a bathrobe," Wendell once said in response to someone who claimed that God doesn't answer prayers directly, "but my God can do whatever He pleases."

The men deliver their testimonies. Interrupted only by Prophet's abrupt departure, beseeching the men on his way out the door "to pray for him because God takes care of things"—in this case, an outstanding debt to a former landlord whom he needed to call—the men reflect in succession on their failures small and large, their sufferings endured and overcome, and on the Lord who reached down to them in their fallenness and delivered them their salvation.

Eventually it's Steve's turn. Youthful and militarily kempt, Steve proceeds deliberately, unafraid of the silences that gather as he assembles his words. He starts. "I just want to thank God that I now have my eyes open. And I'm so conscious of all of His blessings." His features soften as he describes a visit last Sunday with all his four kids. "And the thing that killed me the most," Steve says, "is the little one, the three-year-old. He would just follow me around wherever I went. He wouldn't let me out of his sight, like he wanted nothing more than to just be near me. And it's the most beautiful thing that he loves me," Steve pauses, "because I know that it's nothing that I did, so it's just got to be God. So I just want to thank God for all that."

Steve slips into the story of his life. As a kid he'd been a boxing prodigy. He lived with his mom in Camden, across the river in Jersey, but he would fight in a Philly gym. And everything was good. But then he started running with a gang—"a gang that didn't really stand for nothing"—and started getting into trouble. Then, one night, he was fooling with a handgun and, by accident, he shot and killed his cousin. Apart from the five years he got, that really messed with him on a personal level. But when he got out he was doing really good. He started boxing again. At one point, he was number one in the country, number two in the world at his weight. And he'd travel the world for fights. He fought in Germany and Australia, and he was doing good, real good. But then his mom died and it made him lose his faith in everything, and he fell off and started selling drugs and got back into that whole lifestyle. And one day he came home and his girlfriend told him that because of the drugs, they were being evicted. And that's when whatever it was happened and he ended up back at Graterford.

"But when you're down," Steve says, "that's when you're closest to it. It took me being in a place like this for me to find out that the true freedom is the freedom you find in Christ. And the world has nothing to offer me that Christ can't offer me. And what my experience goes to show is that without Jesus you can't accomplish nothing out there, but with Jesus you can accomplish anything. And I just want to thank God that I now have my eyes open. And now there's no excuse for me to do wrong out there because the Lord provided me with guys like these"—he gestures around the room—"to help me learn the words of Jesus."

Taking Steve's testimony to be a sort of valedictory address, I'm brought back to harrowing testimony he delivered last spring. His attorney and family were pressing him to accept a plea that would have gotten him home in six months. As if in a fog, Steve described how he couldn't quite understand what was going on. He'd been about to sign the plan agreement, but the Lord told him to stay put, so he didn't. At the time, choosing God's counsel over that of his lawyer sounded to my ear like an act of catastrophic self-sabotage, but given Steve's allusions to his imminent departure, I'm delighted to have been wrong.

Wendell quibbles slightly with Steve's conclusion. "Yeah, but the thing is that you must *abide* in the Word so it can transform you from the inside out. As you've discovered, it's not enough to study it and talk about it. You've got to live it. Amen?"

"Yeah, amen," Steve says. "But I wouldn't have been able to do it if guys like you hadn't been here to show me the way."

"Nah," Wendell again deflects. "You don't need us. You're never *really* alone, just like I'm never alone, because God is always with me."

Watching Wendell, I'm struck by the irresistible metaphor of his plastered thumb. As a wound fixed in unwavering affirmation, it emblemizes the tireless optimism of guys like Wendell or Daffy Ball—optimism that in a sadder mood calls to mind Candide's take on the condition: "the mania for insisting that all is well when all is by no means well."[40]

Jay, the aging volunteer, asks the men to turn in their Bibles to the *First Letter of John*, chapter one.

"Oh yeah, the anointing," Wendell nods.

Jay reads aloud about those that might seduce you. *"But the anointing which you have received of Him stays in you, and you need not that any man teach you: but as the same anointing teaches you of all things, and is truth, and is no lie, and even as it has taught you, you shall abide in him.*[41]

"That's why you all must take care," Jay says. "God has anointed you with the Holy Spirit so that you may be able to know in your hearts what God wants for you. And that's what John is talking about here, and that's why you must take care to listen to the Word of God and to armor yourself against folks with a game who try to turn you into what they're about. 'Cause, you see, the truth of the world—that which we can see—is only partially true, but *God's* truth is one hundred percent true. Based on this passage, you can be sure that Satan will send people to try to take you away from God, to take you away from what you have learned. That's what Satan does. So you must stay strong in your child-like faith."

Having watched us through the window, Teddy sidles into the room. Jay smiles at him and continues: "So we need teachers. The Bible is clear about that. And in my experience, it's the Word that makes all the difference between staying stuck in the same old patterns and being able to turn your life around." Citing the men's own testimony, Jay stresses the importance of Bible studies.

Anticipating the proof text to come, Teddy pipes in: "Oh, you talking about Hebrews?"

"No," Jay chuckles, "we're just getting to that." At Jay's instruction, an elderly brown croaks out three canonical verses from Hebrews 5, about the need for differing kinds of teaching: for babes who need milk, and for the mature—those able to distinguish between good and evil—who require solid food.[42]

"Without that solid food," Jay says, "you're prey for Satan's temptations. And Satan *will* throw temptations at you." In illustration, Jay
returns to the MLK Day sandwich expedition to reflect on "a recent
disappointment." "We had one guy in the program," Jay says, "he was
doing really well, but then on Martin Luther King Day we went down-
town to give out sandwiches to the homeless."

"Sandwiches?" Teddy barks excitedly.

"Yeah, sandwiches," Jay says.

"What kind of sandwiches?" Teddy asks.

"Ham-and-cheese sandwiches," Jay says.

"Did they have mayonnaise on 'em?" Teddy asks.

"They sure did," Jay says.

"Good God!" Teddy exclaims, licking his lips.

Poor guy, I think. I guess he hasn't had mayonnaise in forever.

Undeterred, Jay says that when they were distributing sandwiches,
a guy who'd been at Liberty for some time took off. "And he's had a lot
of problems with drugs in the past. So now he's violated his parole and
he's going back to prison. The world has a lot of attractions that he's trying to resist. But," Jay concludes, "God's not done with him yet!"

Suddenly, it's time. We rise, clasp hands, and drop heads. Wendell
leads us in prayer: "Thank you, Lord, for sending us Jay, who's been
coming to see us and teach us the Word for such a long time." Amen.
"And thank you for sending us Josh today."

"Thank *you*," I declare to them alongside their "Thank you,
Father," and instantly regret what must sound like gratitude stubbornly
misdirected.

It's creeping up on six when Baumgartner returns from his second institutional meal, on this, his late day. While the dining hall generally
delivers back Baumgartner in a coma, this evening he's eager to talk.
He asks about Liberty.

I say that while they remain a little narrow for my taste, they were
solicitous as ever. I joke that when Jay talks about Satan sending
people to derail you, I can't help but worry that he's talking about me.
"Say what you will, though," I add vacuously, "they are truly full of
love."

"As long as you toe their line," Baumgartner objects. "But deviate a
fraction from what he perceives as *the* correct form of Christianity, and

see how loving Jay is! Plus, the kind of theology he advocates in there, where *everything* is subject to God's will. Sometimes I wonder if that isn't just a continued evasion of personal responsibility."

"What Brian calls 'God the micromanager,'" I say.

"Right," he says. "It's just not a fully mature theology. It doesn't leave any room for the individual. More than that, it barely leaves any room for God! It's so damn concerned with absolute obedience to God's will and the dangers that await those who deviate, it doesn't leave any space for God's abundant grace."

He opens the new issue of *The Lutheran*, which evidently furnished Baumgartner his dinner company. The cover story commemorates the hundredth anniversary of the birth of German theologian and Holocaust martyr Dietrich Bonhoeffer. "Listen to this. *This* is what being a Christian meant to Bonhoeffer: 'It was about authentically experiencing God's presence through active discipleship following Jesus Christ here and now. Bonhoeffer believed living a Christian life wasn't essentially assenting to established dogmas, nor believing particular doctrines, nor only trusting a Risen Savior in one's life and death. Rather, Christian discipleship involves actively *following after* a living Lord.'" Baumgartner continues: "Although Bonhoeffer believed this life question, *Who really is Jesus Christ for us today?*, was to be actively lived— not once and for all answered—he did offer some helpful insights." For Bonhoeffer, "Jesus Christ is the incarnate, crucified, and resurrected presence of God, personified in the church and existing for others in the world."[43]

Baumgartner riffs on what he read: "Actively present, nondogmatic, inspiring people to exist for others . . . now *this* is *my* kind of God. The God Bonhoeffer describes is a being driven by grace, not a God who wants for you something that is diametrically opposed to what you want for yourself. It's a God that wants to *connect* with you, not to *punish* you. And *that* is what religion is all about: God's effort, by means of grace, to reconnect with you. That's where we get the word *religion*, from the Latin *re-ligio*, meaning to retie the individual to God, and then by extension to retie ourselves through Him to one another."[44]

With a preacher's ease, Baumgartner segues into a series of reflections about the condition of fatherhood. He speaks of his son, now in his twenties. He describes watching with frustration and amusement as his son makes the same idiotic mistakes he once made. He sometimes veers close to overbearingness or condemnation, but he always stops himself short. As he knows full well, trial and error is the only way for his son to learn. "You know," Baumgartner says, "I like to think that God feels about me roughly the way I feel about my son—frustrated that I still haven't *gotten it*, but driven by a willingness to allow me to figure it out on my own."

When stars align, Thursday night is the chapel's busiest activity block, with the headlining Spanish service complemented in the conference room by Al's band rehearsal, in the annex (in biannual six-week spurts) by Sister Georgina's interfaith dialogue group, and in the courtyard outside Keita's window (on roughly one Thursday in four) by the "Indians."

The Indians, as they generally call themselves, or the Natives, as they are known in the office, are relative newcomers. The Native American prisoners' rights movement began in the 1980s, adopting tactics developed by the Muslims a generation earlier, but Native American religion didn't come to Pennsylvania's prison system until a decade later.[45]

In the early nineties, the first convocation of what would become the Pennsylvania DOC's Religious Accommodation Committee was convened for the express purpose of determining the parameters for authentic Native American religious worship. Tribal and spiritual leaders were summoned to Camp Hill to present what, in their view, their religion entailed. At that meeting, as Reverend Baumgartner understated it in a subsequent affidavit, he "learned of the difficulties in providing for Native American inmates with diverse beliefs."[46] Miles from consensus, in Baumgartner's telling, the meeting quickly turned rancorous, with the gathered panelists failing to agree on even a baseline for beginning a dialogue.

When, in 1994, the DOC approved an accommodation for Native American prisoners to possess prayer feathers, medicine bags, and simple headbands, only one Graterford resident took advantage. A year later, two new arrivals to Graterford, James Hunt Warcloud, who traced his lineage to the Cherokee and the Lumbee, and Lucas Sparrowhawk Flying Gibson, whose paternal grandmother was Cherokee, founded the Brotherhood of United Tribes (BOUT). As BOUT, the two were authorized to solicit an outside volunteer. In the interim, Baumgartner took to hosting the smudging ritual and the ritual of the pipe in his office on Thursdays, his late night. While the raid put a temporary halt to the search, Baumgartner eventually found BOUT a volunteer to supervise its rites. By then, Warcloud and Sparrowhawk had successfully pushed for and won accommodations for additional ceremonial objects, including dream catchers, smudging shells, and tree bark. The pugnacious Warcloud, however, was unsatisfied. Impugning the authenticity of both the volunteer (whom they presumed to be a DOC operative) and their "polluted" fellow ritual participants (whose growing ranks they saw as a bunch of poseurs), Warcloud and Sparrowhawk boycotted the rituals they themselves had spearheaded.

So Baumgartner found Bobby Hawk, a member of the Lenape tribe, who remains the Native American volunteer to this day. In the gruffly magnetic Hawk, Warcloud smelled another rat. "Enough is enough!!!!!" Warcloud wrote to Baumgartner. "Either he is for ensuring the Native Americans' religious and cultural freedom or he is a part of the administration wearing the false face of an alleged legitimate Native American Representative. I have spoken!"[47]

Warcloud filed suit, demanding that Native American prisoners be allowed to meet with the same frequency as other religious groups; have a space of their own like the Jews; have the right to engage in the practice of gifting; be able to smudge in their cells; *and*, foremost, to have a sweat lodge like the one up at the federal penitentiary in Lewisburg. Playing the security trump card afforded by the Religious Freedom Restoration Act, which allowed restrictions to First Amendment rights "in furtherance of a compelling governmental interest" provided that the means adopted were the "least restrictive" ones, the DOC stood fast.[48] The federal court agreed, and shortly thereafter Warcloud was shipped to another institution. Years later, with Baumgartner and Bobby Hawk's support, the institution allowed the Natives to build, in the corner yard, wedged between E Block, the main corridor, and the newly expanded chapel offices, a Cherokee prayer circle. While for years they met weekly, that frequency recently dropped when Bobby Hawk left Montgomery County, returning to the mountains of his boyhood.

Baumgartner, who has been administering to Jefferson the Moorish Scientist a solid dressing-down in his office, is interrupted by the three

Indian leaders, here to fetch their ritual paraphernalia. When they reemerge, eagle wing, turtle shell, and worn trash bag in hand, I exchange curt hellos with Claw.

As always, Claw presents as sharp-tempered and cagey. These days, because he is mourning his mother, except for a long tress in the back his head is shaved to the skin. A former biker and a lifer, Claw is one of the men that one comes across when doing newspaper searches on Graterford, in his case, for the time when, while grazing the jail's 300 head of cattle in a ravine, he stumbled upon a set of dinosaur fossil footprints. This was back in '94, when the agricultural program was still operational, lifers still ventured beyond the walls, and the theory of evolution was not yet in Pennsylvania the hot-button issue it has more recently become.[49]

Due to their tough-guy appearance and their alien ritual setting, of the chapel's many groups I was most timid in approaching the Natives. Not until midsummer, when on a Sunday morning I saw them assembled through the window of the main corridor, did I venture outside and introduce myself. Bobby Hawk and Gram—whom I took to be the Natives' leader—knew who I was, and welcomed me back anytime. When next they met, I joined them along E Block's yellow-brick façade. The men, mostly long-haired and decked out in headbands, beads, and feathers, loitered along the wall in small groups, smoking hand-rolled cigarettes and talking. It was a sunny day.

Eventually, Gram, who exudes latent power and could pass for Metallica's James Hetfield from back in his longhair days, took his position beside Chipmunk, his second. Standing side by side between the clustered men and the prayer circle, the two men mounded the mixture of sage, sweetgrass, and tobacco into their overturned turtle shells. Each of the firekeepers lit his mixture, fanned it with an eagle wing to a quick flame, and then snuffed it out to a smolder. From the top of two jagged queues, the men then presented themselves for smudging.

The ritual, which takes perhaps forty-five seconds per person to perform, goes like this: One stands with one's arms outstretched. Moving from feet to head in a sequence vaguely reminiscent of a thorough pat-down, the firekeeper fans smoke toward each of one's extremities. When he eventually arrives at one's face, the firekeeper pauses, at which point, with cupped hands, the recipient wafts the smoke into his nose and mouth. One then rotates clockwise 180 degrees, and the firekeeper slowly works his way back down to the ground. The smudging is finished when the firekeeper drags the eagle wing down to the small of the recipient's back.

Afterward, moving clockwise, each man took a seat in the prayer circle, which is delineated by red stones ringing a wooden pole—the Tree of Life that connects the earth to the heavens. When everyone was on the ground, Bobby Hawk asked the spirits to remember the four-leggers, the two-leggers, the ones that crawl on the ground. He asked the great eagle to take the smoke up to the spirits, bearing with it the memory of those who are sick, those who are in the hole, and those who are currently suffering. Following his prayer, Bobby Hawk delivered an ecological lamentation in which he preemptively mourned the world seven generations hence, by which time the bears will have been exterminated, sons will not learn to hunt and forage from their fathers, and the woods will have been wholly conquered by the strip malls and subdivisions that the European man brings with him when he comes.

One bright fall morning, so as to draw connections between imperial conquest, ecological devastation, and the sorts of violent crimes for which the assembled men were being punished, Bobby Hawk told an allegory: Man finds a bear. The bear is where nature has put it, but man moves in, and he doesn't want the bear there anymore. So he shoots the bear with a tranquilizer dart, loads it into a truck, and hauls it off. The bear wakes up in a new place. While in its natural state the bear posed little danger, in its unfamiliar new environment, it feels threatened and confused. Rendered vulnerable, the bear attacks, and man shoots and kills the bear. Now the bear is dead when what man should have done was merely leave it alone in its natural place. Elegantly, Hawk offered no translation.

My first time with the Indians, I was especially self-conscious since a day earlier the New York Times had run a piece detailing a visit to a prison sweat lodge. Seeking a journalistic middle-of-the-road tenor, the piece nonetheless took as its subject matter—in the manner that such things are unselfconsciously presumed—bad men. "Worship, Dark and Steamy, for Murderers and Rapists," it was titled. After recounting the ritual, and the Native community's successful campaign to overcome the state's foot-dragging, the piece reported the men's claims of the ritual's therapeutic value, its offerings of feelings of rebirth and forgiveness. It then stated flatly: "Still, at prayer circle one day, all those gathered were asked to mention whom they were praying for. Not one mentioned a victim of his crime." To me, the intimation was clear. To the extent that the Indians' religious rituals *felt* therapeutic, such feelings were undeserved. Through their religion, these men were not properly atoning for their sins; they were merely papering them over.[50]

Peering through the steam and sweat, the *Times* reporter saw less men than their unrepented crimes, and I presumed that Graterford's Indians would see in me little more than the impulse to do the same. As I should have by then expected, however, the Natives greeted me warmly. Having come only to observe, I was besieged by nonchalant outreach. I was taught the Indians' special handshake, instructed in the ritual forms, and at once invited to be smudged and to join the prayer circle.

The next time went the same way. As it goes, I began to trade hellos and small talk with the Indians when I saw them around. It was during the hang-and-smoke of my third visit that Gram and Claw pulled me aside and informed me that it had been decided that the circle was for Indians only. It had been Claw's decision. Gram explained that while as a Lakota he was in charge of the smudging, the prayer circle was a Cherokee ritual, and hence Claw's call.

"It's just for Indians," Claw explained. "It's bad juju to open it up to just any curiosity seeker." He quickly added, "Not that you're one of them."

"But I most certainly am!" I assured him. Moreover, I explained, perhaps a bit too apologetically, that as a Jew I understood the imperative to draw ritual boundaries between insiders and outsiders. The decision had nothing to do with me, Claw insisted. It was about reserving the prayer circle for those in the "proper frame of mind." Perhaps to help me get there, or perhaps to change the subject, Claw went on to detail a thing or two about the Great Mystery and about the three kinds of spirit. At conversation's end, I couldn't tell whether the exclusion was personal—directed perhaps at my position as a scholar, as a free person, or as a white man—or whether I was simply collateral damage, a demonstration to those of dubious lineage or conviction that they weren't particularly welcome, either.

The Indians are nothing if not an eclectic bunch. Of the minority who were brought up around traditional practices, the bulk identify as Lakota. The rest are a hodgepodge of bikers, hippies, perhaps a Nazi or two, and, increasingly, Puerto Ricans who trace their ancestry to the Taino, or Arawak, Indians, and who connect Indian religion back to the Santería practices of their mothers and grandmothers.[51] As such, to find a self-identified native-born Indian like Claw policing boundaries made perfect sense. This is especially so because in the case of Graterford's Indians, ulterior motives above and beyond religious sincerity have an obvious material purpose: a coveted hair exemption.

While other routes to long hair exist—some identify as Rastafarians and others proclaim Nazirite vows (the ascetic discipline detailed in Numbers that was responsible for Samson's long locks)—recognition as a Native American carries an automatic exemption. This presumed motive for trying to pass as an Indian extends not only to white guys thought to be hippies, bikers, and metalheads, and now to Puerto Ricans, but also—I realized one day when discovering in the prayer circle the religiously eclectic Charles of EFM, his cornrows unleashed into a frizzy afro—to black guys, too.[52] While Charles credited his attendance to spiritual curiosity, for a purist like Claw, it would appear, the earnestness of the curiosity seeker versus the cynicism of the fraud is largely a distinction without a difference.

A number of men were visibly upset by my exclusion. As the prayer circle filled out, two men persistently tried to wave me in, not grasping why I was sitting against the wall. When I explained it afterward, one guy told me it was total bullshit. Another said he would boycott. A third promised to take it to Claw. I thanked these dissidents profusely, but defended the legitimacy of Claw's proscription and insisted that I took no offense.

The event would have a conciliatory dénouement. A couple of days later, Baraka handed me a blank envelope, its flap folded in, in which I found a typed, two-page document titled "Analytical Concepts of Lakota Beliefs." Though it was unsigned and Baraka wouldn't tell me who gave it to him, its authorship was unambiguous. The document explained the Great Mystery "represented in the embodiment of all supernatural beings and powers in the universe" and broke down the three spirits inside us: Ni, our breath, which is immortal; Sicun, a spirit not limited to the animate that comes into being with us and serves as our guardian spirit; and Nagi, our shadow, or shade.

When next I saw him, Claw shrugged off my thanks. He'd just wanted to make sure I'd understood it wasn't anything personal. Plus, with so much misinformation out there about Indian beliefs and practices, he wanted me to get the straight dope. There are limits, though, he quickly added. Some things shouldn't be spoken of, not just to an outsider, but to anyone.

"Some intimacies ought to be shared with God alone," he said. "It's like bragging to your friends about how good your wife's pussy is. It's just not something you do."

Stepping out of fluorescence and into the bracing darkness, I join the twenty Indians milling about in the nighttime shadow of the E Block wall. Beside the wall lies a mound of coats. Some of the men have retained their corduroy shells, but more are in only their burgundy fleece sweatshirts or white thermal undershirts. Only a few are wearing their knit DOC hats. Back in the summer's heat there was much talk about how as Indians they prefer the cold. Inasmuch as it's thirty degrees outside, now, it would appear, is the time to prove it. Lucas Sparrowhawk—a Vietnam vet, a lifer, and the remaining founding member of BOUT— is talking quietly with Rico, the Puerto Rican cohort's self-appointed spokesman. Rubbing his hands together to reclaim their feeling, Sparrowhawk rolls a cigarette, lights it, and cradles it in his hand for heat.

Beyond the softly talking men are the E Block yards, enclosed in chain link and barbed wire, their basketball hoops swaying in the icy wind. Higher up, where the matte black of the wall gives way to the grayer black of the sky, the earth coughs up a modest rise where the peaks of two bare maples are all the tree that most here ever see.

Ordinarily I chat with Rico, who is generally up for a telling anecdote or a mildly mournful complaint. Last time we discussed his Villanova course, where he is struggling with Sister Barkley's exacting but somewhat unspecified standards. Years later, in a similar setting, Rico will articulate his deep skepticism of the anthropologist, whose mere presence, as he sees it, inescapably affects the behavior of his subjects—most insidiously by seducing the observed into vainly protesting, on behalf of his or her people, their heart-wrenching victimhood.[53] But tonight Rico is preoccupied, so I listen instead to a silver-haired wraith of a man reminisce about Graterford's once vibrant, but since terminated, music program.[54]

The wind picks up, chilling my spine. Sooner than normal, Gram and a second man (not the usual Chipmunk) mound their turtle shells with tobacco, sage, and sweetgrass, assume their spots, and set the contents aflame. At a tempo double that of a languorous summer Sunday, the men are smudged, and, moving over to the prayer circle, they take fidgety seats on the frozen ground.

When my turn arrives, the smudging is strong as always. The feel of the sweet smoke on my body and in my lungs is calming. Oddly assuring, too, is the suspension of the normal order under which standing, eyes closed, exposed, is in this place an act of madness. Not to be overlooked either are the simple pleasures: being outside, the feeling of the driven air, and the lush tones—the ritual's heightened awareness allows me to notice—of sound not penned in by concrete.

When the wing drags down my back, I turn and head for a corner spot beyond the prayer circle, along the wall, where I sit, then kneel, then balance on my heels with my back against the wall, and then kneel again, as the brick proves no less frigid than the ground. I thank the Lord above for my outsider-hood that leaves me little stake in displaying my fortitude. The more I squirm, I console myself, the more Indian I allow the men in the circle to become. Among the pale-skinned longhairs tonight are a couple of dreamy older black guys and an equal number of Latino kids, one of whose bulging braids peek out from under a fishing hat that canopies, too, the unlit stogie jammed between his lips. One man gestures for me to join them, and I stoically return a *thank-you-but-no-thank-you* hand. Glancing to my right, I inadvertently catch, in the office window, Teddy and Vic, who are looking out at me, making faces. I can only hope they didn't see me getting smudged.

Gram thanks the Great Spirit for the cold. Referring to last night's storm, he welcomes the thunder people, but notes their arrival in winter as an alarming sign. He comments how crazy the weather has been until now, how balmy for winter.

"Yeah," Rico interrupts, "I like it like that." Rico is the only man standing.

"Not me," Gram says, "I like it cold." Hearing the thunder people in January removes for Gram any doubt that something is way out of whack. Gram asks the spirits to take care of everyone's families, especially

Chipmunk, who's in the hole, and two others who got shipped. For many in the circle, the latter comes as news, with surprise leading to bitter commentary on the connection between totalitarian policies and environmental destruction. Such, in the collective judgment, is the white man's way. With squinty terseness, Lucas Sparrowhawk reports the harassment he endured this week. It was above and beyond the usual pestering about his hair and his beads that has led him to carry at all times, laminated in Scotch tape, a copy of his approved religious accommodation form. Sparrowhawk relates how somebody sent a couple of emptied packets of barbeque sauce in his name to the deputy's secretary, making it look like blood, and how he got hauled off. "But it's not me!" he says. "They should DNA it and they'll see it's not me. My fingerprints aren't on it." Murmurings attest to comparable intimidations. There are complaints about the "random" urine tests that, in fact, aren't. Being an Indian in a European land is not easy, the men agree. Claw sums it up: "They say that *we're* the heathens but *they're* the ones with the abortion clinics!"

Conversation is sparer than usual. Never reluctant to hold forth, Rico introduces a topic for discussion. He knows it's early to begin thinking about September's Green Corn Feast but he just wants to get on the record now that he doesn't want non–Native Americans preparing it. "That's how the Muslims and Jews have it," he says, "and that's how *we* should have it, too." And while he agrees that leftovers shouldn't be thrown out, and while it's fine for the helpers to have the leftovers, they shouldn't take food before the feast takes place. "The feast is real sacrilegious to us," Rico says. (I take him to mean *sacred.*) What matters most, though, is that *all* the food should be prepared by Native Americans, at least that's how he feels about it, and that's how he thinks they should do it next time around.

"Even bean pies?" Gram asks in his muscular baritone, referring to the dish once heralded by Elijah Muhammad for its health value and which remains, to this day, a chapel feast staple across the denominational spectrum. "Bean pies aren't gonna get made by us, so either we buy theirs or we don't have them at all."

Even more than hair exemptions, feasts are magnets for charges of religious insincerity. During the era of prisoners' power and institutional largesse, a feast became the cherry on top of religious accommodation. The Nation had Saviours' Day, the Sunnis got the two Eid feasts, the Jews got Yom Kippur break-fast and a Passover seder, and the Protestants got Christmas and Easter. As for the Catholics, under the rubric of the Holy Name Society, they would feast on up to seven saints' days throughout the liturgical calendar, with the surplus unexhausted ingredients ending up on the blocks, where the mob guys would allegedly employ personal chefs to dine Goodfellas-style.[55] The confraternity came to be known by the mocking moniker the Hoagie Name Society, after the common Philly designation for a submarine sandwich. After the raid, the feasts were scaled back considerably, as even the religion-friendly Religious Freedom Restoration Act afforded First Amendment protection only to those observances deemed to be "central" to a given religion's practice. While the Jews and Muslims retained their accommodations, the Protestants and Catholics lost everything. As the DOC argued, successfully, in court, with support from Father Gorski's predecessor, such feasts were in kind more cultural than religious, and peripheral to the core practices of Catholicism.[56]

Among the chaplains' more obnoxious tasks is ensuring that all feast participants have paid their ten-dollar fee, and making sure that no one annually partakes in feasts of more than one religious group. In this year's cycle, additional rancor lingers around the newly instituted administrative proscription against "carrying." Carrying was a practice through which faith communities were allowed to cover collectively the fees of their leaders and of the indigent. For many religious prisoners, carrying presented the opportunity to enact in their immediate communities an important charitable principle. From the administration's perspective, though, the practice was one that simply begged for abuse.

With his bean pie objection, Gram quietly reassumes control over the gathered men, more than a few of whom have begun, following Rico's lead, to stand. Most are smoking. My two pairs of woolen socks are proving no match for the frozen earth.

"I love the cold," Gram declares, breaking the silence. Turning to his left, he commends his co-firekeeper on his job filling in for Chipmunk.

"I was a nervous wreck," the guy says matter-of-factly.

"Yup," Gram says. "You never get over it, either."

Gram juts out his jaw and glances dramatically at the watch on the fill-in's wrist. While in summer the Natives will sit for an hour at least, fifteen freezing minutes already feels like forever. Gram, the avowed lover of the cold, remains silent. Fortunately for everyone, as a tropical Indian, Rico's sense of self is in no way tied to the same professed predilection.

"Warm it up!" Rico calls out, and Gram begins the closing prayer.

Bass and drums throb from the conference room where Al's band is rehearsing. The Catholic side remains as dark as it's been since the afternoon, and except for Baumgartner and Vic, who are chatting in Baumgartner's office, the suite is quiet. As expected, Vic rags me mercilessly. He says he never appreciated just how tough my job was until he saw me sitting on the ground, shivering my ass off. I assure him that what he doesn't understand—as a non-scholar—is the essential role my discomfort played in the ritual's performance. Vic tells me that I'm full of shit, and points out, correctly, that I'm still shivering.

The chapel is no warmer. Forty to fifty Latino guys are scattered throughout the pews, everywhere but in the final five rows, which have been blocked off with police tape for density's sake. To a spare crowd divided between burgundies and powder blues, the outside preacher spews forth a verbal frenzy, whose tempo would thwart my meager Spanish even were it not distorted by the PA system and the chapel's acoustics into a slush of feedback and echo.

In Classroom A, two of the lower-ranking members of the Sunday Service Usher Board are sorting Valentine's Day cards to be distributed at this Sunday's service, while in the vestibule, two uncommonly natty white-skinned and -shirted COs are shooting the shit over Bird's desk. The officers are musing on the smell of the smudging smoke, which a good half hour later still permeates the room. They can't get over how much it smells like weed.

"More like angel dust," Bird contends.

"No, weed," insists one.

"I think it *is* weed," says the other.

If so, I say, then burning it up in the open air wouldn't make for a terribly efficient delivery device.

"Not if they were getting it from the street," Bird says.

"That would be the way to do it."

"Like hiding an elephant in plain sight."

The COs are giving the conspiracy only half of their mind, the other half dedicated to Al's band practice, which is rattling the vestibule. They take turns watching through the square window in the conference room door. When they've both lost interest, I take their place.

The Keepers of the Faith, as Al's band is called, is one of five Gospel bands that trade off Sunday services, with three performing every week. If belonging to the same tradition, the music they all play has little relation to the Liberty Ministries repertoire. If those numbers evoke Methodist camp meetings, the Sunday bands channel the last forty years of black popular music, yielding a pastiche of Motown and soul, funk and gospel, R&B and hip-hop.

Nine men are packed into the ten-foot-square conference room, most all of whom I know by face if not by name. Al is seated on the left, his brow tense in concentration, his massive body stuffed behind his tiny guitar like some sort of funk-era Schroeder. Wild Mustache is on the bass, reliably on time, while shaved-head Baby Face is on keys, seemingly as tentative as ever. Smedley, a Muslim who moonlights with a number of the groups, is behind the drum kit—the latest contestant for the position vacated when Al's previous drummer maxed out in early fall. A steady drummer is especially important at Graterford where most rehearsing is done solo, in one's cell, and consequently, according to Al, guys tend to have trouble keeping time. Confident that God will send him the drummer he needs, Al is leaving no stone unturned, even going so far as auditioning Mac Swan of the Moorish Science Temple who, according to Bird, who listened in on the audition, is quite possibly the world's worst drummer. "Straight up romper room," Al judged his performance.

In the corner, Stringy Braids Long Face awaits his turn next to Wire Rim Specs, who bops his head to the beat. To the right of the door, standing mic in hand, is none other than the suddenly ubiquitous Prophet. Opposite Prophet, in the far corner, two upper I Block guys slide in and out of key, with High Forehead holding the mic and Doughy Face hanging on his arm. In his own band, as well as in his recent stint as choir director, Al has made a concerted effort to include the mentally disabled men who live in the new side's specially designated upper I Block. If not for the music's sake, by including them Al hopes to lure them closer to Jesus. To help them along, he lays out conditions for their participation, like that they abstain from homo-sexual acts. "You can't do that while you're in the choir," Al tells them. While Baumgartner is impressed with Al's outreach, not everyone is so certain. Telling me that Al "is not who he says he is," Charles obliquely referred to a recent incident where Al threatened to kill one of the upper I Block guys. Al, for one, would be the first to admit that he's not always the easiest guy to work with. "You can't work with Al," he says. "You've got to work with the Al that loves Jesus."

I, for one, can't get enough of Al in his bandleader mode. It's something that Al has always done—even back in his Muslim years—and never does Al seem fuller in his being than when he's arranging music. Best is his ability to deliver criticism as encouragement. "That's good!" I've heard him shout to a meandering keyboardist. "You've got your time. Now why don't you pick up the *drummer's* time?"

Upon meeting my eyes through the window, Al smiles and signals I should enter. Cracking the door open, I'm engulfed by the cloying heat of crammed bodies at play. Without modulating his metronomic upbeat head bobs, Al shouts, "Hey, Josh! Come in here and get some of this here *heeeeeeat!*"

The room is steam-room warm. I lean against the wall with eyes closed and open myself to its atmosphere, which despite its density of men doesn't feel the least bit claustrophobic.

Giving myself over to the music, I make little effort to catalogue what comes. Without break, a contemporary-sounding track gives way to a traditional gospel number. When that one ends, Stringy Braids takes over on keys. Al cues Wild Mustache on bass, who sets the tone with a walking bass line. After a couple of free measures, Prophet starts rhyming some lyrics, but Al cuts him off. He asks Mustache to take it from the top, and then, one by one, he brings the rest of the band mem-bers in. After a couple of aborted efforts they manage to get all the pieces together, but when Prophet jumps in with the lyric, their fragile communion again crumbles apart.

"Stop," Al says. "Say what I'm saying." Al recites the words and Prophet repeats after. Expectation builds as they get it going a second time, but once again Prophet falls off the beat.

"Don't look at me like that there!" Al says. "You got to hit it in the groove. If you miss it, just wait to the next time around. And don't look at me. And don't look at me on Sunday, either."

Prophet agrees, and soon the gears are meshing. When Al trusts that his concerted maintenance is expendable, he drops in a spacey guitar lick. After a couple of nonfatal missteps, they come to a steady groove. They hit a change in rhythm and then, as one, everyone starts to shout:

You've got the Holy Ghost! . . . Ahh!
You've got the Holy Ghost! . . . Ahh!

Everybody shouts the refrain. And then it gets personal.

Mark's got the Holy Ghost! . . . Ahh!
Mark's got the Holy Ghost! . . . Ahh!

For the duration of the eight repetitions of his name, Mark does a little dance. Then it's my turn:

Josh's got the Holy Ghost! . . . Ahh!
Josh's got the Holy Ghost! . . . Ahh!

And my head bops in time. The Holy Ghost moves through the band, one by one, before finally coming to rest in Al's guitar. The freaky lick returns, and Al's head jabs up and down, side to side.

Al's lick deteriorates into a dissonant scratch, which issues forth on the *one* and *three*. Then, with Al bellowing its passage, the Spirit moves sometimes smoothly, sometimes in a stutter, to the keys, the bass, and then the drums, before coming home to Al's guitar, Al's hands and arms, his shoulders, neck, and head. A couple more barks and they're done.

The band reshuffles to play one that Al has been working up for months. Finding myself on the far side of enraptured, I have no trouble catching the lyrics, which cast salvation's bounty in sharp relief against worldly suffering. Adopting the vantage point of a homeless person, the lyrics speak of being stuck out on the streets. "That's my life," the singers bemoan; "ain't got nowhere else I could go." For this wretched condition, the chorus brings the answer:

I'm just a nobody
So I gotta tell everybody
About somebody
Who can save anybody.

Cracking the door, Bird gives Al five fingers, and Al nods. The musicians play on and the vocalists sing on—souls once lost, now found, vowing to testify to God's salvific power.[57]

"Heavenly Father," Al prays when they finish. "I just want to thank You for allowing us to come together like this to sing Your praises. Please take care of Josh when he drives back to his level, just like you watch over us on this here level in the shadow of the valley of death. In the name of Jesus, amen."

The COs are gone, the offices are locked, and the classrooms are dark. In the dull chapel light, the Spanish service is still going on; and from the rolling of the preacher's words, one on top of the next, it's plain that the Holy Spirit has moved in there. The congregation sways in silence, many arms outstretched.

Bird is reading the *Daily News*.

I ask him where he got it.

"Kaz," he says. "I had to outsource."

Bird and I discuss the suddenly omnipresent Prophet—we're debating, ungenerously, whether, as Bird thinks, he's a "bullshit artist," or whether, as I argue, he's quite insane—until the chapel clogs with Spanish speakers. Amid the hubbub, Rafael, a puffy and pockmarked Puerto Rican with an Abraham Lincoln beard, makes a point of introducing me to tonight's volunteer. The petite but fierce woman, dressed in black, introduces herself as Rita. Gesturing at Rita, Rafael explains that she's the Spanish-language chaplain from the Philadelphia County Jail.

"*Y el*," he says to her, pointing at me, "*el es un judío*"—a Jew.

Having grown up in what he characterized as an Apostolic Christian community that observed the Sabbath and Mosaic dietary restrictions, Rafael seems to see in me a kindred spirit. For that reason, among others, Rafael perennially encourages me to attend Spanish services, and generously insists on translating when I do. Rafael tells me to come Saturday when a man from his church will be preaching. I promise him I will.

Shyly, Rafael's frequent companion, the shorter, quieter José, tells me he has a book he'd like for me to have, which he presents to me. Called *The Last Lap*, it's a first-person testimonial by a Jew who embraced Christ.[58]

Thanking José for his generosity, I slip the book inside my folder.

FRIDAY

THESIS 4

The order observed by men at Graterford conforms as a rule to a Manichaean logic: the self wars for sovereignty with its baser inclinations, a dynamic that recapitulates the agony of a universe torn between God and the Adversary. Between the psyche and its cosmic mirror, we find a social realm similarly divided. Indeed, it may well be the social world of the Philly ghetto and its epic history of tribal warfare that furnishes the template. Much blood was spilled. With each man sacrificed, the once arbitrary boundary between gang and gang, neighborhood and neighborhood, was reinforced. And for every man left standing today, another, at least, lies underground.

While the aging lifers no longer swear allegiance to the degraded symbols those men died for, the habits of rancor persevere. Here acculturation to the prison plays a regenerative role: *If I didn't know a guy on the outside, I sure as hell ain't gonna get to know him in this place!* While this doctrine isn't always lived in practice, it is lived enough to preserve, in the chapel's religious subgroups, the trenches of gang and neighborhood along which men died and killed. Before the stakes of existence became eternal life and death, the vicissitudes of life and death were already too real. Before a man came to assiduously police himself against the deviations and innovations of men who would lead him off God's path, he already policed street corners and back alleys for men who wished him harm. If a man is a lifer, then on at least one of those occasions another life (or lives) ended and his own was destroyed. As long as the exiled lifer wanders in this desert, the umbrella he has jerry-rigged to provide him just a little bit of shade will recast the shadow of the Angel of Death. In this shadow grows resentment.

Here, too, exceptions prove an opposing rule. In spite of the psychic, social, and cosmic forces driving toward war, men labor concertedly to impede such percolating tribulations. Rancor seethes, but *wiser heads prevail.*

Vic is mopping the vestibule floor. Baraka and the Imam are in the Imam's office, quietly talking. Teddy is at his desk, looking shellshocked.

"Did you sleep?" I ask him.

He shakes his head no. Kazi arrives with a "What's going on?" and sits down at Sayyid's desk. Baraka closes the door to the Imam's office. Across the hall on the Catholic side, Mike sits at his desk, reading the paper. In the chapel, Santana and Muti—the lowest-profile chapel worker—are lining up mics along the front of the stage. Al walks the center aisle in my direction, a coil of stereo wire draped over his shoulder. "*Josh's got the Holy Ghost,*" he sings at me, as if only to himself, inducing in me a head bop for the same audience.

"So, that Prophet," I say, "he's sure got a lot of energy, that guy."

"Sure does," Al says. "Him and the other three people that live in his head. That's why I say to him, 'What one am I talking to? Can I talk to the one that loves Jesus?' I tell him, 'I used to talk to those voices, too!'"

"And what does he say to that?"

"Yeah, he know," Al says. "He say he got to stay on the medication or else another four will come out!" With a deep belly laugh, Al rolls on into the Catholic office, where, I figure, he'll mooch a snack or idly gnaw with Mike on one of their outstanding bones of contention, perhaps upping the stakes in their handball feud, or hammering yet again at Mike that since Mike did nothing to stop his high school principal from giving him a blow job, that makes him a faggot, too.

Leaning on the terra-cotta rampart separating the shoe area from the rest of the annex is a heavyset dark-skinned man whose billowy white shirt and red fez can only make him a Moorish Science Temple volunteer.

This is the first outside volunteer to the Moors that I've seen. Baumgartner claims he would have no difficulty fielding a volunteer-led Protestant Bible study every day of the week, but volunteers for the Muslim and the para-Muslim groups are harder to come by. According to Baumgartner, local representatives of the Nation and Muhammad's Temple profess their eagerness but invariably fail to follow through. The situation with the Sunni congregation is more opaque. Prisoners and chaplains agree that many who might be interested in volunteering couldn't pass the background check, either because of their own criminal histories or because of known associations with one or another Graterford resident. Beyond that, there is no consensus. Mamduh and others say that the Imam refuses to take the necessary steps to bring people in, while Namir claims he's issued many invitations but that no one answers the call.

Baumgartner arrives and, rejecting the chair that was set out for him, leans against the wall next to the door. Jefferson, the Moors' prisoner leader, approaches and takes a position by his side. With their eyes trained forward, the two men have a brief exchange, which concludes when Baumgartner hustles off with a sense of purpose.

From the lectern, a sharp-featured brown reads from chapter twelve of Noble Drew Ali's *The Holy Koran*, in which the twentieth-century prophet details Jesus' teaching to the downtrodden laborers at a spring. To these men who knew no happiness and thought heaven to be unreachably far, Jesus counseled: "'My brother man, your thoughts are wrong; your heaven is not far away, and it is not a place of metes and bounds, is not a country to be reached; it is a state of mind! Allah never made a heaven for man; He never made a hell; we are creators and we make our own. Now cease to seek for heaven in the sky; just open up the windows of the hearts, and, like a flood of light, a heaven will come and bring a boundless joy; then toil will be no cruel task.'"[1]

While in earlier centuries African Muslims sounded the call to prayer on North American shores, by the dawn of the twentieth century these were but distant echoes. Unlike in the Caribbean, where the slave trade went on longer and where the permeability between West African and Catholic devotional practices spawned new traditions such as Voodoo, Santería, and Candomblé, in the States, the traditions the Africans brought with them largely died off. Trace elements carried over—but none more salient than the absent presence that is irreparable collective loss. This loss of the former slaves' traditional folkways was the problem to which Noble Drew Ali's revelation was both a symptom and a proposed remedy.[2]

Like Elijah Muhammad, who was born Elijah Poole, the son of Georgia sharecroppers, Noble Drew Ali was born Timothy Drew, in North Carolina. Along with millions of other black men and women of their era, both men migrated north—Poole to Detroit and Drew to Newark, New Jersey, where in 1913 he founded his first temple. A decade later, in Chicago, Noble Drew Ali registered the Moorish Science Temple.

An American religion *par excellence*, the Moorish Science Temple was and residually remains a hodgepodge of Protestantism, modern black nationalism, mysticism, mind cure, and fraternal order.[3] Seemingly cribbed from two preexisting volumes of scriptural esoterica, *The Holy Koran* transmits the further revelations of Jesus, Muhammad, and the Buddha, and offers supplementary holy instruction from the final prophet, Drew Ali.[4] Chief among these instructions was the disclosure, to an audience erroneously known as Negro, black, and colored, of their true national and religious identities: they were the descendants of the biblical tribe of Moab, which in its time also founded the city of Mecca; and they were members of the Asiatic Nation of North America, otherwise known as Moorish Americans. That this august lineage was unknown to the so-called Negro, black, and colored was a larceny of slavery. Rendered ignorant of themselves, the lost Moors strayed after the gods of Europe. It was this collective state of confusion about self, folk, and God that Noble Drew Ali hoped to rectify by reintroducing to the Moorish people the true religion of their forefathers: the religion he called "Islam."

To understand how twentieth-century black nationalists expropriated elements of Islamic tradition for their spiritual projects necessitates accounting for what we might think of as "the missing Muslims." For just as the story of Islamic practice at Graterford today begins with the oddity of finding empty spaces in the chapel where the Muslims are supposed to be, so, too, must a history of African-American Islam first make sense of a similar absence. The missing Muslims of this more epochal story are what we might sloppily call the "real" Muslims. Meaning where, during the emergence of these new American Islams, were the native-born traditionalist Muslims?

With rare exceptions, the answer was that they were back overseas.[5] For while immigrants from the Middle East, Africa, and Asia had begun to trickle into the United States at the turn of the century, this diversifying drift was halted in 1924 with the National Origins Act. By tying quotas to expatriate populations in the states as represented in the 1890 census, the Act rolled back the demographics of American immigration by a generation. Until 1965, when this racist law was abolished, legal immigration was de facto limited to Europeans, and citizens of Muslim lands were barred from naturalization.[6] If, as some allege, Nation of Islam founder Wallace Fard Muhammad, who established Temple Number One in Detroit in 1930 only to vanish shortly thereafter, was himself of Middle Eastern or Central Asian origin, he was one of the few.[7] Without an appreciable population of natural-born Muslims on hand to police its boundaries, "Islam" became pure Orientalist fantasy, and an empty vessel to be filled as the religiously inventive saw fit.

During the war years, the Moorish Science Temple was but one node in Philadelphia's burgeoning religious culture. In his 1944 classic *Black Gods of the Metropolis*, the homegrown biracial anthropologist Arthur Huff Fauset located the Moorish Science Temple alongside a host of other storefront churches, some fleeting and some seminal: Holiness Christianity, Pentecostalism, Black Judaism, and the Father Divine Peace Mission Movement. In Fauset's influential interpretation, these religious cults were generated by and appealed to a black population that had recently arrived from the rural South and was collectively hungry for a sense of place and a sense of self.[8]

If in the Moors Fauset saw the Negro Church's drive toward freedom taken to its racially separatist limit, subsequent developments would show this impulse still had a ways to go. A full generation before the followers of Elijah Muhammad, who, sporting bow ties and trading their slave names for X's, would bring Islam into mainstream visibility, it was Noble Drew Ali's Moors, who, donning red fezes and with "Bey" or "El" appended to their last names, first made something called "Islam" accessible to black Philadelphians.

"The brain is the most powerful machine known to man," the Moor at the podium explains, "but when we give our thoughts to negative things, we're using our own power against us. We have the power to do anything with our minds, but because of our own pettiness, we suffer.

It all comes from our consciousness. Our thoughts harvest the magnetic force from the ether, positive and negative, so you got to be careful about what you think about. 'Cause when we let our minds run rampant, it's like letting a machine run wild. And then we just *react* because we have no control of our thoughts.

"Nothing originates in the physical realm." The Moor's pitch rises with emphasis. "The physical realm is only a mirror of the mind, reflecting our thoughts back at us. What you see is what you get. Like Jesus talking to the common people because they had unhappy thoughts," he says, referring back to the passage from Drew Ali's *Holy Koran*. "It's like when you get back to your cell and you're reminiscing, thinking: 'I can't believe I did that.' Well, thoughts travel out in the ether realm and manifest themselves in the physical realm. That's why it's important to always stay positive. We reap the fruits of our thoughts, and then we can't believe that things are so bad for us! Our thoughts are actions just like our actions are actions. It all depends on how much you meditate on it.

"Thing is, you got your higher self and your lower self. When you're thinking about something you did wrong and a voice in your head goes, '*Nah!*' Well, that's your higher self checking your lower self. Because the two are always battling, you know? The good lies in everybody. Those who falter are just the ones who let their lower selves take over. It's easy for the lower self to do bad. It's easy to take a gun and shoot people in our culture. What's hard to do is to go up to a brother and say, '*I love you.*'"

In their talk of higher and lower selves, the Moorish Scientists offer the chapel's clearest account of what Baraka and Al both pinpoint as the crux of doing religion in prison: the struggle for self-control, in mind and body. In its drive toward the sensuous, the lower self is a constant saboteur. That's why, in their rearticulation of the Apostle Paul's demand for daily death, the Moors preach how, with discipline, a man can subject the lower, carnal, self to his higher, spiritual, self, his ideal self. Fasting is critical. By fasting, one cleans his body of toxins and returns the body to its natural state of health. People are "addicted to eating"—I've heard it said here, which is why their lower selves run roughshod. That so-called black people, who have been separated from their natural folkways, should suffer from self-destructive diets is, to the Moors, entirely unsurprising. But via Noble Drew Ali's divinely inspired scientific method for healthy living, Moorish Americans can transcend the life of vice and sin and move collectively in the direction of truth and justice.

Jefferson approaches the lectern and offers a salute, which the previous speaker returns. "Islam!" they shout at one another.

Not too many years my senior, Jefferson, I learned one fall afternoon in Baumgartner's office, is also a native New Yorker, though he is from Brooklyn. One-on-one, as before his congregation, he is well-spoken, if a bit distant. That day especially, his affect could have been described as slick, but he might just as easily have been sad. Or perhaps it was me that was somehow off.

Jefferson broke down for me how the labels that have historically been thrown onto black people—Negro, black, colored—have been used to segregate blacks off from other races, from one another, and from themselves. "We're the only race that has all these different labels, which is evidence of the uncertainty of who we are and where we come from."

Jefferson knows that at Graterford his odds in recruitment are long. I asked him why guys here tend to choose Sunni Islam.

"Some guys cling to the majority Orthodox out of a form of protection, or so as to be accepted in prison," he said. "I know from being in institutions that when guys come to prison, they feel the need for protection and acceptance, and to be a part of a family or brotherhood."

"Is this why folks get involved with the Moorish Science Temple?" I asked.

"If it were," he answered, "then we'd have a lot more people, so that's not the answer. Once people come down, and they understand the religion and they understand the belief system, and the knowledge and wisdom they receive, if they feel it in their hearts, that's what makes them a member."

As a religious minority at Graterford, the Moors are at their greatest disadvantage when trying to stake a claim on turf regarded by the majority as unequivocally its own. While the Moors used to be included in the Sunnis' Ramadan observance, in response to a popular upsurge, Namir made clear that as non-Muslims who take guidance from a prophet after Muhammad, the Moors, as a group, were not welcome. Jefferson has a request for a separate Moorish Ramadan before the Religious Accommodation Committee, but his case, which Baumgartner showed me, cited no sources and offered no precedent from the Moorish tradition. Not that, these days, a scholarly treatise would necessarily fare any better.

The Sunni majority's exclusivism frustrates Jefferson. "We don't tell them *they're* not Muslim. They tell us that *we're* not." In fact, the very openness of Moorish Science, its reluctance to denounce other religions as false, is part of what attracted Jefferson in the first place. Contrary to the Jehovah's Witnesses with whom he grew up, who were smugly confident that theirs was the only true path, the Moors claim no monopoly on how to get right with God. "I always wondered: What about a kid that was born a Buddhist? A just God will accept his children and judge them for their deeds on earth." As for the varieties of religion, Jefferson takes a liberal stance. "The journey to God is always the same," he said, "even if the paths are different."

Ordinarily two flags flank the lectern—the stars and stripes on one side and the Moroccan green star on a red field on the other—but today there are none. Crouching slightly, Jefferson lays his forearms on the lectern's ridged edge. He bites his bottom lip, pauses, runs his tongue along the dimple below his mouth and tongues his bottom lip again. "There's some sort of problem with the tapes," he says. His facial tic repeats. "They're not here. Reverend Baumgartner has gone up to try to get them." Before Jefferson turns it over to the "Grand Sheik"—he gestures deferentially toward the volunteer—he's got a word to say about unity. Jefferson reads from *The Holy Koran*:

"'Let the bonds of affection, therefore, unite thee with thy brothers, that peace and happiness may dwell in thy father's house. And when ye separate in the world, remember the relation that bindeth you to love and unity; and prefer not a stranger before thy own blood. If thy brother is in adversity, assist him; if thy sister is in trouble, forsake her not. So shall the fortunes of thy father contribute to the support of his whole race.'"[9]

Jefferson pauses. "You see, we've got to stand together. If we stand together we will find peace and happiness. The only thing that separates us is ignorance. God is in everyone. Isms have always separated us. If you look back at our movements in the sixties and the seventies, they were trying to come together, but tactics were used to destroy them. But they also did things that contributed to their destruction. Because we come from a vicious state of slavery, and a lot of us haven't recovered from it yet.

"The Prophet says, 'We need to learn to love instead of hate.' People are killing each other over sneakers, for looking at each other wrong. There's so much hate in us. We need healing. The first step is to know *who we are*. We are *not* niggers. N, B, C—Negro, black, and colored—these were the names given to us by the slave owners. That's why the Prophet taught us that we should proclaim our free national identity to the government in which we live. We are Moorish Americans. Moorish from Moor, which is from the land of Moab, part of the universal family.

"During the postslavery period, there was a lot of chaos. The Prophet had a different vision. We didn't need to whine for the government to help us. We *are* the government. All we have to do is get together, unify, get people into Congress. If we knew back then what we know now, where would we be at? Now that I know Noble Drew Ali's teachings, I see the whole world different. Allah says that struggle brings out the best in us. The first step is to know who we are. A couple of guys was talking yesterday on the block about trying to get some finances together, but as I told them, the first step is to come down to the Moorish Science Temple and learn who you are. Because it all starts with yourself. You need mental food and spiritual food, not just physical food. It's like a fuel. To understand yourself, your history, your place in this country. Why would you settle for money on the corner when you can make the same money in a legitimate way?

"The game is rigged. Prosecutors cheat, and the laws are set up to put you here. Three strikes and you're out. We can't win that game. The very fact that we're *here* talking today is evidence of that. We've got to start playing a new game. The game we been playing has got a lot of wins. A hell of a lot more than us. We saw the old heads in prison, and what do you know, we fell into the same traps that they did. We've got to find a new game, and that's *this*," he holds up *The Holy Koran*.

"This is life," he says. "Allah has a way of showing us stuff. This is the new way. You can get the same money in a legitimate way. We've got the Internet now. When I was on the street it was just starting, but now we got the whole world at the tap of a few keys. We got foreigners coming to this country who are making it. We built this country, and we're filling up the penitentiaries!"

Jefferson's voice lilts toward a conclusion. "The actions we take affect everyone around us," he explains. "When I first fell, someone told me that when a man is sent to prison, it's like his mother has been sent to prison, too. Now, twelve years later, I understand the burden I've placed on my family. I mean, what happens when your kid at school hears his pal talking about all the things his daddy does for him?" He pauses. "We've got to respond positively." Conclusive nods bring a ripple of applause.

The red-fezzed volunteer rises and faces Jefferson. "Islam!" they half-shout at one another. The Sheik takes the lectern. Holding up five fingers on his left hand and two fingers on his right—a mystical seven in all—the Sheik leads the men in responsive prayer.

"Islam." . . . "Islam."
"Allah." . . . "Allah."
"Father of the Universe." . . . "Father of the Universe."
"Of Love." . . . "Of Love."
"Truth." . . . "Truth."
"Peace." . . . "Peace."
"Freedom." . . . "Freedom."
"Justice." . . . "Justice."
"Allah is my partner." . . . "Allah is my partner."
"And God." . . . "And God."
"Of salvation." . . . "Of salvation."
"In the night and day." . . . "In the night and day."
"Islam." . . . "Islam."
"Takbir." . . . "Takbir."
"Allahu Akbar." . . . "Allahu Akbar."

Following the pledges of allegiance to the Moorish people and to the United States of America, the Sheik ("not Grand Sheik," he corrects Jefferson, "just Sheik") fields a fusillade of inquiries, some guileless, some skeptical. Asked about a dragon symbol, Moorish holiday observances, and whether a man can give birth ("Yes, a womb-man can"), the Sheik splices zany readings of the pledge of allegiance ("We pledge allegiance to the Republic because it was the *Republican* Party that freed the slaves, not the Democrats" and "The pledge is *one nation under God, with liberty and Jesus for all,* because *Jesus* is another name for *justice"*) into an address extolling sovereignty and the self-control and self-governance that sovereignty entails.

The moment the service ends, Mamduh and Muti rush in and hastily begin unrolling the carpets in preparation for Jum'ah.

Al and Papa ask me where I've been.

"Moorish Science Temple," I say.

"And how was it?" Al asks.

"Interesting," I say, "very interesting."

In response to Al's mild guffaw, I voice my sympathies for groups like the Moors and the Nation.

And I mean it. Still vital outposts in their own right, these groups are most notable as residual forms in the chapel's living genealogy of black religion. Without the groundwork laid by these inventive American traditions, it is simply unthinkable that on an evening in the ninth month of the Muslim calendar in rural Pennsylvania, seven hundred black men would come together to break fast and pray in Arabic. Because the "second resurrection" superseded what would retroactively become "the first," it's hard not to see the eventual eclipse of black nationalist Islam as somehow inevitable. But that would be a mistake. There are good reasons—both world-historical and idiosyncratic—for the eventual triumph of Sunni Islam at Graterford, but it is important to remember that history needn't have turned out the way it thus far has. While Sunni Islam, whether of the Warith Deen or the Salafi sort, is indisputably a richer religious tradition than its black nationalist predecessors, history is not the story of the systematic elimination of antiquated forms by their rightful successors. Especially with regard to the most triumphant social forms, it is important always to remember: no regime of truth was foreordained, just as none of its vanquished counterparts was somehow intrinsically in error.

To this day, moreover, the Moorish Science Temple's framing of the intractable predicament of black men in America lives on. As I often hear it—from Muslims and Christians no less so than from Moors or members of the Nation—because of slavery, black Americans are unique the world over for their culturelessness. While I contest this point, arguing not only that African-Americans have a robust culture all their own but that this culture is, in many ways, the vibrant core of *American* culture, I take as authentic the sense of unparalleled loss that men here articulate. For those whose culture had been torn away, the manufactured histories and identities of the Moorish Science Temple and the Nation of Islam offered a place to stand, and a way to stand up. If nowadays their incessant talk of "science" and "nation" seems hokey and their self-styled ancestries manifestly fanciful, their principal diagnosis remains no less true. As Jefferson characterized the practical imperative behind these once innovative religious forms: *We've got to start playing a new game.*

Where my sympathies become outright appreciation is in how, even at their more militant edges, groups like the Moors and the Nation practice a form of multiculturalism that necessitates moving beyond the wan mutual condescension of "tolerance" and into something kinetic requiring coalition and compromise.[10] At least at Graterford, Moors and members of the Nation are careful to foreground their truths as historically constituted and culturally specific, as but one set among many. Not simply the realpolitik of the minority faction, this philosophical modesty is a function of the black nationalists' insight into how a people's collective experience shapes its sense of the world. Especially against the backdrop of the expansionist universalism common to the chapel's Muslims and Christians, as a Jew and a pluralist, I very much appreciate this philosophical modesty. And all the better that it comes with a side of undisguised textual and ritual creativity!

With less economy and clarity, some of this I communicate to Al and Papa.

"The thing that I find admirable in them," Papa says, "is their call for unity."

"Sure," Al asks, "but why do they have to separate themselves? Why can't we all just get along? Why can't we all *come together* and unify? Why do they have to unify all by themselves?"

I protest that while that sounds great in the abstract, in his call for unity, isn't Al really demanding that the marginal group suck it up and sign on to the dominant group's agenda? "Like, 'Hey, you Jews,'" I say, "'can't we all just put aside our differences and come together in Christ?'"

Al shakes his head. "That's not what I'm talking about. I'm not talking about doctrine. I'm talking about everybody coming together and talking. And taking it from there."

"Nah," Papa counters. "Maybe in God's time"—meaning, in the end of days—"not our time."

Al and Papa go back and forth, with Al arguing that such unity is not merely a reasonable hope, but that it's our duty to build it, and Papa standing firm that while unity in time is inevitable, its implementation is wholly in God's hands.

I suggest to Papa that if he takes a look at the unity between faiths that we find in the chapel, maybe he needn't be so pessimistic.

This neither of them is buying.

The conversation drifts. Somehow Baraka comes up.

"That's a wise man," Papa says.

"Arguably the wisest that I know," I say, "excluding, perhaps, my father." Loosened by intellectual stimulation and concord, I speak before I think and launch into a tangential anecdote from a couple of years back, recalling how in a grim winter of the soul I mustered the energy to communicate to my parents that, lest I somehow fail to mention it again, they should know that I would miss them when they were gone.

Without skipping a beat, my father, a lifelong observant Jew and a man of letters, though arguably also a man of greater comedic than emotional intelligence, fired back: "Don't worry. Someday we'll all be together with Jesus."

It was the perfect thing to say. By burlesquing with a heavy and misplaced theological hand what, in that moment, was the unbearable burden of human terminableness, my father gave me cause to laugh in the face of the absurd. Absent the balm of a viable solution to the precipitating problem, I've come to believe that such laughter is a tactic worth trying to cultivate.[11]

At present, my own speech has been less propitious. From the looks on their faces, Al and Papa are, at best, puzzled, and, in a way I wouldn't begrudge them, perhaps a bit offended. If for me, counseling courageous mirth was an act of love, for them, Jesus hardly belongs in a punch line.

As I quietly thrash about hoping to somehow hit the switch that will clean up the mess I've made, grace comes in the unexpected form of Mamduh and Muti, who arrive in search of Al's technical assistance.

Trying to get the PA system up and running, they've hit a snag. With a halfhearted show of reluctance, Al hauls himself up and lumbers after them annex-ward.

Redeemed by interfaith logistics, I follow along. As Al fiddles with the wires and connections, Mamduh grabs the live mic and dates us all with a prophecy from hip-hop's golden age:

"Sucka MCs who did not learn, if you don't this time we shall return!"[12]

Back from escorting the Sheik out, Baumgartner flops down in a chair.

"He seems like a lovely guy," I say, which is what I always say.

Baumgartner is more circumspect. "The Sheik is eager to get things rolling, but he doesn't quite understand how things work here."

"How so?" I ask.

The Sheik, Baumgartner explains, is on a temporary pass and has yet to undergo the whole security protocol—a background check and so on—but he's already talking about adding a second weekly service and getting his wife involved. "He doesn't get that things don't happen overnight here. He needs to learn to exhibit a little patience."

"A trait that wouldn't hurt Jefferson, either," I say.

Baumgartner laughs. "No, it certainly wouldn't."

"So where were the flags today?" I ask.

"Oh, didn't you notice? They didn't have *any* of their stuff today." Which brings Baumgartner to the saga of the Moorish Science Temple paraphernalia cart. He tells the story. A few weeks back Jefferson expressed his desire to have their cart repainted. Jefferson asked Baumgartner to put in for a painting order so that he might wheel it to the paint shop. Knowing the pace of this place, Baumgartner suggested that they wait until the folks at the paint shop were ready for them, and when they were, the paint shop could send somebody to pick it up. Jefferson suggested they remove the cart's contents now, but Baumgartner again countered that they should wait for the paint shop's go-ahead. Jefferson agreed to do it Baumgartner's way.

Fast-forward a couple of weeks. Baumgartner comes back from vacation to find Jefferson in his office, wanting to "inventory" the cart's contents. The cart, however, is nowhere to be found. Baumgartner looks for it. Jefferson looks for it. They look for it together. No cart. After a quarter hour of this fruitless hunt, Jefferson turns to Baumgartner and says, "You know, I think somebody took it down to the paint shop." Meeting Jefferson's eye, Baumgartner asks, "Okay, if the cart was taken down to the paint shop, then why are you *here* looking for it, and why am I here *helping* you look for it?"

So is this why Baumgartner was castigating Jefferson last night in his office? I ask.

That's only half of it, Baumgartner says. *This* week Jefferson put in a request slip for a couple guys to come down early this morning to set up. Having dealt with Jefferson before, though, Baumgartner checks the names and numbers on the computer. Lo and behold, one of the numbers is off. Not just slightly off, but totally off. And it wasn't simply an honest mistake—Baumgartner answers my question—because if you know nothing else in this jail, you know your own number. So last night, Baumgartner asked Jefferson what was up. Jefferson took responsibility, saying that he'd somehow messed up the name and number. Baumgartner shakes his head. His intention, he says, was less to ascertain the facts, than to reestablish his authority.

Which brings us to this morning, when Jefferson comes up to Baumgartner and says, "Okay, why don't you write someone a pass and we'll go get the cart?" To which Baumgartner replies, "No, why don't *you* choose someone to go with me?" All of which went for naught, of course, because when they went to the paint shop, they couldn't find the cart there, either.

"So what's going on?" I ask.

"Who knows?" Baumgartner is a "w" of shoulders and upturned palms.

"The cart is locked?"

"Sure, it's *locked*," he says, between air quotes. "But that's no obstacle. It wouldn't be hard in this place to find somebody with the skills to pick it."

"So they're trying to move something?" I ask.

"Could be."

"What?"

"Could be anything," he says. "Drugs, a cell phone, oil. Could be anything. Or it could be that it's got nothing in it now, but they're doing a test run to see if it gets through."

"In order to later do *what?*"

Baumgartner shrugs again. "It could be oil," he says. "That's what they're saying about Sayyid. That that's what *he* was smuggling."

"Well," I sigh. "I suppose that when you're living in a place like this, you just don't get the presumption of innocence anymore."

Baumgartner disagrees. "It's not that I don't give guys the presumption of innocence. If it's a guy I know well—say, a guy who works down here—I don't presume that he's up to something. It's just when there's a confluence of certain odd occurrences that I begin to get my hump up. And the Moorish Science Temple, well, they've been having a lot of those. But still I don't presume anything. That's how we're different from the guys in the bubble. They *do* presume that all these guys are criminals, always up to something dirty, always hatching a plan. I don't assume that they *are*, but I'm not about to put my head in the sand and say that they aren't. Obviously, if I only thought of these guys as criminals, I couldn't do my job. But by the same token, if I wasn't open to being suspicious, I couldn't do my job effectively, either."

In a speech Baumgartner gave me last month that struck me as plainly rehearsed with the destination of my field notes in mind, he described a range of attitudes toward the prisoners. At the anti-inmate end—Security Captain Simpson's—prisoners are regarded as nothing more than criminals in need of surveillance. At the other extreme—that of Reverend Carvel, the notoriously pollyannaish St. Dismas volunteer—prisoners are nothing more than unfortunates in need of love. According to Baumgartner, these attitudes on the ground mirror broader American outlooks toward prisoners, with "fry 'em" at one end, and "there but for the grace of God go I" at the other.

"I want to reject both those extremes," Baumgartner said. "I don't get to do the ministry at all if I'm not compliant with the rules of the system, and yet at the same time I want to bring a message to the guys that this *system* is not your lord and master. This system is not the definition of your life, of who you are, and I want you to find a sense of freedom, joy, contentment, and accomplishment, even in the midst of what this place is, even in the face of everything that you have been and can never quite escape. I want to toe the line of the institution on one side, deny the authority of the institution on the other side, and feed my family and pay my mortgage in the process. If that's not the definition of a tightrope, I don't know what is." He concluded: "We live in a system that insists on everything being either black or white, but the reality is just a fog of grays."

Not that the job's uncommonly rough edges are without their pleasures. Intrigues aside, Baumgartner appreciates as well the license to deliver the sort of tough talk that might cost a more conventionally placed pastor his or her job. "On the outside, one can't just say, '*Cut the shit, bitch,*'" Baumgartner has said. At Graterford, by contrast, such speech is well within bounds. "God put you here for a reason?" Baumgartner likes to say. "No he didn't. You were an idiot. Now that you're here, though, what are you gonna do about it?"

While Baumgartner vocally takes pride in his staff—which he refers to as "the most subversive in the institution"—for its ability to operate within the ruling custodial logic without buckling under it, sometimes he is less than confident. "To what extent am I a part of an oppressive system?" Baumgartner once wondered aloud. "To what extent do I subvert an oppressive system, provide opportunities for self-definition in terms other than those that the system provides? For chaplains this is an ongoing struggle." On his more pessimistic days, Baumgartner suspects the administration sees his staff as little more than affable opiate peddlers—feeding inmates false hopes that make them, if nothing else, better prisoners. And because prison management relies on communal substructures to maintain order, theological content is, in this regard, perhaps secondary to social form. As Baumgartner acknowledged, the applicability of the tutelage that helps a man survive prison is severely limited: "The guys are taught how to live *in here*, not how to live out there."

Speaking of oil, I ask Baumgartner about why I haven't smelled any this week. To the best of his knowledge, Baumgartner says, the Moors, the Nation, and Muhammad's Temple are all out. Pulling at another loose thread, I ask him about his comment from Wednesday about "having handed Simpson the——on a platter"—I refer to the notorious street gang. Baumgartner lights up and launches back into narrative.

Well, it all started about a month ago when he got a tip. (Baumgartner pauses to let me *not* ask what precisely he means by a "tip," which I dutifully don't.) The tip was that the gang was using the Thursday-night Spanish service as cover for their meetings. The Spanish regulars were none too pleased, of course, and a couple of them gingerly approached the purported gang members, asked them to leave, and were told to fuck off. Baumgartner waited until Thursday night and went looking for the gangsters. Finding them there, all tattooed and sinister in the back of the chapel, he hung around. After the service, he noticed that the whole crew was deferential to one guy in particular, whom

Baumgartner took to be the leader. Baumgartner fired off an e-mail to security, and the following Thursday, a four-man search team showed up ready to bust them. The gangsters, however, were a no-show. The search team hung out for a while but then left, taking a little bit of Baumgartner's face with them. The following week the team returned, but again, no discernible gang. Baumgartner sensed his stock drop even lower in the security bubble. Finally, as is often the case in jokes, folktales, and other yarns, on the search team's third try, the gangsters appeared. The service was allowed to commence, but then, with the visiting preacher on the dais, the search team struck. They pulled the suspected gangsters into Classroom B, where they patted them down and found evidence connecting them to the gang. I ask what precisely they had. Baumgartner assumes that it was their tattoos that gave them away.

"Oh, so *that's* who those two COs were last night," I say, finally getting it.

This Baumgartner confirms. Having rounded up the majority last week, the COs came back around for one final sweep.

The Imam's office bustles. Guys drop in to fetch their prayer robes, emerging, quite a few *Assalamu alaikums* later, draped in white. Others stay on, laughing and touching. The atmosphere is light, the air perfumed. Salat al-Jum'ah—Friday prayer—will soon begin.

Muslims flow into the chapel—a steady mixture of blues and browns, black kufis and white kufis, mass-produced kufis and makeshift, knotted-cloth kufis, punctuated by the stray uncovered head. The faces—but for one or two, all black—are obscured by beards, full and partial, unkempt and manicured, though here and there a cleanly shaven chin shines out from the rest.

At the doorway to the annex vestibule, Muti dispenses drops of oil from a small plastic squeeze bottle. Spreading the substance between their hands, the recipients trace their fragranced fingers on the backs of their necks and cheeks, before wiping dry onto their shirts whatever vestige of scent might linger.

Inside the annex door, three old heads exchange numbered slips for shoes. Past this bottleneck, cliquey clusters are forming. On the annex's eastern wall, another old head directs traffic, pointing barefoot men to bald patches on the floor. In places, these sprawled bodies hint at the rows they will soon become.

Back in the chapel, I take a front-row seat to watch the crush. Insights sometimes arrive via drive-by: "Write how obedient we was, how disciplined we was. Write good stuff about us," a young Muslim once called out to me without adjusting his gait. More often, engagement is more concerted, with ongoing conversations furthered and new relationships sparked. For gaining insight into Islam at Graterford, such cultivation has been especially vital. For unlike the chapel's Protestant practices, which to a substantial degree manifest legibly on the chapel's surface, Graterford's subterranean Muslim culture required some excavation. By pointing me toward some of what had been lost, the chapel workers started me off. Then, once I'd been told what to look for, the unpast history of Islam at Graterford began to stuff up through the cracks of the ethnographic present.

Given all the things that Islam has meant here, the differences between the fading Warith Deen faction and the ascendant Salafi ought not be overstated. Each asserts there to be one God, a God whose final Revelation was delivered through the Prophet Muhammad in the form of the Qur'an and the Sunnah. For each, a Muslim who has declared his faith is ideally to pray five times a day, be charitable, fast during the Muslim month of Ramadan, and, should he be afforded the opportunity, make pilgrimage to Mecca. The list goes on, well beyond the fundament of the Five Pillars. Not least among this common ground is the unequivocal assertion of Osama bin Laden's apostasy.[13]

But the conflicts are real, too. The obligatory, public rituals provide the main stage of contestation. As the majority, the Salafi nowadays dictate the public terms of the debate. Qasim, the final imam of Masjid Sajdah, noted how because Imam Namir relies on an unsubstantiated hadith, at Jum'ah, he erroneously addresses the community *before* praying; or how on the day of the Eid, "Imam Namir was chanting *Takbir*—God is Great—and the Warith Deen guys were shouting it along with him." But not the Salafi. "The Salafi were just there for the prayer"—meaning, enacting the Sunnah without man-made embellishment.

Mamduh, who before he accepted the Salafi *da'wah* (call) used to pray with Masjid Warith Deen Muhammad, pointed to how his former co-congregants circle their hands, one over the other, prior to eating. "That's a *bid'ah*," an innovation, he says. "All the Prophet says is that one has to say the *Bismillah* before one eats and *el-hamdullilah* afterwards." The followers of Warith Deen are similarly mistaken when they greet one another on Ramadan with the formulae *"Ramadan Kareem"* and *"Ramadan Mubarak"*—the Prophet said neither. Another Ramadan *bid'ah* is their distribution of raisins after the evening prayer, which they do, according to Mamduh, in imitation of the Christian ushers who circulate holiday cards and prayer requests.

For the religiously maximalist Salafi, for whom there is no boundary where the obligations of *ibadah* (religious worship) leave off and something like the private sphere or secular citizenship begins, the Warith Deen group's ceremonial missteps are only the beginning. "We have not left out anything in this book," Qasim quoted from the Qur'an.[14] With every action sanctified, the practices of everyday life become a minefield of potential errors. While all avow the standard prohibitions against alcohol, drugs, fornication, gambling, and eating pork, the Salafi go further. The prohibition against listening to music showcases the thinking. Since music possesses you, it is analogous to drinking, and therefore *haram* (forbidden). Demonstrated, as well, is the gap between such dogmata and people's actual behavior, since though frequently cited, the prohibition, I'm told, is rarely if ever observed here.[15]

That the body is a key site of distinction should by now be clear. As a testament to the thoroughness of their prostrations, some Salafi have scarred foreheads. Less onerous are the Salafis' beards, kufis, and the high-water pants worn to honor a statement of the Prophet that any garment that hangs below the ankle is in the hellfire.[16] By contrast, the Warith Deen guys are, in style, both less uniform and less emphatic. Some have beards, but an equal number sport goatees, and some wear no beard at all. Nor is their clothing particularly telling. They are aware of the hadith about garment length but read it homiletically, as an admonition against wastefulness and the arrogance of the rich man who would let his garments tatter. The prescription, for them, is an ethical one, with pant length being only a symbol. As long as one is being neither profligate nor haughty, he is being a good Muslim. As such, they maintain, it is the Salafi who in their literalist overreach fall short of the Prophet's ideals.

As a place where offense is easily given and taken, the cellblocks are a crucible. Members of each Muslim faction maintain that those in the opposing group lob insults like *kafir* (infidel), *dalala* (deviant), or *la madhhab* (one without loyalty to a school of law). Men on both sides lamented as well the tendency of the other group's youth to pass by the aged without properly greeting them first, as has long been the custom, or by failing to make the proper amends for interpersonal trespasses within the mandated three-day period.[17]

As I canvassed the Muslims from both sides of the aisle, everyone told me to talk to Abdullah Shah, Masjid Warith Deen Muhammad's onetime spiritual leader. In the back of the empty chapel, I asked him what he says when confronted with the prohibition against music. "They know better than to come to me with that stuff. I would say, 'Present me with the proof.' If there is one, I'll abide by it." If Abdullah Shah showed respect for the Salafis' methodology, Mubdi was more polemical. Questioning the aspiration to religious perfection, he asked: "What? Are you going to stop needing to shit just because you're study-ing *Tawhid* [Islamic monotheism]?"

One way to cast these sectarian differences is as a dispute over reli-gious authority.[18] Evincing Salafism's originalist sensibility, Qasim claimed that to know Islam, one has only to look to the Qur'an and the hadith. One needn't get too caught up in distinctions between the vari-ous legal traditions that came after. Making a similar case, but revealing the conduit through which the foundational texts are accessed, Yunus said, "Salafi is about doing what the predecessors did. We're like the Wahabbis. Or what in Egypt was called the Muslim Brotherhood. We're about not introducing any innovations. That's what we do. Don't veer to the left. Don't veer to the right. Sajdah always took the middle course."[19]

Residually attuned to cultural factors, the Warith Deen guys are quick to note how there's nothing middling about the specific form of Islam propagated in the tracts the Salafi acquire directly or, via family members, from West or North Philly bookstores and Salafi websites. Karl, a meandering but incisive Warith Deen old head who first talked me up at the chapel's Veterans Day service, assessed the situation as follows: "They take the old ideas from across the pond and not the lead-ership that's been sent to them. They read these foreign books that's not feasible for our situation in America." By contrast, he explained, "We adhere to the traditions but we use a new method, a new approach, an approach suited to *this* time and place." It is a talking point taken from Warith Deen himself who, back in 1975, borrowing a move from the Ahmadiyya, alluded to himself as a *mujaddid*, a renewer as per the hadith, stating that "every 100 years the religion has to be revised."[20]

Like those in the Nation and the Moorish Science Temple, then, Warith Deen Muhammad's followers, in their embrace of his message, see themselves as privy to a fresh, modern Islam, one culturally suited to the experiences of black people in America. Conversely, the Salafi outsourcing of religious authority to the Arabian Peninsula is indicative, as they see it, of the residual dysfunctions wrought by slavery. In their ignorance of self, the Salafi are easy prey for the Saudis, who exploit black rootlessness, resentment, and, indeed, self-hatred, to spread the Saudis' own nationalist version of Islam. As Karl said: "Many of them are trying to dress and to be like the Arabs because they don't have their own identity. I like who I am, and that's the big difference." The purported self-hatred also accounts for the Salafis' rejection of Warith Deen as an interpreter of the tradition. Defenders of Warith Deen recite the Qur'an's counsel against rejecting a bearer of wisdom "simply because he is one of you." Or as Omar, the aging chapel worker, cut it to the bone: "They don't think a nigger has anything worthwhile to say."[21]

Which, in turn, provides their Salafi detractors the opportunity for amusement. As they see it, Warith Deen Muhammad's demigod status among his flock is embarrassingly reminiscent of his father's onetime position. Just as the members of the Nation used to turn to the newspaper *Muhammad Speaks* to get their marching orders, so today do they subscribe to Warith Deen's *Muslim Journal*. As an interpreter of the tradition, moreover, Warith Deen is a hack. Sure, he might have studied the Sunnah and gone on the *haj*, but he never fully escaped his father's essentially political, and therefore un-Islamic, worldview. As such, his cult is little more than zombie black nationalism. Parodying their purported posture, Mamduh said, "'We don't care about the white man in Europe! We want to hear it from somebody in America!' They want to hear it from somebody who came through the gang wars. They think they shouldn't have to turn to anyone else. But everything they know they learned in 1981!"

For the pluralist Mubdi, the conflict over authority is as much a matter of tone as of content. More than anything, what he objects to is the Salafis' stiff-necked absolutism. He asked rhetorically, "After all the things that African-Americans went through, you're going to tell me what I can and can't read?" In defending his allegiance to Warith Deen, Karl is pragmatic. He's a Muslim because, as he says, "like a good pair of shoes," he feels "comfortable in it." He extolled, as well, the Muslim American Society's economic-empowerment programs that work to retain wealth *within* the black community.[22] Mubdi underscored the same economic operations. "Religion is just a cover," he said, "a tool for extracting emotions. What's really going on is economics."

It is precisely this underlying materialism that, for Qasim, evidences the two groups' "different mindsets." "Our concept is based on religion," he said. "They don't look at it that way. They are interested in politics, getting things together, but the Salafi position is this: We need to get our *own* house in order, and become good Muslims before we can do anything else. But they'll say: *We've got to deal with the real world!* You'll bring them a hadith, and they'll say: *I won't work with that; that was then.* They'll reject verses of the Qur'an. See? Different mindsets." Whatever Warith Deen Islam might be, in Qasim's view it is not religion. "Warith Deen is an *aqeedah* [creed] based on economic empowerment, not on *din* [religion]." By subordinating God to worldly affairs, the very practical-mindedness that to Mubdi and Karl makes their version of Islam worth practicing renders Warith Deen Islam, for Qasim, not merely a misconstruction of Islam, but *shirk* (idolatry), and therefore, in the final analysis, not Islam at all.

The protest politics of their counterparts' youths is to the Salafi another false god. "The Qur'an and Sunnah boys," Qasim said, referring to the former members of Masjid Sajdah, "we're not racists, we're just into the Qur'an and Sunnah." The more accommodationist attitudes into which the Warith Deen guys have matured are little more palatable. "What's up with *that?*" Mamduh said, pointing to the American flag on the cover of the *Muslim Journal.*[23] If for Mamduh the entanglement of faith with patriotism—especially amid the current American military incursions into Muslim lands—is farcical, Karl is unapologetic. Recounting his cohort's evolution out of the Nation of Islam and into the political mainstream, Karl said: "Back in the day we weren't as political as we are today. We were separatists, too. We were told not to vote. When Warith Deen became imam, he made a hundred-and-eighty-degree turn. It was nothing short of a miracle."[24] And now? "I'm as American as Pepsi Cola, hot dogs, and apple pie."

In that way that one is especially irked by someone else's bad behavior that calls one's own foibles to mind, Karl is unforgiving of the Salafis for their abdication of civic pride and civic duty: "They don't understand what America is about: freedom. We have the right to practice our religion. Yes, they're apolitical. Isolate, alienate yourself from everyone else because you don't know how to deal with the rest of humanity. But you shouldn't live like a monk. You should be part of society." Karl noted: "They have politics, but that politics is about alienation."

If, over time, the followers of Warith Deen Muhammad have taken the integrationist route, in their refusal of civic engagement the Salafi have, in a roundabout way, taken up the Nation's mantle of protest. In their uncompromisingly apolitical religious maximalism, they express the "cosmic *No!*" that is one of black religion's defining themes even as, in the same breath, they simultaneously negate the tradition of black religion itself. Whereas the Moorish Science Temple, the Nation of Islam, and the Warith Deen guys continue the Sisyphean pursuit of erecting for themselves, as black men, a place in contemporary America, the Salafi plumb a deeper well. The problem is not political or economic, and it's not about figuring out their true identity as a people. While distancing themselves from such modern distinctions, the Salafi seek to solve those problems, too, but only as fully integrated into the comprehensive web of prescriptions and restrictions mandated for man by God.

Ironically, then, the Salafis' repudiation of political engagement at long last brings Islam at Graterford into proper conformity with what *religion* is supposed to be. Recall that in the Supreme Court's 1965 appropriation of theologian Paul Tillich's "ultimate concern"—which to this day marks the Court's deepest incursion into theology—"political, sociological, or philosophical views" were cast as subordinate, not ultimate, concerns, and deemed therefore unworthy of First Amendment protection.[25] What the secular Court didn't spell out, Tillich himself did: the mistaken "elevation of a preliminary concern to ultimacy" was "idolatry"—or, as the Salafi call it, *shirk*.[26] Mid-twentieth-century white liberal Protestantism and early twenty-first-century black Muslim ultra-orthodoxy have a great many dissimilarities. And yet, it is according to the religious logic they share—a logic that has in time carried the day—that the doddering dinosaurs who follow Warith Deen Muhammad increasingly look to would-be Graterford adapters like quasi-Muslims, and the Salafi hardliners, whose otherworldly piety once evoked for many the self-defeating dreams of hoodwinked slaves, have become, for most here, the guardians of true Islam.

Struggling to make sense of this all, after Jum'ah one Friday, I huddled with Baraka in the chapel and outlined the dynamics of Graterford's Muslim communities as they then appeared to me. When he was done nodding his head at my account, he took my pen and diagrammed black Islam's parentage.

N.O.I.	*Sunni*
Nationalist	Orthodox
Defiant	Passive
Movers	Observers
Encompassing	Exclusive

To which I added, with vocalized question marks:

Particularist	Universalist
Aggressive	Gentle
Foolish	Sophisticated

Baraka made no objection. Where on the chart, I asked him, would he place the Warith Deen Muhammad version of Islam? To my softball, Baraka offered a dialectic. "We combine the wisdom of each," he said. The Nation, he explained, was the father, aggressive and directed. Orthodoxy was the mother, providing instruction of what to do and what not to do. Gesturing toward a more general sociological truth, Baraka observed, "There have always been a group of guys who represented that kind of purism and practiced that kind of intolerance." He added: "A wise member of the moderate middle would wish for the Salafi to continue to grow." That is, nothing is more conducive to the march of progress at the center than vibrant zealotry at the margin. But this takes the long view.

The funniest thing about the Salafi, as Baraka sees it, is that in spite of their vehement renunciation of politics and social action, they continue to stoke the administration's paranoia. "They think that *they* are us," he said, "but they are nothing like us." Meaning, the administration mistakes the avowedly *apolitical* religious radicalism of today's Muslim majority for the *political* radicalism of yesteryear's. What the administration doesn't realize, according to Baraka, is that the Salafi don't have a seditious bone in their collective body. The administration wrings its hands, monitoring the Salafis' presumed Jihadist tendencies, but the paradigm is ill-fitting. Unlike their predecessors, who in pursuit of their rights were willing to adopt *any means necessary*, the Salafi—as Baraka put it—are merely struggling to comport their personal hygiene according to the appropriate seventh-century standard.[27]

Nevertheless, it now stands as common knowledge in the chapel that the FBI is embedding informants at Graterford. Paranoid, perhaps, but could it really be otherwise? In this Age of Terror, in which the protectors of the state have shown little appetite for drawing fine-grained distinctions between, say, Shia and Sunni, or secular nationalist Iraq and Islamist al Qaeda, are we really to expect the authorities to distinguish between the Nation of Islam and the Salafi? And that goes double for today's "jailhouse Muslims," who, fantastically conjured in the muddled shadows of two mythic types—the black nationalist revolutionary and the bin Ladenist terrorist—can only spur public paranoia.

For what it's worth, in my time in the chapel, I've heard *nothing* remotely resembling Jihadist speech—though, admittedly, a would-be Jihadist would know better than to talk to a snooping scholar of religion about it. But the anxiety—and the concomitant excesses of control that the anxiety underwrites—is overdetermined. Between indiscriminate violence in Muslim countries and the mass incarceration of African-American men at home, if it was our express intention, could we design a system any more conducive to generating insurrectionist ire among black Muslim men than the one we've already erected?[28]

Donning his trademark rasta-colored knit kufi, Sabir sidles down the pew and starts talking to me like we're already mid-conversation: "The thing you need to understand about all of this," he says, "is the way that all of us coexist here." Soft-spoken almost to the point of inaudibility, Sabir is a People Against Recidivism counselor and an old Nation guy from Holmesburg days.

"How do you pull it off?" I ask.

"It stems from a willingness to endure and survive together. If there was conflict, there would be a lot of useless taking of life."

"Are you talking about the Muslims or about everybody?" I ask him.

"Everybody," he says. "Men in each religion have the same capabilities. Each has a right to believe and to practice that belief. We don't intrude on the other."

"And how is this done?" I ask.

"Because wiser minds prevail," he says. "If more ignorant minds were in positions of power, then ignorant things would happen."

What role do the chaplains play?

"Nah, not much," he says. "It starts with us. We've been functioning this way long before there even was an outside imam." Sabir relates some history, about the old days of the basement mosques, and about other splinter groups that met in the school and the hospital—most of which I'm familiar with.

I ask Sabir how he would characterize his own Islamic affiliation.

"I'm part of the Sunni group," he says, "but I'm a follower of the teachings of Warith Deen Muhammad."

Sabir surveys the gathering throng: "There was a time when they wouldn't let even four or five of us walk together. It took a lot of work to get this."

The chapel is mostly bare. On the pews neighboring mine, a handful of men sit and listen; while spanning the T of the dais and center aisle, seven Warith Deen old heads—Baraka, Peanut, and Carlos at the top, Ahmed and Mikhael halfway down, and Chuck Crews and Sabir at the bottom—honor tradition by providing security. Some stand in place, while others roam. Now and again, as the sentries pace past one another, heads are dropped, and whispers, nods, and smiles are shared.

"Avoid Shaytan."

The injunction comes from the speaker on the dais, which is broadcasting the Imam's *khutbah* (Friday sermon) from the annex. "We pray for God to give us strength to follow the Prophet," Namir says in his accented, almost tonal English. "We need two things, according to the Qur'an. We need hope, and we need fear of Allah. We cannot be arrogant as to be sure of where we are going, but we need to have hope. That is our prayer."

Last week's *khutbah*, the Imam reminds the assembled men, was about a hadith that states: "Beware of unlawful things. If you distance yourself from the unlawful, you'll be the most righteous on earth. And if you are contented with what Allah has provided for you, you will be the richest." Today's *khutbah* turns to that hadith's second part: "Be good, be kind to your neighbor, and you will be a believer. Whoever is good to his neighbor, that is the proof of his faith."[29]

For faith to be complete, the Imam says, one must respect his neighbors. In Islam, the Imam explains, it is forbidden to cause one's neighbor to live in fear, just as it is forbidden to take life or destroy someone else's property. He quotes the Prophet Muhammad: "One must stop such things if he is to be counted among the believers." As additional support, the Imam cites hadith from al-Bukhari and al-Muslim—the two most prolific and authoritative of the ninth-century compilers of hadith.

With the exception of Sabir and Peanut, who remain standing by the rear chapel door, the rest of the security detail is now huddled by the speaker.

"True faith keeps one from doing atrocities to his neighbor. If, however, a man's faith is only surface, and not affecting his actions, then the Prophet wanted nothing to do with him. People give excuses, that his neighbor is from another race, that his neighbor is from another culture, that he speaks another language. Islam doesn't care about any of that *crap*. What Islam is saying is that you are all one.

"And what if he is not a Muslim?" the Imam asks. "Well, the cook in the Prophet's home, he was instructed to give food to the neighbor, who was *not* a Muslim. So Muslim, not Muslim, it doesn't matter." While I've never heard it expressly avowed, it is claimed by many of their detractors that the Salafi preach against associating with non-Muslims. For the Imam in his *khutbah* to tack directly into this thicket of contention strikes me as daring.

In Arabic and English, the Imam recites another hadith in which the Prophet declared: *Be good to your neighbor.* "And what is a neighbor?" he asks. "Count forty houses to your left, forty houses to your right, forty houses in front of you. All these people who live in these houses, they are all your neighbors. That is why it says: 'Be good to your neighbor and you will be a believer.' And that is why we make prayer to give us *iman*" (faith). "Because without *iman* we're nowhere."

Qasim, Masjid Sajdah's final imam and, for many Salafi, Graterford's true imam to this day, arrives in a white prayer robe and a harried air. Knowing the Salafis' reservations about the Imam's authority, I've long taken Qasim's perennial Friday lateness as a subtle signal—nestled within his obedience to the Prophet's mandate that one listen to the

Friday *khutbah*—of insubordination toward the DOC employee who happens to be delivering it. I haven't begrudged him his apparent resentment. The animating disputes between the Salafi and the Warith Deen guys strike me as real and pressing and cut to the heart of how one is to stand in relation to his maker, to his fellow man, and, therefore, to himself.

And this is before one pays any mind to the burdens and coercions of history.

In the chapel one fall Friday, a man I didn't know approached me and introduced himself as Jamar. In order to understand the split between the Salafi and his own group, Masjid Warith Deen Muhammad, Jamar said, I needed to factor in the "gang tendency in African-American culture." It was hardly the first time at Graterford that I'd encountered gangs used as a heuristic. Most commonly, the gang is invoked to disparage some party not currently present, whether they be the Warith Deen guys, Muslims in general, or some other faction. More ecumenically, Bible-believing Christians speak of gangs when calling out those seen as concerning themselves unduly with religion's ceremonial and sociological components. One, it is said, has a *relationship* with God, but has a *gang relationship* with his religion.

Not until talking with Jamar, however, had I encountered someone who evoked the gang in a way that implicated his *own* group as much as the other guy's. I was all ears. Jamar explained that when guys get to prison, they tend to gravitate to the people they knew on the outside, which for many of them means their fellow gang members. The next time I talked to someone, he said, I should find out what part of Philly he grew up in. What I would find, he promised, is that the vast majority of Sajdah guys grew up in either West Philly or North Philly, while the vast majority of Warith Deen guys grew up in South Philly or North Philly. "When I look around during Jum'ah, I see it plain as day," Jamar said, sweeping his forearm across the chapel. "North Philly guys standing along the wall over here," he pointed. "South Philly guys over here," he pointed again. The exchange lasted fewer than five minutes, but it was as ground-shifting to me as it would later be astonishing to Teddy and Khalifa that anyone could be oblivious to something so obvious.

Returning to the office after Jum'ah, I asked Baraka, Kaz, Teddy, and Sayyid where they'd grown up. South Philly, I learned. In fact, Kazi, Teddy, and Sayyid had grown up together on the same city block. I burst out laughing. What I'd taken as a paragon of ecumenism—of Christians and Muslims who, stuffed in cramped quarters, managed to do a great deal more than merely coexist—was, in addition to that, *also* just a bunch of old friends hanging out.

That very night I caught up at length with Qasim. Because Masjid Sajdah's former imam is standoffish, because I am wary of forcing myself on people, and because of my intuitive and conditioned loyalties to Baraka and his crew, we'd not yet sat down together. I proposed that we do so, and he agreed.

Belying his brusque public persona, one-on-one Qasim proved exceedingly gracious. I had some questions about some of the Qur'anic verses and hadith I'd heard cited, so, pulling books off of the Imam's shelf, Qasim answered my questions in sequence. I queried him about the early history of Sunni Islam in Philadelphia and the days of Masjid Sajdah. Then I probed the conflict between the Salafi and the followers of Warith Deen Muhammad. While he was initially reticent to say anything, wary of stoking the fires of *fitnah* (conflict), eventually he opened up about that, too.

When it was almost time for lockup, Qasim showed me a yellowed book-pressed clipping from the *Philadelphia Tribune*, a black newspaper, about his case. It had been a murder case, and the article focused on the plea for clemency made by a local civic organization on Qasim's behalf. When the killing took place, Qasim was sixteen and his codefendant only a year his senior. The victim, age twenty-four, was "a well known heroin pusher" affiliated with the Black Mafia and the Nation of Islam, who, according to the article, had been "trying to put pressure on them to sell narcotics." The boys were noncompliant. A fight ensued. The young man was shot dead. Whereas his codefendant struck a deal with the DA and got off with a few years, Qasim refused to cop a plea, maintaining throughout the trial that he'd been acting only in self-defense. The jury didn't see it that way, and at age seventeen, for killing a guy in the Nation, the future imam of Masjid Sajdah was sentenced to life in prison without the possibility of parole. This was in 1974.

Like many of Graterford's juvenile lifers, Qasim's manner has the rough edges of a man raised by this place. Qasim's full beard is almost done graying, and he is recently married. He is learned in the tradition, and, as the Salafi imam, is often asked to settle disagreements. As imam, he also takes it as his duty to sniff out percolating strife and head it off before anyone loses control. As someone who, temperamentally, would just as soon be left alone with his books, Qasim doesn't necessarily excel at this task. Though Imam Namir, who once a season has Qasim deliver the Friday *khutbah,* says he's improving.

As far as his serial lateness goes, Qasim assured me he intends no disrespect. He expressed horror when I told him how it looked and vowed to do more to nullify this possible interpretation. He's not trying to make any sort of political statement, he said, it's just that he works in the prison's underwear plant, where, in a month, when he makes his bonus, he nets $135 for 120 hours of work. The longer he's away for Jum'ah, the less money he makes. He needs the money primarily for the phone calls he places to his wife, which for a fifteen-minute call cost five dollars. Not infrequently, as I'm told, the lines cross, and the system, having mistaken the crossed line for the unlawful engagement of a third party, terminates the call. When that happens, Qasim loses his money and, frequently, depending on who's around, also his place in line.[30]

"That is why we have freedom," the Imam continues. "So we can do what we want to do, and so we can be accountable for it. We have a choice: Do what the Qur'an says or do what I have to do? Doing what I *have to* do—that is the language of *jahaliyya,*" the period of ignorance that preceded Islam. "To be in *jahaliyya* is to be handcuffed, because that is what the Qur'an says. The Prophet Muhammad, *salla ilahu alehi wasalam*" [Peace Be Upon Him] says *byoot*—houses—showing that your neighbor is not merely the house *next* to you, but many, many houses.

"There is an *ayah* [a Qur'anic verse] that says: 'When a conscious greeting is offered you, you should greet with an even more conscious greeting in return.'[31] Greeting one another is part of being good to your neighbor. Allah takes careful account of all things that we do.

"Another *ayah* says: 'Restrain anger and pardon all men.'[32] Don't carry a grudge. This is part of what's destroying us. You can't give it up: revenge. You don't do anything *now* because you don't have a chance. You're nice, you're good, for thirty years even, but then if you get out, all those thirty years are out the window." Again, I'm a bit taken aback by how confrontational the Imam is being. "In Islam, with *iman*"—faith—"you say: 'In *jahaliyya* this is what I will do, but he—the one who did bad to you—is lucky because now I am in Islam, so I will pardon him.' Allah loves those who do right.

"It's not easy. But nothing is easy in this life. The Qur'an says that, too. It's not easy, but it's the same for everybody. That it isn't easy is no excuse to not be kind and humble in our nature.

"We make reference to the *salaf*, the men who received direct, pure, Islamic education from the Prophet. They are human beings like us, but they are special, because they let Islam be their lead. In *jahaliyya*, Umar—you know Umar," he refers to the second caliph. "In *jahaliyya*, Umar was a hater and persecutor of Islam. And then look at what he became. He became the Umar that you know!

"So you must know *jahaliyya* before you know Islam. You want to know all the bad things that happened in *jahaliyya*, then when you make the transition into Islam, you will appreciate the difference it makes in your life. In *jahaliyya*, life is nothing. It has no value. For Umar, for example, his intention had been to kill Rasul Allah"—the Messenger of God—"because that's the language he knows. All he knows is the sword. Like guns today. But when Islam opened his heart and when he took the *shahaddah*"—the Imam recites the declaration of faith in Arabic and then repeats it in English: " '*There is no God but Allah and Muhammad is the Messenger of Allah.*'

"When they found out that Umar became a Muslim, those in *jahaliyya* said, 'Oh, we are in trouble.' *ALLAHU AKBAR!*" the Imam yells. "Before Umar, everyone could say only, 'Allahu Akbar' "—he drops to a whisper. "But after Umar came into Islam, Umar told everyone to sing it aloud. Umar was transformed! ALLAHU AKBAR!

"That's the real Islam, the Islam that can *transform*. From bad to good and from good to best. '*Be good to your neighbor and you will be a believer.*' It's not me who's saying that. It's Rasul Allah who's saying that."

Through the speaker on the stage, I hear the Imam's hushed voice recite a benediction in Arabic. After which, I needn't see any longer to know, he sits down, then stands again, for the brief, second *khutbah*.

First in Arabic, then in English, the Imam reads in honor of Hijjah, the final lunar month, what, he will later explain, is commonly regarded as Muhammad's final sermon, in which the Prophet, Peace Be Upon Him, counsels the Muslim to respect the life and property of every Muslim and forgo violence and usury, and warns that he will one day face the ultimate judgment. He instructs the believer to treat his women well, to worship five times daily, fast during Ramadan, pay his alms, and make pilgrimage to Mecca if he can afford it. "Every Muslim is the brother of another Muslim," the Prophet says. "You are all equal. Nobody has superiority over another except by piety and good action." Declaring himself to be the last prophet, Muhammad instructs the Muslim that should he abide by the laws and examples laid out in the Qur'an and the Sunnah, he will never go astray.[33]

A silence, and then quietly, more Arabic. The few guys remaining in the chapel file into the vestibule. Then the muezzin recites the call to prayer.

The first half-dozen times I attended Jum'ah, I observed the men worship from the shoe area inside the annex, where four rows of plastic chairs are set up for guys too old, infirm, or, it is said, too lazy, to sit on the floor. I sat, unmoving, my head bowed slightly. Wary of giving any indication of trying to pass, I was equally wary of being reduced to a gawker by the mesmerizing spectacle of hundreds of uniformed black male bodies lined up in disciplined rows uniformly standing, bowing, prostrating, and chanting. Unable to resist taking what felt like fugitive glances, I soon found myself in the habit of taking in Jum'ah blindly from the chapel.

Prayer comes to an end. In the annex doorway, men and their shoes reunite in a jumble, and the chapel begins to fill. I try to make it back to the office but, with the door to the main corridor still apparently locked, the mass of bodies is too dense.

The office, when I finally arrive, is no less packed. Unable to secure a vacated corner, I stand by the door and look on as a tattooed blue shows Khalifa a stack of photographs of faces and places they must share in common.

From the vestibule, the unmistakable command of authority can be heard scattering the Muslims back to their blocks. A minute later, a "whitecap"—as Graterford's ranking officers are known—steps into the office.

"All right," the captain says, "move it out." And the remaining Muslims do.

When the office is empty, a scowling Teddy emerges from Keita's office. "Close that door!" he shouts acidly, traversing the room. Teddy kicks the doorstop, and the door slams shut, trapping Papa and me inside the office's suddenly soured air.

Dumbly, I follow Baraka back into the Imam's office. The intensity of Jum'ah now fully dissipated, I find the world largely stripped of coherence.

"So, what's going on?" he asks.

"The Imam was on fire today, no?" I say.

Baraka agrees. He "felt violated almost," and was "forced to think hard about real and present things in his life." I think back to Wednesday's conversation and Baraka's avowed reluctance to have his mood affected by another. "That's why some of the guys don't like him," Baraka says. "He makes them think about things they'd rather not think about. So, what's going on?" he repeats.

Incoherent from fatigue and exuberant from the power of Jum'ah, I splutter out something to that effect.

Baraka looks at me askance. "Oh, I don't trust you."

"Bar," I say, "you know me. I hide my elephants right in plain sight."

"Sure you do," he says, "but there are some smells that even sights can't see." I don't understand, and tell him so. He demonstrates his frustration at my noncomprehension. That he is being abstruse, I am certain, but whether deliberately or not, I cannot say. The Imam arrives and sits behind his desk. I commend him on his *khutbah* and he thanks me.

When next I register stimulus, Baraka is full tilt on a rant about how everything has its threshold, and everything has a safety valve where its maker can shut it off. He speaks of the natural order generated by the Creator in which everything is in its proper place and will remain in its proper place long after we're all gone. Lost as I am, I nonetheless try to counter, suggesting that the existing order is far more fragile than he gives it credit for, and that ecologically, for example, there is no guarantee that the earth as we know it will be around for our children. He scoffs at that, saying that we overestimate our own capability. We are talking past each other. Mistaking what I take to be mutual confusion for disagreement, he turns to the Imam to arbitrate.

"What do you think, brother Imam?" he asks Namir.

"Oh, I agree with you, Baraka," the Imam says without pressing for clarification.

Satisfied, Baraka looks at me.

"Oh, come on, Bar," I say. "He's only placating you. He didn't even hear what you said."

"Is that true?" Baraka asks.

"Of course I am," the Imam concedes. "I have to live with you!"

Apropos of little, I ask Baraka if he's seen Werner Herzog's *Grizzly Man*, which I've been chewing over since I Netflixed it the other night. Using found footage, the film documents the story of a wayward soul named Timothy Treadwell, who for many summers had lived in Alaska among the grizzlies, until one day when, with his camera rolling but the lens cap still on, he and his girlfriend were killed and devoured by a bear.[34] Baraka knows of it but hasn't seen it. I tell him he should if he gets a chance. He asks me why I've thought of it. It's crossed my mind, I say, that a comparison could be drawn between Treadwell's Alaskan folly and my time at Graterford. Should I somehow manage to get myself mauled in here, I say, I can picture the perspective from which that outcome would seem a fitting comeuppance for such deathwishingly dilettantish behavior. As I'm tiredly reporting this private musing to Baraka, I grow sickened by my likening of men like him to wild beasts and let it drop.

Only much later, upon further reflection, will I come to realize that I needn't have been so prudish, and that, if anything, such an obliquely associated dangerousness is, to Baraka, not the least bit unflattering. Not that the man is interested in being confused for a devil, only that he'd even less like to be mistaken for a saint. For a fox like Baraka, who only plays at being the hedgehog, the role of saint is simply too dull. For my benefit he may play the character of the Magical Negro, dutifully helping this clueless but well-meaning white boy along on my way, but then he may lurch into a more menacing persona.[35] For sure, some of this is about the pleasure of play. It is also a matter of style. Not to be overlooked, however, in Baraka's performance of a self that falls on the shadier side of virtue are the dictates of his ethics. For unless it is my fantasy, and I don't believe it is, Baraka regards the drive to mere goodness as a temptation to be resisted.

For what, in this world, without final judgment or even medial relief, is the point to goodness? Once, acute goodness might have gotten a man home, but in this era of life without the possibility of parole or commutation, even the best of men can't win that game. And so, just as there is neither sense nor honor in groveling before the parole board, neither is it fruitful to go about proclaiming one's moral transformation. Both can do little more than reaffirm the contempt of those who would disdain you, and reaffirm the pity of those who (more grotesquely still) might wish to be of help.

And so, instead of the vanity of goodness, Baraka has, over the years, cultivated a character of a different kind. It is a persona that has served him well in the chapel, and perfectly positions him to flypaper the next intellectual or otherwise sticky stranger to come along. His is a social strategy that takes without asking the recognitions and license that all the chapel's *transformed* men plaintively clamor for, and proceeds from there into terrain as yet uncharted. If not quite beyond good and evil, Baraka is, at the very least, spectacularly askew of these prefabricated poles.

Let the less talented content themselves with the pursuit of goodness. Baraka's game is something rarer and more refined. What Baraka manages to be is *interesting*.

Left by ourselves, Namir and I fall into an ongoing conversation about recidivism. Of all the chaplains, Namir is the one on whom the problem weighs heaviest. Recidivism weighs on him since there are more young Muslims than Christians, and so the revolving door leads right past his desk. Moreover, as a relative newcomer, he still retains the greenhorn's capacity to be shocked by things to which others around him have become inured, such as the frequency in which a young man living in the city of Philadelphia will pick up a gun and shoot another young man. To make sense of the weird corner of the world he has found himself in, he draws on a hadith foretelling the final days. One of the signs, it is said, is that "men will be killing one another without cause. They will be asked why they kill one another and they will say, 'I don't know.'"[36]

When guys are leaving on parole, Namir tells them, "Just remember to feel Allah wherever you go." But most return. The other day, he reports incredulously, he asked Mamduh about one guy who recently got out. Mamduh told him, "Oh, he's good." But then, Namir says, his voice rising in pitch, "Just the other day I saw him in the chapel and found out he'd been in county for the last six weeks! And when I see him at Jum'ah he acts as if nothing happened!"

For all the religious discipline they cultivate on the inside, I say, no analogous structure exists to support them on the street.

This the Imam concedes. More basic than that, though, he says, is the problem that going to prison is, for them, a legitimate option. "That's why it's not fair to compare these guys to people who come to this country with nothing in their pockets. Because the immigrants, even those who don't have anything, don't know that prison is an option that's there for when things get tough. Nothing is easy in this world," he repeats from his *khutbah*. "Like your project," he says, commending me for the hours I'm putting in this week.

Embarrassed by his praise, I look away, and notice, as I have on many occasions, the two index cards on his desk laminated under clear tape. Written in Arabic in time-faded pencil are two verses: "For the sake of them, don't let your soul flee" and Jacob's instruction to his sons: "Do not lose hope. Go and find your brother."[37]

Keita waddles in. Lately he's been gravitating to the Imam's office for its more functional radiator. The three of us get to talking about Hamas's landslide victory in yesterday's Palestinian parliamentary elections, which Keita interprets as a huge *screw you* to President Bush and to Israeli prime minister Ariel Sharon, but which Namir and I presume reflects factors closer to the ground.

As the Imam packs away his desktop for the weekend, Keita asks if he thinks their rumored pay raise might come through. Namir hasn't heard one way or another, but he figures to find out now.

From his pocket, Keita pulls a handful of Reese's peanut-butter cups, which he extends to me, and I take. He saw Sayyid, he says. The Imam asks how he seemed. His mouth full of Teddy's chocolate, Keita reports that he seemed fine.

When we're alone, Keita explains what happened earlier to piss Teddy off. Returning from the Restricted Housing Unit, Keita found the office overrun with prisoners who'd "come to Jum'ah" but weren't, in fact, at Jum'ah. He called Teddy into his office and instructed him to shoo them out. Teddy took the instruction as an ascription of personal blame.

"I didn't tell them to come down!" Teddy snapped back.

"Okay," Keita responded. "Then I'll get someone to do it for you." So he picked up the phone and called for the whitecap.

First back, Teddy flops down at Al's desk.

He's having it real hard, he says, rubbing his eyes. Every night he's up until five a.m., and he hasn't talked to God all week. He says he's thinking: "I tried it your way, Lord, but I'm just gonna do it my way now."

I understand better Teddy's moodiness this week. As he's told me, Christ is his "venting system"—how he "disposes" of his negative feelings. If he's not talking to Jesus, then he's lugging all that garbage around.

I understand, I say, how I *don't* understand just how tough it must be to stay positive in here, but that it's obvious to me how hard he works at it. So if he's talking about it, I know he must truly be suffering.

"You don't know the half of it," he says. "You don't see the stuff that I see. Guys crying in their cells at night. Guys who've just given up, who just lie there all day in their cells."

"How many guys are like that?" I ask.

"Sheez, I don't know. You got cell after cell of them."

"What percentage?"

"Maybe half," he says. "You'd just never see these dudes, these dudes that just lie there. These dudes never come off the blocks. They don't get visits. They have no connection to the outside world. They just know that this is the rest of their life, and they're gonna die here. I don't even like to tell 'em I have visits."

It's that much harder on the white guys, Khalifa told me last week. Black people are accustomed to hardship. But the white guys, they've had so much and have fallen so far. That's why only the white guys kill themselves. Khalifa loves himself too much to do that to himself. Plus, he remembers that if he does do it he'll burn in hell forever. But the white guys, they feel like they've already lost everything and have nothing left to lose.

I ask Teddy when he's next going to see his lady.

"Tomorrow." He closes his eyes, shakes his head, and says, "Thank you, Jesus." She'll get here at seven, first thing, he says, so she can be in the visiting room when it opens at nine. All told, they'll have six hours together.

"That's a beautiful thing," I say. "You're a fortunate man."

"Ain't *that* the truth," he says.

I ask where Al is. Al never comes down Friday nights, Teddy reminds me, he's got his Bible study. Who runs the Bible study on D Block? I ask. Teddy doesn't know—he's still new there.

Teddy had been on B Block, but switched to D a few weeks back "for a change." An honor block with lighter security measures, B was just too dead, he said, which was making him soft and was lulling him into a dangerous place. I've made no attempt to confirm Teddy's account, but it wouldn't surprise me if his move was somehow less than voluntary, just as it seemed to me likely that his recent block detention hadn't been for rejecting the advances of a female CO who refused to take no for an answer.

Teddy says that having tired of the squabbling, he doesn't participate in block Bible studies anymore. Guys would agree about the stories, but when they'd talk about an individual verse, everyone would just spout off about what they thought it meant, and it would get wild. In defending their understandings, guys would get angry. "Some guys just can't take the disagreement," Teddy says. "Skins aren't thick enough." He pivots. "But the blocks is crazy, for real."

"Not like it used to be," I say, showing that I'm down.

"No," he concedes, "not like it used to be, but these dudes is still crazy here." He launches into a story he's told me before, about how, a few years back, there was this new kid on his block, a wide-eyed kid who'd just fallen for the first time and a couple of bad actors brought him under their wing, were looking after him, "protecting him," all the while letting the kid fall farther and farther into their debt. They were setting the kid up to be victimized sexually. Teddy watched the whole thing unfold, how these vultures were setting the kid up to turn him out. So even though he doesn't like to get involved, he went to the kid, who seemed like a nice kid. Teddy took the kid aside and said, "You know they're going to rape you, right?" Of course the kid was shocked. "You see, when you're new to this place you don't understand how things are," Teddy explains. But Teddy reassured the kid: "Don't worry, I'll make sure nothing happens to you." So the kid distanced himself from the predators. But then, when they figured out it was Teddy who'd thwarted their plan, the would-be rapists came looking for him. Teddy said to them: "Look, if you want him you're gonna have to go through me." Promising Teddy they'd get him later, the guys left. One evening soon thereafter, they came and stepped to Teddy in his cell. Teddy told them to back off but they wouldn't, and so—bam!—Teddy clocked one of them. The guy stepped again and—bam!—Teddy put him down again. But that's when Teddy realized that he'd been "brought back to that *conviction*" (he uses the word to indicate something like moving back over to his lower self) and he felt remorse at having resorted to violence. So he said, *"Come here!"* He pantomimes picking a guy up and pulling him into an embrace. And that's the story of how by means of righteous vengeance Teddy saved an innocent from being raped, and at the same time managed to overcome the impulse to commit righteous vengeance.

With a squint and a pout, I evince my incredulity about Teddy's story. The moral clarity, courage, *and* mercy described strike me as an unlikely combination, especially when the purported hero happens to be the narrator. Teddy waves off my skepticism.

Kazi slides in and sits down.

I tell Teddy how my heart broke a little bit yesterday during Liberty Ministries when I realized that he hadn't had mayonnaise in years. He has no clue what I'm talking about. "Jay and the sandwiches?" I try.

He bursts out laughing. "Nah, I was just messing with him." Apparently, he loves messing with Jay. "That guy is so *serious*. Like a sandwich is gonna save a homeless guy . . . please!" Only via a sucker's pity, it would seem, does mayonnaise become a coveted delicacy.

I ask Kaz if the Imam's *khutbah* hit him hard today. I know from Teddy that some Muslims—Kazi and Sayyid among them, I can only presume—criticize the Imam for passing judgment on guys for things like violating parole, when he's never had to walk in their shoes.

"Well, you know," Kaz says, chuckling in deflection, "I'm used to his *jawns*." *Jawns* is Philly for *joint*, an all-purpose nominal stand-in.

Teddy pounces. "Don't duck the question!"

"Ah, let him duck it," I say, trying to respect Kazi's reluctance to talk shit.

We jump to the less precarious topic of illicit contraband. "These dudes is crazy," Teddy says. "You know there're dudes have *cell* phones up in here? I'm telling you, these dudes is crazy. Some of these guys talk to their lady every day. But what are you gonna say?" Teddy's voice deepens its pitch: *"Yeah, baby, I'm lying here in my cell . . ."*

Khalifa arrives with a plastic-wrapped brick of tea bags. Teddy puts up the kettle, and when prompted, I pull a tower of Styrofoam cups from Al's desk drawer.

The water is boiled and poured. The tea bags are dropped and steeped. Sugar packets are torn, emptied, and the resulting mixture is poured back and forth between two Styrofoam cups. Refusing their offer of tea, I accept a cup of steaming water, which I cradle beneath my chin for warmth.

Once again, Teddy shepherds conversation to the topic of conjugal visits. This time he wants to know what the chaplains think.

Wondering if this is perhaps not for me to report, I say, simply, "We all agree."

"Agree to what?" Khalifa presses.

"That when you suppress basic human drives, they're gonna squeeze out in some other way."

Khalifa seems satisfied by my answer. "It just doesn't make any sense from a management perspective," he says. "Driving dudes crazy like that."

"It's not motivated by a desire to manage," I say. "It's motivated by a desire to punish." I ask if whether, in spite of the lack of lawful opportunity, men nonetheless manage to have sex with their wives.

Teddy has, he says, in the visiting room once. He got sent to the hole for it, though. This was in 2000, back when his mom was dying. Even after his ninety days, he was barred from receiving visitors for six months, so he didn't get to see her before she died. When the probationary period ended, his brothers and sisters came to see him. Teddy told them: "Look, the one who held us all together, she's gone now. I don't want to see none of y'all anymore. I'll see y'all when I'm out of here." And he hasn't seen any of them since.

We talk further nonsense. Sex, contraband, fighting. Khalifa and Teddy trade allusions to their bygone youths during the era that was theirs, before they were drawn into this crazy time warp where, according to Teddy, old heads argue endlessly about how things are when what they're really arguing about is how things were in 1975.

They reminisce about the "schools" they got sentenced to. Khalifa didn't enter the system until he was pushing eighteen, but Teddy was fourteen when he first got sentenced to a youth facility. That place, he says, was *far worse* than this jail is now. Much more violent. Unlike this place, rape was prevalent there, and the only way to survive was to fight. So Teddy learned to fight. What he didn't learn to do was read. It was only later on, well into adulthood, when he'd been in Graterford for some time, that he learned how to do that. He'd always passed like he could, but the shame was beginning to wear him down. His wife would beg him to write her cards, and he wanted to, but he couldn't. So one day he told his wife: "I have a secret that only God knows." He showed her a letter he'd started, which demonstrated his illiteracy. "I'm so sorry, baby!" Lily said, and took him in her arms. And ashamed as he was, he hauled his ass down to the school and got himself some help. But more than from the tutoring, he learned to read in his cell, from his Bible. And then one day he finally *got* it. Able to read with some proficiency, he finally understood what Jesus was saying. After that he was able to participate in Bible studies—participate for real, not just like another faker who comes down and gives a bunch of testimony to cover up the fact that he can't read what the Word says.

I say I hadn't realized that that's what was going on.

Of course, Teddy says, that's what testimonies are for. So that guys who can't read can have a Bible study of their own. He used to be the same way, he says. And now look at him—he knows the Bible practically by heart. And even though he's only got a GED, Teddy's told me, the administration respects him, and the other guys look up to him.

So they didn't learn how to read, but they did learn how to fight. They would fight in closets the size of Baumgartner's bathroom, fewer than three foot square. So he learned to fight like *this*, he demonstrates, ducking in and under, springing up and jabbing tight. Amid the punches, Teddy again references the vigilante justice he was forced to exact in support of the kid who'd nearly been raped. Once again I play like I know better. This time, seeking to tip the balance, I try to enlist Khalifa in my skepticism, but Khalifa is having none of it.

"Look," Khalifa says, "I lied when I was back on the street, but as soon as I got life in prison, I didn't have to lie anymore." To counter the idea that as a "jailhouse Muslim" he's merely faking his faith, Mamduh once said something similar: "I don't know who we're trying to impress," he said, looking from side to side. "Ain't nobody round here to impress."

Feeling rebuked, I try to roll with it. "I never learned how to fight," I say. "It's different when you're Jewish. When I was a kid, all I was taught about fighting was that if I was mugged I ought to give the muggers whatever they asked for. That's what Jews are taught."

Khalifa looks at me cross-eyed. "All parents teach their kids that. That's not a Jewish thing. That's just common sense."

Just to have something to say, I ask, "So did you guys know any Jews growing up?"

"Yeah, there was *one* Jew," Teddy says. Once, he explains, the neighborhood had lots of them, but by the time he and 'Lifa were coming up, there was only one left. "He was the grocer, and your mom bought insurance from him, and before school started in the fall, you'd buy your school clothes from him. And then, on the last Friday of the month, after he made his rounds to collect his insurance checks, he was the guy you would rob!" Teddy cracks up and solicits from me a five of medium height.

I take him to be joking.

"No, it's true," Khalifa insists.

"Huh," I say, referring back to Tuesday's conversation. "And you don't think that maybe the muggings had something to do with why the Jews left the neighborhood?"

Now it's their turn to be incredulous—incredulous that I would so blatantly mistake an effect for a cause.

"Nah," Khalifa says, "they left because they finished taking all the money out."

We've been here before.

"Speaking of Jews," I say, "I'm late for a date with my peoples."

"Oh, that's right," Teddy says, "it's Friday." Generally, when I take my leave, Teddy complains that I spend all my time with the Jews and the Muslims, but tonight he raises no protest.

In the bustling vestibule, I happen upon Damon, the Rastafarian, and Rudy, the prisoner leader of St. Dismas. Both are here for rehearsal, Damon for Sunday choir practice in the chapel, and Rudy for his group the Mighty Way, which uses the conference room. The two middle-aged men cut quite the Afrocentric pair—Damon with his dreadlocks, wooden bead necklace, and black leather Africa medallion, and Rudy with his long braids and thick beard. In addition to a romantic commitment to a promised land lost, at one time such symbols must have also signaled fiery youth. No longer.

They ask me what I've been up to, and I enthusiastically report back.

"You think a lot's going on now?" Damon asks. "You should have seen it before '95. We had Bible studies every day of the week."

"It wasn't just the Christians that were affected by the raid," Rudy adds. "They took away the beautiful Muslim space downstairs, too. They let the Jews keep their place upstairs as a study, but they moved their services to the annex. That was the compromise."

Pulling on a new thread, I ask about Bible studies on the block.

Not much going on there, they agree.

"The COs try to snuff them out," Damon says. "Whenever they come upon three or four of us together."

"What they're really concerned about," Rudy adds candidly, "is that if they let four or five Christians meet, then the Muslims will want to meet, too, and then suddenly you'll have ten Muslims meeting."

Damon recalls the best Bible study from back in the day. It took place in the school, and "the teacher would do hermeneutics." I ask Damon what he means.

"I mean going back to the original word," he explains. "Because the original word in the ancient Hebrew can mean so many different things." Among those here who've experimented with such methods, biblical Hebrew seems endowed with an inordinate amount of linguistic play. Rather than seeing the elasticity of meaning they encounter in Hebrew as a property of language as such, they appear to regard Hebrew, specifically, as some sort of *Ursprache*, with a unique mystical openness. An analogous Hebraic exception is found in allusions to the Hebrew "culture" of the Old Testament. For while Teddy and Al are quick to identify the prohibition against eating shellfish as a "custom of the people," they would never think to historicize similarly, say, Paul's attitudes toward homosexuality. And so, the fact that a man's access to God is circumscribed by his culture remains, in the chapel, more or less, a Jewish problem.

"*Shabbat shalom*," Damon shouts over my shoulder at—I turn to find—the matronly Steinberg sisters, tonight's Jewish volunteers. Damon, as I know from past conversation, grew up a half generation prior to Teddy and Khalifa, when the Jews were still around. His best friend was Jewish and the friend's mother was like Damon's second mom. "I may be *goyim*," Damon likes to say, "but I'm not *meshugannah*. I'm *mishpachah*."

Damon excuses himself for choir practice, and I follow him into the chapel. I ask how the choir is faring under Santana's renewed watch. It's coming together, he says, but *now* he's got to step up and solo, which he doesn't like to do. Pulling on his dreads and fingering his Africa medallion, Damon reminds me that he used to be choir director. While as far as I know Damon's dual religious allegiance doesn't garner him too much grief, Reverend Baumgartner drew the line at having an avowed Rastafarian serve as the Sunday service choral director.

"Excuse me, Josh," Santana snipes. "We've got to get to work." I apologize, and beat it.

In Classroom A, in what must be an ad hoc Baptism class, Keita is pressing eight men to weigh the importance of faith versus that of actions.

"How does one know faith?" he asks me directly. Having heard this formula enough times over the past year, I believe I know the right answer.

"By its fruits?" I tepidly suggest.

Keita laughs, though whether what's funny is that I'm in the know or that I remain outside of it, I can't judge. Without settling my uncertainty, Keita introduces a hypothetical. Say you're living next to a crack dealer—do you turn him in? "What," he asks, "is the Christian thing to do?" Though I long to hear the answer, to hear Keita's students wrestle not between good and evil but between two goods pitted tragically in mutual exclusion, I feel bound by my date upstairs.

I bid everyone a *Gut Shabbos* and grab a seat.

Brian is arguing about *Collins*, this time with Eugene, a half-black, half-Jewish Vietnam vet. What *Collins* means, Eugene says, is that the federal court recognizes that a "Sixth Amendment violation deserves a merit-based analysis if you can get past the gatekeeper."

"No, that's not it at all," Brian corrects him. "*Collins* will be instrumental because if you have a *Brady* claim, the system is more apt to grant a Sixth Amendment ineffective-assistance-of-counsel claim than to implicate their own for having committed errors."

Brian asks me what I think. I say that it's all over my head, which it is. Brian rolls his eyes but explains nonetheless. "Let's say you assert a *Brady* violation, that being that the prosecution withheld, willfully or otherwise, potentially exculpatory evidence. What I submit to you is that what *Collins* does is give the court a way to grant relief *without* implicating its own. *Collins* allows them to reverse not because the DA lied and cheated, but because the defense attorney was an ass. My contention to you is that for the court, this is a far more palatable proposition."

For Eugene, paramount is *Collins*'s potential payoff. So as he did this week for Baraka and Teddy, among countless others, surely, Brian shifts from legal interpreter into dream crusher, informing Eugene that *Collins* does *not* mean that you'll automatically get back into court just because you had a *Brady* claim. "Look, if the court already ruled on you, then whether it addressed your *Brady* claim or not, you're done."

Having seemingly honored his other extracurricular obligations, Lenny arrives earlier than usual. He circles the table and extends an affectionate hand to both Steinberg sisters and, upon sitting down, makes inquiries into family and health.

With sitcom pacing, no sooner has Lenny settled down than David lumbers in.

"What's up?" I ask.

He says, "I've started reading Forster's *A Passage to India*, and to be quite honest, I don't see what all the fuss is about." He shrugs and disappears into the kitchenette, presumably to make coffee.

The seven of us continue to warm each other up with small side conversations, which, absent the Rabbi's stewardship (the Rabbi comes in Saturday mornings instead), forms—along with candles and coffee— the substance of Kabbalat Shabbat services. As a bunch of people talking over one another with a mixture of rudeness and affection, Friday-night service is an unmistakably Jewish species, and its patter makes me feel unselfconsciously myself in a way unique for the chapel week.

The headline that has everybody's attention is Hamas's victory. Staking out the Darwinian right, Lenny declares that "the history of the world is people conquering one another"—meaning, it's time for the Palestinians to get over it. With a commensurate escalation of pitch, David lends his support. "Stalin took this swath of Poland"—he gesticulates over here—"this swath of Germany"—he gesticulates over there. "Twenty-five million people moved, and nobody did a thing! Israel conquers a piece of the Arab world half the size of Delaware and suddenly it's the greatest injustice the world has ever seen? I mean, come *on!*"

"The Jews came to the desert and made it flow with milk and honey!" someone shouts, a founding cliché drowned out in the emerging tumult between David and Brian.

Though hardly the dove that the Rabbi is, with David sounding the alarm about Hamas, Brian is forced to the center. "David," he says in that way that naming one's interlocutor signals a muted assault, "it's not the end of the world. It's just like with the Irgun. With legitimacy, they will become more moderate in time."

David rejects the comparison between Mandate-era Jewish militants and Hamas, and offers a litany of factual distinctions between them. "Come on, they're Nazis," he says of Hamas. "They're very clear about their desire to push the Jews into the sea."

Perhaps feeling impelled to represent leftist orthodoxy in the Rabbi's stead, or perhaps yelling simply because it's what I know how to do, I decry David's double standard, and the carte blanche it issues Israel to lob bombs, assassinate, and bulldoze homes. Lenny defends Israel's behavior as the necessary outcome of the Arab states' unwillingness to repatriate refugees after '48 and '67—they exploit Israel as a wedge issue to curry the world's sympathy at the expense of their own people.

"Sure," I shout back, "and the Arab media sensationalizes Palestinian suffering to justify retaliatory violence—just as I'm sure there are Iraqi factions that torture people. But oughtn't we to hold our own to a higher standard?"

"And who is 'our own'?" David asks.

"At this point?" I say. "Black hats from Brooklyn, Baruch Goldstein . . ." I refer to the ultraorthodox settler who murdered twenty-nine Palestinians in Hebron in 1994.

"Ahh!" David waves his hand. "Those are just nuts!"

"No," Brian corrects him. "Those are *our* nuts!"

Righteous Lenny is easy prey for my exceptionalist "higher standards" argument. "Look," he says, "we ought to give Hamas a shot. Either we'll get peace or, more likely, they'll continue with the terror, and then we'll have the right to go in and kick the shit out of them." Running with my allusion to torture, Lenny segues into a rant on the criminal immorality of our current regime—the wanton destruction that has been wrought in democracy's name. "It's a *shanda*," he shrieks—it's shameful.

With utmost moral seriousness, I muse on my feelings of complicity in our country's military excesses. David looks at me like I'm crazy.

In David's bemusement, I'm made suddenly cognizant of the radical distance between his citizenship and mine. "Huh," I say. "I guess you don't necessarily feel part of all this. Or maybe you're *not* part of this, you being this weird class also subject to the repressive apparatus of American imperial power, and without a voice in the process." Realizing that I needn't speculate, I ask, "I mean, how exactly *do* you feel?"

"What do you mean?" David asks, spit flying from his lips. "Of course I want to overthrow the government!" If at Graterford a Salafi Muslim must be exceedingly vigilant as to what he says to whom in his desire to see the Union destroyed, a white man enjoys significantly more freedom to sound off.

"Sure," I say, unsure as to how to navigate the escalation. "Don't we all?"

"Fine," he says, "we're all *implicated*"—he overenunciates mockingly. "And what are *you* doing about it?"

"What do you mean?" I ask, taking faux affront. "I'm sitting right here *talking* about it, aren't I?" Which is to concede David's point.

As frequently happens, David links the subject matter at hand to his personal history, his reported experience of state negligence and persecution, first when his daughter was being abused, and then again, when prosecuted for going after the animal who was doing it to her.

"Get to the point, David!" Brian barks.

"Okay, okay," Lenny pleads. "You're a professional victim. We understand, already!" Nothing aligns Lenny and Brian quite like David discussing his case. An unfamiliar CO cautiously pokes his head in—"to check on the ladies"—declines a cup of coffee, and leaves.

When the door closes, Brian seizes control.

"Why don't you tell them"—the Steinberg sisters, that is—"about your project?" which, despite his great curiosity, he professes to know next to nothing about. I try to beg off. He insists. I resist. He insists again. No one else makes a move. With a mildly malevolent smile, Brian pleads: "You never debrief me!"

"So? What have you found?" the sisters ask.

"Well," I say, hoping to move on to something else, "based on my careful study, it appears as if religion at Graterford provides a super-interesting set of phenomena and that the guys who live here are, in fact, human beings."

Brian tells me not to be obtuse, so I talk about pluralism, about how I was early on struck by the range of religious practices here, and how due to a set of historical contingencies—some of which I recount— Graterford's chapel ranks among the world's most religiously diverse places. Simultaneously, however, the chapel remains, I argue, a thoroughly Protestant space, both in the sense that the vast majority of groups practicing here have emerged from that tradition, and also in the sense that the rules of the game by which religion is regulated, rules that conceive of religion foremost as a matter of individual belief, are residually Protestant rules. That said, I acknowledge what, all things considered, is an extraordinary amicability among the chapel's many groups. Noting the discriminatory and divisive place that the chapel, in more sectarian hands, could be, I give some credit for this tolerant mood to Reverend Baumgartner. "But," I add, "I am not to be trusted on this."

"Why not?" Lenny asks.

"Because Baumgartner has had a large role in shaping my thinking about this place. Plus, I like him quite a bit and suspect I might be something of his booster."

"That's Josh," Brian tells the sisters. "Always qualifying."

"What?" I say. "Am I talking to Teddy here? I didn't know I was required to give yes or no answers." It's Teddy who most often harangues me for my alleged evasiveness, when what I'm being, I believe, is nuanced.

"You know very well what you do," Brian says.

"Do I?" I say.

"There you go again," Brian says, looking back to the sisters.

"What?" I plead. "I can't answer a question with a question? I mean, aren't we all Jews here?"

One of the sisters interjects. "But how do you know that what you're seeing here is representative? Aren't you going to compare your findings with other jails?" It's a reasonable objection.

"No," I say. "Certainly I'd be curious to someday compare Graterford to other prisons, but for the time being I'm content to simply treat Graterford in the full splendor of its particularity. I mean, in this jail alone, there's far too much going on to be captured in one book. In places, I would hope to indicate what's Graterford-specific and what might be indicative of things one might find across the system. But, quite honestly, I'm more than happy to give a partial representation of what the practice of religion is like at one particular prison at one particular moment in time. In fact, I very much want to interrupt the reader's desire to know what 'religion in prison,' as such, is all about."

They look confused.

While it's been some time since an ethnographer could unselfconsciously presume that by scrutinizing a single African or Indonesian village, he might unearth the social logic by which primitive peoples live always and everywhere, in the project at hand I am exceedingly wary of this temptation of overgeneralization. As was once true of the "primitive," the "prisoner" is a fantastical persona, a figure shrouded by distance, an object of curiosity and desire. Because prisoners are largely rendered silent and invisible, it is easy enough to let one small set stand in for them all. Such, anyway, was the standard operating procedure during prison ethnography's mid-century heyday. Through observation at one Southern Illinois state penitentiary (the proclaimed "Middletown" of American prisons), sociologist Donald Clemmer could abstract "prisonization" as the force through which members of *The Prison Community* became socialized into a particular set of attitudes. And by interviewing prisoners at New Jersey's Trenton State, Gresham Sykes could theorize subcultural identification as a prisoner's sole means for surviving *The Society of Captives*.[38]

Claims of this size and scope have their place, but I have long suspected myself, in the present case at least, to be constitutionally unwilling to make them. As I maintained going in, Graterford is no more just "a prison" (and therefore *all* prisons) than Philadelphia is just "a city." Idiosyncrasies—of locality, of history, and of personality—matter too much to be rubbed away. (If Graterford were simply a run-of-the-mill maximum-security prison, one could well ask, would *I* really be on hand to see it?) If I was cognizant of some of my limits, I was a bit shakier as to what precisely I was up to. Before I'd found my way to the office, I started with the chapel's formal rituals. Primarily because mixing it up came to me more naturally than did quietly watching and writing it down, I found my footing in dialogue. And so, when in the course of introducing myself, people would ask me what it was I was writing about, I would say that this was precisely what I was hoping they would tell me.

Some months into my time at Graterford, I arrived in the chapel to find Baraka in Chaplain Keita's office with a stocky, white-bearded Muslim I'd never met. The two of them were sampling some VHS recordings of the Masjid Warith Deen Muhammad community in its heyday. In the video, silent at least in this playback, a couple dozen men are gathered in the garden that used to lie outside the chapel's southeast corner. They are executing some sort of military-style drill; a cut, and now the men are milling about. Riveted by these images, I was distracted when the white-bearded Muslim called me slowly by name. I asked him his. Musa, he said. He had a grounded presence and a mischievous eye. I asked Musa how long he'd been at Graterford. Since the seventies, he told me. What I needed to understand, Musa instructed me, half-watching the video, was that back in the day, they hadn't had *any* of this; that before the agitations of *his* Muslim community, prayer rugs, kufis, and all religious literature up to and including the Qur'an had been contraband.

I asked Musa whether he'd been in the Nation back then or whether he'd been a Sunni. Two questions was fine, Musa said, but three was an interrogation. *He* asked me what exactly I was planning to write about religion in prison. I explained, as I was in the habit of doing, that I wasn't testing out a theory per se. Instead, I was trying to get a sense of how Graterford's prisoners themselves conceptualized their religion; as I figured it, the insights of those who thought about it and lived it here would prove both more surprising and more revealing than the scholarly frameworks I was coming out of. Musa looked at me without speaking. I continued, rattling on about how while I was for sure curious about how people at Graterford might generalize about "prison religion," in my perspective a given prison was a particularity, socially contingent in time and space. At this point it would have been polite (in my world, anyhow) to respond with a question, an objection, or at the very least an "uh-huh" to signal engagement, but Musa just kept looking at me unblinkingly. Struggling to fill the silence, I asked him if he got what I was saying. He shrugged the question off like there was nothing to get.

Musa said flatly, "So you're an empiricist."[39]

"In my judgment," I say, back at *shabbos*, "the impulse to generalize broadly about a class of people often accompanies an unwillingness to see that class of people *as* people." Consequently, I explain, I'm reluctant to compress the men of Graterford into one conceptual box. "People are simply too interesting to be reduced down to one or two generalizations."

Eugene nods, but the Steinberg sisters seem unmoved. I try again: "Look, the landscape of religious practice in this place *now* is radically different than it was pre-raid, right?"

"Right," Eugene says. "And religion at Graterford is *way* different than religion at Dallas. They've got so many things going on up there."

"Right," I say. "Dallas is a medium-security institution. It's in the mountains. Different prisoners, different chaplains, different COs, different culture. That is to say, it's different up there from down here, right?"

Brian seems predictably annoyed. "And that's it?" he says. "Your advisors up at Princeton are going to be satisfied with a dissertation that says *that*? That says that religion at Graterford is . . . *different?*"

"It's true," I concede. "It will require a wee bit more obfuscation than that if it's gonna pass."

"Why are you interested in prisons at all?" Brian shifts. "Why do you care about what we lowlifes are doing in here?"

I recount how when I was small, my mother worked at Rikers Island and how, from adult dinner table discussions, I became horrified and transfixed by emergent American mass incarceration. Later, when I began to think about what to do with my life, prisons seemed like a place to make some sort of intervention.

"So what have you done before now?" Brian asks.

I explain that upon graduating from college, I went down south to work for an organization that provides legal representation to people on death row. How, I wondered at the time, could anyone do anything else? Had I been slightly more self-aware, I might have acknowledged such reasoned righteousness as only part of the call. Another was the ecstatic American imperative to go forth and experience the world for oneself, to see it, touch it, and feel it; to override, that is, a competing injunction: how for a Jew, as my father has put it without a shred of shame, "primary experience is reading about it."

Brian leans over to the sisters and—loud enough for me to hear—says, "Quite simply, religion here, like everything else, is a game. Guys do it for the privileges, for the power it gives them in this place and the power it gives them over other prisoners. That and for protection."

"Oh, come on," I object. "That's the sort of thing they say on the outside. And that way of thinking exhibits a profound lack of sympathy for the very real struggles one engages in here, physically, psychologically, emotionally, *as well as* spiritually. And while I'm somewhat skeptical of discussions of religion that overemphasize religion's meaning-making function, this place *is* something of an existential boot camp, and guys' involvement with whatever religious discipline they're involved with certainly addresses those needs, too."

Lenny asks me what I mean. To a certain extent, I say, I can only project my own experience as one who wrestles with bad thoughts. "And if I have thoughts out *there* that I can't shake, I can only imagine what it's like to be in here for sixteen hours a day locked in a bathroom."

"In a cage," Brian corrects me, even though by calling cells bathrooms, I'm parroting back his words.

I press Brian on his suggestion that folks *only* get involved with religion for the purposes of protection—meaning that the chapel regulars are little more than bottom-feeding *bad men*. "Let's say that one becomes religious only for 'protection.' How different is that from folks on the outside going to church for a sense of 'community'? Is the desire for community *merely* a game? Protection: that's a discourse that is dominant about prisoners' religion because it's not generally acknowledged that men in here have needs above and beyond physical protection. But of course you have those needs! Who doesn't? And folks in here disproportionately turn to religion to fill them. Why? Well, for one, because of the accidents of the First Amendment, the prisoners'-rights movement, the waning of the rehabilitative ideal in the eighties, and the legislative push to promote free religious exercise for all (this time around, largely from the right), religion is by now one of the few games left. I mean, where *else* are you gonna go? Furthermore, the suggestion that protection can be opposed to something like authentic religion strikes me as patently absurd. As if the desire to stay alive isn't sincere enough!"

What I really ought to write about, David says, is "that Todorov thing." He's referring to philosopher Tzvetan Todorov's *Facing the Extreme*, which makes the case, as David has explained before, for the perseverance, even in the inhuman hell of the concentration camps, of an inextinguishable moral sensibility among the inmates. In David's view, if acts of generosity and kindness could survive ultra-efficient

German evil, then half-assed Pennsylvanian ineptitude has little chance to eradicate them either.[40]

Eugene draws the express link between the practice of religion and the survival of one's soul. "More than anything else, though," he says, "what religion in here is about is that they can have this"—he touches his body—"but they can't have this"—he points to his head. "They can't have my mind. Spirituality is a way to keep a part of you in reserve that's not caught up by the system. The unfortunate thing is that at the same time, this thing that helps keep you free is also the thing that divides us. Why do there have to be factions?" Eugene continues. "I say this as someone who's white and black, and Jewish. *Religion* is from the Latin, meaning 'to tie,' and it's supposed to be something that ties us together, not something that drives us apart. Can't we just see the humanity in each other that religion helps us maintain, the humanity that cannot be snuffed out by this system around us?"

I want to engage Eugene, to question his presumption of an inherent humanism that religious factionalism serves to undermine, and to probe him directly on what precisely religion *does* to preserve within captivity a sort of freedom, but I'm distracted by what Brian is saying to Vickie Steinberg.

"Nothing is real here," Brian says to the volunteer. "Nothing is authentic. Everything is a ruse, a game. I always have to debrief Josh on this."

I take for granted that Brian has far greater intimacy than I do with the darker sides of the human animal, part of which—in spite of what Teddy and Khalifa might claim about lifers and truth-telling—is undoubtedly people's capacity for bald-faced deception. Nonetheless, I am, in this regard, only half as naïve as Brian thinks. From a theoretical standpoint, I take little issue with Brian's characterization of religion as a "game." Contrary, however, to his intimation that gamesmanship entails insincerity, as I see it, for all of us game players—and, in this view, we *all* are—there is no more effective way to play the game than to suspend disbelief and actually effect the interior state corresponding to the requisite moves.[41] And while, methodologically, I do presume the sincerity of those with whom I am talking, this is less because I take them all to be engaged in plainspoken earnest speech (what a tedious world that would be!) and more because I believe that instead of acting as a corrective, an alternative presumption would only add another layer of distortion.[42]

"I think you both have good points," Vickie says to Brian. "Josh has a point—that religion fulfills needs. And you have a point—that it's not *real* religion."

Brian watches me watch him. "So tell me," he says, "why be Jewish? What do we get from it?"

The day has primed me with a readymade answer. "Look," I say. "Among the African-American prisoners in the jail, there is an abiding sense that the collective experience of slavery stole their identity from them, and that much of the trouble they find themselves in stems from the fact that they don't know who or what they are. It is this profound sense of having lost their culture that is the driving impetus for groups like the Nation of Islam and the Moorish Science Temple. From guys in the Nation to the Salafi Muslims, they're all trying to fill that perceived gap, that sense of absence that haunts their identities." I look around the room. "None of *us* in this room is similarly troubled. As Jews, we know all too well who we are. Such is the nature of what my good Italian friend calls our cumbersome inheritance."

At the mention of the Nation of Islam, David pipes in, "Oh, do you mean *Poolism?*"

"What?" I say.

"As in Elijah Poole," he says. "Elijah *Muhammad* was really Elijah *Poole.*"

"Sure," I say, "but by that logic," in which the prophet and God are made one and used to define the faith, "Islam becomes *Mohammedanism,*" as in the nineteenth century it was indeed called.[43] "Trying to make other religious traditions conform to a Christian template often obscures more than it reveals."

"Look, Josh," Brian says, fully exasperated. "I want you to give me one straight answer."

"Okay," I say. "What's the question?"

"Are people here people of faith?"

I consider my answer only so long as to correctly anticipate Brian's reaction.

"What do you mean by faith?" I say.

"*No!*" he shrills. "Answer the question! Do they *believe?*"

"It all depends what you mean by *believe,*" I say.

"Come on!" Brian yells. His fury seems authentic.

I rehearse a genealogy of the category "religion." Playing for them what is by now a religious-studies standard, I explain that while the notion of religion may be traced back toward Athens and Jerusalem, in its contemporary form, "religion" is a child of Protestant theology. For in contrast to the medieval Church's premium on ceremony, sacrament, and deed, it was the Reformation that made personal belief the essence of Christianity. The modern concept of religion, then, emerges from a polemic against the Church's empty forms, a charge that recapitulates the Apostle Paul's beef with the Pharisees 1,500 years earlier. As is the case with all descriptions of how things are, the distillation of religion to a condition of interiority—to faith, to conscience—takes a strong, normative stance on how things ought to be.

In its ongoing life as a concept, I argue, *bona fide* faith depends in part on how it excludes its others. If in the authenticity of their beliefs, Protestants have been credited with having *true religion*, in their ritualism, Catholics and Jews have been thought of as doing something that falls just a bit shy. While for conservative Protestants like most of the guys downstairs, personal salvation remains predicated on faithful belief in biblical doctrines, over the last hundred and fifty years, the liberal wing of the Protestant intellectual tradition, in scouring its ever more pluralizing surroundings for common ground, has extrapolated from the particular case of Christianity a universal rule. At the core of each "world religion" was placed the individual and his relationship to his God, which is how we got the categories of Buddhism, Zoroastrianism, and Mohammedanism.[44] If, after further study, the presumed object of faith proved somewhat misplaced, faith as the defining characteristic of religion has nonetheless been preserved. In asking whether chapel men are *people of faith* or, alternatively, whether or not *they really believe*, I argue, Brian is unwittingly applying precisely this Protestant standard.

"Well, I don't know about you," I say with one finger to my head and another to my heart, "but my insides are a lot more garbled than that. Sometimes I go to *shul*"—synagogue—"to pray; sometimes I go to *shul* to be with my family; sometimes I go to *shul* because I feel like I have to. I feel as though we must historicize and deconstruct the insistence that in order to be authentic, religion has to be about the relationship between the individual and the divine. As an alleged universal, religion as a condition of belief strikes me as far too restrictive. At the very least, it in no way jibes with my own experience."

As an enterprise of personal meaning-making, the recitation of a liturgy may be direct, but more often it is oblique, or even askew. Words alienate, or lead one astray, or pass by unnoticed. From time to time they hit their mark. In the day-to-day, religious meanings may be critically important, but not solely as the substance of creed or conviction. Religious language also gives us food for thinking through history, people, and ethics, and furnishes resources for ritual, argument, and play. To conclude, I refer back to David's comment. "It's a Christian logic that makes the Nation *Poolism*. But by that same logic wouldn't we call Judaism *Mosesism* and drastically miss the point as a result?"

No longer suspicious of his fellow prisoners' religious surfaces, Brian comes at me again; he now seeks to describe the *depths* of us all.[45] "But aren't we innately religious?" he asks. "As human beings, do we not inherently have the need to connect with that which created us? Do you not believe that?"

Homo religiosus is what, in a more confident era for the study of religion, historian of religion Mircea Eliade famously dubbed this purported human condition. As I've been schooled to see it, however, to posit in each man and woman something that clamors for the Creator is to mistake an affective consequence of one religious tradition for the cause of them all.[46]

"No," I begin, "I don't believe that I—"

"I don't care what *you* are!" Brian shouts. "Do you not believe that *we* are?"

"No, I don't necessarily believe that *we* necessarily are, Brian," I say. "Certainly not in any kind of simple way."

Calmly, Brian asks: "So if it's not about the individual and God, then why do *you* study religion?"

It is, admittedly, an odd vocation. I recount my background, how I grew up in a home of agnostic observant Jews. "Where I'm from," I explain, "we're *shomer shabbos* and keep kosher and my father puts on tefillin every day, but nobody believes in God in any literal sort of way."[47] Somehow, it took me until I was eighteen to figure this out. Though unnerved, I was also quite intrigued. As a college freshman, I took some religion classes. When provoked by William James's suggestion that one might—for the sake of a healthy psyche—*will* belief, my father pointed out that in Hebrew, the word for belief, *ma'amin*, exists only in the causative form, meaning: *I will myself to believe*.[48]

While this portrait of my family's agnostic observance strikes most of those around the table as nonsensical, to Lenny it's not unfamiliar. "My grandparents were the same way," he says. "Kosher, *shabbos*, the whole nine. It wasn't until later that I realized they didn't believe in God."

For Brian, however, who favors clean and orderly distinctions, the model remains distasteful. "So why be Jewish? Why your father? Why does he do that? Why does he waste his time?"

"Because it works," I explain. According to my father, the moment in the morning that he finishes *davening* and puts away his tefillin offers him his day's greatest peace (he calls it "relief"). "But more important are all the other moments. My father is a very contented individual. And while he might simply be temperamentally inclined toward contentment on the one hand, or full of grace on the other, I can only assume that his practical relationship with Judaism is part of what makes his life work so well."

Brian on redirect: "And what have you learned about Christians here?"

I want to tell him about Paul on contentment, about the perils of visceral reaction, about the optimism of rebirth, about gratitude, but as is often the case, by the time I've gotten three words out, Brian has had enough: "Please answer the question at hand! Are the Christians here people of faith?"

"What do you mean by *faith*?"

"Come on!" he yells. "Are they or aren't they?"

Outscreaming him, I demonstrate my position with the example of the Native Americans. "Let's take the Native Americans," I say. At the mention of these notorious fakers, David laughs derisively. Undeterred, I continue: "Do the Native Americans believe in all the spirits that inhabit the yard and in the Great Spirit in the sky? I would assume that of those who come down on Thursday nights, some do, some don't, and some enjoy entertaining such a notion as a metaphysical possibility. However, of the Natives who come down, do I believe that each and every one of them believes in sitting for an hour on the frozen ground on a winter's night in order to feel the feelings and think the thoughts that such a practice evokes? Meaning, do they believe in sitting on the freezing ground for an hour for *its own sake*? For those who attend, the answer evidently is yes. It is *this* conviction, to come sit on the freezing ground, rather than their presumed conviction in the literal reality of the spirit world they describe, that is of paramount interest to me."

"So what you're saying is that religion is essentially activity," David deduces.

"Could be," I say. "Religion could be any of a number of things, depending on what we ask of it."

As I will later write in one of this book's many discarded introductions: "Inasmuch as rich texts are always elastic texts, whatever religion at Graterford might be said to be depends largely on the eyes one brings to it. In the chapel's fellowship, a Christian might well see the power of the Lord at work; a Muslim, the transformative effect of righteous submission. A humanist might see how the men at Graterford employ religious practices to live meaningful lives in spite of the soul-crushing weight of their surroundings. A suspicious secularist, by contrast, might see how religious discourses at Graterford use these men, enlisting them to accept their gratuitous suffering as requisite. A bit more mutedly, a liberal might see in the chapel's vibrancy the lamentable absence of other opportunities for intellectual and spiritual development. An anthropologist might notice the ways that religion fosters tribal identities, an essential function in this atomizing and dangerous environment, while a psychologist might see how through religion, men who have struggled with controlling their impulses gain a handle on them. An ethicist might see the role played by spiritual practices in the formation of character, while a reader sensitive to gender might note how religion allows formerly aggressive men to transvalue the brutal masculinity of the streets into one that celebrates self-sacrifice. An idealist might see how religion allows these men to live in a world within yet somehow outside state power, while the unsentimental might see in chapel activity merely a flimsy bulwark against boredom. None of these encapsulations is without its truth. Rather than commit myself to any one of them, however, my hope in this book is to inhabit the space vacated after such abstractions have been given a chance to temporarily thaw, a space of novelistic indeterminacy and, just maybe, of ethical possibility too."

That religion at Graterford is an entity as variable as the perspectives from which it may be described is perhaps Brian's least favorite formulation yet. "Come on!" he says. "What do *you* think religion is?"

Not merely out of a lack of conviction or so as to rile Brian am I reluctant to characterize religion too neatly. As I see it, rather than in the discretely mapped forest, it is in the territorial mess of trees and shrubs, undergrowth and earth, where the stuff of religion takes place.

And if religion might be cleanly designated in theory, in practice it is a messy glut of particulars, with overarching conceptualization being just one of these many burls. As I fear, any attempt to sum up what religion at Graterford is about would necessitate sacrificing the unruly breadth and depth of the chapel's religious practices for the overdetermined subset of elements that lend themselves to expedient summation. Quite simply, the world as it unfolds in time is far more extravagant and intricate than scholarly argument can possibly allow.[49] If not theological per se, the devotion to describe this reality justly is arguably as close as I get.

Nonetheless, conditioned by a ritual sense to know that the hour for resolution is at hand, I succumb, and offer up for Brian a watery, secular Jewish twist on liberal Protestant universalism. "If forced to argue, *al regel achat*"—meaning "on one leg," I say, referring no doubt obscurely to the Mishnaic story of Rabbi Hillel, who when asked if he could recite the entire Torah while standing on one leg, said simply, *Love thy neighbor as thyself*—"religion would be *this*."[50] I sweep my arm around the table. "Religion would be something like eating food and drinking coffee with one's friends, with one's *people*. The Creator would be more than welcome but his attendance would be in no way compulsory. And *this*"—I gesture again—"is a beautiful, meaningful activity. And no scholar of religion and no court of law should be able to suggest that as far as religion goes, *this* activity somehow falls short. And," I add with complete candor, "I'm tremendously grateful that you're all willing to share it with me."

When David has cleared the coffee and Brian has choked out the candles, we descend to the vestibule to await the sisters' escort.

"Jesus Christ," I say to David, "Brian can be so *fucking* narrow."

David, who has been known to call Brian "Little Hitler" for his tightfisted manner, whirls around. "You don't say!" He performs epiphany. "Do you really think so?"

"What's that?" Brian asks, having overheard.

"Nothing," I say. "I was just saying that you're a goddamn fundamentalist. But don't worry about it. I'm one, too. Just of a different stripe." Brian's smile doesn't waver.

Having locked up the office, Keita joins us in the vestibule. When the escort arrives, we traverse the empty corridor, our soles kicking up squeaks from the freshly washed floor. At B Block—"Bagel Boulevard," as it was known back in days of denser *Yiddishkeit*—we bid the remaining prisoners goodbye.

Keita, the sisters, and I sign out and pass through the gate. To the right of the double doors separating us from the cold, Keita pushes the dispenser and dollops his hands with a puff of soapy foam. He rubs his hands, front-to-front, circles one in the other, and then the other in the one. I do the same.

"It's a ritual," he explains to the sisters.

SATURDAY

How, in God's name, has it come to this?

Any answer can only be partial, but here's a survey: by a bounteous universe (honor it by whatever name you choose), by a sun that makes things outgrow their bounds, by a nature that continues to slowly come undone, and, lastly, at the fragile margins, by the actions and inactions of women and men.[1]

Somewhere along the way, eons after it all began, clans of men, women, and children began to till the earth. Affixing themselves to the land and to the calendar by which their crops were sown and reaped, these men and women gradually developed a set of activities, some immediately germane to material flourishing and some seemingly extraneous to it. Here we might take special interest in the "less useful" activities: Our forebears cut symbols into rock, they fashioned semblances out of pigment, they made music, and they danced. They played games. The children watched them do it, the parents showed them how, and the practices survived them all.[2]

Much later, in the same corner of the world, in a trend spanning roughly a millennium and a half—and henceforth the historical record will substantiate our conjecture—a handful of influential visionaries were credited with gaining access to a realm of reality beyond reality, whereby they received, from an invisible being regarded as to some degree sovereign over all that they saw and didn't see, a set of amendments to the laws by which they lived. Let us call the commemoration of these wondrous encounters and the enactment of their consequent prescriptions *religion* (though as a category presuming to isolate an elementary component of our species' nature, *religion* will only emerge much later).[3] On their merits, too, as well as via conquest, trade, and emigration, these cultural and religious forms spread, mutating with each and every transmission. Eventually, they even traversed the ocean. Toward the very end of our story, in a uniquely idealistic and opportunistic hour, a country was founded.

It is here, in the new American republic, that we stumble upon the curious innovation that will one day furnish our seven days their improbable setting. For it was in Ben Franklin's Philadelphia that a group of middle-class Quakers and their fellow religious progressives, having grown disgusted and horrified with the going forms through which public depravity was censured, revolutionized punishment.[4] On the strength of their mobilization, the age of the stockade, the whip, and the gallows was declared over. In the modern era, punishment was to be softened, transformed from a system that extracted recompense from the body into one intent on mending the soul. Henceforth, the debauched offender was to be removed from his corrupting environment and placed in a *penitentiary*, where, by means of a solitary encounter with the divine light dwelling within him, he would be reformed. At Philadelphia's famed Eastern State Penitentiary, which opened in 1829, the aspiration of holy encounter was literalized architecturally with the placement of skylights—"eyes of God"—through which the sequestered prisoner might come to see himself as the Almighty saw him, slough off his sin, and repent.[5]

In theory, the penitentiary was to have been the quintessentially modern institution. And by means of surveillance and instruction, its product, the transformed man, henceforth to be known as the *prisoner*, was to be the archetypal bearer of what theorist Michel Foucault would a century and a half later call the "modern soul." As iconically illustrated via Jeremy Bentham's idealized prison, the panopticon, Foucault's elegantly simple idea was this: if people are unsure whether or not they are being watched, they will assume responsibility for policing themselves.[6] In this manner, as a properly disciplined modern *subject*, the prisoner was to have been rougher hewn, for sure, but in the end fashioned not all that differently than the factory worker, the soldier, the student, and the patient—a man endowed in body and mind with the requisite know-how to act (and *only* to act) in the productive manner befitting his peculiar social position.[7]

Things didn't turn out as planned. The silence and solitude of

Eastern State inspired madness more than rectitude.[8] Before long, as incarceration became the norm, solitude itself was sacrificed to overcrowding. Reformist zeal proved fleeting. By the mid-nineteenth century, the penitentiary's founding aspiration had been largely abandoned, leaving the institution branded with its name to hobble on without coherent philosophical justification, a machine without a ghost.[9] In the public conceptualization of crime, the pendulum swung—much like it did again in the final decades of the twentieth century—from Quaker environmentalism to Calvinist fatalism. Moral turpitude came to be seen not as a collective product of rotten environments but as the intrinsic nature of rotten men, and, gradually, as driven by the shaping power of the ownership class and the spirit of American racism, the modern prison grew into the appropriate instrument for the infliction of just deserts.[10]

In the chapel, this epic history is also local history. For when Eastern State was mothballed in 1971, its prisoners were dispatched to Graterford. Back then Graterford's population was only half of what it is today. But then came the wars on crime, then on drugs, and, eventually, on terror. Interests lobbied, people organized (and failed to organize), government officials did their things, and the system changed with the times. More and more prison time was handed out to more and more people, such that something like 2.3 million Americans will spend tonight in prison or in jail.[11]

THESIS 5

American religious history provides one way to account for the array of dispositions on display in the chapel. By linking imprisonment to reform, the religious beginnings of the penitentiary left their institutional traces, as did, more diffusely, the second and third Great Awakenings, when practices empowering individuals to draw their own theological conclusions proliferated, thereby presaging ever more innovation. Recent trends have been more directly determinative: the Great Migration north of African-Americans during the early decades of the twentieth century and the attendant urban improvisations that made Islam in its varied articulations part of the black religious vernacular; mid-century litigation undertaken by religious outsiders that stretched the narrow conception of what qualified as protected free exercise under the First Amendment; the prisoners'-rights movement of the 1960s, in which religious prisoners, predominantly members of the Nation of Islam, agitated for and won rights to possess religious literature and ritual implements and to assemble for prayer; the explosion by more than six hundred percent of the national prison population over the final three decades of the millennium; the pro-religion spirit of our political era that has brought new public and private support for religious programming on behalf of incarcerated men and women even as other educational and therapeutic opportunities have dissipated; and, at Graterford, the 1995 raid and subsequent chapel shake-up. By enabling some moves and circumscribing others, this unlikely sequence of historical contingencies—sometimes recalled, mostly forgotten, and always contested—lives on in the chapel's practices.[12]

THESIS 6

For an account more attentive to religious *experience,* individual men may furnish a second starting point. At Graterford, one could make the case, religion truly starts where William James says it does: with "the feelings, acts, and experiences of individual men in their solitude."[13] Having arrived in the prison undone, men must learn to survive confinement, one another, and themselves. Many did not have rich interior lives before, but now the thoughts come in a flood: anxiety in search of assurance, suffering in search of language, anger in search of a foe, chaos in search of order.[14]

Of course, these men were once children, too, and do not arrive in the prison as blank slates. They come equipped with religious proclivities born of their families and communities: in the past, there was a grandmother or mother who preached the Word at them, in vain; there was a voice inside their head that knew when they were doing wrong; like the majority of Americans, without thinking about it too much, they've always known that God is who He said He was.

Whether in solitary confinement or in the general population, days at Graterford are frightening, boring, and exhausting. One gets by the best he can. At night, the distractions fade away and the thoughts rush in. It is here where the prisoner is forced, in James's language, to "stand in relation to whatever [he] consider[s] the divine"—which is how many religious men will soon conceptualize the echo of their thoughts. Here anxiety comes for assurance, suffering to make sense, and anger to be honed; here the self begins to erect an order, and here the terrible secrets that a man must keep to survive become the things that *only me and God know about.*

THESIS 7

From the prison's vantage point, however, all this comes only later. First come the steel and concrete, then authority structures, regulations, and only then the prisoners' religious ideas and practices. And what may we say of these practices? Foremost, as can be said of any social forms that have been around since longer than yesterday: they *work.* Just as mass incarceration *works*—not to rehabilitate and reintegrate prisoners (far from it!) but rather to reproduce itself, grow, crowd out alternatives, and become *normal*—so, too, for these men is religion made to *work.*

Living in prison is a crazy thing to make men do, but the overwhelming majority of convicts will give it a shot. Strangely and twistedly, men are conditioned by the building, the administration, by the staff, by their peers, and by themselves into making it through another day, another week, another year. The incarcerated men draw on all resources available, and toward this end, religion proves a trove. An illustration might help:

If the convict is alone, shared tribal marks suggest religious faith to be one way of finding his people. More likely, if one already has people from back in the street, then their differentiating symbols and postures are easy to assimilate into one's style, one's affect, and one's language. By aping those who've already figured out how to do it, men begin to make their lives in here.

In this process, there is certainly room for religious meaning. From their pockets, the acculturators pull out penciled Bible verses or Qur'anic surahs, words that they say help them get by. But these bulbs will take a while to flower. More critical at this stage is finding one's footing. Because early on danger is especially acute, one must pay close attention, and check his impulses. If one forgets to mind himself, then a prisoner or a guard will serve as an instructor and burn the memory into his body. But this is less common than it used to be. More likely, should one forget, the task of building self-awareness will be sub-contracted to time, a bottomless stock of which is stored in the hole. After ninety days, the prisoner returns to the block one didactic scar richer. Following a brief spell of clairvoyance, anguish dissipates and boredom returns.

Primed for action by his fellow prisoners, by his cousin who once did time, and, principally—like the rest of us—by what he's seen on television, the convict is pleasantly disappointed to discover that very little, in fact, happens here. Bored one night, with his cellie asleep, the TV out, but the light still on—it could be weeks or years into his sentence—he picks up his Bible. After flipping through its crisp pages, he finds the recommended verses. For the first time in ages, he reads. Now something is happening. The next night he picks up where he left off. Maybe it's his need, maybe it's his vague sense of readiness, maybe it's the brute power of the printed word, but for whatever reason, he finds that when he reads these verses, he suddenly knows something in a way that he hasn't known anything before.

Or perhaps the novice is illiterate. Religious traditions are transmit-ted orally most of the time, and here it is no different. Through a third party, he receives word to come down to the chapel on Sunday, that his cousin will be there to meet him. He goes. Jesus, it's good to see him. They hug and reminisce and get dirty looks from the ushers. When it's over, they agree to do it again. And another time. Before long, going to the chapel becomes a normal thing to do. It proves much more enjoy-able here than when he was a kid. He enjoys listening to the gospel music, or even to the sermon. Even when he's bored, there's a feeling of camaraderie in being bored with others. And while two years back he wouldn't have believed you if you'd told him, when Sunday comes around he's as excited for chapel as he is for the Eagles. Well, almost.

One tough Wednesday, he gets bullied on the shop floor. He tells himself that if he can just hold it together until Sunday, everything will be okay.

Meanwhile, some of the dudes he saw in the chapel, he sees around on the block. They share a laugh. They start sitting together in the chow hall. These guys give praise to Jesus a lot, and that's a bit odd, as is their talk of how they were saved on such and such a day. Other behaviors make more immediate sense. He becomes attentive to what he's eating: *I mean, this food will kill you if you don't watch out!* Once a week his new buddies walk the yard, and he joins them. Other than to work, his weekly trips to the chapel and the yard are the only times he gets off the block.

One Sunday during service, the sun is shining and the choir is singing, he is overcome by a strange sense of euphoria, a feeling that the worst has passed and that, in the end, everything is going to be all right. He tells the other guys about it over chow. That feeling, they tell him, is the Holy Spirit reaching out to save him. A few weeks later, maybe something happens again. As he's been prepped to expect, he feels somehow like a new man: clean, absolved, and deeply grateful.

Or maybe nothing happens at all. Instead, ever so slowly, the Jesus-talk that once seemed so weird ceases to be so. The man begins to make the religious language his own and, as such, comes to understand his own experience through it. One of the things he understands intuitively is that he is no longer the same person he was when he first came to prison.

So religion at Graterford *works*: it works to replicate itself inside its residents' bodies and minds; once there, it helps to pass the time, to give a man tools to survive this boring, scary, and sad place, both in isolation and together with his fellow men. It works to institute self-control, conditions discipline of conduct, of diet, and, especially, of thought. It gives the prisoner the framework to think through who he is, what he has done, what will happen when he dies, and how he might never *go home*. Or, just as likely, it provides objects for contemplation so that he *doesn't* have to think about such dire things. If perhaps never to the stark degree achieved by the jail's edifice and regimen, as a lived practice, a prisoner's religion gives shape to his world.

In its perverse and roundabout way, then, religion at Graterford honors the penitentiary's founding mission, producing men who regard themselves as transformed, and indeed, in a variety of ways, they are.

"Religion?" the squat Spanish volunteer howls.

"Yes," I shout back over the slushy reverberations of conga, tambourines, maracas, and guiro. "Religion."

Having goaded me into introductions, Rafael has proceeded to inform the volunteer of my disciplinary allegiance as a religious studies scholar, just as on Thursday he clued in Rita, the tiny Philadelphia county chaplain, to the fact of my cumbersome inheritance as a child of Israel. Rita is also back, and, once again, from her miniature beehive down to her patent leather shoes, she is a composition in luminous black. When it's her turn at the lectern, Rita will tell how, yesterday, in *her* chapel, two guys badly beat up a third—this after a special service where fifteen people gave their hearts to God, which obviously the devil didn't like.

But the morning will belong to the third volunteer, a pale, sunken-eyed Dominican named Mota, who will rail against religion and against the Jews.

"You people who think you came here this morning just to hang out, just to speak to a friend?" Mota will shout once he's caught his stride. "You're wrong! Because God has a different purpose for you. God brought you here to hear the Word. God has a big promise for us, and through Jesus Christ, He confirmed it. Moses asked, *Who are you?* God answered, saying, *I am that I am.* But *Jesus* said, *Blessed are those who haven't seen, but who believe!*"

As he promised, Rafael is translating for me. Half-deaf from his years on the blocks, he has sat us in the front row, where he can read Mota's lips.

"Religions are wrong!" Rafael bellows in English on top of Mota's Spanish. "Religions submit men to their own willingness. But Jesus Christ sets you free. Jesus Christ says, *I am the Truth, the Way, and the Life; and no one comes to heaven but through Me.* Only through Jesus can you come to the Father. But *everyone* who embraces Jesus will be saved!" That is to say, codes of conduct, ritual observance, charity—in the final analysis, these are vanities. Faith in Christ is the thing.

"If you think that God has forgotten you, you're wrong! It's *you* that has departed from God! God does not depart from us. The devil tries to put your self-esteem down so that you think that you're a nobody. He tries to tell you that you're no good. He hopes that you will kill yourself. He wants you to break all the vehicles of salvation. That's why we must believe God. I've got problems, too, even if I'm in the street. Maybe even my problems are bigger than yours! But I am with God, and God's promises are unchanging and eternal. What God promised to Abraham, Moses, and to the Jewish people? He has promised the same to you!"

Mota reads from the twenty-first chapter of Matthew, in which, by parable, Jesus warns the Pharisees that the kingdom of God will be taken from them, and its fruits brought forth by another.[15] Mota prays: "We should all overcome our stubbornness and open up our hearts to Jesus Christ.

"Jesus spoke to the people of Israel but they did not listen to Him. So they fell. To this *day* the people of Israel do not believe. They are still waiting for another messiah. But when He comes, they will see that *He* is their messiah. Those who believe, they will be edified. But those who do not believe . . . they will have a big problem. For *religious* people, Jesus will never come. That's why we must seek the truth.

"Because He's continued doing miracles, and because you and I live, He lives. *Out of the midst of you I will rise up!*"[16]

"Yes! Praise Jesus! Hallelujah!" the assembled men shout in Spanish and English.

From First Peter, Mota recites the admonition and promise that if a man is humble before God and vigilant in the face of the devil, God will take him from his afflictions and restore him.[17]

"A *Jew* said this!" Mota screams, and, factoring for the amplified reverb and Rafael's hearing-impaired echoes, I'm fairly certain that he's screaming at me.

"Jesus confirmed the Word with His sacrament. And Peter and Paul gave testimony to Christ of the glory. It is necessary that we study this Word, that we submit ourselves to the Word. There are a lot of *religions*, it's true. But there is only one *truth*. And that's the truth of Jesus Christ."

Pounded in time, the lectern emits dull thuds. "The Jews continue to have problems. Do you want to know why? Because they have the Word but they don't want to know it. They think *He* is a stumbling stone. As it promises in Luke 2:34, Jesus is for the falling and lifting of the people of Israel. All who believe are risen up! All those who do not, fall! We need to be ready for His return. The young people say, *The world is mine.* And the old man says, *I've been waiting all my life but He still hasn't come.* But we're going to see Him with our own eyes!

"Hallelujah! Jesus Christ separated himself from God the Father so you can sacrifice and be holy. We like to say that we can't be holy, but that's not true! All those who believe in Jesus Christ can be holy. God doesn't see us for what we *do*. If He did, then we wouldn't be here. He sees us through His Son, Jesus Christ. Don't despair just because you have problems. You're holy! He said it and I believe it. None of us in this world is just!

"Wow," Rafael says, "I wish I could write like you!" It takes me a second to understand that these are Rafael's own words, rather than Mota's. I look up and he's pointing at my scribbled transcript. Rafael suffers from dyslexia, he's told me, but when he was a kid nobody told him, so he figured he was just stupid. At Graterford, he's learned to read and write Spanish. English is next.

Rafael returns to channeling Mota: "Christ started working on your life ever since the day you came to Jesus. Abraham received God's promise—*Like the stars in the sky, like the sand in the sea will be your descendants.* And he believed! The most beautiful thing about God is this: we don't *want* to submit. Instead we want to manipulate the Word of God. But we *can't* manipulate the Word of God. God says that to all the nations, in all the tongues, first to Jerusalem, and then to Greece, and then to Rome, and then to Philadelphia. So the Word of Jesus Christ is being fulfilled. Wherever they try to stop us, we break the locks and come in. He's going to break down the walls, the jails, the chains. Because this is the Word of God, the Word that edifies and constructs.

"Jesus spoke in parables," Mota says. "But what was hidden the Lord brought forth into the light. Sure, it was hidden, but who can hide the Word of God? It is *religion* that tries to hide the truth of God. But God has taken the truth and made it known so that people can know Him. The trunk of the tree is Israel—but it is *we* that are the spiritual descendants. We abide in the promises of God, not the promises of man. Jesus is our spiritual house.

"Like it says in John 8:36," Mota roars. "Jesus said to those Jews who believe in Him: *Know the truth and the truth will set you free.* The truth of Christ will free you from all titles and all religions. They said: *We are from Abraham, how can you say that we aren't free?* But Jesus Christ said to them: *You can't be free and still be tied with sin.* So the Jews couldn't be free. They prescribe laws that they can't observe themselves! To ogle, to deceive a brother—these are sins before God! But the Son will make us free. This is *not* about deeds. It is about faith. Faith in what? Faith in Christ! Hallelujah!"

Mota's frenzy crashes into the lagoon of the altar call. Softening his tone, "Does anyone need prayer?" Answered back with silence, gently he asks again, the prosecutor suddenly a counselor.

A solitary brown approaches the dais and stands at the base of the step, his head held down but his shoulders broad.

Am I Mota's Jew? Or is Mota's Jew merely a Pauline trope for the half-stepping wretch who lives—infuriatingly and piteously—in each of us? I'm tempted to approach Mota, to ask him what precisely Jewishness means to him, to interrogate him and, in all likelihood, be interrogated in turn. But I opt to let it go.

Instead I seek out Rafael, who's wandered off, to thank him. I find him at the mouth of the aisle, standing beside the altar call's sole responder and across the table from a young white CO.

"Whatever it is," the CO passionately pleads with the altar-call-responder, "you've got to keep your hands *off* the situation. Whatever it is, you've just got to let *God* take care of it." Turning to Rafael, the CO points at the brown. "Tell him I'm a Christian. And tell him that God just spoke to me right now, and told me I needed to talk to him." He turns back to the brown and implores: "I don't know your situation, but God just told me that you've got to keep your hands off it!"

Rafael translates the CO's instruction into Spanish.

"Thank you," the brown says back to the CO in heavily accented English, "'cause I'm going through something really hard right now."

"See?" The CO turns to Rafael and me, his eyes sparkling. "I don't even speak Spanish! God just spoke to me. Told me I had to come over here and tell this man to keep his hands off his situation. Because God is going to take care of it!"

Santana and Papa are chatting on the Catholic side and Philly soul oozes from the conference room.

Baraka is in the office with David and Vic. When queried, David fills me in on this morning's activities, where upstairs they discussed the rise of vernacular Hebrew until David and the Rabbi got into a kerfuffle, something about the ideological agenda of Leon Uris's *Exodus*.[18]

Baraka and David have been reminiscing about Watergate.

"Nixon was simply the best president ever," Baraka says without looking up from a letter he's redrafting. "There was a man wholly unafraid to use the power of the post."

Still somewhat mystified myself, I ask David what he makes of Baraka's professed Republicanism.

David looks at me with his wild eyes. "He's black and he's Republican. I figure it's got to be mental illness." Still without looking up, Baraka smiles.

The Rabbi passes through. "Did you know Baraka's a Republican?" I ask. The Rabbi's mouth drops open. Even in a place like this, some revelations retain the power to shock.

"Look," I chide Baraka, "now you've upset the Rabbi."

Baraka and David find common ground in Pennsylvania's Senator Arlen Specter. He was the DA on Baraka's case, I learn from Baraka, and the author of the single-bullet theory in the Warren Commission Report, I learn from David. As a railroader and whitewasher both, Specter, they agree, is a scoundrel of the first order.

Father Gorski pokes in an exuberant nose. In his hands, he holds copies of Pope Benedict's encyclical on love, the first of the pontiff's new papacy, which Gorski plans to distribute. I ask if his anticipated pay-raise came through. He laughs like I've made a joke.

Baraka explains that he's only down for a minute, and that he's got an afternoon appointment with the Flyers game on TV. Early on, when he was still feeling me out and our exchanges hovered around politics and sports, Baraka described his youthful career as a cleats-up tackling soccer defender. Only later in life did he get turned on to hockey.

Soon it's just Vic and me.

"So what's going on in the world of religion?" the resident atheist asks.

"A little of this . . ." I say.

"You know," Vic says, "religion is the perfect example of how twisted we are as a species. All you need to do to see how sick, self-loathing, and paranoid we can be is look at religion."

I laugh with the pleasure of unanticipated recognition and deliver a short spiel on the nineteenth-century German philosopher Ludwig Feuerbach and his touchstone inversion of the principle that man is made in God's image. According to Feuerbach, precisely the opposite is the case. It's God who's made in *our* image, not vice versa. As an imagined ideal, God is the projection of human capacities. However, in the process of building up God, according to Feuerbach, we sell ourselves short. In relegating our strength, love, and justice onto God, we debase the human—disowning the virtues that are rightfully ours and asserting in their stead a vitiated nature of rot and sin.

"No, that part religion gets right," Vic laughs. "We *are* a bunch of dirty rotten sinners. So is he your guy, this Feuerbach?"

I detail for Vic the special place that Feuerbach occupies for the study of religion. How if you take Karl Marx's word for it, Feuerbach was the beginning and end of the criticism of religion, which for Marx provided the template for all social criticism. Just as Feuerbach read theology anthropologically, so too would Marx encourage us to scrutinize economics, philosophy, and law. As presently constituted (whenever our present might happen to be), the ideas of God, the Good, the Law, and the Market—indeed, all our abstractions—are reflections through the fun-house mirror of our uneven social relations, and serve the interests of the owners over the laborers. If, according to Christian theology, man is a dirty rotten sinner, that's only because his dirty rotten social relations make it appear so.[19] Should we ever overcome social and economic injustice, the scales would fall from the eyes of the religious, and the pernicious nonsense of religion would be cast off.

"And for you?" Vic asks.

Well, I venture, you might say that Feuerbach's materialism represents my point of departure. Coming out of this tradition, I see religion less as a study of gods in heaven than of people here on earth. However, while Feuerbach and Marx are key way stations on the road to the anthropological study of religion, I don't see them as suitable stopping points. While with Marx I see ideas as wholly enmeshed in the social world—and not merely *reflective* of our material world but, rather, decisively implicated in how this world is constituted and reconstituted—religion as mass delusion doesn't strike me as a particularly interesting story to tell.[20]

"True but boring, huh?" Vic interjects.

More like true but hardly exceptional, and, more perniciously, badly conducive to reinforcing the blind spots for comfortably godless men like Vic and myself. In lieu of *real* political and economic power, the poor man, it is said, has his religion.[21] In its materialist metaphysics, its normative liberalism, and in its haughty universalism, *the poor man of religion* is a quintessential Enlightenment defamation. Hemmed in by modernity or capital, estranged, relegated to nonage, or enrapt by illusion, the poor man (and, perhaps more commonly, the poor *woman*) is nothing less than the religious subject as configured in the secularist imagination.[22] For those operating within this conceptual framework, the poor man of religion applies wherever one finds people who for whatever mindless, brave, or sad reason avow an untenable and injurious faith in the caring nature of the cosmos. As encapsulated in Charles's reduction of Daffy Ball's fervent faith at EFM—*Oh massah! I's is just so privileged to be a slave!*—the poor man of religion is the pitiful soul who, by means of religion, comes to embrace the inhuman conditions of his or her enslavement.[23]

The poor man of religion does get something important right. Namely, that in adopting the descriptions of the world available to us, people affirm the existing social order. Contrary to what some of its more fetishistic critics might allege, however, religion is hardly unique in its propensity for fallacy or in its support of systemic injustice. If it is delusional to believe in something too much, which is to say in a manner partially oblivious to its sources and social consequences, then we are all of us delusional—those of us who structure our lives around a given scholarly conversation, musical subculture, sports franchise, or political party no less than those of us who profess a particular religious conviction. Ergo my principal reluctance to pity too much the purported poor man of religion: by mistakenly regarding the general conditions of ideology and practice as somehow specific to religion, the invocation of the poor man scapegoats religion so as to let the rest of us off the hook.[24]

The framing poses other dangers as well. Though not as directly conducive to the use of brutalizing force as is his *bad man* counterpart, the poor man of religion may also turn deadly. Consider, for example, the specter of the burka'ed woman, who in the run-up to the Bush wars became a quandary for which benevolent military intervention was the necessary solution.[25] Indeed, far from being the bad man of religion's opposite, the poor man is, in fact, its ready complement. After all, without a brainwashed flock on hand to execute his will, the false prophet is no more dangerous than the neighborhood crackpot.

As I argue to Vic, for purposes of rendering religion as a scholar, the poor man framing would be especially toxic. By presuming to know religion's essence and function at the outset, the pathologizing move succeeds in capturing little of what religion is and does for those who practice it. Dismiss the beatific Daffy Ball as a deranged poor man and one misses all the things that, through his faith, Daffy is enabled to do. I note how humbling it was to find people in this place who manage to direct their psychic energies not toward anger and resentment, but toward gratitude. It is a focus that inspires Daffy to serve his fellow men in a variety of ways, the social utility of which—as his hospice patients would be the first to attest—are readily intelligible beyond Daffy's Christ-centered framework.

In making this case, one may certainly err in the opposite direction. As regrettable as it would be both analytically and politically to deny the poor man the entitlement to his convictions, it would also be wrong to fully concede him his claim to freedom. While Daffy's claim on freedom is true in its own fashion—and true in a way that as a fellow struggler I would be a fool to reject out of hand—in a country that incarcerates so many, it would be cynical and defeatist for the non-incarcerated among us to endorse a version of freedom that erases the distinction between a life spent behind bars and a life *not* spent behind bars.[26] To raise the poor man up from the dust and dunghill and declare him by virtue of his religious faith free is to validate his place and to relinquish the prophetic disgust that the system we have collectively wrought is rightfully due.[27]

Cast in the role of the holy unvanquished, Daffy Ball becomes a sacrifice offered for the pleasure and enrichment of those unincarcerated religious believers who might draw strength from the spectacle of his enduring faith; or, alternatively, a sacrifice made on behalf of seculars like me, who via the same saintly spectacle are, in their bad faith, somehow redeemed from their lingering obligation to practice religion at all. But if we remain on the wire between pity and glorification, we may unsentimentally observe that through his relationship with Christ, Daffy Ball, in his small way, works wonders.

It's funny, I say to Vic, how differently the same set of data may be processed. Take the premise that life is short. With that recognition, one may curse the world for not being some other way. Buried in that discontent, however, is the affirmation of the extraordinary and precious thing that life is. It seems to me, I say, that especially in this place, it's by means of a committed engagement with a religious discipline that folks overcome the disempowering trap of resentment and embrace instead an orientation of wonder and thankfulness. In this way, faith is decidedly its own reward, regardless of where we might or might not go when we die.

Vic shakes his head. "You know," he says, "I never understood all the angst that people have about death. Death is simply part of life. There's no point in fearing it or hating it. I mean, you don't hate eating or taking a shit, do you? So why hate dying? But on the other side of the coin, don't be in such a rush to die. There's always pleasure to be squeezed out of life." He waves an arm. "Even in a shithole like this."

"It must be truly miserable to live here," I say.

"No," he assures me. "This place isn't misery. This place is a joke. It's a comedy they're staging in here, pure and simple. Now, Camp Hill"—the DOC flagship—"now *there's* an institution that's run by the book. Up there they'll send you to the hole for having two guys in a cell." Vic chuckles, noting how cruel and unusual it is to send black guys from Philadelphia and Pittsburgh into the center of the state. "You know what they say about Pennsylvania," he says. "It's Philly in the east and Pittsburgh in the west and Alabama in between. It's rough up there. At least down here you got a lot of COs who are more or less from the same population as the prison population. Up there? It's all white people on one side of the bars and all black people on the other."

I ask Vic to remind me where he's from.

"Lebanon," he says. "That's midstate."

"What's that like?"

He mouths a couple of measures of "Dueling Banjos."[28] I get it. Even though it's Klan country up there, Vic says, he always related well to black people.

The door swings open and the fat dwarf from St. Dismas's Communion asks, "Do you have any toilet tissue?" We shake our heads no, and the door closes.

The vestibule sound track has taken a strong turn toward the liturgical. For those for whom religion is something housed in stained glass and stone, the trebly organ and two-part harmonies of Peter's Catholic trio might well sound like the week's first *religious* music. Which, on his more truculent days, is how Father Gorski sees it.

In recent chaplains' meetings, Gorski has complained of the racket that sometimes rages in the conference room. Not discernibly practice or rehearsal, sometimes, according to Gorski, it's just "a bunch of guys holding a jam session." By Gorski's traditionalist ritual aesthetics, there's nothing holy about a jam session. As a liberal and a jazz musician, however, Reverend Baumgartner has a much more expansive conception of the sonically sacred. At least so long as Baumgartner's the FCPD, it's his sensibility that will hold sway; and on those Saturday evenings when Al sits in with True Vine, the music bumps, and Gorski once again decides he's had enough, he and Al will continue to skirmish.

Down for the sparsely attended Seventh-Day Adventist service, Oscar the musician enters the vestibule from the chapel, a *Daily News* word-find in hand, and asks Father Gorski to lend him some Wite-Out.

"No," Gorski curtly responds, "can't give it to you. It's contraband." Oscar slumps back into the chapel, his puzzle uncorrected.

I ask the Father if he was kidding.

"Not in the least," he says. "Wite-Out can be used to alter clothes." Because browns' uniforms are frequently adorned in white with nicknames and slogans, it hadn't crossed my mind that doing so might be against the rules.

A motley crowd has gathered in Classroom A to pray the rosary with the Legion of Mary. Among them is Michael. Twenty years old, if that, Michael has a soft, round face and a big rear end, which he advances in a duck-footed waddle. Of all the chapel regulars, Michael is the one who inspires in me the most sadness. Developmentally delayed, Michael comes across as painfully free of guile. Only once have we spoken: "Gotta go to school," he said, seemingly to no one. We were in the main corridor. "Very important to go to school," he repeated. I told him that I agreed.

While childlike faith is often extolled here, Michael is well beyond the pale. Not that his unnerving simplicity is, at Graterford, in any way unique. Beneath the hospital, the Special Needs Unit is full of such men. I've seen them: squeezed there amid the wild and irrepressible, the shit-throwers and the self-harmers, are men who present not too differently than Michael, men wide-eyed and disconnected, who whether by chemistry innate or administered, seem largely unaware of where they are.

Perhaps it's the weekend quiet—the bare corridors, darkened shop floors and vacant side yards—but on Saturdays, the prison's social function as dumping ground for the unwanted is difficult to ignore. Add to that the refusal of Catholic ritual to brush death under the rug, and, even when I'm not depleted, like today, Saturdays tend to be more contemplative than is comfortable.

Lap, who has hollow cheeks, stringy long hair, and might himself pass for Jesus were it not for the three wooden crosses around his neck, has been reading aloud from a medieval hagiography of Saint Thomas Aquinas. In the far corner of the tiny room, a cart draped with a white tablecloth supports two burning candles, two vases of red plastic roses, and two statues—a matronly blue-and-white Mary, and the birdlike figure that is the lay Marian order's insignia. Scattered on the end-to-end tables are tangles of plastic rosaries; a cascade of rosary pamphlets, some crisp and glossy, some sticky; a teetered stack of handouts; and a beat-up White Pages with "CLAW" scribbled in indelible marker across its bottom.

When Lap finishes, the Legion's ancient, bony-beaked volunteer reminds the men of the five glorious mysteries: the resurrection of Jesus Christ, the ascension of Jesus up to heaven, the descent of the Holy Spirit to the Disciples, the assumption of the Virgin Mary into heaven, and her subsequent coronation as Queen of Heaven and Earth. Until the Lenten season begins and they turn to the sorrowful mysteries, it is these five beautiful and unfathomable events, when the rigid boundary between heaven and earth was temporarily breached, that will remain the focus of their prayers.

Unlike most of the chapel's religious languages, which are designed to feel accessible at first encounter, the universe of concepts revealed through the rosary remains for me inaccessible and strange. Form is easier to fathom. Moving clockwise, the men take turns reciting the five glorious mysteries and the biblical passages on which they are founded. After recounting a mystery, the reader leads the group in responsive recitations of one "Our Father," ten "Hail Marys," and one "Glory Be"—which Lap counts with upheld fingers. The cycle finishes with the singing of "Ave Maria."

Sometimes smoothly, sometimes joltingly, the mysteries circle the room.

"Hail Mary, full of grace, the Lord is with thee; blessed art thou among women and blessed is the fruit of thy womb, Jesus."

"Holy Mary, Mother of God, pray for our sinners, now and at the hour of our death, Amen."

As the chorus issues forth its dissonant affirmation, Lap holds his rosary aloft and toward the altar, his eyes shut. Soon it's Michael's turn.

After reciting the opening words intelligibly, toward the middle of the mystery, Michael's delivery deteriorates into a muddled mumble. By his fourth or fifth repetition, he's turned the reading into a joke, slowing it down, raising and dropping his pitch in a sarcastic singsong cadence, unpersuasively suggesting that he could read it better if only he cared to.

As the rotation leaves him behind, Michael leaves. In watching him go, I can't avoid thinking something Baumgartner said of a similarly piteous Saturday regular who got shipped last spring: "He simply never had a chance." Not all are so sentimental. According to Bird, Michael is a convicted rapist, and knows full well that what he did was wrong. Same as he knows that it's wrong when he slips away to have sex with a guy.

While prison ethnographers generally turned a blind eye to prisoners' religion until the 1970s, when the Nation of Islam's spectacular militancy made religion impossible to disregard, a notable exception was a purported correlation between chapel attendance and sexual deviance. At Donald Clemmer's Depression–era Illinois penitentiary, for example, it was "the opinion of numerous inmates that those who attend because of a religious drive are usually the intellectually dull, the emotional, the provincial, and the aged. Criminologically, these same observers report that sex offenders, murderers, and embezzlers are in attendance at the service in a much greater proportion than their share of the total population."[29] If at Graterford, embezzlement and murder carry no special stigma, the sex criminal remains a pariah, and the chapel a place where even the most despised can go without fear of being turned away.

Lap, whose mother is deaf and who signs along with the mass from the dais, recites a mystery with a deaf man. With Lap's accompaniment, the man, who has thick plastic glasses, a palsied left arm, and a large wooden cross around his neck, jarringly exclaims the mystery, spit flying from his mouth. Again with Lap's help, a deaf five-foot-tall Vietnamese man-child makes an indecipherable go of it. When next it's Lap's own turn, he and the man-child repeat it the same way.

•

Vic the heathen and Peter the Catholic have known each other for decades, dating back to the early eighties at Camp Hill, although back then—I won't discover until later—Vic was the Catholic one.

No one in the chapel is more serious about his religion than Peter. Born to unaffiliated Protestant parents, at twelve Peter started attending church on his own. Already a seeker in his youth, after receiving life for murder, Peter began his studies in earnest. At Frackville, in the mountains, he started studying Greek and Hebrew. The latter he continues with the Rabbi to this day—carving, in seven years of Tuesday evenings, a sizable path through the canon of late biblical and early rabbinic literature. After exploring the gamut of available practices (among them, Buddhist meditation), Peter was baptized a Catholic. Of the many traditions he studied, Peter determined, Catholicism afforded him the best techniques for accessing what he characterizes as "both the numinous and the mystical facets of religious experience." Through the Catholic tradition Peter has come to know God both as separated and transcendent—what, after German theologian Rudolph Otto, Peter dubs the "wholly other"—and as radically present.[30]

Though an indefatigable student of the text, for Peter the project of knowing God is something altogether different. "Trying to understand God through language," Peter explained, "is like trying to taste grapefruit with your eyes." For Peter, knowing God is an urgent undertaking. "With love," Peter said, "God allows you to become something more than what you were." But concerted spiritual discipline can only get you to God's doorstep. Admission requires grace. "You can't expect it," Peter said. "If you expect it, it's lost its *giftness*." Peter sees the need for God as universal, but he understands the special function religion provides in his daily life as a prisoner. "In prison," he said, "those who try to be *hard* inevitably break. Religion allows one the give to be *strong*."

While Vic schmoozes with the shaggy white CO on duty—playing a listing game of COs who ended up on the other side of the bars—Peter inquires if I've yet read the proposal that he gave me back in December. I confess that I haven't, and ask Peter to jog my memory. It's a protocol, he reminds me, for a restorative-justice program based on the model of Franciscan penance. His intention is to run the program in conjunction with the Secular Franciscan Order that with Father Gorski's assistance he's in the process of bringing to Graterford. His driving motivation, he explains, is to do anything in his power that might give his victim's family a chance to heal.

Taking a hard line utterly discordant with Peter's tone, I ask Peter if in his hunger for absolution, he might unintentionally be trespassing on his victim's family's right to be left alone. That is, what if what they want from him is nothing other than distance? Peter is momentarily quiet, making me fear that I've come on too strong. Seeking to fill the silence, I make a borderline snide aside about victims—a demographic whose pain, as I see it, is too often cynically mobilized for the purposes of ever harsher punishment. Chiding me gently, Peter draws a distinction. It's the public-advocacy victims'-rights groups he can't stand. "They don't care about victims at all," he says. "They just use them, and perpetuate their hurt for political end."[31] For the victims of crime and their families, however, he has nothing but respect and compassion. I don't at all disagree, and feel properly chastened for my indiscretion.

"Shift change!" Vic barks. Through the glass window of the chapel complex door, a couple of whitecaps are nearing the corridor's end. Vic proposes we move into the office, which we do.

Peter continues. Given the debt accrued through his crime, he just wants to help out his victim's family any little way he can. Even the littlest thing, like sending a birthday card on their daughter's birthday. With modestly greater care than before, I wonder aloud if that isn't something of a fairy tale.

Not at all, Vic says, tuning in. At his trial, members of his victim's family made a plea on his behalf, and now and again they send him a ten-dollar money order. Moreover, he does send them cards on the holidays, which, to the best of his knowledge, they appreciate.

It *does* happen, Peter insists. He relates an anecdote from South Africa's Truth and Reconciliation Commission. A woman whose son and husband were killed under apartheid had the opportunity to confront their killer. But instead of responding with vengeance, she converted her loss into love: "You took away the people that I love," she reportedly told the man, "so let me love you."[32]

When he later returns for mass, Peter will show me two letters he received in response to his proposal—one from a Villanova grad student who is eager to help, the other from a victims'-rights group that is predictably aloof. He will hand me, as well, a second copy, blued at the edges from carbon paper, of his "A Path of Penance: A Reflection upon Living St. Francis' Exhortation to Penance."[33]

In the eight-page, single-spaced proposal, Peter humbly articulates his intention—as a Christian, as a Catholic, and as a Secular Franciscan—to pursue a path of personal penance. This pursuit begins conceptually with a critique of the existing order of punishment. According to Peter, our retributive system injures, hardens, and isolates. It rapes. Acting coercively from without, it can do nothing to change hearts, to instill love or contrition, or to inspire actions of atonement. As such, it does nothing to address the offender's broken relationships with his God or his neighbor, or to address the harms inflicted through his criminal acts.[34]

Penance means responding to Christ's call to an abundant life and freedom. Setting off on this journey of faith requires that one renounce the things of the world. To those skeptics who might dismiss as trifling the renunciation of the world by a prisoner who, seemingly, has already lost everything, Peter insists that reluctant renunciation is hardly enough. One must, rather, issue his renunciation affirmatively— a maneuver that the prisoner's history of loss and everyday precariousness makes all the more difficult. But one has no choice but to begin where one is, which in Peter's case is in the condition of guilt. While his guilt, as Peter sees it, is defined not by his crime but by his common heritage as a son of Adam, he acknowledges the special responsibility he bears as someone who through grave sin has injured his neighbors. Reconciliation with Jesus Christ entails that he, in Paul's language to the Ephesians, "put away the old self . . . and put on the new self,"[35] so as to go forward, seeking "what is noble in the sight of all."[36]

Coupling penance for past wrongs with an ethics going forward, Peter describes this requisite death and rebirth as a *conscientization*. Conscientization is the ongoing critical self-examination that lies at the core of personal and spiritual growth. This process does not take place in isolation. Rather, full fidelity to a faith through which, as Paul says to the Romans, one is not conquered by evil, but conquers evil with good, necessarily requires fierce engagement with one's circumstances.[37] In the case of the prisoner, penance requires that one refuse the habits of dehumanization, vengeance, and wrath to which our criminal justice system has acclimated him. Because this system expediently sacrifices the true needs of victims and offenders for short-term political ends, at the heart of this transformation, penance requires that one transcend as well the dehumanizing binary of victimizer and victimized.

As to the nuts and bolts, Peter vows and advocates four practical measures, two more or less discrete and immediate, and two comprehensive and ongoing. They are, first, an expression of regret; second, a full confession; third, making amends as far as possible; and, lastly, working toward creating positive relations in the place of the division, hurt, and harm wrought by his crime. By adopting these measures and by calling upon others to do the same, Peter hopes to impart healing on a world ravaged by sin.[38]

It is difficult to capture by means of synopsis alone the erudition on display in Peter's proposal, and its exquisite balance of qualities often in tension: commitment and humility, diagnostic precision and idealistic courage. Plainly, it is a considered stab at making good. What grabs me most about the document is Peter's refusal, in spite of the change he is desperate to effect, to delude himself about the difficulties of the task at hand. Channeling Paul, Peter exhorts himself and the reader not to "conform to this age but be transformed by the renewal of your mind."[39] As Peter repeatedly stresses, however, an "age" is a pervasive and resilient entity. No quick fix will abolish this age of "criminality, victimization, and even victimhood." Transformation, both individual and collective, and the freedom that such transformation will enable, are not present conditions but horizons to strive for. The journey ahead is as impossible as it is necessary.

Much in the way, then, that Baraka, as would-be bad man, resists the pull of facile virtue unto putative "goodness," so does Peter—whose impassioned faith might qualify him a poor man—refuse the ready elixir of declaring himself already liberated. Freedom, for Peter, is not to be had via instantaneous grace or merely by affirming it so. Freedom will require the grinding, self-critical commitment to the life of love that is Jesus' mandate for women and men on earth. As subjects of this fallen age, we are *all* of us spiritually impoverished and psychically yoked. If his criminal guilt and the material fact of his incarceration make Peter an exceptional case, in his dire need for comprehensive overhaul, he epitomizes as well the fallenness that is the human condition. Freedom—the freedom to which we are all obligated to strive—will arrive eventually. But in the meantime, as a freshly fallen Adam learned and a weathered Candide affirmed, there's work to be done.[40]

By some kink of fortune, minutes after I receive Peter's reissued proposal, Vic will hand me four essays of varied lengths, which document, in sum, a history of his gathering frustration with (and presage his eventual break from) Inside-Out, the prisoner/outside college student dialogue group. While Vic's papers lack the acute sobriety of Peter's program, that is not their game. At once more confrontational and more playful, Vic's efforts are no less learned or critically engaged. Peppered with scattershot citations of Seneca, Eminem, Carol Gilligan, Karl Popper, Martin Luther King, Nietzsche, Joseph Heller, Pink Floyd, and Michel Foucault, among others, the papers represent a challenge to the program's director, an exhortation to his fellow course participants (the prisoner "insiders," especially), and a demonstration (to himself, principally) of his own sovereignty. In style, the pieces modulate back and forth between bald polemic and a more probing mode of immanent critique that judges the program against its own ideals. At the papers' core lies the following argument: If, by fostering dialogue and collaboration between insiders and outsiders Inside-Out is hoping to follow the lead of educators John Dewey and Paulo Freire and use education to overcome oppression, then, as Vic sees it, the program is falling miserably short of its goals.[41]

Vic's grievances are concrete: the diminishing number of outsiders, the shadowy procedure by which insiders are tapped for inclusion, the mechanisms by which insider authors are not credited individually, the overwillingness of the director to speak on prisoners' behalf, and the overly regimented course structure that leaves little time for spontaneous exchange—all of which reduces the insiders to little more than animals in a petting zoo. This litany of irritations betrays a coherent picture, one that Vic renders using the tools of critical theory. To wit, while Inside-Out may *talk* about combating prisoners' isolation, disempowerment, and infantilization, in the process of becoming an organization, these animating goals have been sacrificed for the putative "greater good" of preserving the organization itself. Rather than informing the group's actual practices, then, these ideals have become little more than an ideology, one used to crush dissent and prop up the extant regime of power. Having drunk the program's Kool-Aid, Vic's fellow insiders have become principals in their own subjugation, whereby— much like the docile schoolboy, the prostrate parishioner, and the flag-waving citizen—they sacrifice the possibility of true individual and social freedom for the sycophantic acquiescence to local authority. In the end, far from troubling the structures of power through which prisoners are dominated, the program merely serves to reinforce them.

While I will be floored by the simultaneous receipt of Peter's and Vic's papers, I will be unsure of what precisely to make of their juxtaposition. For the longest time I will presume that the insight embedded in this shard of serendipity is to be found in the contrast between the two men's texts: the contrast between religion and secularism, between proposal and critique, and, ultimately, in extrapolating from text to character, that between Peter's enabling optimism and Vic's self-defeating resignation. But after repeated readings, I will come to read these texts not for what they suggest about their authors' inner lives, but for what they reveal about their capacities for action. Arguably influenced as much by Baraka's take on honor as by Kierkegaard's take on Abraham, and in a way that perhaps renders religion a red herring, I will come to see in Peter's and Vic's texts not the contrast between contentment and frustration, but parallel evidence of two men struggling with the tools they have come by to reshape, in ways small and big, the world as they find it.[42] In each case, the odds are as long as the power is unequally distributed. But against a world set in its crummy ways, each man pushes incrementally on toward its remediation. In Vic's case, righteous struggle will soon yield to bitterness. The condition is a fragile one, and courage will require renewal. But at least for the moments captured by Vic's and Peter's prose, two selves stoked toward transformation catch fire and threaten to engulf others.

Albeit far too late, in this dual characterization of Peter's proposal and Vic's papers I can't help but believe I hold the kernel for an affirmative response to Brian's badgering inquiry from last night as to whether or not there are at Graterford men of faith.

Before the office empties, Gorski fetches me to accompany him, as he occasionally does, on his rounds of the Restricted Housing Units.

Both of us coatless in the unseasonably warm sun, we pass the defunct garden, where, before the raid, as Baraka tells it, a guy could forget he was even in prison. To our right is L Block, where Sayyid is. Behind the barbed wire, prisoners out from the hole for their daily hour of air pace and idle in the sideways stack of ten-by-fifty-foot chain-link cages, one man to a cage. Just shy of the prison's eastern wall, we hang a left and pass through the barbed wire that cordons off J Block and the rear sally port.

The J Block tiers, which house a mixture of men in the hole and some of the commonwealth's 225-plus death row prisoners, are stubby old things. Each one consists of eight cells flanked by doubled hallways that leave eight feet of clearance between these special prisoners and the free people who come to see them. Using the inner hallway, we tour Gorski's regulars: a flabby but frail seventy-something with a death sentence, a cloudy right eye, and a table littered with orange silos of meds; Shepherd, one of four brothers serving life or on death row, whom the grinding industrial fan renders all but inaudible; a tenderized African-American man whose crossbars are stuffed with sci-fi paperbacks; a second black guy who blurs with the first; a deeply decent-seeming Latino death row prisoner roughly my age whose photographs of his kid disappear now and again behind an armada's worth of flapping laundry; and Andy, who once he's done his 120 days for having lost it at a CO, will rejoin Gorski's monthly session where he'll make clear to kids from nearby St. Gabe's reformatory school that prison is simply no place for them. Andy, who's white and whose brother just won a Rhodes scholarship, teases me about my dissertation's lack of a thesis, wonders whether what I've seen at Graterford has made me more willing to forgive, and lauds proposed legislation that would make lifers over fifty who've served twenty-five years parole-eligible.[43] Only when our exchange is almost over do I notice that half-obscured by laundry and gloom, huddling against the bars by my feet, there is an elf of a boy, his torso covered in Celtic tattoos and shirtless in the hotbox heat.

When Gorski has bestowed upon each of his regulars the Eucharist, a prayer, or just a few minutes of company, we leave J Block for the rapidly dwindling sunlight. Gorski emphasizes the importance, for the death row guys especially, of "a ministry of presence." How critical it is for them just to have somebody drop in now and again to say hi. "It doesn't even have to be particularly religious," he says. "Just to show them that they're remembered."

Pennsylvania has a long tradition of such meager but lifesaving ministry. In 1835, a Prussian visitor to Eastern State Penitentiary quoted one anonymous prisoner who noted that his "greatest joy was the visit of a cricket or a butterfly because it seemed like company." The visitor, a

Doctor Julius, observed: "The Bible also became a document of interest to the prisoner, because his possession of it was a favor during his good behavior. The infrequent visit of the moral instructor, or of some visitor from the outside world, might be lengthened or made more frequent if the prisoner would try to learn to read from the Bible as a textbook. Moreover, any visit from an officer came to have an intense meaning to the prisoner. Such visits alone connected him with the world of living beings."[44]

"You know," Gorski says. "The administration instructs staff to alter their routines so prisoners can't anticipate your movements, but in the case of the death row guys, I do my best to have precisely the same routine every week. They depend on it so much." I realize as he says it how many of our J Block exchanges concluded with the caged man half stating, half pleading, "See you next week?"

I couldn't help but notice how fiercely present the ordinarily acerbic and uncoddling Gorski was with the guys on J Block, and I tell him so. Gorski acknowledges how much he likes it, ministering to the guys on the RHU. Indeed, from the tempo of his speech and the glimmer in his eye, Gorski seems elated—elated in a way seemingly common to chapel volunteers following their services, elated much in a way that I myself frequently feel when released into the parking lot after an intense day. What a crazy thing we've built in the penitentiary, I think to myself. How truly bizarre that this awful place should afford such profound pleasure to those who feel called to enter into it and partake in its overflowing meaningfulness.

With L Block on our left, I ask Gorski if he's planning on going to see Sayyid.

"I'd rather not," he says.

I'm disappointed but remain silent.

"It has nothing to do with Sayyid," he says. "It's just that they've already started feeding the guys, so they have things to throw now."

Gorski is harassed in the RHU much less now than when the Church's sexual abuse scandal was raging.[45] Back then, on visits to J and L, he was sure to get called "baby raper" and worse. The charcoal-hued Keita, who's greeted with shouts of "Ooga booga" and "Shaku Zulu" is, nowadays, more of a target.

●

Andy, Gorski says over dinner in the dimming staff dining hall, is not generally one to make trouble. He grew up in a $400,000 home and he went to high school with the son of Gorski's friend. With Andy, Gorski says, it was really driven home for the first time: how these people are from the same world that he's from. And though, as I know, he is quite conservative, he honestly believes that Andy is innocent of the crime for which he was convicted.

Gorski scans my face for surprise. The proclamation is indeed out of character. Gorski is acutely allergic to liberal sentimentalists who cast prisoners as helpless and lodge all blame on the *system* and its operators. "Yeah, he can be an angel for an hour, sure," Gorski wants to say to such idiots, "but you don't see him raping somebody back on the block." More than once, with joyous incredulity Gorski has told me about the time he took Reverend Carvel, the aging St. Dismas volunteer, back to L Block, and how, when Carvel couldn't hear the prisoner through the small, square, eye-level window, the foolish priest got down on his knees and spoke through the knee-high slot where the food tray goes, practically begging for a face full of feces.

Gorski is not alone. The volunteers can drive Baumgartner nuts, too: the sanctimonious supporters of convicted cop-killer *cum* political prisoner, Mumia Abu-Jamal; the white volunteers who play black; and the egomaniacs who treat saving souls like notches on a bedpost.[46] Baumgartner told the story of one such preacher. At the close of his service, he pled and pled for someone to answer the call. Eventually one guy approached the altar—a demonstrably mentally ill new-sider who came up more or less every week. The volunteer left wholly delighted with himself, beaming at his morning's work. When he returned to the jail six months later, he asked Baumgartner: "And how is that young man?" Baumgartner didn't have the heart to tell him that he'd hanged himself in his cell.

Gorski tells me Andy's story. In college, Andy got mixed up with drugs and one night a girl ended up dead. The DA put the pinch on a local drug dealer who was somehow involved. In exchange for a deal, the dealer ratted out Andy who, though innocent, had no alibi for the hours in question.

While I have no judgment about this account on its merits, I suggest to Gorski the possibility that his empathy might say more about his own positioning than about the facts of the case. The key variable, I say, might be the $400,000 home that locates Andy within the recognizable domain of Gorski's own world.

Father Gorski disagrees. There's something particular about Andy that makes Gorski doubt he did the crime for which he was sentenced.

For scholarly and civic reasons both, I'm not particularly interested in the facts of men's crimes. In light of how we think about prisoners, I concede that the preoccupation with such facts seems merely "common sense"—and it is. But tethering the substance of each man's character to his crime is no less bluntly unreasoned than if, as one with a fondness for psychoanalysis, I made a point of probing each man about his relationship to his mother. Yes, each man at Graterford has a mother from whose womb he sprung, just as each man has a crime for which he was convicted. Neither, however, is necessarily my business, nor necessarily determinative of his character. From a political standpoint, moreover, undue attention to individual criminal acts obscures the root causes that bring men here for life. Take Teddy, Sayyid, and Kazi. Inasmuch as these three men grew up on the same block, the crimes for which they were convicted were plainly symptomatic of other precipitating factors.[47] As for an ethics of engagement, am I truly obligated to probe a man about the worst thing he's ever done? Would anyone think to impose such a brutal hermeneutic on me or Father Gorski?

If I've been more than happy to avoid the specifics of crime, the men of the chapel have proven unwilling to follow suit. As I tell Gorski now, of those prisoners I get to know beyond *"how you feeling?"* sooner or later, the majority make a point of telling me about their cases. Of these, roughly half—like Baraka and Teddy—want me to know that they *didn't* do it, and half—like Peter and Lenny—want me to know that they *did*, and that they take full responsibility for what they have done. As far as claims to innocence go, I'm effortlessly agnostic as to the relationship between these declarations and the blurred facts on the bygone ground. When men like Baraka, Teddy, and, in this case, Andy, claim innocence, I presume that they truly *believe* themselves to be so. However, whether they were factually innocent of the crime for which they were convicted or whether, after years of denial and magical thinking, they've somehow managed to convince themselves they were, I'm in no position to judge.[48] Just as there are, no doubt, men in Graterford for crimes for which they have zero culpability, I figure that there's a lot a man can avoid knowing when his last shot at freedom depends on it. In either case, as far as my own civic entanglement is concerned, whatever evil these men might have done is secondary to what we have collectively decided to do to them—which in the case of a man like Baraka, for example, is to imprison him for longer than I've been alive.[49]

, As I reassert to Gorski, should we factor out Andy's race and class—elements which, I say, make Andy an easier object for his empathy and mine—I have no reason to presume Andy as more viable a candidate for innocence than, say, Teddy.

But in Teddy's case, Gorski pushes back, there is a long history of crime, a long track record with which to make sense of his arson-murder.

But that, I counter, is the flip side of the $400,000 home thing. Most people who grow up in $400,000 homes don't have lengthy rap sheets. Whereas a former drug addict from the ghetto . . .

Shifting from the fact of Teddy's guilt to its psychic consequences, Gorski pinpoints the absence in Evangelical Protestantism of anything like the sacrament of reconciliation. Without reconciliation—that is to say, the Catholic rite of confession—a guy like Teddy will never have peace. He'll always have to carry around the burden of the lie.

I detail for Gorski the Protestant guys' frequent invocation of the distinction between the virtue that Paul counsels to the Philippians of finding contentment wherever one happens to be, versus the vice of acceptance, which to them is tantamount to soul suicide. Seems to me, I say, that a good number of the Evangelicals here—the lifers especially—display an astounding capacity for achieving this frangible equanimity.

Gorski doesn't buy it. In his perspective, the simplistic formula of Christ's instant and unconditional forgiveness is thin and wholly unsustainable. Meaning: in placing his faith in the insufficiently exacting God of Evangelical Protestantism, a bad man like Teddy deceives only himself, and only fleetingly at that. Roman Catholicism, by contrast, is the one tradition that institutionally ritualizes forgiveness. It's the guys who experience *that*, Gorski argues—*especially* the lifers—who are most at peace because they've been given the tools to assimilate what they've done and a ritual process for ongoing absolution.

"It's just good psychology," Gorski says. As far as Teddy goes, he'll never be at peace because he's never asked for forgiveness. *"Faith alone* can be a dangerous crutch. Some truly live it, but for others . . ." He trails off.

Talk turns to the Legion of Mary and the ragtag bunch that congregates there. "I-tards," Father Gorski says, alluding to a horrible quip I recently made about the developmentally disabled men who live on upper I Block. He laughs and reminisces about how back when Al was running the choir, it was full of "I-tards." We share a guilty chuckle. Knowing that Al and Father Gorski have had their run-ins, I come to Al's defense, saying that I found his outreach to upper I Block guys quite admirable, perhaps even "Christian."

Bypassing my sentimentalist bait, Gorski sticks to the absurdist, launching into an impression of his parishioner, the frantically insane Anthony Lukes. In a rough approximation of Lukes's inimitable oratorical style, Gorski delivers a breathy diatribe about the "political, economic, social, critical forces" that are shaping the present historic moment, and the "political, economic, social, and critical aspects" of the situation at hand. It is, in fact, true that Lukes speaks like the skipping recording of a sociology graduate student. Sticking with Lukes, Gorski says that while under his regime only baptized Catholics can receive Communion, his predecessor, Father Rzonka, gave Communion to anyone who asked. When he came on, Gorski took Lukes, who is black, to be one of these newly unsanctioned holdovers. But Lukes gave him his mom's phone number. "Turns out she's more Catholic than I am!" Gorski quips. "Go figure."

On the topic of his mentally challenged parishioners, I ask Gorski about the disturbingly childlike Michael. Shaking his head, Gorski says he has to watch Michael carefully because he has sex issues, and that if Michael leaves for the bathroom and is followed out by another guy, odds are they're having sex in there. I tell Gorski I've heard this same thing from Bird. Gorski agrees with Bird that guys like Michael know full well what they're doing and need to be held responsible for their actions.

We head for the chapel. Soaking in the tranquillity of the deserted corridor, Gorski muses rhapsodically on the moment following Saturday night mass when he first leaves the prison. He loves that moment, he says. That regardless of season, at that hour the parking lot feels so quiet and serene. I say I know exactly what he means.

Gorski asks what my friends think about what I do. I tell him about the so-called "Capote effect," where, by spilling over with arresting details of prison life, I rudely relegate everyone else's dinner table conversation to an afterthought. (The effect is named after a scene in the recent biopic when, after spinning some stunning yarn about the Clutter murders, Capote breaks the resulting silence by sarcastically inquiring, "And what have *you* been doing?")[50]

Gorski concedes that he, too, is always the hit of the cocktail party.

Baumgartner's phone is ringing off the hook. In all likelihood someone is dead, but nobody is finding out about it until Monday.

Kazi arrives and sits down unassumingly at Sayyid's desk. More convivial solo than when around others, he asks how my project is going. I tell him about the week I've spent and how I'm beginning to suspect that it might furnish the structure not just for a chapter but for the book as a whole. He asks me when I'm out of here for good.

Perhaps due to this week's heightened intensity, I'm beginning to sense the guys' awareness that I'm not long here. It feels to me like anticipated abandonment, but that might be a projection of my own discomfort, my first stirrings of fear about what will happen when these men of flesh and blood are flattened out by distance and craft into something more closely resembling characters. What will happen when they lose the power to hail me in return? In what I write, will I do them justice? Or will time and distance facilitate betrayal? When I bring these worries to Lenny, he'll backhandedly reassure me that, as prisoners, they simply assume people like me will screw them over; but they're open to being pleasantly surprised in the event that I don't.

I still have lots of folks to talk to, I stress. Kazi nods, saying that there are some really low-profile guys, guys who rarely speak but whom I should definitely track down. I ask for names. He singles out Qasim, Yunus, and a couple of other Sajdah elders, all of whom I've heard of, I say, but none of whom I've talked to yet. I ask Kaz why he's down this evening. He explains that he's here to work on his postconviction writ, whose filing date is fast approaching.

While I resist the impulse now, next week I'll ask Kazi about how he figures Sayyid is faring in the hole. "You gotta adjust," the notoriously institutionalized Kazi will say. "In prison you really got to adjust."

For now, though, we each write in silence.

Al lights up and says he would've come down earlier if he knew I was here. I pepper him with questions about last night's Bible study. It takes place in the kitchen in the back of B Block, usually with four other guys. It was blessed, he says. And was he teaching or preaching? Some of each, he says, but a lot of preaching, which he doesn't like because it makes him too emotional. I ask him what he was preaching about. Al's face tightens in search of the right word. Moments pass. Gratitude? I ask, more probably because it's on my mind than any other reason. Yeah, he says, making me wish I'd outlasted his silence.

When Al asks me how I'm feeling, I confess my incipient separation anxiety.

"When are you gonna disappear?" he asks.

"One more month as it's been, and then back when necessary."

"Like a couple of times a month?"

"Something like that," I say, though I doubt it'll be that frequent. Silence. "It's going to be pretty boring without me, huh?"

"Your presence will be missed," Al says. He can't believe it's been almost a year already.

As will shortly become clear, I'm not the only one for whom the emptying of the hourglass sparks concern. If by last summer Al and Teddy first jokingly put a bounty on my soul, with my departure now looming, Al will begin to make his play for real. As he'll tell me next week, he's been worrying about me, worried about what's going to happen to me during the tribulation—the tumultuous period described in *Revelation* after the faithful are raptured but before Christ's return. For while he knows that Enoch and Elijah will eventually advocate on the Jews' behalf, he'll just want to make sure "I wasn't going to be going through all that." Because I know him and Teddy, he'll stress, the Word has been made available to me, so I'm going to be held to that higher standard. He'll press me: What exactly is my plan for what's going to happen to me after I die, when I'm forced to stand before God's judgment?[51]

I will concede that as far as personal salvation goes, I really don't have much of a strategy. As best I can tell, I'll divulge, before we're born and after we die, we're like water in the ocean—wholly undifferentiated. For the brief, thrilling, and sometimes lonely time that we're here, we're like water in the toilet bowl—discretely contained, and, as such, seemingly disconnected from all the other water that is. Then, at the end of our days: flush. And back to the oceanic oneness we return.

At one time that might well have been true, Al will reply as if what I'm saying isn't too far out—but everything changed when the spirit was breathed into Adam. And while there was a time in his life when he knew he was doing wrong, God came to him and saved him. And because God already did that for an animal like him, he's certain that eternal life is to follow. "The spirit dwells with me forever," Al will say, "and I have salvation because Christ Jesus died on the cross. Jesus Christ took my place for me."

For me, I'll try to explain, the most pressing order of business is less what's going to happen when I die than how I'm to live in the meantime. Digging back into my day school training, I'll detail the rabbinic distinction between *mitzvoth bein adam l'makom* and *mitzvoth bein adam l'havero*—commandments regulating the relationship between man and God versus those regulating man's relationship with his fellow man. For me, I'll say, one's relationship with God is essentially a private matter. What concerns me more is how I might live up to my obligations to my fellow woman and man.

Because Al's own sense of duty—the one that drives him to do everything in his power to save my soul—is inextricable from his relationship to God, he'll struggle to understand *who* exactly my relationship is with. I'll explain that while for him, as I understand it, one voice inside his head—the one he calls God—speaks louder and clearer than all others, my mind houses only a jumbled chorus, whose voices I take to be aspects of myself. But who is my relationship with? he'll again probe. Rather than with God above, I'll say, with whom my exchanges historically proved to be frustratingly monological, for me, relationship inheres in the social, in moments such as the present one when we are moved by the ideas and feelings of one another.

After thirty more minutes of conduits and cul-de-sacs, we'll return to the problem of salvation. "If Jesus Christ isn't who He says He is," Al will confidently declare, "then let God do whatever He wants to me." Meaning, all he can do is live and die with his conviction, and if that conviction proves to be wrong, well, then he's willing to face the consequences. Excitedly, I'll tell Al that in my more confident moments, this is *precisely* how my godless ethical convictions feel to me. Maybe I'm wrong in discounting personal salvation, I say, but I'm doing the very best I can with the information I have, and if one day I'm forced to stand before God and defend the choices I've made, I'm willing to make my case.

What will have begun in rancor will give way to an extraordinary moment of translation. I will be engulfed in a sense of fellowship, forged through hard-won mutual recognition—a sense that perhaps our two worldviews aren't so irreconcilable after all. Seemingly, something similar will happen for Al. As he'll say to me the following day, he figures that if we just took the time to talk it all out, we'd discover that when it comes down to it, we don't really disagree about anything.

Vic arrives and parks himself at Sayyid's desk, which Kazi has vacated. Al asks him how long he thinks I've been around. "Dunno, six months?" Vic hazards. "A year," Al corrects him.

"So when are you out of here?" Vic asks. I tell him what I told Al.

"I don't get it," he says, "why can't you stick around?"

"Because I have *no function* here," I say.

"You and seventy-five percent of our staff!" Vic declares.

I laugh, but Vic is adamant that my purposelessness around here is a wholly generic condition.

"Do you drink?" Al asks.

Having been browbeaten before for my admittedly intemperate, fornicating lifestyle, I hesitate to give an answer. "Yeah," I tentatively say, "a bit."

"Then you could do Baumgartner's job. Baumgartner drinks." I can't tell whether this is empathy or censure.

I tell them about how I'm working on landing a Villanova class for next winter, so that'll guarantee me an ongoing presence (though not necessarily with men like Al). And then there's the pending mid-state job opportunity. If that works out, I say, then I can pretty much stay on forever. Furthermore, should that come through, I could figure out ways to bring in students. In such an event, I ask, what sorts of things might they want to do with a bunch of college students?

"Sex show," Vic says, to Al's delight.

"No, really," I say.

"I'm serious!" Vic pleads.

"Come on."

"Well, let's see," Vic tries again. "Some kind of religion thing . . ." He fades out in search of some kind of religion thing.

"It doesn't have to be a religion thing per se," I say. "Just something educational that might involve them and you. Can you think of anything between religion and a sex show?"

"Nude show?" Vic tries, and again Al loses it.

From atop the CO's desk, Kazi gazes into the corridor past the first trickle of men arriving for mass. In the conference room, Ezra, one of the stately old heads who pomades his hair and carries a comb in his breast pocket, is rehearsing True Vine. In Baumgartner's assessment, Ezra is the chapel's most talented musician. Although according to the same source, during performances, Ezra likes to mess with the tempo to throw the other guys off.

Next door, in the Catholic office, Jack, dressed tonight as an altar boy, is holding forth in culture-warrior mode for some of the usual suspects. Emboldened by my arrival, Jack rails on about the liberals.

"How can you be so mad at the liberals," I ask, "when the conservatives have control of the executive, the legislative, and the judiciary branches?"

"Well," Jack says, "Philly's still run by Democrats and they screw that up plenty. Tax and spend, tax and spend." Jeff, a second Catholic regular, is slight in frame, and he too is one of Gorski's altar boys. He also objects. Even with Alito, Jeff says, the Supreme Court still has only three true conservatives.

"If the conservatives are pro-life," an incessant yeller yells, "then why don't they support health insurance covering fertility treatments!"

"Because they're not natural," Jeff explains, favoring the restriction.

The office grows increasingly cramped as the gathering horde— fifteen men, all white—cluster for confession.

In the back of the chapel, I find Gorski's clerk, Mike Callahan, whom I take as a fellow refugee from his coworker's vitriol. "Why do you think Jack's so pissed off at liberals?" I ask.

"Yeah," Mike says, "it's Ridge he ought to be mad at." In a well-worn lament, Mike rues the political climate that brought on the raid. He invokes Mudman Simon and Reginald McFadden, perpetrators of two high-profile, media-electrifying crimes, which the new Ridge administration exploited so as to lengthen and harden punishment. While I'm quite familiar with Mudman the biker, who, out on parole from Graterford, shot and killed a New Jersey state trooper, I ask Mike to remind me of the details of the McFadden case. Mike recounts how upon his release from Graterford, McFadden went up to New York and killed a whole bunch of white people. He expresses sympathy for McFadden, who was only sixteen when he was sentenced to prison for a black-on-white murder, and then snitched his way to a commutation. "He didn't know any better," Mike says. "You know? What do you expect from someone who was raised here from the time he was a kid? He learns to deal."[52]

Santana sidles over to join us. When the beleaguered choir director discovers that we're talking about the raid, he snarls his disgust and gestures goodbye with both hands.

"Had enough of this topic?" I ask.

"Look," he says, "if guys want to live with that for the rest of their lives, then that's fine, but I live for today."

Perhaps, I say in Mike's defense, part of living for today is teaching newcomers like me how today came to be like it is and not some other way.

That's fine, Santana says, he just doesn't want any part of it.

It's a fair position. There is, admittedly, an indulgent quality to the unflagging ruminations about the raid. Here especially, it must feel good to tell stories in which, for instance, other people are the guilty ones.

If Saturday is a theme on human sadness played in a minor key, it is during mass that the score reaches its crescendo. No doubt some of it is mine, but whether in the summer's long light or the blackest winter night, Catholic mass invariably brings home the horribleness of this place and the loneliness that must haunt the men who pass their days here.

In the distance, two small white statues, one of Mary and the other of Joseph, sit atop the altar, while on the chapel's flanks, fourteen wooden boxes have been unshuttered to reveal, in carved relief, the stations of the cross. Two-thirds of the 130 men assembled are browns and the remainder are blues, though of the browns a sizable share have dressed up for the occasion in white T-shirts. A scattering of small caucuses, some sober, some frolicsome, fill the chapel with a beehive buzz. As generally comes with a crowd here, there are some fearsome characters, too. Not too far from where I'm standing in the back, in the last pew before the final six that have been sectioned off with yellow police tape, the customary cluster of shiny white heads and inked bodies pulse with effortless aggression. From the back of one bulldog head, a pair of tattooed eyes—seductively lashed and meth-head wide—stare back at me.

Without forewarning, Father Gorski enters the chapel along with four green-robed altar boys. Between them, the men carry a bowl, a chalice, and a large gold cross. As the procession hustles toward the altar, the din of chatter rises and deadens. At stage left, Peter's trio sits at the ready, while at the foot of stage right, Lap faces the pews, poised to translate. When the procession hits the stage, the music starts.

In spite of my expectations, mass, when it arrives, proves itself to be—disappointingly, and mercifully—a dead letter. Hymns are sung, their exultant lyrics seemingly belied by the trio's plaintive, reedy sound. A prayer for the sick is offered. Two Bible readings are recited, the first from the Old Testament, by Father Gorski, and the second, from the New, by tonight's guest, Peter's invitee, a lay Franciscan sister. Both passages are didactic in kind, with the former cautioning against false prophets, and the latter a reflection on the unmarried man's anxiety about and devotion to the Lord. From where I stand along the back wall, in the worn-down, somewhat disassociated state in which I find myself, the Bible readings might as well be in Greek.

My incontinent attention is claimed by a CO who approaches Jack at the aisle's mouth and hands him a note. Pulling plastic tiles from the green box that sits on the back pew, Jack spells out a two-letter, four-numeral DOC number on a hand-held placard, which he hands to a black guy in white who parades it down the leftward aisle until it catches the designated eye. His number recognized, the seated man springs up and hustles out to receive his visitor.

Dutifully, I transcribe the homily, which Gorski delivers like he's got a plane to catch. "In tonight's Gospel reading," he says, "we read the verse from which priestly celibacy is derived. While marriage is a holy sacrament, the Church Fathers decided it would be a good thing for a priest to be freed from the obligations and demands of family so he may dedicate himself entirely to God." Gorski notes the Church Fathers' wisdom in this regard. Though a decidedly different path from that of having a family, being a priest is, Gorski argues, an exceedingly rewarding vocation.

"Many of you are caught in the middle, too," Gorski says. "Even though many of you are married, you are living celibate lives. This is a challenge, I know. How can you do this in a way that will give you strength? The only way is to sacrifice yourself in prayer, to offer yourself up in prayer for your friends and family outside. Bishop Fulton Sheen"— the former American archbishop and radio and television broadcaster— "thought that the question Jesus would ask at the pearly gates to each arrival is: 'Where are your children?'[53] Even those of you who don't have biological children still have the obligation to bring forth spiritual children. And those of you who *do* have children—you need to do what you can so that they will lead righteous paths and enter heaven."

The Apostles' Creed is recited. The Lord is asked to reach out to the politicians and victims of violence and war so that people will hear Jesus' Word. He is asked to provide safe schools, and to look after those who serve the poor.

The band sings another song, this one in two-part harmony, with Peter singing tenor and Jeff the altar boy in falsetto. "*We hold a treasure,*" goes its refrain. For a moment, the music's unanticipated ethereal beauty blows away the fog and restores in me the feeling of permeability we sometimes call presence.

But that mood also passes quickly.

Father Gorski chants the liturgy of the Communion cycle. Twice— when the wine has been turned to Christ's blood and when the host has become Christ's body—a bell is sounded.

The Lord's Prayer is recited, and amens aver it.

"Peace be unto you," Father Gorski declares, and the men respond. Turning to greet one another, they trade embraces and words of peace. When all those within reach have been blessed, some turn and wave peace symbols across the chapel, halting their outstretched Vs where eye contact is made.

Jack finds me where I am. "In all seriousness," he says, "peace be unto you and your family." I echo back his words, and we embrace.

"*Lamb of God, who takes away the sins of the world, grant us peace.*"

Gorski invites the practicing Roman Catholics to come up and receive Communion, and welcomes members of other Christian communities of faith to come up for a special blessing. A queue forms down the central aisle, granting cover for conversations to recommence. As the body and blood of Christ are dispensed, the line grows shorter, and a second wave rises up for its turn. Among them is the mentally disabled Michael, who joins the line straight from the vestibule. As the ranks of the reseated grow, the din of chatter crests into a sharp *shhhhhh*.

Following announcements, the recessional begins. "Lead me, Lord, lead me in Thy righteousness," Peter sings.

I'm relieved mass is over, relieved not only to be set free of my sense of disconnect, but freed, too, from the potential catharsis immanent to it—an unbidden undoing for which I currently lack the stamina.

For what feels like the thousandth time, I'm approached by a blue. What am I doing? he wants to know. Am I getting paid for it? How much am I getting paid? In six months he'll be maxing out. It'll be the second time. In the interim, he's doing what he can to get off E and onto one of the brown blocks—"the blues still think that they're on the streets over there!" This blue is a Muslim, and he's been wondering about me since he saw me at Jum'ah. Does he go to a masjid on the street? I ask. Yeah, he says, Masjid Warith al-Deen. He was in Graterford back in '89, he tells me. Things have changed a ton since then.

In a frenzy of blinks and twitches, Anthony Lukes kicks off the third installment of Peter's fledgling group of Secular Franciscans with an opening prayer.[54]

When Lukes finishes, the ebullient volunteer welcomes the fifteen or so men assembled. In addition to a mountain of literature, the sister distributes handcrafted strings of crown rosary. She encourages each man to take one but warns she's been counseled that if they wear them around, they'll be confiscated.

A rapping behind me calls my eyes to the small window in the door leading from Classroom A to the chapel. I turn to find Gorski's face, which is quickly replaced by a beckoning hand.

Aside from Santana, who is tidying the altar, the chapel is empty.

"What's up?" I ask.

"It's quite unfortunate," Gorski says. "You just missed something special for your book."

"What's that?"

"Well," he says, "Michael was helping collect books when four COs showed up in formation, and led him away by the arm."

I ask Gorski what that means.

"He must have reported that *something* happened," Gorski says matter-of-factly, or perhaps euphemistically, but which in either case means rape.

I don't say anything.

Gorski spoke to one of the COs, who told him that Michael had reported an incident from earlier this afternoon.

"What'll happen now?" I ask.

"He'll be taken away," Gorski says, "and matters will be investigated. Whatever they find, he's most likely headed to the hole for a while."

Having nothing to say, I flimsily shake my head and return to my seat in classroom A, where in lieu of thinking and feeling, I lower my head and record another round of clockwise-moving recitations of men's derelict loyalty to a loving God, and of their earnest efforts, at this late hour, to finally do right by Him.

As I enter a vestibule still banging and humming with Ezra's jam, Anthony Lukes creeps over to me, tilts his bug-eyed face too closely into mine, and whispers, "I know you're writing a masterpiece, a masterpiece." As an advance review, it's more heartening than the biting feedback he gave me last month, when, with equally inappropriate proximity, he said, "I heard you on NPR. You were doing an exposé on us animals." (I had not, in fact, been on NPR.) With one hand pressed on my shoulder, Anthony pulls Father Gorski in with the other: "He's writing a masterpiece, Father. A masterpiece, I tell you!"

Egged on by a madman, I find myself entertaining, as I gather my things from Baumgartner's office, the grandiose thought that I might, indeed, be in the midst of producing something special. Inflated with this promise, I head for the front gate. Behind me, Ezra's groove reverberates, then echoes, and finally goes silent.

Only miles down the road, my euphoria darkens and I tear up from excitement, empathy, and exhaustion. In ways I couldn't possibly yet conceive, the interval contained in these pages will reverberate for me for a very long time. In and beyond the writing of this book, this week will acquire—both as an object of compulsive repetition, and as a spur for my most spiritually nourishing and ethically ambitious actions—an unmistakable family resemblance to those transformative events in proclaimed fidelity to which so many in the chapel live their lives.[55]

But it will be years before I'm capable of this conceptualization.

What I understand already, however, as I will earnestly but self-consciously confess to my friend and colleague Maggie at the other end of the drive, over an uncommonly potent Belgian beer in our neighborhood bar, is that my fieldwork will shortly be finished and that the conditions of my life will change. And I pray, or something roughly equivalent, for the strength of character to prove myself deserving of the trust these men have invested in me.

SUNDAY

THESIS 8

There is no general rule that characterizes the relationship between the chapel man and his religion. For some, a given religious tradition provides one additional set of elements in a mosaic of ideas and practices. Others *sell out* and come to act and think the entirety of their lives through the terms of their adopted tradition. Some cultivate rage, and others gratitude. Some become monks, and some scholars. Some become apostles and share the good news. Some explore other religions. In pursuit of truth or justice, many become good. A select few are extraordinary. Some travel the world through texts. Some backslide. Some wander away. Some commit themselves to repaying the debt incurred through their crime. Some skirt on the surface of practice and hang out with their homies. Some make friends. Some band together and build institutions. Some take advantage, some make peace, some don't give a shit about much. Most all, in their own way, struggle. Inevitably, through genius and frailty, imitation and innovation, as finished men and as works in progress, each man will make his religious practices uniquely his own. The permutations are endless, and each is worth taking seriously as religion.

THESIS 9

From a sociological perspective, however, chapel religion does one thing principally: it helps to transform convicts into prisoners—by which we mean those with the embodied know-how to survive prison. Often, by hailing men into the monkish disciplines befitting such a cellular edifice, religion at Graterford makes incarcerated men feel free even as it crafts the cosmos in the prison's regimented image. If prone to hyperbole, one could well speak of the Warden-God—or, at Graterford, the Superintendent-God. The Superintendent-God's law is extreme but eccentric. Those subject to this law are frequently intolerant of trivial behaviors and permissive of other ones that under a less capricious deity would surely be prohibited. Or, just as likely, the law's letter has only a tenuous relationship to daily practice. While the proof, it is frequently said, is in the pudding, in this fishbowl, where every foible and trespass is visible, no one is unfallen. "Deviance is normal here," Baraka said. "If you didn't have deviance, you wouldn't have daily repentance." And so it *works*.

This disciplining works through groups, and it works *for* groups. As frequently cited, then, there are, indeed, social advantages to be garnered from these practices, with fellowship, protection, solidarity, and company as only some of the relevant yields. Upon reading these theses, however, and concluding that I'd overemphasized the ways that religion authorizes religious groups, Vic will accuse me of "having drunk too much of the Kool-Aid some in the chapel were serving." Never forget, he will remind me, that what I've observed in the chapel is only what the authorities have allowed to exist. "If a particular religion becomes too much of a problem, it will be stifled and its adherents scattered into the four winds of the U.S. correctional system."[1]

As a reflection of institutional priorities, then, and of the social reality of the prisoners who, with their bodies and minds, bring them to life, Graterford's religious practices are principally geared to help a man survive only in the conditions he currently finds himself.

But given a sufficiently materialist perspective, the charge that chapel religion is reactionary in character might convincingly be levied not only against all religion but, indeed, against all but the most inscrutable and daring social practices.

THESIS 10

Religion at Graterford is decidedly of its time. In this era of carceral control, as educational and therapeutic opportunities have withered, increasingly, if a prisoner is looking to work on himself spiritually or intellectually, he will venture down to the chapel to do so. Timely as well is the *kind* of religion we find here. Figuratively and literally, the crusaders for social justice on the religious left have all but lost their teeth. As rehabilitation has given way to corrections, and now to warehousing, the aspiration to systemic change has largely been abandoned. As sentences have grown in number and duration and prisoner populations have been atomized by administrative brutality and cunning, ever more inventive and stringent forms of personal purity have flourished. Changing oneself, it is said, is the way to change the world.

This formula is not delusional. These religious goals are real, and in their pursuit, the selves these men become and the gods to whom they relate are as real as the principals in any way of life. Inescapably, however, the renunciation of transformative politics in favor of personal transformation means, in practice, the de facto acceptance of our present *system*. Mass incarceration is here to stay; best that one should learn to live *in* it but not *of* it.

Graterford has more than its share of religious radicals. Contrary to the public's fears and wishes, though, these radicals are ascetics, not revolutionaries. Nowadays, only an old man or a madman would think to talk about revolution. For the time being, Graterford no longer produces Malcolm Xs. It produces prisoners. Not system shatterers, today's religious prisoners are, in their own quiet and righteous way—much like the overwhelming majority of us—system sustainers.

First comes the thumping of the bass and the bass drum. Then, through the jostle of bodies, come the claps and shouts that burst forth from the chapel every time the steel door is swung open. In the shaking vestibule, the joyousness is palpable.

Thank you, Jesus, for saving me!
Thank you, Jesus, for saving me!

While there's been contention lately over whether or not chapel workers should be allowed to use the office during the chapel's abbreviated Sunday program, the collective presence of Kazi, Teddy, and Al tells me that the fragile status quo has survived another week.

Teddy asks me what's up with my hair, so I head to the Imam's bathroom to tamp it down. In the Imam's office, Baraka sits at his desk, writing poetry. There are a slew of things I want to discuss with him, but it's nothing that can't wait until Tuesday.

In the conference room, half a dozen men—Jack among them—await the arrival of the Christian Science volunteer. Alex, the group's dreadlocked and sad-eyed prisoner leader, greets me unassumingly.

I ask Alex how his Villanova class is going. Thanking me for asking, he says he's doing his best to get into the "Ethics of War" class. Which reminds him, he needs to talk to somebody about it this morning: "You know that Muslim brother across the hall—Crocket?"

"Yeah," I say, "Sayyid?" Sayyid's been gone less than five days but I'm already surprised to hear him mentioned.

"Yes. Is he there?" he asks.

"No," I say, and nothing more.

Alex asks me, "So, are you giving the appeal this morning?"

I don't understand.

He means the sermon.

"No, no, no," I say, laughing. "I'm not qualified for that."

In a cloud of perfume at the chapel door, two Protestant ushers are distributing slips of paper for prayer requests to those in need, and emphatic handshakes to everyone.

The crowd of browns, blues, and two varieties of special-occasion whites—the dozen buttoned-down ushers, and scores dressed up in long white undershirts—fills the pews to the last row. I shimmy past the overturned chair and green plastic watering can that block the back leftward pew at the center aisle, and take a seat.

The Mighty Way is on the stage.

> *Because of who You are, I give you glory*
> *Because of who You are, I give you praise*
> *Because of who You are . . .*

Teddy plops down to my left. "Oh, man," he says, "watch this." He points to a guy in the row in front of us, a blue with a salt-and-pepper beard and an old-school flattop that's graying at the temples. "This dude used to be in another gang," Teddy says. "He used to beat me up."

He laughs from his stomach. Finding a hand on his shoulder, the blue turns around. Seeing Teddy, he breaks into a wide grin. The two of them stand and slam right shoulders affectionately. "He was from on down Khalifa's way," Teddy explains to me after the two men retake their seats. The Mighty Way plays on.

If your soul's not hanging with Jesus
It will surely drift away

Of the two hundred men in the chapel, eight out of ten are black. Most sit, but a couple dozen remain on their feet, where they sway back and forth, clapping.

O give thanks to the Lord
He is good.
He is good.
Hallelujah.

From the lectern, Amos, a Spanish service principal and this morning's worship leader, prays: "Let's take a minute to thank the King of Kings, who woke me up this morning, who saved me this morning, who died on the cross at Calvary. Let me understand Your greatness. We praise You, we glorify You, Lord, the Rose of Sharon, the shining star of Bethlehem, in Jesus' glorious name for the glory of God." Having risen in volume along with the prayer, the congregation quiets into the amen.

"Although we find ourselves behind these penitentiary walls," Amos says, "though we've even been back a couple of times . . . that's by the grace of God, because by all rights we should be dead already!"

Amos cues the band, which plays "In the Sanctuary." The hoppier number gets the congregation moving, and stirs me from the inside.

We lift our hands to give you the glory.
We lift our hands to give you the praise.
And we will praise you for the rest of our days.

A third of the men are now standing, clapping with arms upraised. One by one, Oscar, Damon, and John pass me by, each bestowing on me a hug as he does. Reverend Baumgartner comes over. Seeming especially jocular, he grabs Teddy and me each by the upper arm. "Teddy will interpret the sermon for you," he instructs the two of us.

While the bullish egalitarian in me viscerally bristles at Baumgartner's joke, he is surely right: the critical dimension of religion is indeed more my forte than Teddy's. Baumgartner himself brilliantly characterized the anticlerical, antiliturgical form of worship favored by Teddy, most of his fellow congregants, and a plurality of his countryfolk, too: "What Teddy prefers is the closely guarded illusion of unstructured prayer . . . just as long as it goes exactly as planned." And so it does. No priests, no sacraments, just the messy and putatively noncoercive assemblage of music, altar patter, and Bible readings, which semireliably makes a sufferer like Teddy feel and know God's glorious presence for what it is claimed to be, and prompts him—for the duration of the worship, and in recurring moments during the hours and days to follow—to renew his commitment to the life that these thoughts and feelings demand. So far as I can tell from the outside, for Teddy the dominant mood of this recentering experience is that of gratitude. In the culminating altar call especially, I have, on previous Sundays, stolen sidelong glances at Teddy and watched him weep and whisper: *Thank you, Jesus, Thank you, Jesus, Thank you, Jesus.*

"It's not about us," Amos says. "It's not about entertainment. It's about acknowledging, making praise." Everyone stands. Amos asks the men to turn their Bible to the Book of Galatians, sixth chapter, and proceeds to read the first ten verses.

I zone out. And then, unexpectedly, a voice very close: "That was it." Standing at my ear is Al. He repeats the language of the final verse. "*Do good to all men, especially to them who are of the household of faith.*" This is the verse from Galatians he had in mind Wednesday when we were talking about Ephraim's obligations to the community.

Slick-faced from his set, Gary of the Mighty Way joins us, and asks me how I'm feeling. I tell him I was feeling it, and I was.

"Well, *hallelujah!*" Gary shouts.

Oscar and Santana's group, the Gospel Messengers, take the stage.

"Don't look at *me*," one band member pleads into the microphone. "Look at God!"

"I just want to thank *God*," says a second.

"Brother here," the first guy adds, pointing to someone in the first row. "I saw him in the infirmary last night and he couldn't move a muscle. So to see him here this morning? Thank you, Jesus!" The men applaud.

The Messengers do one they've been doing forever: Wilson Pickett's "Ninety-nine and a Half Won't Do." The arrangement is tight, their harmonies precise.

We got to bring it all down, start getting it right.
We got to stop this messing around, and keep the thing uptight.

I ask Teddy how he would characterize this sound. "That's that old southern sound," he says assuredly.

All right, sugar.
Got to have a hundred,
Got to have a hundred . . .

A minute later, Teddy walks himself back, saying that he isn't quite sure.

If sound is hard to capture in words, atmosphere is similarly elusive. But it's warm, and though the sunlight is still filtered through the winnowing morning clouds, the chapel *feels* bright—as it generally does on Sunday mornings when it's packed full of men praising the Lord, measure by jubilant measure, and I'm fresh, focused, and only dropping in. Suffice it to say, it feels a long, long way from mass.

The band starts up another number, this one marked by a walking keyboard line and chorus of falsetto "oohs."

"*Take me to Jesus,*" they plead as one.

"Now, *that's* that old southern sound," Teddy says. "Back in the woods." He shakes his head in time.

Take it to Jesus
Take it to Jesus
Take it to Jesus

The soloist descends the stage and comes a third of the way down the aisle, both feeding and feeding off of the celebratory vibe.

Teddy has wandered off. At the center end of my row, Daffy Ball bounces along with the music. Daffy has the placard at the ready, should word come down that somebody has a visit. Wendell of Liberty Ministry approaches from the front with a smile, his big white thumbs-up thumb still upstretched and unbent. He's on his way to the infirmary to get it cleaned and replastered, and I wish him well.

The song ends, the chapel quiets, the seated stand, and Amos reads two selections from Isaiah. In the first, the Hebrew prophet counsels those with thirst but without money to delight their soul in the everlasting covenant. In the latter passage, a messianic prophecy foretells a man to come, one reviled and rejected by men, a man wounded by and for our sins, through whom we are healed.[2]

"So if you're thirsty and hungry?" Amos says. "Even if you're broke, come and drink. Drink from the rock of the living waters, Jesus Christ. Because he'll quench your thirst, Jesus Christ, who took away our sins and granted us eternal life."

The Mighty Way retake the stage.

Think about His love.
Think about His goodness.
Think about His grace that brought us through.

Twice, a cappella, the Mighty Way declare the greatness of the measure of our Father's love. Then Ezra drops the beat. Down my row, Daffy sorts through white slips of paper. The band doubles the tempo and pushes through into another of its standards, "You Ought to Run and Tell That." Teddy leans over and grabs my shoulder: "Now *this* is the soul sound!" And it sounds good.

Let me tell you about a man from Galilee
He loosed the shackles
He loosed the shackles
He loosed the shackles and set me free.

Again Amos takes the mic. He tells the story of a congregant's nephew who went before the parole board. "He went ahead and did his thing—you know how it is. They said they were going to give him a six-month hit. And he was a humble guy. Not that he was pretending, he was a truly humble guy, the kind of humbleness you get with fasting and prayer. And they saw he was so humble that they knocked three months off the hit. So, you know, with all that crazy law stuff, God will always find a way!"

Santana calls the Gospel Messengers back to the stage. I turn to Teddy. "I thought Santana *was* the Gospel Messengers."

"Yeah," Teddy says, "he was. He stopped singing with them two weeks ago. But now he wants them back." He shakes his head. "Santana be crazy."

"Yeah," I say. "He seems stressed lately. You know what it is?"

Teddy looks at me cockeyed. "I've got *my own*," he says. "I don't worry none about his."

I ask Teddy about how his visit went yesterday with Lily, his wife. "Beautiful," he says. "She is a strong woman."

He will find a way.
He will forgive you for all of your sins.
Open your heart and let me in.

Santana solos, his crystal voice exuding guileless goodness. Were the devil to sing, he'd probably sound like this. Without compromising force or clarity, Santana goes falsetto.

Tell God about it.
He will make a way.

On behalf of the Usher Board, Amos asks everyone to be quiet and attentive during the sermon, and reminds everyone that chapel schedules are also available.

Rudy of the Mighty Way and St. Dismas takes the lectern in order to read from the prayer slips: "Brother Edward thanks God for letting him get his test results that came back negative." There is widespread applause. "Ralph thanks God for the light of Christ now glowing in his heart." More applause. "Reggie finally heard from his sister after two years. He gives God the glory that he can make it through difficult situations with humility. He asks everyone to pray for his marriage, his family, friends, for the guys on death row, and for the guys in the hospital." More applause.

Amos adds one final request. He says: "May the Lord save the soldiers and the boy who was critically shot by gun violence in Philadelphia last night." Amos asks for new guys and first-timers to stand up, and a handful of men rise, to warm applause. He then calls forward the guys celebrating their birthdays this week. Three men approach the stage.

The first guy gives his name and his block. Then: "Tuesday I'll be fifty-six."

The second guy remains anonymous: "Today I'm too old," he says. "I wish I were younger."

Last is DeeDee. Born Dwight, DeeDee is a former bodybuilder, a former Fruit of Islam, and a transsexual. Last year DeeDee was a St. Dismas regular but these days stays away, reportedly because Rudy refuses to call her by her preferred name.

"My birthday passed," she says. "I didn't want to come up because usually they give me dinosaurs." She laughs at the embarrassment of years. "Today I'm forty-nine."[3]

Gary takes the mic. "I'm going to do it like Charley did it," he says. Charley was a beloved community member who died last spring. Gary sings:

Happy Birthday to you
Happy Birthday to you
Happy Birthday, dear brothers,
And may God bless you.[4]

The congregation breaks into applause.

A brown I don't know reads from the fourteenth chapter of the Book of Matthew. Some open their Bibles and others bow their heads. The brown reads about how Jesus coaxed his disciples into a boat on the Galilee only to disappear up a mountainside to pray. Night fell to find the disciples far from shore, buffeted by wind and wave. Long into the night, Jesus appeared to them, walking on the surface of the lake. The disciples were terrified.

"It's a ghost," they cried.

"Take courage!" Jesus said. *"It is I. Don't be afraid."*

"Lord, if it's you," Peter replied, *"tell me to come to you on the water."*

Jesus said to come. So Peter got out of the boat and walked toward Jesus on the water. But when the wind picked up, he started to sink, and cried out, *"Lord, save me!"*

Jesus reached out and caught Peter, before famously chastising him, "*You of little faith, why did you doubt?*"

They climbed back into the boat, the wind died down, and the disciples declared, "*Truly you are the Son of God.*"

On the other side of the sea, word was sent around that Jesus had arrived, and people from all around brought their sick to be healed. And healed they were.

The brown concludes: "May the Lord bless us with an understanding of His Word. Amen."

Retaking the lectern, Amos acknowledges the reader, to booming applause. To even greater applause, Amos introduces Reverend Baumgartner, who wishes everyone "Good morning" until the applause dies down. Baumgartner begins:

"Many of us remember with great fondness our brother, Harry Birdsong," Baumgartner says. "Sweets." Recognition flickers through the chapel. "Sweets helped me kill many an hour in my office, talking about music.

"Harry used to tell me this as a true story. You can decide whether you think it's true or not. Harry was living in Cleveland, down by the lake, and an itinerant evangelist was coming to town for a revival, and all the pre-revival hype said he was going to walk on the water. And then the night of the revival came. And he was standing down by the waterfront, and everybody there was hooting and clapping. And the preacher said, 'Do you believe?' They all shouted, 'YES!' And he said, 'Do you *really* believe?' And they all shouted, 'YES!' And he said, 'Do you *truly, in your heart of hearts*, believe that I can walk on this here water?' And they shouted, 'YES! We believe!'" Baumgartner pauses. "And the preacher said, 'If you *really* believe, if you *truly* believe, then I don't have to show you.'"

He delivers this with a showman's timing. The resulting ripples of laughter are not merely polite. Baumgartner continues: "Harry swore it was a true story. I don't know about you, but for *me* to believe, the man would've had to have taken at least a couple of steps out onto that lake.

"Today we read from Matthew's Gospel." Baumgartner provides some context: "So the disciples had been following Jesus for some time. And then, in the fourteenth chapter, John the Baptist is executed, and Jesus, being grief-stricken, goes away by himself, and the disciples are left alone, confused about what just happened. And then the people hear that Jesus is in the area and they all come out to see him. And then you have the story of the five thousand, plus women and children. Between you and me," Baumgartner adds as an aside, "women and children were people, too.

"Anyway, Jesus tells the disciples that he'll catch up with them later but, quite obviously, they don't assume he's going to catch up with them in the middle of the sea. And suddenly, there he is, walking on the water. And Peter says, 'Is that You, Lord? If it is, I'll join You on the water.' And Jesus says, 'Come.'

"Peter obeys and jumps in with two feet. So there he is, walking on water. And then suddenly he loses his nerve and starts to sink." A stray chortle rises from the pews.

"Yeah," Baumgartner guffaws toward the laughter, "as if you would do any better.

"And then Jesus calms the storm, and the next thing we know, He and the disciples are on the other side of the lake in Gennesaret, and the people there recognize Him and send word to all their family and friends, and the next thing we know, Jesus is healing all of the sick people in town through His touch." Baumgartner looks around. "You know, that's a lot of stuff for the disciples to witness, and it seems like it all happens in a twenty-four-hour period."

Baumgartner waits. "What I want to remind you of today is that these astonishing stories never happened for their own sake. The miracles always happen in order to point you to something else. *Miracle*, in Greek, means 'a sign.' And a miracle is always a sign of something. So whenever we find a miracle, we need to figure out what it's pointing to. Miracles are always signs to show just who Jesus is, and to remind us of all the promises that He is the incarnation of the loving and gracious God.

"You see, talk is cheap, and at some point a guy has to demonstrate all the claims that he's made. Obviously, Jesus had a great following and He was an inspired and insightful teacher. Obviously, He was very good at telling stories, so people were drawn to hear Him. But He is not the only good storyteller that ever was. So if the claims about Him, about His messiah-ship, about His incarnate presence, about Him being the Son of God, are all to be believed, there would need to be some demonstration that He truly *is* what is claimed of Him, and that He truly has the authority to deliver what has been promised through Him.

"Remember the TV show *Happy Days?*" Baumgartner asks to more oohs of recognition. "Old TV shows never die, they just go into syndication. Well, in one old episode Richie decides that he's tired of being bullied, so he decides to stand up to this bully who's been picking on him. He goes to Fonzi and asks him to teach him how to be tough. The biggest thing, Fonzi says, is attitude. If you act tough and intimidating, then people won't bother you. This calms Richie down a bit. Later in the episode, though, it comes time for the predicted confrontation and, unfortunately, the other guy isn't backing down. Richie asks Fonzi what's wrong. Why isn't the other guy backing down? Fonzi says to him, 'I forgot to tell you one thing: somewhere along the line you actually have to hit somebody so people know that you can.'"

This round of laughter comes peppered with knowing murmurings of approval.

"At some point, it's not enough to *act* tough. At some point you actually have to hit somebody so people know that you can do it! When we talk about Jesus, *that* is what we are talking about. We can *talk* about Jesus being the Messiah. We can *talk* about Jesus being the savior. But until He actually *saves* somebody, none of what we say about Him means a thing. It's like the guy in Cleveland that Sweets told me about. It's easy to *talk* about walking on water but *I*, for one, need to see at least a couple of steps. Without proof, this preacher is just another in a long line of people that have disappointed us. So sooner or later, if you're going to get me to believe in you, you've got to put your money where your mouth is and *save* somebody."

Up the left aisle, an usher parades the placard overhead, a DOC number now inset. A visit is about to be bingoed.

"Only a month ago we celebrated Christmas, and heard the proclamation of a tremendous promise: the birth of the child who is promised to be the Messiah, Emanuel, the savior. In one verse, these promises are made, and all of a sudden, in the next verse, Jesus is all grown up and people are wondering if all that has been promised is truly so.

"But without any demonstration, they're just another batch of failed promises. We have experienced so many failed promises that we've grown accustomed to *failure* being the norm. So unless there is some sort of demonstration, a promise means nothing. In Matthew fourteen, the disciples finally witness, finally experience, that such power to save as has been promised is demonstrably present. It's no longer a matter of promise. It's no longer a matter of hope. It's no longer a matter of someday. It's now a matter of witnessing it—*firsthand*—and knowing that the promise is true. What becomes vividly observable for believers in this chapter is that in the presence of this Jesus"—Baumgartner repeats the phrase—"is that in the presence of *this* Jesus, there is compassion for the needs of all people, and there is nourishment for all those who hunger and thirst for righteousness, for those who hunger and thirst for God's peace, for those who hunger and thirst for God's healing power to save us through all the diseases of life. That's *disease* but also *dis-ease,*" Baumgartner pronounces the word like it's two. "So often in life, when we have no peace, and no certainty, we confront dis-eases. In the presence of this Jesus, though, as the story tells us, there *is* healing. There *is* calm in the storm that is this life. There is deliverance from that feeling of being overwhelmed by fear and doubt. Why does Peter sink? He sinks because he is afraid, and because he doubts."

Shouts of approval greet the denunciation of doubt.

"And if it had been me?" Baumgartner slickly pivots, "I wouldn't have even gotten out of the boat! But as the story says, there is no place, even in the midst of turbulent seas, where *He* cannot find us. All of us must deal with fears. All of us must deal with uncertainties. All of us must deal with dis-eases. But in all of the experiences, all of the changes, all of the dis-eases of *my* life, the healing of my spirit, the nourishment of my soul, and the calms in my turmoil have *always* and *only* been in the presence of Jesus. This is not hearsay. It's not a claim. And it's not a promise. It has been demonstrated to me and I have experienced it—all of my calms, and respites, and deliverances have been in the presence of Jesus. And when I look for calm someplace else, I start to flail, I start to experience supreme dis-ease. When I look for it someplace else, I find that I can't sleep at night and my relationships become stress-filled and I start to sink. But in the presence of the promise of Jesus of Nazareth, I find the presence of peace and wholeness and certainty and love and salvation and the lack of being afraid.

"In all of our doubts, in all of our tribulations, in all of our diseases, it is our experience of the presence of Jesus that we can feel secure in. Amid all of this uncertainty, and pressure, and pain, we hear the voice. And the voice . . . and the voice says: *Don't worry, it is I. Do not be afraid.*

"And then, when we *experience* that, no longer do we merely have promises. What kind of God would it be that would make us believe without seeing something? God doesn't hide behind the cloud and say"—suddenly Baumgartner is the Wizard of Oz—'*YOU GUYS BETTER BELIEVE, OR ELSE!*' No, this God shows us something. That's what the Gospels are about. He comes and dwells in our midst so we can touch Him and feel that there is no reason to be afraid. And, with the disciples, we can put all of our trust, all of our faith, all of our confidence in Him that is truly the Son of God." The booming voice returns: "'*DO YOU BELIEVE?*' Good, then I don't have to show you. I don't have to show you because the presence of Jesus in all the moments and circumstances of your life up to now has already made the truth of His promises abundantly clear.

"See it, know it, trust it, confess it, live it. For the demonstration of His power to be the Savior has already been shown clearly in our presence. I'm not going to walk on anything other than the solid ground of my life, and I'm not going to ask you to walk on anything other than the solid ground of your experience of your life."

An airy riff begins to waft from Santana's fingertips. The altar call has arrived.

Baumgartner says: "All those who have experienced Jesus in a new way today, please walk forward and share the Gospel of Jesus."

More with pure melody than with words, Santana begins to sing.

Baumgartner continues: "All those who have known Jesus but have felt far away, please come forward. All those who are experiencing disease, come step over the side of the boat and *trust*. Just put your foot forward and feel how He brings us to Himself."

Perhaps a dozen men approach and take their place at the foot of the dais, below the large gold cross and beside David's *etrog* tree.

At this very spot, on one of my sporadic visits in the spring, Al will show me how without any outside horticultural intervention, the branches of the *etrog* tree will have become conjoined with its neighbor's such that each plant sprouts the leaves of the other. As I marvel at this miraculous portent of pluralist concord, Al will admonish me that the body of Christ was *grafted onto the true vine.* Caught off guard by the sternness of Al's tone, I'll suddenly get it. In the two plants' spontaneous hybridity, Al will have read not the promise of amicable Jewish-Christian coexistence, but rather the inevitable overcoming of this difference in Christ. That is, in fulfilling the covenant, the body of Christ took Israel's place and I had best act accordingly. After an awkward embrace, I'll push back. With less passion than came naturally when I was an everyday presence, I'll try to pry open the holy community Al envisions to make room for all the righteous, whether they know Christ in the way Al does or whether they pursue truth and justice some other way. But quoting John, Al will stand fast: "Except a man be born again, he cannot see the kingdom of God."[5]

Santana's heavenly intonations continue. At the altar, prayer warriors lay hands on those men who answered the call, and who stand before them, both tall and bent, swaying and still. As it goes, when the service is over these needy souls will leave their names and cell numbers. Later on, they'll be paid a visit in their cell by someone looking to help, someone whose ideas about who God is and what that means for their life are much closer to Al's than to Baumgartner's.

Throughout the chapel, hands are raised up as bodies sway in time to Santana's keyboard and voice. The minutes pass luxuriously, and I have no desire for any of this to end.

Eventually Baumgartner prays. "Heavenly Father, we have heard Your promises. But we want and pray for Your presence to be shown to us. We no longer live in hope. We live in certainty. Heavenly Father, make clear the certainties of our salvation. Heavenly Father, we pray that the whole of Graterford may come to know the certainty of Your promise, that all in this world might come to know it, too. Heavenly Father, take away from us our fears, our confusions, our turmoils, and embrace us with Your peace and love that we may live in the wholeness of Your demonstrated promise. In Your name and in the name of Your Son, Jesus Christ, we declare as He taught us:

Our Father, who art in heaven,
Hallowed be Thy name.
Thy kingdom come.
Thy will be done,
On earth as it is in heaven.
Give us this day our daily bread.
And forgive us our trespasses,

As we forgive those who trespass against us.
And lead us not into temptation,
But deliver us from evil.

The recitation rises to a shout.

For Thine is the kingdom,
And the power, and the glory,
FOREVER AND EVER!
AMEN.

Baumgartner concludes: "In a manner that surpasses all understanding, keep Jesus Christ in your hearts. Go in peace and serve the
Lord." With this closing injunction, the vessel of ritual tension cracks
and the congregation begins to ooze from the chapel. I am scribbling
feverishly, trying to capture as much of the altar call's script as I can,
and to corral into language the texture of the elation that still permeates the emptying chapel.

A tap lands on my shoulder. I look up to find Charles—Charles
the religious eclectic, Charles the provocateur, Charles the wounded,
Charles of video ministry, of EFM, occasionally of the Indians' circle,
and, this week, Charles of nowhere at all.

Charles gives me a warm if not strained smile. When last I saw him
his hair was getting on scraggly, but his cornrows have since been im-
peccably rebraided so that not a single hair escapes. Taking my pen in
my right hand, I hop to my feet and we hug. Stumbling a bit, I inadvertently dig my pen into his back. In a manner that, absent the din of the
receding multitude, might well be suspect, our heads remain pressed
close.

I tell him I missed him on Wednesday and ask how he's been.

"I'm struggling," he says. From his absence, I had assumed as
much. "But I don't know . . ." He shrugs. "Maybe I'll give it over to the
Lord soon. Maybe even today." His eyes are glassy.

Then, intemperately, like an evangelist for a church dedicated to
the sorts of peculiarities by which I swear, I ramble: "You know, Charles,
guys at EFM like Daffy and Al, they love you, and you're lucky to have
them, and I don't begrudge anyone who's figured out how to make it in
this place, but—though I hesitate to say this because I can't imagine

carrying what you're carrying—I feel that everybody's got to figure out his *own* way. And that's true in here no less so than out on the street. You've got a super-inquisitive mind. So your resistance to what *they* believe might not be simply a matter of pride. Maybe you think some things that they *can't* think, and perhaps even some things that you can't *not* think. So I don't think it's just a matter of you hopping out of your boat and into their truth. It might be harder than that, I fear. Messier than that."

Charles nods soberly. He suggests we talk sometime. I say I'd like that, and we agree on Wednesday afternoon. We embrace again. Neglecting to take proper care, I again jab the nub of my pen into the cavity between Charles's shoulder blades.

"Sorry if I just stabbed you in the back with my pen," I say, without immediate recognition of the full significance of my words.

NOTES

These notes exist for the conventional scholarly purposes of citation attribution, clarification, and supplementation. For those wishing to pull on this or that thread, I have also included some suggestions for further reading. If you are incarcerated and are interested in receiving selections from one or more of the cited sources to which you otherwise have no access, please write me at the Department of Religion and Classics, University of Rochester, Box 270074, Rochester, NY, 14627–0074, and I'll do my best to honor your request.

PREFACE

1. With the exception of public personages, all names have been changed.
2. Isaiah 1:7. A note on biblical translation: when the Bible is quoted, I try to use the translation most commonly used by the relevant community. For Protestants, that means either the American King James or the New International Version. For Catholics, that means the New American Bible.
3. According to internal statistics from the time of this book's action, Graterford's permanent population broke down demographically as follows: 67% African-American, 20% white, and 12% Hispanic. With respect to religious identifications checked off upon a convict's first entry into the system, or as changed thereafter at a prisoner's own initiative, 30% of Graterford's residents identified as Protestant, 26% as Muslim, and 16% as Catholic.
4. As of 2010, Pennsylvania trails only Florida and Louisiana in its number of state prisoners serving life without the possibility of parole (LWOP), also known as "death in prison." Of the 41,095 people serving LWOP nationwide, 4,343 are in Pennsylvania state prisons. At 9.4 percent of Pennsylvania's prison population as a whole, there are a third again as many people serving LWOP in Pennsylvania as there are people on death row in the United States. See Ashley Nellis and Ryan S. King, "No Exit: The Expanding Use of Life Sentences in America," The Sentencing Project (July 2009); and Ashley Nellis, "Throwing Away the Key: The Expansion of Life Without Parole Sentences in the United States," *Federal Sentencing Reporter*, Vol. 23, No. 1 (October 2010). For a Pennsylvania lifer's first-person account of everyday life, see James A. Paluch, Jr., Thomas J. Bernard (ed.), and Robert Johnson (ed.), *A Life for a Life: Life in Prison: America's Other Death Penalty*

(Roxbury Publishing Company, 2004). On lifers at California's San Quentin State Prison, see John Irwin, *Lifers: Seeking Redemption in Prison* (Routledge, 2009).

5. On race and mass incarceration, see Michelle Alexander, *The New Jim Crow: Mass Incarceration in the Age of Colorblindness* (New Press, 2010); and "Uneven Justice: State Rates of Incarceration By Race and Ethnicity" (The Sentencing Project, 2007).

THE MEN OF GRATERFORD'S CHAPEL

1. Few of those men classed by the Department of Corrections as "Protestants" would actively affirm this identity. Some call themselves "Christian," but others, like Al, do not. In most cases, on account of the presence of Bebbington's hallmark characteristics of Biblicism, crucicentrism (an orientation toward the atoning work of Christ on the cross), conversionism, and activism, it would not be wrong to group these men as "Evangelicals." See David Bebbington, *Evangelicalism in Modern Britain: A History from the 1730s to the 1980s* (Routledge, 1989). A similarly apposite label could be "Bible believers," or its more practical correlate, "Bible-carrying Christians." See Nancy Ammerman, *Bible Believers: Fundamentalists in the Modern World* (Rutgers University Press, 1987); and David Harrington Watt, *Bible-Carrying Christians: Conservative Protestants and Social Power* (Oxford University Press, 2002).

MONDAY

1. "200 Convicts Riot at Graterford," *New York Times*, August 26, 1934.
2. This architectural form is commonly called a "telephone pole design." See Norman Johnson, *Forms of Constraint: A History of Prison Architecture* (University of Illinois Press, 2006).
3. Douglas Brinkley and Julie M. Fenster, *Parish Priest* (William Morrow, 2006).
4. Michael Medved, *Right Turns* (Crown Forum, 2004). For an ethnography about reading in prison, see Megan Sweeney, *Reading Is My Window: Books and the Art of Reading in Women's Prisons* (University of North Carolina Press, 2010).
5. See David Stoll, *Is Latin America Turning Protestant?: The Politics of Evangelical Growth* (University of California Press, 1990). For a global perspective see Mark A. Noll, *The New Shape of World Christianity: How American Experience Reflects Global Faith* (IVP Academic, 2009).
6. On Christian Science in historical perspective, see Willa Cather and Georgine Milmine, *The Life of Mary Baker G. Eddy and the History of Christian Science* (University of Nebraska Press, 1993); and Claire Hoertz Badaracco, *Prescribing Faith: Medicine, Media and Religion in American Culture* (Baylor University Press, 2007), pp. 49–89.
7. The term *interlocutor*, which I favor for its dialogical resonances, was suggested by Amira Mittermaier. See Amira Mittermaier, *Dreams That Matter: Egyptian Landscapes of the Imagination* (University of California Press, 2011), pp. 22–23.
8. Baraka has quoted to me the Stoic emperor Marcus Aurelius as saying "Our life is what our thoughts make it"; and, in a similar vein, "*Vincit qui se vincit*—he conquers who overcomes himself." For more, see Marcus Aurelius, *Meditations* (Penguin Classics, 2006).
9. On American religious pluralism, see Diana Eck, *A New Religious America: How*

a *"Christian Country"* Has Become the World's Most Religiously Diverse Nation (Harper San Francisco, 2002). For pluralism in historical perspective, see William R. Hutchison, *Religious Pluralism in America* (Yale University Press, 2004). For critiques of the pluralist project, see William E. Connolly, *Pluralism* (Duke University Press, 2005); and Pamela E. Klassen and Courtney Bender, "Introduction: Habits of Pluralism," in Bender and Klassen (eds.), *After Pluralism: Reimagining Religious Engagement* (Columbia University Press, 2010), pp. 1–28.

10. Jeffrey Stout specifically touted a narrative form as conducive to getting at the chapel's "lived religion." See Robert Orsi, "Everyday Miracles: The Study of Lived Religion," in David Hall (ed.), *Lived Religion in America: Toward a History of Practice* (Princeton University Press, 1997), pp. 3–21.

11. Since 1941, Pennsylvania law has required all life sentences be imposed without the possibility of parole. See Marc Mauer, Ryan S. King, and Malcolm C. Young, "The Meaning of Life: Long Sentences in Context," *Sentencing Project* (2004), p. 7, and http://www.sentencingproject.org/doc/publications/inc_meaningoflife.pdf.

12. My position in this argument is informed by John McDowell, "Two Sorts of Naturalism," in *Mind, Value, and Reality* (Harvard University Press, 1998), pp. 167–97, and Richard Rorty, "Non-reductive Physicalism" in *Objectivity, Relativism, Truth: Philosophical Papers, Volume I* (Cambridge University Press, 1999), pp. 113–25. In support of his position, Vic repeatedly invoked "constructs" in what he dubbed "the Chomskyan sense," through which reality is hardwired into the brain. See Noam Chomsky, *Syntactic Structures* (Walter de Gruyter, 2002).

13. Andy and Lana Wachowski (dirs.), *The Matrix* (1999).

14. On postmodernism, see Jean-François Lyotard, *The Postmodern Condition: A Report on Knowledge* (University of Minnesota Press, 1984); and Fredric Jameson, *Postmodernism, or, the Cultural Logic of Late Capitalism* (Duke University Press, 1991), pp. 1–66.

15. See Jonathan Z. Smith, "Religion, Religions, Religious," in Mark C. Taylor (ed.), *Critical Terms for Religious Study* (University of Chicago Press, 1998), pp. 269–84. For a survey of touchstones, see Daniel L. Pals, *Eight Theories of Religion* (Oxford University Press, 2006); and Ivan Strenski, *Thinking about Religion: An Historical Introduction to Theories of Religion* (Wiley-Blackwell, 2006). On the civic stakes of this scholarly enterprise, see Russell T. McCutcheon, *Religion and the Domestication of Dissent: Or, How to Live in a Less Than Perfect Nation* (Equinox Publishing, Limited, 2005).

16. During the three-year period ending in 2005, the reincarceration rate for men released from Pennsylvania state prisons was 47%. See *Recidivism in Pennsylvania State Correctional Institutions* (Pennsylvania Department of Corrections, December 2006). This figure is in line with national numbers. According to a frequently cited statistic with a lower threshold: two out of three prisoners released from prison will be *rearrested* within three years of their release. For these statistics, and other recidivism data, see the Bureau of Justice Statistics' website: http://bjs.ojp.usdoj.gov/index.cfm?ty=tp&tid=17.

17. See Rules and Regulations, Title 37—Law, Board of Pardons [37 PA. CODE CH. 81], http://www.pabulletin.com/secure/data/vol28/28-22/849.html; Act 1995–8 (SS1), http://www.palrb.us/pamphletlaws/19001999/1995/1/act/0008.pdf; and "A Call to Make Pardons Tougher to Get for Lifers/The Effort to Change the Rules Is Being Put before Pa. Voters on Next Month's Ballot," *Philadelphia Inquirer*, October 26, 1997. For commutations by gubernatorial administration see http://www.portal.state

.pa.us/portal/server.pt/community/statistics/19543/commutation_of_life_sentence
_1971_-_present/765885. In the 1970s, when Omar came to Graterford, a Pennsylvania lifer could expect to serve, on average, eighteen and a half years. See Vaughan Booker with David Phelps, *From Prison to Pulpit* (Cadell & Davies, 1994), p. 122.

18. In his 2004 State of the Union address, President George W. Bush called for $300 million to be directed toward prisoner reentry. See http://www.justice.gov/archive/fbci/docs/fed-prisoner-reentry-resources.pdf.

19. The pop song was Sheryl Crow's "If It Makes You Happy" (1996).

20. Marcel Mauss, *The Gift* (W. W. Norton and Co., 2000).

21. Under the then-existing contract, base pay for rank-and-file COs ranged from $23,660 to $38,369, with overtime compensated at time and a half. See http://www.pscoa.org/wp-content/uploads/H1_Contract_2005-2008.pdf.

22. The one-in-three figure refers to black men in their twenties and can be found in "Young Black Americans and the Criminal Justice System: Five Years Later," The Sentencing Project (1995). In "Uneven Justice" (The Sentencing Project, 2007) the same dispiriting fraction is used to designate the third of black males born today who can expect to spend some time in prison should "current trends continue."

23. On the racialization of Jesus in America, see Edward J. Blum and Paul Harvey, *The Color of Christ: The Son of God and the Saga of Race in America* (University of North Carolina Press, 2012).

24. The version of the Book of Jasher Watkins found was probably the one originally published in seventeenth-century Venice, translated into English in 1840, and republished in 1887 by a Salt Lake City press, before being uploaded to the Internet sometime prior to 2006. In all likelihood, this Jasher was uploaded by a member of the Church of Latter Day Saints, among whom, evidence suggests, there is some belief in the text's authenticity. See http://www.ccel.org/a/anonymous/jasher/home.html.

25. As de Tocqueville noted: "Americans so completely identify the spirit of Christianity with freedom in their minds that it is almost impossible to get them to conceive of the one without the other; and this is not one of those sterile ideas bequeathed by the past to the present nor one which seems to vegetate in the soul rather than to live." Alexis de Tocqueville (trans., Gerald E. Bevan), *Democracy in America* (Penguin, 2003), p. 343.

26. See Whitney Cross, *The Burned-Over District: The Social and Intellectual History of Enthusiastic Religion in Western New York, 1800–1850* (Cornell University Press, 2006); Nathan O. Hatch, *The Democratization of American Christianity* (Yale University Press, 1991); and Ann Braude, *Radical Spirits: Spiritualism and Women's Rights in Nineteenth-Century America* (Indiana University Press, 2001). On the awakenings in sum, see William G. McLoughlin, *Revivals, Awakenings, and Reform* (University of Chicago Press, 1980).

27. As of 2006, according to one survey, more than a quarter of all Americans had read *The Da Vinci Code*. See "American Piety in the 21st Century" (Baylor Institute for Studies of Religion, September 2006). On black biblical hermeneutics among African-Americans, see Vincent L. Wimbush, "Reading Darkness, Reading Scriptures," in Vincent L. Wimbush (ed.), *African Americans and the Bible: Sacred Texts and Social Textures* (Continuum International Publishing Group, Inc., 2003), pp. 1–43. On the hermeneutics of paranoia in black America, see Patricia A. Turner, *I Heard It through the Grapevine: Rumor in African-American Culture* (University of California Press, 1994).

28. To this point, it is worth noting that the language of "a house of prayer for all peoples" itself comes from Isaiah 56:7.

29. Talal Asad, "Reading a Modern Classic: W. C. Smith's 'The Meaning and the End of Religion,'" *History of Religions*, Vol. 40, No. 3 (Feb., 2001), pp. 205–22; Robert A. Orsi, *Between Heaven and Earth: The Religious Worlds People Make and the Scholars Who Study Them* (Princeton University Press, 2005), pp. 177–204; and Jonathan Z. Smith, *Relating Religion: Essays in the Study of Religion* (University of Chicago Press, 2004), pp. 375–90. On liberal Protestantism beyond the study of religion, see Leigh E. Schmidt and Sally M. Promey (eds.), *American Religious Liberalism* (Indiana University Press, 2012).

30. For a variety of conceptualizations of the secular and secularism, see Talal Asad, *Formations of the Secular* (Stanford University Press, 2003); William E. Connolly, *Why I Am Not a Secularist* (University of Minnesota Press, 2000); Janet R. Jakobsen and Ann Pellegrini (eds.), *Secularisms* (Duke University Press, 2008); and Charles Taylor, *A Secular Age* (Belknap Press of Harvard University Press, 2007).

31. See *United States v. Seeger*, 380 U.S. 163 (1965), and Paul Tillich, *Shaking the Foundations* (Charles Scribner's Sons, 1948), p. 57. *Seeger* further quotes Tillich: "The source of this affirmation of meaning within meaninglessness, of certitude within doubt, is not the God of traditional theism but the 'God above God,' the power of being, which works through those who have no name for it, not even the name God." Tillich, *Systematic Theology, Vol. Two* (University of Chicago Press, 1975), p. 12. For a critical assessment of the legal appropriation of Paul Tillich's thought, see James McBride, "Paul Tillich and the Supreme Court: Tillich's 'Ultimate Concern' as a Standard in Judicial Interpretation," *Journal of Church and State* (1988) 30(2): 245–72.

32. See Winnifred Fallers Sullivan, *The Impossibility of Religious Freedom* (Princeton University Press, 2005); and Winnifred Fallers Sullivan, *Prison Religion* (Princeton University Press, 2009). For prisoners' religious rights, see John W. Palmer and Stephen E. Palmer, "Religion in Prison," in *Constitutional Rights of Prisoners* (Anderson Publishing, 2006), pp. 105–42. For critical appraisals of the Supreme Court's attempts to define religion, see "Note: Toward a Constitutional Definition of Religion," *Harvard Law Review* 91 (March, 1978): pp. 1056–89; and Eduardo Peñalver, "The Concept of Religion," *Yale Law Journal*, Vol. 107, No. 3 (December, 1997), pp. 791–822. For critical histories see Courtney Bender and Jennifer Snow, "From Alleged Buddhists to Unreasonable Hindus: First Amendment Jurisprudence after 1965" in Stephen Prothero (ed.), *A Nation of Religions* (University of North Carolina Press, 2006), pp. 181–204; Sarah Barringer Gordon, *The Spirit of the Law: Religious Voices and the Constitution in Modern America* (Belknap Press of Harvard University Press, 2010); and Eric Michael Mazur, *The Americanization of Religious Minorities* (Johns Hopkins University Press, 1999).

33. *Africa v. Commonwealth of Pennsylvania* 662 F.2d 1025. On MOVE, see John Anderson and Hilary Hevenor, *Burning Down the House* (Norton, 1987); and Robin Wagner-Pacifici, *Discourse and Destruction: The City of Philadelphia versus MOVE* (University of Chicago Press, 1994). On the Five Percenters, see Felicia Miyakawa, *Five Percenter Rap: God Hop's Music, Message, and Black Muslim Mission* (Indiana University Press, 2005), pp. 1–37. While Five Percenters have generally been classed by prison administrators as a street gang, in 2003 the Southern District of New York recognized the Five Percenters' First Amendment right to free religious exercise. See *Marria v. Broaddus* 2003 U.S. Dist. Lexis 13329.

34. Inmate Religious Accommodation Request Form, DC-ADM 819-1 (September 17, 2004).
35. See The Religious Land Use and Institutionalized Persons Act (RLUIPA), Pub.L. 106–274, codified as 42 U.S.C. § 2000cc-1, which the Supreme Court upheld in *Cutter v. Wilkinson*, 544 U.S. 709 (2005). RLUIPA was Congress's response to the Supreme Court's invalidation of 1993's Religious Freedom Restoration Act in *City of Boerne v. Flores*, 521 U.S. 507 (1997). Like its predecessor, RLUIPA preserved for all institutions receiving federal or state funding the two-pronged "Sherbert test." Pursuant to the Sherbert test, the government may "substantially burden a person's exercise of religion only if it demonstrates that application of the burden to the person—(1) is in furtherance of a compelling governmental interest; and (2) is the least restrictive means of furthering that compelling governmental interest." *Sherbert v. Verner*, 374 U.S. 398 (1963). For federal enforcement data, see "Enforcing Religious Freedom in Prison," *U.S. Commission on Civil Rights* (2008).
36. Exodus 22:18.
37. According to internal statistics, in the eighteen months preceding June 2005, the Religious Accommodation Committee (RAC) fielded ninety-two requests for accommodation and approved eleven.
38. For an ethnographic study of neopaganism, see Sarah Pike, *Earthly Bodies, Magical Selves: Contemporary Pagans and the Search for Community* (University of California Press, 2001).
39. As an archetypal and consequential instance of this critical impulse, recall then Texas governor George W. Bush shedding mock tears on behalf of born-again and soon to be executed Karla Faye Tucker.
40. The "jailhouse Muslims" as gang motif featured prominently in the HBO prison drama series *Oz*, which aired from 1997 to 2003.
41. Walter Kaufmann, "Who Thinks Abstractly?" In *Hegel: Texts and Commentary* (Anchor Books, 1966), pp. 113–18.
42. See Joshua Dubler, "The Secular Bad Faith of Harry Theriault, the Bishop of Tellus," *Soundings: An Interdisciplinary Journal* 92.1-2 (Spring/Summer 2009), pp. 21–50. On sincerity, see Lionel Trilling, *Sincerity and Authenticity* (Harvard University Press, 1972); and R. Jay Magill, *Sincerity* (W. W. Norton & Co., 2012).
43. See Edward E. Curtis IV, *Black Muslim Religion in the Nation of Islam, 1960–1975* (University of North Carolina Press, 2006). For a searchable archive of the complete works of Elijah Muhammad, go to http://www.seventhfam.com/.
44. See David Harrington Watt, "What's In a Name?: The Meaning of 'Muslim Fundamentalist,'" *Origins* 1 (June 2008), pp. 1–5. See also Bruce Lincoln, *Holy Terrors: Thinking about Religion after September 11* (University of Chicago Press, 2003).
45. See Ernest Sandeen, *The Roots of Fundamentalism: British and American Millenarianism 1800–1930* (University of Chicago Press, 1970); and George M. Marsden, *Fundamentalism and American Culture: The Shaping of Twentieth-Century Evangelicalism, 1870–1925* (Oxford University Press, 1980). For an ethnography of contemporary fundamentalists, see Susan Friend Harding, *The Book of Jerry Falwell* (Princeton University Press, 2001). For his part, Falwell has been known to define a fundamentalist as "an evangelical who [is] mad about something" (Harding, p. 16).
46. Inasmuch as all quests for origins are to some degree bound by their point of departure, the principal parameter for Abdul Wahhab's excavation of the tradition was the Hanbali School of Law, and in particular, the work of fourteenth-century

Hanbali scholar Ibn Taymiyya. On the roots of contemporary Salafism, see Richard P. Mitchell, *The Society of the Muslim Brothers* (Oxford University Press, 1993); and Henri Lauzière, "The Construction of Salafiyya: Reconsidering Salafism from the Perspective of Conceptual History," *International Journal of Middle East Studies* 42 (2010), pp. 369–89. For Salafism as a global movement, see Olivier Roy, *Globalized Islam: The Search for the New Ummah* (Columbia University Press, 2004); and Roel Meijer (ed.), *Global Salafism: Islam's New Religious Movement* (Columbia University Press, 2009). For a critique of Salafism, see Khaled Abou El Fadl, "The Ugly Modern and the Modern Ugly," in Omid Safi (ed.), *Progressive Muslims: On Justice, Gender, and Pluralism* (Oneworld Publications, 2003), pp. 33–77. For a defense of Salafism widely read at Graterford, see Haneef James Oliver, *The "Wahhabi" Myth: Dispelling Prevalent Fallacies and the Fictitious Link with Bin Laden* (T.R.O.I.D. Publications, 2004).

47. On originalism, see Antonin Scalia and Amy Guttman, *A Matter of Interpretation: Federal Courts and the Law* (Princeton University Press, 1998); and David Strauss, *The Living Constitution* (Oxford University Press, 2010), pp. 7–32. For a reflection on the ascendancy of an originalist practical perfectionism among contemporary Orthodox Jews, see Haym Soloveitchik, "Rupture and Reconstruction: The Transformation of Contemporary Orthodoxy," *Tradition*, Vol. 28, No. 4 (Summer 1994), pp. 64–130.

48. Ninian Smart, *Worldviews: Crosscultural Explorations of Human Beliefs* (Prentice Hall, 2000).

49. James Crocket [pseudonym], "Ninian Smart's 'Doctrine Dimensions' Explained by Karen Armstrong," final paper for *Religion, Faith, and Reason*, a course in Villanova's Program at Graterford (Fall 2005). In addition to Smart's *Worldviews*, Crocket's unpublished paper is directly in dialogue with Karen Armstrong's *A History of God* (Ballantine Books, 1994). More obliquely, Crocket's essay engages a scholarly paper by Robert J. Schreiter, which he gave me along with his own work, about religion in the age of globalization and postmodernity. See Schreiter, CPPS. "A New Modernity: Living and Believing in an Unstable World," paper presented at the Anthony Jordan Lectures, Newman Theological College, Edmonton, Alberta, March 18–19, 2005.

50. Abu Bilal Mustafa al-Kanadi, *The Islamic Rulings on Music and Singing* (Abul Qasim, 1991); and Saleh as-Saleh, *The Three Letters: The Beard, Isbaal, Smoking* (Daar al-Bukhari, 1995). http://abdurrahman.org/character/Isbal-Dr-Saleh-as-Saleh.pdf.

51. Surat Al-'Aḥzāb, 33:36.

52. From conversation, I know, for example, that Sayyid rejects the notion of *epoché*— the conceit shared by some scholars of religion that an observer may simply bracket his own prejudices so to access the experience of religion from the insider's perspective. On *epoché* in the study of religion, see Robert A. Segal, "In Defense of Reductionism"; and Peter Donovan, "Neutrality in Religious Studies," both in Russell T. McCutcheon (ed.), *The Insider/Outsider Problem in the Study of Religion: A Reader* (Cassell, 1999), pp. 139–63 and 235–47.

53. Romans 13:12.

54. Hannah Arendt, *Eichmann in Jerusalem: A Report on the Banality of Evil* (Penguin, 2006).

55. Expert opinion yields little more certitude. A recent in-house study conducted by the Pennsylvania Department of Corrections estimated that 7% of Pennsylvania

prisoners have been victims of sexual assault, and in 2010 the Bureau of Justice Statistics reported that 4.4% of prison inmates are sexually abused annually. See "Special Issue: Prison Rape Elimination Act," *Research in Review,* Volume 10, Number 4 (Pennsylvania Department of Corrections, December 2007); and "Sexual Victimization in Prisons and Jails Reported by Inmates, 2008–2009" (U.S. Department of Justice, August 2010). Pressed in part by a series of articles in the *New York Review of Books,* in January 2011, the Justice Department released a new set of numbers according to which, in 2008, more than 216,600 American prisoners were sexually abused—a figure closer to one in ten. The *NYRB* authors suspect that number also understates the reality. See David Kaiser and Lovisa Stannow, "The Rape of American Prisoners," "The Way to Stop Prison Rape," and "Prison Rape and the Government," in *New York Review of Books,* March 11, 2010, March 25, 2010, and March 24, 2011. On the place of the prison in the construction of modern American sexuality, see Regina Kunzel, *Criminal Intimacy* (University of Chicago Press, 2008).

TUESDAY
1. The spokesman for this nation of religiously *confident* men could well be the nineteenth-century preacher Alexander Campbell, who detailed his methods as follows: "I have endeavored to read the scriptures as though no one had read them before me. And I am as much on my guard against reading them today, through the medium of my own views yesterday, or a week ago, as I am against being influenced by any name, authority or system whatsoever." (Quoted in Nathan Hatch, *The Democratization of American Christianity* [Yale University Press, 1991], p. 179.)
2. See Susan Jacoby, *Freethinkers: A History of American Secularism* (Metropolitan Books, 2004). For data on the self-identified unreligious today, see "'Nones on the Rise: One-in-Five Adults Have No Religious Affiliation," *Pew Forum on Religion and Public Life* (October 9, 2012).
3. On Joseph Smith as the quintessential American religionist, see Harold Bloom, *The American Religion* (Simon & Schuster, 1992), pp. 69–130.
4. See Mary Douglas, *Natural Symbols: Explorations in Cosmology* (Routledge, 1996), pp. 37–68; and "Grid and Group, New Developments," paper presented at the London School of Economics, June 27, 2005, available on the Web at www.psych.lse.ac.uk/complexity/Workshops/MaryDouglas.pdf.
5. According to one study, black men in prison do indeed outlive their nonincarcerated counterparts. See David L. Rosen, David A. Wohl, and Victor J. Schoenbach, "All-Cause and Cause-Specific Mortality Among Black and White North Carolina State Prisoners, 1995–2005," *Annals of Epidemiology* 21 (2011), pp. 719–26.
6. Only the United States and Somalia sentence juveniles to life in prison without the possibility of parole. See "Amicus Brief on Behalf of Petitioners Miller and Jackson," *Human Rights Watch* (January 26, 2012), p. 4. Pennsylvania is the national leader in sentencing juveniles to die in prison. While figures, even at the state level, are difficult to ascertain definitively, according to one set, of the 2,570 juvenile lifers in state prisons nationwide, 444 are in Pennsylvania. See http://www.endjlwop.org/the-issue/stats-by-state/. On June 25, 2012, the U.S. Supreme Court ruled that *mandatorily* sentencing juveniles to die in prison constitutes cruel and unusual punishment. See *Miller v. Alabama,* 132 S.Ct. 2455 (2012). The following October, Governor Tom Corbett signed into law legislation that makes

thirteen- and fourteen-year-olds convicted of first-degree murder eligible for parole after twenty-five years. Fifteen-to-seventeen-year-olds will now be parole eligible after thirty-five years. The law is not retroactive.

7. For phenomenologies of "prison time," see George Jackson, *Soledad Brother: The Prison Letters of George Jackson* (Chicago Review Press, 1994); and Jack Henry Abbott, *In the Belly of the Beast: Letters from Prison* (Vintage, 1991); for Jean Genet's version, see Michael Hardt, "Prison Time," *Yale French Studies*, No. 91 (1997), pp. 64–79.

8. The biweekly pamphlet, called *Our Daily Bread*, is distributed around the world by RBC Ministries of Grand Rapids, Michigan.

9. For an ethnographic study of Jehovah's Witnesses, see Andrew Holden, *Jehovah's Witnesses: Portrait of a Contemporary Religious Movement* (Routledge, 2002). On the seminal place of Jehovah's Witnesses in the twentieth-century expansion of First Amendment religious rights, see Shawn Francis Peters, *Judging Jehovah's Witnesses: Religious Persecution and the Dawn of the Rights Revolution* (University Press of Kansas, 2002).

10. On performativity, see John L. Austin, *How to Do Things with Words* (Clarendon Press, 1962); and Judith Butler, *Excitable Speech: A Politics of the Performative* (Routledge, 1997).

11. In a scholarly article authored by members of the Graterford's LIFERS association, rehabilitation and transformation are contrasted as follows: "Rehabilitation seeks to change the way a person behaves; transformation changes how a person thinks. Rehabilitation looks to the past; transformation is future oriented. Rehabilitation often occurs externally; transformation originates from within. To transform a person, one must first empower that person to see the world differently; to reconfigure one's way of not only relating to the world, but also fundamentally changing his or her way of perceiving that world as well." The LIFERS Public Safety Steering Committee of the State Correctional Institution at Graterford, Pennsylvania, "Ending the Culture of Street Crime," *The Prison Journal* (2004) 84: 48S–68S, p. 61S.

12. "Transformation" is the driving metaphor for InnerChange Freedom Initiative, the state-partnered, faith-based reentry program sponsored by Charles Colson's Prison Fellowship. Founded in 1976 by convicted Watergate coconspirator and best-selling author Charles Colson, Prison Fellowship offers a range of Christian-based services to prisoners and their families in over a hundred countries. See http://www.prisonfellowship.org/why-pf. For a critique of Colson's rhetoric of transformation, see Tanya Erzen, "Testimonial Politics: The Christian Right's Faith-Based Approach to Marriage and Imprisonment," *American Quarterly*, Volume 59, Number 3, September 2007, pp. 991–1015. For a critical account of *Americans United for the Separation of Church and State v. Prison Fellowship Ministries*, 432 F. Supp. 2d 862 (S.D. Iowa), which found against InnerChange's constitutionality, see Winnifred Fallers Sullivan, *Prison Religion* (Princeton University Press, 2009).

13. See http://endviolence.org/evp/index.shtml. The End Violence Program is run by people affiliated with Landmark Education. A corporate-age reconfiguration of the seventies' self-help group est, Landmark is a for-profit organization that develops curricula and offers a series of programs—most notably the Landmark Forum—geared toward personal improvement and self-actualization. The influence of Landmark Education's "educational technology" on the End Violence Program is prominently credited in the LIFERS' "Ending the Culture of Street Crime," *The Prison Journal*

(2004) pp. 52S and 68S (note). On Landmark Education, see "Do You Believe in Miracles?" *Elle* (August 1998). On est, see William Warren Bartley III, *Werner Erhard: The Transformation of a Man: The Founding of est* (Clarkson Potter, 1978).

14. On Malcolm X in prison, see Malcolm X and Alex Haley, *The Autobiography of Malcolm X* (Ballantine, 1973), pp. 154–94; and Manning Marable, *Malcolm X: A Life of Reinvention* (Viking, 2011), pp. 70–99.

15. In his cell, Sayyid has the Qur'anic commentary of the fourteenth-century scholar Ibn Kathir—the same collection that the Imam has in his office. Sa'di was a twentieth-century Saudi scholar. On Tafsir, see Muhammad Ayoub, *The Qur'ān and Its Interpreters* (SUNY Press, 1984); Walid A. Saleh, *The Formation of the Classical Tafsīr Tradition* (Brill Academic Publishers, 2004); and Norman Calder, "Tafsir from Tabari to Ibn Kathir," in G. R. Hawting and A.-K. Shareef (eds.), *Approaches to the Qur'an* (RoutledgeCurzon, 1993), pp. 101–40.

16. The last time the Bureau of Justice Statistics produced a report, roughly one in ten incarcerated Americans were military veterans. See "Special Report: Veterans in State and Federal Prison, 2004," *Bureau of Justice Statistics* (May 2007), http:// bjs.ojp.usdoj.gov/content/pub/pdf/vsfp04.pdf. But at this point, the wars in Iraq and Afghanistan had just begun.

17. This quotation is commonly attributed to Dostoyevsky and, more specifically, to Constance Garnett's translation of *The House of the Dead*. However, I have been unable to confirm it.

18. According to the U.S. Department of Justice, more than half of prisoners nationwide suffer from mental health disorders. See "Special Report: Mental Health Problems of Prison and Jail Inmates," *Bureau of Justice Statistics* (September 2006). http://bjs.ojp.usdoj.gov/content/pub/pdf/mhppji.pdf. On treatment and custody, see Lorna Rhodes, *Total Confinement: Madness and Reason in the Maximum Security Prison* (University of California Press, 2004), pp. 99–160 especially.

19. A Negro spiritual.

20. For a cultural history, see Marni Davis, *Jews and Booze* (NYU Press, 2012).

21. *The Watchtower*, December 15, 2005, pp. 24–29.

22. Ergo the rabbinic rhetoric of *Yam ha-talmud*—the Sea of the Talmud.

23. For this alternative genealogy of Ashkenazi Jews, see Arthur Koestler, *The Thirteenth Tribe: The Kazar Empire and Its Heritage* (Fawcett Popular Library, 1978). On African-American appropriations of Judaism, see Yvonne Chireau and Nathaniel Deutsch (eds.), *Black Zion: African American Religious Encounters with Judaism* (Oxford, 2000), pp. 15–90.

24. Counselors are the other.

25. This widely collected and cited hadith may be found in Shaikh Ali Hasan Alee Abdul Hameed's *Forty Hadith on the Call to Islam and the Caller* (al-Hidaayah Publishing, 1994). Hameed was a student of the Salafi scholar Muhammad Nasiruddin al-Albani.

26. On violence, see Hannah Arendt, *On Violence* (Harcourt Brace Jovanovich, 1970); Walter Benjamin, "Critique of Violence" in *Reflections* (Schocken Books, 1978), pp. 277–300; Michael Taussig, *The Nervous System* (Routledge, 1991), pp. 1–36 and 111–40; and Max Weber, "Politics as a Vocation" in *The Vocation Lectures: Science as a Vocation, Politics as a Vocation* (Hackett, 2004), pp. 32–94.

27. Vic's initial question was why anyone would possibly assume that Noam Chomsky would have any sympathies with Zionism as an ideology. On Zionism, see Arthur

Hertzberg, *The Zionist Idea: A Historical Analysis and Reader* (Jewish Publication Society, 1997). For a critical history see Gabriel Piterberg, *The Returns of Zionism: Myths, Politics and Scholarship in Israel* (Verso, 2008).

28. On T. D. Jakes, see Jonathan Walton, *Watch This!: The Ethics and Aesthetics of Black Televangelism* (NYU Press, 2009), pp. 103–24.

29. For an ethnographic study of purity practices among Cairo's Salafi Muslims, see Richard Gauvain, *Salafi Ritual Purity: In the Presence of God* (Routledge, 2013).

30. This count includes the black nationalist Nation of Islam, Mohammed's Temple, and Moorish Science Temple, and a handful of other neotraditionalist sects.

31. "At Graterford, Officials Collected Stories Along with the Contraband," *Philadelphia Inquirer*, October 27, 1995.

32. See William J. Bennett, John J. Dilulio, Jr., and John P. Walters, *Body Count: Moral Poverty . . . And How to Win America's War Against Crime and Drugs* (Simon and Schuster, 1996). For a critique, see Steve Macek, *Urban Nightmares: The Media, the Right, and the Moral Panic over the City* (University of Minnesota Press, 2006). On candidate Bill Clinton's pivot to toughness on crime, see Marshall Frady, "Death in Arkansas," *The New Yorker* (February 22, 1993). As president, Clinton finished his triangulation on criminal justice with the 1996 passage of the Antiterrorism and Effective Death Penalty Act (AEDPA), which severely limited the conditions under which prisoners could file habeas corpus petitions. See the Antiterrorism and Effective Death Penalty Act of 1996, Pub. L. No. 104–132, 110 Stat. 1214 (1996).

33. On neoliberal penality see David Garland, *The Culture of Control* (University of Chicago Press, 2001); and Loïc Wacquant, *Punishing the Poor: The Neoliberal Government of Social Insecurity* (Duke University Press, 2009). On the economic and social logic of neoliberalism more generally, see David Harvey, *A Brief History of Neoliberalism* (Oxford University Press, 2007). For a periodization of American mass incarceration that takes a somewhat longer view, see Bernard E. Harcourt, *The Illusion of Free Markets: Punishment and the Myth of Natural Order* (Harvard University Press, 2011).

34. Angela Y. Davis, "Masked Racism: Reflections on the Prison Industrial Complex," *ColorLines* (Fall 1998). On the historical emergence of mass incarceration, see Ruth Wilson Gilmore, *Golden Gulag: Prisons, Surplus, Crisis, and Opposition in Globalizing California* (University of California Press, 2007); and Marie Gottschalk, *The Prison and the Gallows: The Politics of Mass Incarceration in America* (Cambridge University Press, 2006). For ethnographic studies of the now dominant custodial logic, see John Irwin, *The Warehouse Prison: Disposal of the New Dangerous Class* (Oxford University Press, 2004), and Lorna Rhodes, *Total Confinement: Madness and Reason in the Maximum Security Prison* (University of California Press, 2004).

35. For a current map of the Pennsylvania Department of Corrections system, see http://www.cor.state.pa.us/portal/server.pt/community/institutions/5270.

36. In 1980, the state of Pennsylvania had 8,582 prisoners, representing 72.3 people for every 100,000 members of the population. By 1995, the state prison population had nearly quadrupled to 32,410, representing 269.1 per 100,000 Pennsylvanians. See the Pennsylvania Commission on Crime and Delinquency 2002 Fact Sheet at www.pccd.state.pa.us/pccd/lib/pccd/stats/criminaljusticetrends/prisonsandjails/prisonpop2002.pdf.

37. Designed as streamlined "pods" rather than ungainly tiers, the new blocks allow two COs to effectively oversee forty men. This compared to the old side blocks, where, all concede, the six COs on duty couldn't possibly look after the 500 men in their charge.
38. Figure given in "Schools to Use Inmate's Book," *York Daily Record*, August 13, 1996.
39. See "Hits and Misses in Candidates' War of Words over Crime," *Philadelphia Inquirer*, October 23, 1994, and "GOP Looking to Revive Crime Bills That Failed," *Philadelphia Inquirer*, November 28, 1994.
40. The guarantee of ceremonial autonomy was enshrined in the Religious Activities Handbook (BC ADM-819). On February 3, 1995, a bulletin from the deputy commissioner informed correctional staff and inmates that the relevant section had been deleted.
41. "Prison Swept for Drugs Cell by Cell," *Philadelphia Inquirer*, October 25, 1995.
42. "Flush with Success?" *Philadelphia Daily News*, October 27, 1995.
43. "Graterford Raid Paid Off," *Philadelphia Inquirer*, December 5, 1995.
44. "Inmate Throne for a Loss," *Philadelphia Daily News*, October 26, 1995.
45. "Staying Alive Was the Name of the Game for Ex-Inmate," *Philadelphia Daily News*, October 25, 1995.
46. On the professionalization of the figure of the imam in the United States, see John H. Morgan, *Muslim Clergy in America: Ministry as Profession in the Islamic Community* (Wyndham Hall, 2010).
47. Quoted in *al-Samad v. Horn*, 913 F. Supp. 373 (E.D. Pa. 1995), trial record.
48. Ibid.
49. Among the new technologies adopted at Graterford are horse patrols, canine units, drug detection devices, and bioscans.
50. According to other data presented at my Graterford orientation, the same three-year period saw a 65% drop in positive drug tests.
51. For an insider portrait of the pre-raid era, authored by a member of Graterford's Jewish community, see Victor Hassine, *Life without Parole* (Roxbury Publishing, 1999); for a post-raid analysis by a Graterford employee, see B. Scott Gallie, Sr., *Circle of Conviction* (First Books, 2000).
52. *Brady v. Maryland*, 373 U.S. 83 (1963). In addition to *Brady* and *ineffective assistance of counsel*, for long-term prisoners, one of the few available avenues for judicial relief is *Batson v. Kentucky*, 476 U.S. 79 (1986), which prohibits the striking of potential jurors solely on the basis of their race. This issue is especially salient for many at Graterford due to the existence of a 1996 Philadelphia district attorney's office training video that explicitly stressed the importance of excluding potential black jurors (along with seemingly intelligent candidates of any race). See http://video.google.com/videoplay?docid=-5102834972975877286.
53. Sean Patrick Griffin, *Black Brothers, Inc.: The Violent Rise and Fall of Philadelphia's Black Mafia* (Milo Books, 2005).
54. Four civil society organizations survived the raid: the Brotherhood Jaycees, the NAACP, LACEO (the Latino Prisoners' Association), and LIFERS; and each has an annual fundraiser. While the leadership cadre of all four groups is made up largely of lifers, LIFERS (long-incarcerated fraternity engaging release studies) is not limited to men serving life. For a study of the LIFERS at Pennsylvania's State Correctional Institution at Huntingdon, see Frances N. Huber, *Communicating Social Support Behind Bars: Experiences with the Pennsylvania Lifers' Association*

(Ph.D. dissertation in Communication Arts and Sciences, Pennsylvania State University, 2005).

55. Though they differed in their specifics, many medieval scholars enumerated the commandments at 613, with the most influential tally belonging to Maimonides.

56. Up to a quarter of Pennsylvania's death row prisoners are imprisoned on Graterford's J Block. Pennsylvania's death row is the fourth-largest in the country.

57. Nas, "One Love" (1994).

58. On the metaphor of the game and its application to language and practice, see Ludwig Wittgenstein, *Philosophical Investigations* (Prentice Hall, 1958), especially pp. 30–34, and Pierre Bourdieu, *The Logic of Practice* (Stanford University Press, 1990), especially pp. 66–82. For a contemporary take on blacks and Jews *in the game*, watch the sixth episode of the second season of *The Wire*, in which Omar, who robs drug dealers for a living, says to Levy, the Jewish lawyer: "I got the shotgun. You got the briefcase. It's all in the game, though, right?" http://www.youtube.com/watch?v=oYj7q_by_2E.

59. In the image, Day, ancient and defiant, is framed by the torsos of two armed law enforcement officials. For Day's quotation in context, see Daniela Gioseffi (ed.), *Women on War: Essential Voices for the Nuclear Age* (Touchstone Books, 1988), p. 103.

60. See Louis Althusser, "Ideology and Ideological State Apparatuses," in his *Lenin and Philosophy, and Other Essays* (New Left Books, 1972), pp. 136–70. http://www.marxists.org/reference/archive/althusser/1970/ideology.htm; Raymond Williams, *Marxism and Literature* (Oxford University Press, 1977), pp. 108–14; and Andrea Sun-Mee Jones and Joshua Dubler, *Bang! Thud: World Spirit from a Texas School Book Depository* (Autraumaton, 2006).

61. Exempla of this prevailing democratic impulse in the Princeton Religion Department include Eddie S. Glaude, *In a Shade of Blue: Pragmatism and the Politics of Black America* (University of Chicago Press, 2008); Elaine Pagels, *Beyond Belief: The Secret Gospel of Thomas* (Vintage, 2004); Leigh Schmidt, *Restless Souls: The Making of American Spirituality* (HarperOne, 2005); Jeffrey Stout, *Democracy and Tradition* (Princeton University Press, 2004); and Cornel West, *Race Matters* (Vintage, 1994).

62. This reification of the *system* calls to mind Michael Taussig's discussion of State fetishism, in which the capital S of the State is forged at the intersection of reason and terror. Michael Taussig, *The Nervous System* (Routledge, 1991), pp. 111–40.

63. Queer theorist Eve Kosofsky Sedgwick used the example of the mass incarceration of African-American youth to question the impulse behind "paranoid reading" practices that purport to unmask appearances and expose what's *really* going on: "Why bother exposing the ruses of power in a country where, at any given moment, 40 percent of young black men are enrolled in the penal system? In the United States and internationally, while there is plenty of hidden violence that requires exposure, there is also, and increasingly, an ethos where forms of violence that are hyper-visible from the state may be offered as an exemplary spectacle, rather than remaining to be unveiled as a scandalous secret." Eve Kosofsky Sedgwick, *Novel Gazing* (Duke University Press, 1997), p. 18.

64. According to press reports from the time of his trial, David accused the boyfriend of molesting his daughter, a charge that was denied by the boyfriend and seemingly did nothing to aid David's defense.

65. It is impossible here not to think of Agamben's "bare life." See Giorgio Agamben, *Homo Sacer: Sovereign Power and Bare Life* (Stanford University Press, 1998). On bare life in the context of the concentration camps, see Giorgio Agamben, *Remnants of Auschwitz* (Zone, 2002).
66. Leviticus Rabba 30:12.
67. My general policy—outside of the week at hand—was to take notes during religious rituals only when others were doing so too. I generally composed my field notes in the dead time between activity blocks and via digital recorder on the drive back to Philly.

WEDNESDAY

1. I've come to regard this as the *"City Slickers* principle," after the 1991 film (Ron Underwood, dir.), in which Jack Palance's sage cowboy exhorts a midlife-crisis-torn Billy Crystal that he must identify the "one thing" that matters to him. Reconciling his longing to be a man with his antecedent domestic obligations, the nebbish Crystal rises to the challenge to embrace his "one thing"—his family.
2. Richard Rorty, *Philosophy and Social Hope* (Penguin, 2000), pp. 168–74.
3. On Jesus in American culture, see Stephen Prothero, *American Jesus* (Farrar, Straus and Giroux, 2003).
4. 1 Corinthians 13:11.
5. Habakkuk 1:3.
6. EFM is a lay ministry program, generally administered by correspondence, which is sponsored by the University of the South. See http://www.sewanee.edu/EFM/.
7. Philippians 4:11.
8. Friedrich Nietzsche, *On the Advantages and Disadvantages of History for Life* (Hackett, 1980), p. 8.
9. On "total institutions," see Erving Goffman, *Asylums* (Anchor Books, 1961). In popular culture, the "jailhouse Muslim" also comes in this sadder secondary variety, with religion framed as simply a means of psychical and physical survival. In this vein, I've seen Stephen Colbert and Jon Stewart each make a seemingly unscripted aside about how when he was in prison, he too was a Muslim.
10. On doubt, see René Descartes (ed. and trans. Roger Ariew and Donald Cress), *Meditations, Objections, and Replies* (Hackett Publishing Company, 2006); Søren Kierkegaard, *Johannes Climacus* (Serpent's Tail, 2001); and Jennifer Michael Hecht, *Doubt: A History* (HarperOne, 2004).
11. This deliberation is what, after the Spanish philosopher Miguel de Unamuno, American pragmatists dub "the tragic." See Sidney Hook, *Pragmatism and the Tragic Sense of Life* (Basic Books, 1974); and Cornel West, *The American Evasion of Philosophy* (University of Wisconsin Press, 1989), pp. 114–24.
12. I'm thinking of Derrida's observation that in feeding his or her own mewing companion, the cat lover de facto consigns the rest of the world's hungry cats to starvation. See Jacques Derrida, *The Gift of Death* (University of Chicago Press, 2007), p. 71. For an alternative ethics, see Peter Singer, "Famine, Affluence, and Morality," *Philosophy and Public Affairs*, Vol. 1 (Spring 1972), pp. 229–43, and Peter Singer, "Outsiders: Our Obligations to Those Beyond Our Borders," in *The Ethics of Assistance: Morality and the Distant Needy* (Cambridge University Press, 2004), pp. 11–32.

13. For contemporary assessments of Paul's influence on Western philosophy, politics, and ethics, see Alain Badiou, *St. Paul: The Foundation of Universalism* (Stanford University Press, 1997); Jacob Taubes, *The Political Theology of Paul* (Stanford University Press, 2004); and Slavoj Žižek, *The Puppet and the Dwarf* (MIT Press, 2003).
14. See Martin Heidegger, *Being and Time* (SUNY Press, 1996), pp. 144–49, and Jeffrey Stout, "What Is the Meaning of a Text?" *New Literary History*, Vol. 14, No. 1 (1982), pp. 1–2.
15. On the silent thrust of a social norm and the misrecognition that attends such habituations, Pierre Bourdieu speaks of "The best-kept and worst-kept of secrets (since everybody kept it)." Pierre Bourdieu, *The Logic of Practice* (Stanford University Press, 1990), p. 114.
16. I have been advised to shield the identity of this group.
17. See Michael Taussig, *The Nervous System* (Routledge, 1991), pp. 11–36.
18. See "Old Behind Bars: The Aging Prison Population in the United States" (Human Rights Watch, January 2012), http://www.hrw.org/reports/2012/01/26/old-behind-bars. On Pennsylvania in particular, see "Report of the Advisory Committee on Geriatric and Seriously Ill Inmates" (Joint State Government Commission, June 2005), http://jsg.legis.state.pa.us/publications.cfm?JSPU_PUBLN_ID=40.
19. My project was originally slated to take place in New Jersey's Rahway Prison. However, between May 2005, when my proposal was approved, and September, when my research was to commence, the New Jersey Department of Corrections suspended all research inside its institutions. Six months after the NJ DOC's approval was retracted, the project was approved by the Pennsylvania DOC's Office of Planning, Research & Statistics. Throughout, my research was vetted by Princeton University's Institutional Review Board for Human Subjects. On the institutional obstacles of doing prison ethnography, see Loïc Wacquant, "The Eclipse of Prison Ethnography in the Age of Mass Incarceration," *Ethnography*, 3–4 (2002), pp. 371–97.
20. For the master-slave dialectic, see G.W.F. Hegel, *Phenomenology of Spirit* (Oxford University Press, 1977), pp. 111–19, http://www.marxists.org/reference/archive/hegel/works/ph/phba.htm. For a pragmatist rendering, see this 2008 interview with philosopher Robert Brandom: http://video.google.com/videoplay?docid=-1034802594689246468.
21. Galatians 6:10.
22. On feeling, doing, and knowing as the overlapping faculties at the heart of religious piety, see Friedrich Schleiermacher, *The Christian Faith* (Continuum, 1999), pp. 5–12.
23. Georges Bataille, *The Accursed Share*, Vol. I (Zone Books, 1991). Also referenced in my lecture were Georges Bataille, *Theory of Religion* (Zone Books, 1992); and René Girard, *Violence and the Sacred* (Johns Hopkins University Press, 1977).
24. Bruno Latour, "A Few Steps Toward an Anthropology of the Iconoclastic Gesture," *Science in Context* 10, 1 (1997), p. 77.
25. On self-consciousness as a cornerstone for a revolutionary ethics, another graduate of Graterford's Villanova Program wrote: "For me, I try to operate in the interstices of the architectural and ideological Panopticon as far as I can even recognize its dimensions. And an important part of that attempt is to recognize that I too am subject to the gale of ideologies—panoptic and beyond—that we are all buffeted by. To that end, I try to remember that it is the internal priest, the internal guard and the internal oppressor that is the hardest to overthrow. If I direct

my gaze continuously outward—a panoptic worldview, if you will—I lose sight of what is most crucial to my personal liberation. In my revolution, it is not the Kalashnikov or the Molotov cocktail that will slay the oppressor within; it is not the rat or the video camera that will reveal my truth; and it is not the sword or even the pen that will etch a new meaning onto my existence; what is the most essential tool for my, and, I believe, all meaningful revolution is the mirror . . . and I plan to look into it." From Tom Schilk, "Am I My Brother's Keeper? (Elements of Panopticism in the Modern Prison)," unpublished final paper for Religion in the Tradition of Social Theory, a course in Villanova's program at Graterford, Spring 2007.

26. See Hubert Dreyfus, *Being-in-the-World: A Commentary on Heidegger's Being and Time, Division I* (MIT Press, 1991), pp. 141–67; and Judith Butler, *Gender Trouble: Feminism and the Subversion of Identity* (Routledge, 1999), pp. 194–203 especially.

27. Bryan Singer (dir.), *The Usual Suspects* (1995).

28. W.E.B. Du Bois, *The Souls of Black Folk* (CreateSpace, 2010), p. 8. For the relevant sociology, see W.E.B. Du Bois, *The Philadelphia Negro: A Social Study* (University of Pennsylvania Press, 1996). On Du Bois and religion, see Jonathan Kahn, *Divine Discontent: The Religious Imagination of W.E.B. Du Bois* (Oxford University Press, 2011).

29. See Sigmund Freud, "The Aetiology of Hysteria," in Peter Gay (ed.), *The Freud Reader* (Norton, 1995), pp. 96–110. For a study of Freud's "seduction theory" that contributed to the rubric of "recovered memory," see Jeffrey Masson, *The Assault on Truth: Freud's Suppression of the Seduction Theory* (Farrar, Straus and Giroux, 1984).

30. On "animism" in the modern anthropology of religion, see Pals, *Eight Theories of Religion* (Oxford University Press, 2006), especially pp. 18–52.

31. See Craig Timberg and Daniel Halperin, *Tinderbox: How the West Sparked the AIDS Epidemic and How the World Can Finally Overcome It* (Penguin, 2012).

32. On piety, see "Euthyphro," in Plato, *Five Dialogues* (Hackett, 2002); and "Introduction," by James Gouinlock, in Marianne S. Wokeck and Martin A. Coleman (eds.), *George Santayana, The Life of Reason, or, The Phases of Human Progress: Critical Edition* (MIT Press, 2011). On irony, see Søren Kierkegaard, *On the Concept of Irony with Continual Reference to Socrates* (Princeton University Press, 1992); and Jonathan Lear, "A Lost Conception of Irony," *Berfrois* (January 4, 2012).

33. On Elijah Muhammad, see Claude Andrew Clegg III, *An Original Man: The Life and Times of Elijah Muhammad* (St. Martin's Griffin, 1997); Karl Evanzz, *The Messenger: The Rise and Fall of Elijah Muhammad* (Vintage, 1999); and Herbert Berg, *Elijah Muhammad and Islam* (NYU Press, 2009).

34. In 1983, the name of this holiday was changed from the singular, Saviour's Day, to the plural, Saviours' Day, to emphasize collective responsibility.

35. See Clifton E. Marsh, *From Black Muslims to Muslims: The Transition from Separatism to Islam, 1930–1980* (Scarecrow Press, 1984), pp. 89–124; and Matthias Gardell, *In the Name of Elijah Muhammad: Louis Farrakhan and the Nation of Islam* (Duke University Press, 1996), pp. 99–118. For a video of Wallace Muhammad's Saviour's Day speech, see: http://www.youtube.com/watch?v=vQPe9yAbRqU.

36. Lawrence H. Mamiya, "From Black Muslim to Bilalian: The Evolution of a Movement," *Journal for the Scientific Study of Religion* 21:2 (1982), pp. 138–52.

37. Early in this period, Masjid Sajdah weathered a schism when a dozen men (then a significant fraction of its ranks) pledged their allegiance to the Dar ul-Islam move-

ment. The Dar was a national organization based in New York that was dedicated to spreading Sunni Islam among African-Americans. The faction petitioned Yunus to take Masjid Sajdah in that direction. When the Dar demanded that its affiliate members pledge a *bayat* (oath of loyalty) as a rite of community initiation, Yunus refused: "I understood what they wanted, but in the penitentiary system, we should not pledge that allegiance because we would be transferred." If members of Sajdah were shipped, Yunus doubted the national organization would go to bat for them. On the Dar, see R. M. Mukhar Curtis, "Urban Muslims: The Formation of the Dar ul-Islam Movement," in Yvonne Yazbeck Haddad and Jane Idleman Smith, *Muslim Communities in North America* (SUNY Press, 1994), pp. 51–73.

38. For a dissident account of this history, see Umar Lee, "Rise and Fall of the Salafi Movement," http://www.umarlee.com/rise-fall.html. For an apologetic rejoinder, see the two-part lecture delivered in response by Dawud Adib, formerly imam of the Germantown mosque, in June 2011 at the Salafi Conference in Cherry Hill, New Jersey, http://www.youtube.com/watch?v=tixXMlFkgms and http://www.youtube.com/watch?v=n7mKE-7W6cw&feature=related.

39. Two influential texts were Muhammad ibn Abdul-Wahhab, *Kitab at-Tauhid* (Dar-us-Salam Publications, 1996); and Abu Ameenah Bilal Philips, *The Evolution of Fiqh* (A. S. Noordeen, 1989).

40. While Warith Deen and Sajdah were far and away the most prominent, in the heyday preceding the raid, Graterford had five other traditionalist Muslim groups. Of these secondary groups, the most visible was Masjid Taubah, which conceived of itself as Shia and met in a third room in the basement. No one I've spoken with identifies as having belonged to this masjid, but one young Muslim characterized the bygone sect as follows: "If Warith Deen Muhammad were the political Muslims, and Sajdah were the pious Muslims, Taubah were the *cool* Muslims." More *spiritual* Muslims, meanwhile, would likely have been drawn to the meditation and chanting sessions of the Bawa Muhaiyaddeen Fellowship. This Sufi sect, which was founded by a Sri Lankan guru on the Philadelphia Main Line in the 1960s, still retains a monthly chapel slot, though they meet only sporadically. Others included the Dar ul-Islam–affiliated splinter group; a residual group of Ahmadi Muslims; and, as inspired by a briefly tenured contract chaplain, a group identified with the Habashi sect, which has a mosque in West Philadelphia. As Yunus explained the bygone sectarianism: "Everybody could come up with some kind of gimmick. 'They're Muslim?'" he said, as if speaking for that era's administration. "'As long as we have someone in the street to vouch for them, they can have what they want.'" On the Bawa, see Gisela Webb, "Tradition and Innovation in Contemporary American Islamic Spirituality," in Yvonne Yazbeck Haddad and Jane Idleman Smith (eds.), *Muslim Communities in North America* (SUNY Press, 1994), pp. 75–108; on the Ahmadiyya, see Richard Brent Turner, *Islam in the African-American Experience* (Indiana University Press, 1997), pp. 109–46; and on the Habashi, see A. Nizar Hamzeh and R. Hrair Dekmejian, "A Sufi Response to Political Islamism: Al-Ahbash of Lebanon," *International Journal of Middle East Studies* 28 (1996), pp. 217–29. For comparison's sake, see the history of Masjid Sankor at New York's Green Haven Prison in Robert Dannin, *Black Pilgrimage to Islam* (Oxford University Press, 2002), pp. 165–88.

41. Jochanan Kapliwatsky, *Arabic Language and Grammar, Part III* (Rubin Mass, 1976), pp. 40–42.

42. See Edward Said, *Orientalism* (Vintage, 1979), pp. 1–28. On "Black Orientalism," see Sherman Jackson, *Islam and the Blackamerican* (Oxford University Press, 2005), pp. 99–130. For an oblique cultural history of American Orientalism, see Nathaniel Deutsch, *Inventing America's "Worst" Family: Eugenics, Islam, and the Fall and Rise of the Tribe of Ishmael* (University of California Press, 2009).

THURSDAY

1. Emile Durkheim, *The Elementary Forms of Religious Life* (Free Press, 1995), and Mircea Eliade, *The Sacred and the Profane: The Nature of Religion* (Harcourt Brace Jovanovich, 1987).
2. On "black religion" as distinguished from "African-American religion," see Charles H. Long, *Significations: Signs, Symbols, and Images in the Interpretation of Religion* (Davies Group, 2004), pp. 145–70; and Sherman Jackson, *Islam and the Blackamerican* (Oxford University Press, 2005), pp. 23–58.
3. According to the typology, the fox knows many things, but the hedgehog knows only one thing. See Isaiah Berlin, *The Hedgehog and the Fox: An Essay on Tolstoy's View of History* (Ivan R. Dee, 1993).
4. More than a few Graterford old heads carry scars on their bodies from having been used as human guinea pigs in pharmaceutical and other product testing at Holmesburg. See Allen M. Hornblum, *Acres of Skin: Human Experiments at Holmesburg Prison: A True Story of Abuse and Exploitation in the Name of Medical Science* (Routledge, 1999).
5. In 1960, 26% of Philadelphia's population of two million plus was black. By 1980, African-Americans accounted for 38% of a city population that had fallen to 1.68 million. See Sean Patrick Griffin, *Black Brothers, Inc.* (Milo Books, 2005), p. 14.
6. On Frank Rizzo, see Joseph R. Daughen and Peter Binzen, *The Cop Who Would Be King* (Little, Brown, 1977), and S. A. Paolantonio, *Frank Rizzo* (Camino Books, 1993).
7. "Overcrowded Holmesburg Was Ruled Unconstitutionally Cruel in 1972," *Philadelphia Inquirer*, June 1, 1973, p. 1.
8. Griffin, *Black Brothers, Inc.*, p. 48.
9. Ibid., pp. 196–208.
10. William Brashler, "Black on Black: The Deadly Struggle for Power," *New York* (magazine), June 5, 1975, p. 56. Quoted in Griffin, p. 207.
11. Griffin, p. 97, and Mattias Gardell, *In the Name of Elijah Muhammad* (Duke University Press, 1996), p. 189.
12. For an oral history of Temple Twelve, see Minister Jeremiah Shabazz, *Top of the Clock* (First Impressions, 1997).
13. See Malcolm X and Alex Haley, *The Autobiography of Malcolm X* (Ballantine, 1973), pp. 158–59. On Temple Twelve's founding, see Jeremiah Shabazz, *Top of the Clock* (First Impressions, 1997), p. 17.
14. Sherman Jackson, *Islam and the Blackamerican* (Oxford University Press, 2005), p. 32.
15. See David M. Goldenberg, *The Curse of Ham: Race and Slavery in Early Judaism, Christianity, and Islam* (Princeton University Press, 2003), and Elijah Muhammad, *Yakub: The Father of Mankind* (Secretarius Memps, 2002).
16. On the Nation of Islam as a species of Protestant dispensationalism, see Louis A.

DeCaro, Jr., *Malcolm and the Cross: The Nation of Islam, Malcolm X, and Christianity* (New York University Press, 1998).

17. On African-American Ahmadiyya, see Richard Brent Turner, *Islam in the African-American Experience* (Indiana University Press, 1997), pp. 109–46. On the Ahmadiyya more broadly, see Simon Ross Valentine, *Islam and the Ahmadiyya Jama'at: History, Belief, Practice* (Columbia University Press, 2008). It should be noted that upon his arrival in Philadelphia, the Ahmadiyya missionary Muhammad al Sadiq was taken into custody and detained for a number of weeks. See Turner, pp. 115–16.

18. "Moslem Musicians," *Ebony* (April 1953), pp. 104–10.

19. "2 Arraigned in 2 Killings at Holmesburg," *Philadelphia Inquirer*, June 2, 1973.

20. For a fine-grained history of black politics and social organizing in Philadelphia from the forties to the seventies, see Matthew J. Countryman, *Up South: Civil Rights and Black Power in Philadelphia* (University of Pennsylvania Press, 2006).

21. On the era of penological progressivism, see Erik Olin Wright, *The Politics of Punishment* (Harper Colophon, 1973); James B. Jacobs, *New Perspectives on Prisons and Imprisonment* (Cornell University Press, 1983); and Marie Gottschalk, *The Prison and the Gallows* (Cambridge University Press, 2006), pp. 165–96.

22. For a portrait of Graterford during the Robert Johnson era, see Vaughn Booker and David Phelps, *From Prison to Pulpit* (Cadell & Davies, 1994), pp. 120–41.

23. On the prisoners' rights movement, see Gottschalk, *The Prison and the Gallows*, pp. 77–114. On prison riots, see Bert Useem and Peter Kimball, *States of Siege: U.S. Prison Riots, 1971–1986* (Oxford University Press, 1991).

24. See Kathleen Moore, "Muslims in Prison: Claims to Constitutional Protection of Religious Liberty," in Yvonne Yazbeck Haddad, *The Muslims of America* (Oxford University Press, 1991), pp. 136–55, and Sarah Barringer Gordon, *The Spirit of the Law: Religion and Litigation in Modern America* (Belknap Press of Harvard University Press, 2010), pp. 96–132.

25. As Elijah Muhammad wrote: "Our true God is not like the 'Spook God' of Christianity who demands death for our salvation and redemption. He is offering us Freedom, Liberty and the Pursuit of Happiness on this earth while we live." Elijah Muhammad, *Message to the Blackman in America* (Secretarius Memps, 1973), p. 54.

26. On Shamsud-din's involvement thirty years later in the "pay to play" racketeering of Philadelphia mayor John Street's administration, see Griffin, *Black Brothers, Inc.*, pp. 6–10.

27. While no one in the chapel recalled it for me, on at least one occasion, these disputes allegedly provoked a riot. See "Graterford Riot Blamed on 'Religious Differences,'" *Gettysburg Times*, July 29, 1972.

28. On the resurrection of the Nation of Islam under Louis Farrakhan, see Matthias Gardell, *In the Name of Elijah Muhammad* (Duke University Press, 1996), pp. 119–43.

29. *Allah v. Menei*, 844 F. Supp. 1056 (1994).

30. C. Eric Lincoln's study was published in 1961. See *Black Muslims in America* (Wm. B. Eerdmans, 1994). For other influential early representations see James Baldwin, *The Fire Next Time* (Vintage, 1992), pp. 47–82, and the 1959 documentary produced by Mike Wallace and Louis Lomax for public television, *The Hate That Hate Produced*. http://video.google.com/videoplay?docid=6140647821635049109.

31. Popular especially (but hardly exclusively) among members of peripheral groups like the Nation and the Native Americans are works that self-consciously evince a "conspiratorial view of history." See, e.g., A. Ralph Epperson, *The Unseen Hand* (Publius Press, 1985). In an ideological wrap-around, also common in these marginal discourses are the challenges against governmental authority generally associated with the Sovereign Citizen movement, whose roots are in the white supremacist Christian Identity movement.

32. See "Radical Rhetoric, Conservative Reality: The Nation of Islam as an American Conservative Formation," in Peter Eisenstadt (ed.), *Black Conservatism* (Garland Publishing, 1999), pp. 109–32.

33. As written into the DOC's charter, the Prison Society's official visitors are authorized to be admitted throughout the system—a key reason why in this current era of heightened controls and barriers to access, Pennsylvania's prisons remain relatively permeable.

34. Conspicuous among this pile of texts are copies of a trucker ministry pamphlet called *Highway News* and handfuls of small, cardstock Chick comic booklets. On the latter, see Robert B. Fowler, *The World of Jack T. Chick?* (Last Gasp of San Francisco, 2001).

35. http://www.libertyministries.us/.

36. On Mennonites in Pennsylvania, see John L. Ruth, *Maintaining the Right Fellowship* (Wipf & Stock, 2004).

37. Donald P. Hustad (ed.), *Hymns for the Living Church* (Hope Publishing Company, 1974).

38. Isaiah 11:6.

39. For an ethnography of Evangelical Bible studies, see James S. Bielo, *Words Upon the Word* (New York University Press, 2009).

40. Voltaire, *Candide, or Optimism* (Penguin, 2005), p. 52.

41. 1 John 1: 26–27.

42. Hebrews 5:12–14.

43. John W. Matthews, "Bonhoeffer at 100," *The Lutheran*, February 2006. See Dietrich Bonhoeffer, *Letters and Papers from Prison* (Touchstone, 1997), and Martin Marty, *Dietrich Bonhoeffer's Letters and Papers from Prison* (Princeton University Press, 2011).

44. While noting it is "the subject of considerable Christian homiletic expansion" dating back to the fourth century, J. Z. Smith rejects this purported etymology in favor of a denotation having to do with "the careful performance of ritual obligations." Smith in Mark C. Taylor (ed.), *Critical Terms for Religious Study* (University of Chicago Press, 1998), p. 269.

45. See Carolyn N. Long, *Religious Freedom and Indian Rights: The Case of Oregon v. Smith* (University Press of Kansas, 2000), and Leonard Peltier, *My Life Is a Sun Dance* (St. Martin's Griffin, 2000). See also James B. Waldram, *The Way of the Pipe: Aboriginal Spirituality and Symbolic Healing in Canadian Prisons* (University of Toronto Press, 1997).

46. *Warcloud v. Horn*, 97–3657 (E.D. Pa. 1998). Trial record.

47. Ibid.

48. Passed in 1993, the Religious Freedom Restoration Act was Congress's legislative response to the Supreme Court's *Oregon v. Smith* ruling that free-exercise claims did not trump generally applicable laws. See *The Religious Freedom Restoration Act of 1993*, Pub. L. No. 103–141, 107 Stat. 1488 (November 16, 1993).

49. On the controversy over the inclusion of intelligent design in the Dover County, Pennsylvania, school curriculum, see *Kitzmiller v. Dover Area School District*, 400 F. Supp. 2d 707 (M.D. Pa. 2005), Edward Humes, *Monkey Girl: Evolution, Education, Religion, and the Battle for America's Soul* (ECCO, 2007), and Lauri Lebo, *The Devil in Dover* (New Press, 2008).

50. "Worship, Dark and Steamy, for Murderers and Rapists," *New York Times*, June 25, 2005.

51. See Migene González-Wippler, *Santería: The Religion: Faith, Rites, Magic* (Llewellyn Publications, 2002).

52. The Seventh Circuit recently found in favor of an Illinois prisoner requesting a hair exemption on the basis of a Nazirite vow. *Grayson v. Schuler*, No. 10–3256 (January 13, 2012).

53. Rico wrote his brief polemic against anthropology in the context of a course I taught through the Villanova Program titled "Event, Ethnography, History." That was the third course I taught at Graterford, the prior two being "Religion in the Tradition of Social Theory" and "Freud, Nietzsche, Dostoevsky." With the exception of the allusion above and note 25 for Wednesday, I have not made use of my students' work in the writing of this book. Needless to say, however, while my classroom goals were altogether different, my encounters with my Villanova students greatly broadened my understanding of the terrain chronicled and analyzed in this book—and for that I thank them. For power-conscious critiques of anthropology, see James Clifford and George E. Marcus (eds.), *Writing Culture* (University of California Press, 2010), and Johannes Fabian, *Time and the Other: How Anthropology Makes Its Object* (Columbia University Press, 2002). For an affirmative defense of ethnography, see Michel-Rolph Truillot's "Anthropology and the Savage Slot" in Richard G. Fox (ed.), *Recapturing Anthropology: Working in the Present* (SAR Press, 1991).

54. Having survived the raid, the music program was done in by its success when, in 2002, for the pilot episode of the reality TV program *Music Behind Bars*, VH1 featured a Graterford heavy metal act, Dark Mischief. One of the band members had been convicted of murdering two teenage girls, however, and the airing of the show provoked outrage—outrage that began with the mother of one of the victims and soon made its way to the *O'Reilly Factor*. In the wake of the resulting public relations disaster, the music program was defunded.

55. Martin Scorsese (dir.), *Goodfellas* (1990).

56. *Holy Name Society v. Horn*, Civil Action No. 97–804 (E.D. Pa. 2001), trial record.

57. Williams Brothers, "I'm Just a Nobody" (Blackberry Records, 2005).

58. Sid Roth, *The Last Lap* (MV Press, 2001).

FRIDAY

1. Noble Drew Ali, *The Holy Koran of the Moorish Science Temple of America*, 12:8–10. Also known as the *Circle Seven Koran* for its cover graphic, it may be found online at http://www.hermetic.com/bey/7koran.html.

2. See Albert Raboteau, *Slave Religion: The "Invisible Institution" in the Antebellum South* (Oxford University Press, 1980), pp. 3–92, and Michael Gomez, *Exchanging Our Country Marks: The Transformation of African Identities in the Colonial and Antebellum South* (North Carolina University Press, 1998). For a documentary history, see Allan D. Austin, *African Muslims in Antebellum America: A Sourcebook* (Garland Publishing, 1984).

3. On the Moorish Science Temple, see Gomez, *Exchanging our Country Marks*, pp. 203–205; Richard Brent Turner, *Islam in the African-American Experience* (Indiana University Press, 1997), pp. 71–108; Robert Dannin, *Black Pilgrimage to Islam* (Oxford University Press, 2002), pp. 15–34; Edward E. Curtis IV, *Islam in Black America* (SUNY Press, 2002), pp. 45–62; and Susan Nance, "Mystery of the Moorish Science Temple: Southern Blacks and American Alternative Spirituality in 1920s Chicago," *Religion and American Culture* 12, No. 2 (Summer 2002), pp. 123–66. On mind-cure, see Charles S. Braden, *Spirits in Rebellion: The Rise and Development of New Thought* (Southern Methodist University Press, 1963). On black nationalism, see William L. Van Deburg (ed.), *Modern Black Nationalism: From Marcus Garvey to Louis Farrakhan* (New York University Press, 1996).

4. See Herbert Berg, "Mythmaking in the African American Muslim Context: The Moorish Science Temple, the Nation of Islam, and the American Society of Muslims," *Journal of the American Academy of Religion*, Vol. 73, No. 3 (September 2005), pp. 685–703.

5. See, for example, Linda Walbridge, *Without Forgetting the Imam: Lebanese Shi'ism in an American Community* (Wayne State University Press, 1997), pp. 16–47.

6. For a cultural history, see John Higham, *Strangers in the Land: Patterns of American Nativism, 1860–1925* (Rutgers University Press, 1988). For a critical assessment, see Ian Haney López, *White by Law* (New York University Press, 2006).

7. For speculation on Fard's identity and disappearance, see Richard Brent Turner, *Islam in the African American Experience* (Indiana University Press, 1997), pp. 147–73, and Michael A. Gomez, *Black Crescent* (Cambridge University Press, 2005), pp. 276–92.

8. Arthur Huff Fauset, *Black Gods of the Metropolis* (University of Pennsylvania Press, 1970), pp. 41–51 especially. On the Great Migration, see Isabel Wilkerson, *The Warmth of Other Suns* (Random House, 2010). On religion in particular, see Milton C. Sernett, *Bound for the Promised Land* (Duke University Press, 1997).

9. *Holy Koran* 25:1–5.

10. For a critique of tolerance, see Benjamin L. Berger, "The Cultural Limits of Legal Tolerance, " in Courtney Bender and Pamela E. Klassen (eds.), *After Pluralism* (Columbia University Press, 2010), pp. 98–123; and Slavoj Žižek, "Tolerance as an Ideological Category," *Critical Inquiry* 34 (2008), pp. 660–82.

11. See Søren Kierkegaard (Thomas C. Oden, ed.), *The Humor of Kierkegaard: An Anthology* (Princeton University Press, 2004); Pete A. Gunter, "Nietzschean Laughter," *The Sewanee Review*, Vol. 76, No. 3 (Summer 1968); and Simon Critchley, *Very Little . . . Almost Nothing* (Routledge, 2004).

12. Run-DMC, "Hollis Crew" (1984).

13. To place Islam at Graterford in international perspective, see James A. Beckford, Daniele Joly, and Farhad Khosrokhavar, *Muslims in Prison: Challenge and Change in Britain and France* (Palgrave Macmillan, 2006).

14. Qur'an 6:38. The Salafi favor the *Noble Quran*, edited and translated by Saleem Al Hilaali and Muhsin Khan, http://www.dar-us-salam.com/TheNobleQuran/index.html. Followers of Warith Deen have long used the *Holy Qur'an* translated by Abdullah Yusuf Ali, http://wikilivres.info/wiki/The_Holy_Qur%27an.

15. As a partial explanation of this gap, Qasim invoked the principle of *al-darrur*, pursuant to which that which is proscribed becomes permissible when circumstances make abstention impossible.

16. Saleh as-Saleh, *The Three Letters* (Daar al-Bukhar, 1995).
17. The injunction that a Muslim must reconcile with another Muslim within three days comes from a hadith that appears in both Ṣaḥīḥ al-Bukhārī and Sahih Muslim, which for Sunni Muslims are the two most authenticated hadith collections.
18. On the problem of authority in African-American Islam, see Sherman Jackson, *Islam and the Blackamerican* (Oxford University Press).
19. On the "path of the middle way" (*wasatiyya*) see Brigitte Maréchal, *The Muslim Brothers in Europe: Roots and Discourse* (Brill, 2008), pp. 5, 148; and Muhammad bin Salih Al-Uthaimeen's commentary on Ibn Taymiyyah, *Aqeedatul-Wasitiyyah* (Dar-us-Salam, 2009).
20. On the concept of the *mujaddid* for the Ahmadiyya, see Turner, *Islam in the African-American Experience*, pp. 112–13; for Wallace Muhammad's appropriation see Curtis, *Islam in Black America*, p. 116. For a primary source, see *Bilalian News*, February 15, 1980, p. 17.
21. Warith Deen Muhammad died in 2008. For his obituary, see "W. Deen Mohammed, 74, Top U.S. Imam, Dies," *New York Times*, September 9, 2008. On the "Old Guard" Sunnis' mistrust of Warith Deen Muhammad, see Jackson, *Islam and the Blackamerican* pp. 67–70.
22. Karl specifically referred to the Collective Purchasing Conference (CPC), a Muslim American Society economic initiative.
23. Mamduh, who is politically a leftist, is a reader of Z *Magazine* and a listener to *Democracy Now!*
24. On the transformation of the former Nation of Islam under the leadership of Warith Deen Muhammad, see Clifton E. Marsh, *From Black Muslims to Muslims* (Scarecrow Press, 1984), pp. 89–124, and Matthias Gardell, *In the Name of Elijah Muhammad* (Duke University Press, 1996), pp. 99–118.
25. *U.S. v. Seeger*, 380 U.S. 163 (1965).
26. Paul Tillich, *Systematic Theology*, Vol. I (University of Chicago Press, 1973), p. 13.
27. Malcolm X employed the rhetoric of "by any means necessary" not infrequently. See Malcolm X, *By Any Means Necessary: Malcolm X Speeches & Writings* (Pathfinder Press, 1992).
28. The American public's readiness to cast Muslim prisoners as would-be terrorists is, to a significant degree, I would contend, an expression of this collective bad faith. Consider the case of alleged would-be "dirty bomber" José Padilla. Padilla, a Puerto Rican convert to Islam, it was widely reported, converted to Islam while in prison. In a 2002 op-ed in the *Wall Street Journal*, evangelical prison ministry giant Charles Colson pointed to Padilla to note how "Islam, certainly the radical variety, feeds on resentment and anger all too prevalent in our prisons" and "is raising a class of angry, dangerous men with anti-American, Islamist sympathies." It was Padilla's doubly demonized status as a "jailhouse Muslim"—i.e., both gangster and terrorist—that made him a perfect trial balloon for indefinite extraconstitutional detention of American citizens. After five years in solitude in a South Carolina brig, Padilla was convicted—in a trial that made no mention of "dirty bombs"—of providing material aid to terrorists. By this time, those who cared to could have known that José Padilla had never been in prison, only in a Florida jail, during which time, according to the *New York Times*, he'd read the Bible voraciously. Since the War on Terror began, every couple of years has offered up another jailhouse Muslim terrorist scare, and we may be sure that the next time a handful of

intemperate, feckless, and, in all likelihood, mentally ill cons or ex-cons flatter themselves with delusions of destruction, the demagogues of screen and state will sound the requisite alarms. For examples, Google the phrases "2005 Los Angeles Bomb Plot," "Liberty City Seven," and "2009 Bronx Terrorism Plot." For Colson's op-ed, see Charles Colson, "Evangelizing for Evil in Our Prisons," *Wall Street Journal*, June 24, 2002. On Padilla's personal history, see "Terror Suspect's Path From Streets to Brig," *New York Times*, April 25, 2004. For a recent survey, see SpearIt, "Facts and Fiction About Islam in Prison: Assessing Prisoner Radicalization in Post-9/11 America," Institute for Social Policy and Understanding (December 2012). On bad faith, see Jean-Paul Sartre, *Being and Nothingness* (Washington Square Press, 1992), pp. 86–116, and Slavoj Žižek, "What Rumsfeld Doesn't Know That He Knows about Abu Ghraib," *In These Times* (May 21, 2004).

29. This hadith appears in the collections of Tirmidhi and ibn Majah.
30. On the prison telephone industry, see Steven L. Jackson, "Ex-Communication: Competition and Collusion in the U.S. Prison Telephone Industry," *Critical Studies in Media Communication*, Vol. 22, Issue 4 (2005), and John E. Dannenber, "Nationwide PLN Survey Examines Prison Phone Contracts, Kickbacks," *Prison Legal News*, Vol. 22, No. 4 (April 2011).
31. Qur'an 4:86.
32. Qur'an 3:134.
33. See Alfred Guillaume, *The Life of Muhammad: A Translation of Isḥāq's Sīrat rasūl Allāh* (Oxford University Press, 1967).
34. Werner Herzog (dir.), *Grizzly Man* (2005).
35. Isaiah Berlin, *The Hedgehog and the Fox: An Essay on Tolstoy's View of History* (New American Library, 1986). On the trope of the "Magical Negro" see Krin Gabbard, *Black Magic: White Hollywood and African American Culture* (Rutgers University Press, 2004).
36. This was the Imam's off-the-cuff translation. Similar language may be found in Book 88 of Ṣaḥīḥ al-Bukhārī, which contains hadith about the end times.
37. These verses, too, were the Imam's translations out of Arabic. While the latter seems to reference Qur'an 12:87, I remain uncertain as to the source of the former.
38. Donald Clemmer, *The Prison Community* (Holt, Rinehart, Winston, 1940), and Gresham M. Sykes, *The Society of Captives* (Princeton University Press, 1958). For subsequent touchstones of the genre, see John Irwin, *The Felon* (University of California Press, 1970), and James B. Jacobs, *Statesville* (University of Chicago Press, 1977).
39. See Bas van Fraassen, *The Empirical Stance* (Yale University Press, 2004), pp. 31–63.
40. Tzvetan Todorov, *Facing the Extreme: Moral Life in the Concentration Camps* (Macmillan, 1997).
41. See Pierre Bourdieu, *The Logic of Practice*, pp. 52–97; Jennifer A. Herdt, *Putting On Virtue: The Legacy of Splendid Vices* (University of Chicago Press, 2012), pp. 23–44; and Saba Mahmood, *The Politics of Piety: The Islamic Revival and the Feminist Subject* (Princeton University Press, 2005), pp. 1–39.
42. Jeffrey Stout, *Democracy and Tradition* (Princeton University Press, 2004), p. 176.
43. Among innumerable other examples, see Edward W. Blyden, *Christianity, Islam, and the Negro Race* (W. B. Whittingham & Co, 1887), pp. 1–29.
44. Tomoko Masuzawa, *The Invention of World Religions* (University of Chicago Press, 2005).

45. See Paul Ricoeur, *Freud and Philosophy* (Yale University Press, 1977), pp. 20–36.
46. Mircea Eliade, *The Sacred and the Profane* (Harcourt Brace Jovanovich, 1987), pp. 162–215. For a broad critique, see Russell R. McCutcheon, *Manufacturing Religion: The Discourse on Sui Generis Religion and the Politics of Nostalgia* (Oxford University Press, 1997).
47. Also known as phylacteries, teffilin are black leather boxes containing scribed passages from Exodus and Deuteronomy traditionally worn by Orthodox Jewish men on their forehead and weak arm for non-holiday morning prayers.
48. See William James, "The Will to Believe," in his *Essays in Pragmatism* (Hafner Press, 1948), pp. 88–109.
49. For inspiration, see Annie Dillard, *A Pilgrim at Tinker Creek* (Harper Perennial Modern Classics, 2007); Friedrich Nietzsche, "On Truth and Lies in a Nonmoral Sense" (1873), in Keith Ansell Pearson and Duncan Large (eds.), *The Nietzsche Reader* (Blackwell, 2000), pp. 114–23; and Walter Benjamin, "One-Way Street," in Walter Benjamin (Marcus Bullock and Michael W. Jennings, eds.), *Walter Benjamin: Selected Writings, Volume 1: 1913–1926* (Harvard University Press, 1996), pp. 444–88.
50. Babylonian Talmud, tractate Shabbat, folio 31a.

SATURDAY
1. The domain of these world-making activities in the ongoing present is what I have been calling "practice." See Pierre Bourdieu, *The Logic of Practice* (Stanford University Press). On ritual practices in particular, see Catherine Bell, *Ritual Theory, Ritual Practice* (Oxford University Press, 1992).
2. For an attempt at reconstructing the origins of religion, see Robert N. Bellah, *Religion in Human Evolution: From the Paleolithic to the Axial Age* (Belknap Press of Harvard University Press, 2011). For a critique of the drive toward origins, see Tomoko Masuzawa, *In Search of Dreamtime: The Quest for the Origin of Religion* (University of Chicago Press, 1993).
3. Wilfred Cantwell Smith, *The Meaning and End of Religion* (First Fortress, 1991), pp. 1–79; Jonathan Z. Smith, "Religion, Religions, Religious," in Mark C. Taylor (ed.), *Critical Terms for the Study of Religion* (University of Chicago Press, 1988), pp. 269–84; and Leora Batnitzky, *How Judaism Became a Religion* (Princeton University Press, 2011).
4. The reformists called themselves the Philadelphia Society for Alleviating the Miseries of Public Prisons. In 1886, a century after its founding, the organization changed its name to the Pennsylvania Prison Society. See Benjamin Rush, "An Inquiry into the Effects of Public Punishments upon Criminals and upon Society," in *Essays: Literary, Moral and Philosophical* (Thomas and William Bradford, 1806), pp. 136–63. On the history of the Pennsylvania Prison Society, see Norman Johnston, Kenneth Finkel, and Jeffery A. Cohen, *Eastern State Penitentiary: Crucible of Good Intentions* (Philadelphia Museum of Art, 1994), and "Pennsylvania Prison Society" (Pennsylvania Historical Society, Collection 1946, 2006). On the age's reformist milieu more broadly, see Robert Abzug, *Cosmos Crumbling: American Reform and the Religious Imagination* (Oxford University Press, 1994), pp. 11–29.
5. On the emergence and evolution of the penitentiary, see Orlando Faulkland Lewis, *The Development of American Prisons and Prison Customs, 1776–1845*

(Prison Association of New York, 1922), and David Rothman, *The Discovery of the Asylum: Social Order and Disorder in the New Republic* (Walter de Gruyter, 1977). On the limits of religious reform, see Jennifer Graber, *The Furnace of Affliction: Prisons and Religion in Antebellum America* (University of North Carolina Press, 2011), and Andrew Skotnicki, *Religion and the Development of the American Penal System* (University Press of America, 2000). For thinking about the place of the penitentiary in American culture, see Anne-Marie Cusac, *Cruel and Unusual: The Culture of Punishment in America* (Yale University Press, 2009), and Caleb Smith, *The Prison and the American Imagination* (Yale University Press, 2009).

6. Jeremy Bentham, *The Panopticon Writings* (Verso, 1995), pp. 29–95. On incarceration and liberalism, see Thomas L. Dumm, *Democracy and Punishment* (University of Wisconsin Press, 1987); David Garland, *Punishment and Modern Society* (University of Chicago Press, 1990); and Bernard Harcourt, *The Illusion of Free Markets: Punishment and the Myth of Native Order* (Harvard University Press, 2011).

7. Michel Foucault, *Discipline and Punish* (Vintage, 1995), pp. 195–230 especially.

8. In his essay "Philadelphia, and Its Solitary Prison," Charles Dickens observed: "My firm conviction is that, independent of the mental anguish it occasions—an anguish so acute and so tremendous, that all imagination of it must fall far short of the reality—it wears the mind into a morbid state, which renders it unfit for the rough contact and busy action of the world. It is my fixed opinion that those who have undergone this punishment, MUST pass into society again morally unhealthy and diseased. . . . What monstrous phantoms, bred of despondency and doubt, and born and reared in solitude, have stalked upon the earth, making creation ugly, and darkening the face of Heaven!" Dickens, *American Notes for General Circulation*, Volume I (Chapman and Hall, 1842), p. 262. For other contemporaneous critiques, see Dorothea Dix, *Remarks on Prison and Prison Discipline in the United States* (Joseph Kite & Co., 1845), and Enoch Wines and Theodore Dwight, *Report on the Prisons and Reformatories of the United States and Canada* (Scholarly Publishing Office, University of Michigan Library, 2005). For a more bullish assessment, see Gustave de Beaumont and Alexis de Tocqueville, *On the Penitentiary System in the United States and Its Application in France* (Southern Illinois University Press, 1964).

9. See Jennifer Graber, *The Furnace of Affliction* (University of North Carolina Press, 2011), pp. 157–78, and John Lardes Modern, "Ghosts of Sing Sing, or the Metaphysics of Secularism," *Journal of the American Academy of Religion* Vol. 75, Issue 3 (2007), pp. 615–50.

10. Rebecca M. McLennan, *The Crisis of Imprisonment* (Cambridge University Press, 2008); Douglas Blackmon, *Slavery by Another Name* (Anchor Books, 2008); Marie Gottschalk, *The Prison and the Gallows* (University of Pennsylvania Press, 2006). On turn-of-the-century criminology, see Nicole Hahn Rafter, *Creating Born Criminals* (University of Illinois Press, 1997). On the slipperiness of rationales for punishment, see Friedrich Nietzsche, *The Genealogy of Morals and Ecce Homo* (Vintage, 1989), pp. 57–98.

11. See "The Punishing Decade: Prison and Jail Estimates at the Millennium," *Justice Policy Institute* (May 2000); "Correctional Population in the United States, 2010" (Bureau of Justice Statistics, December 2011), http://bjs.ojp.usdoj.gov/content/pub/pdf/cpus10.pdf. Over the last two decades, as the number of Americans in prison and jail has doubled, rates of violent crime have actually dropped. See Franklin E. Zimring, *The Great American Crime Decline* (Oxford University Press, 2007), and Alfred Blumstein and Joel Wallman (eds.), *The Crime Drop in*

America (Cambridge University Press, 2006). For policy prescriptions, see Mark A. R. Kleiman, *When Brute Force Fails: How to Have Less Crime and Less Punishment* (Princeton University Press, 2009). For critical reappraisals see Heather Ann Thompson, "Why Mass Incarceration Matters: Rethinking Crisis, Decline and Transformations in Postwar American History," *Journal of American History* (December 2010), and Christopher Glazek, "Raise the Crime Rate," *n+1* (January 2012). Toward an abolitionist program, see Angela Y. Davis, *Are Prisons Obsolete?* (Seven Stories Press, 2003). To get involved nationally, go to http://criticalresistance.org/, and, in Pennsylvania specifically, http://decarceratepa.info/.

12. History told with an eye trained on the power-steeped processes through which the contingent elements of our social world have obtained their sheen of necessity, inevitability, and immutability is genealogy. See Michel Foucault, "Nietzsche, Genealogy, History," in D. F. Bouchard (ed.), *Michel Foucault: Language, Counter-Memory, Practice: Selected Essays and Interviews* (Cornell University Press), pp. 139–64.

13. William James, *The Varieties of Religious Experience* (Modern Library, 1999), p. 36.

14. On the ways that religious practices enable assurance, suffering, antipathy, and order, see, in turn, Peter Berger, *The Sacred Canopy: Elements of a Sociological Theory of Religion* (Anchor Books, 1990); Clifford Geertz, *The Interpretation of Cultures* (Basic Books, 1977), pp. 3–43; Nietzsche, *On the Genealogy of Morals*; Mircea Eliade, *The Sacred and the Profane: The Nature of Religion* (Harcourt Brace Jovanovich, 1987).

15. Matthew 21:42–46.

16. Deuteronomy 18:15.

17. 1 Peter 5:6–14.

18. Leon Uris, *Exodus* (1958) is a novel about the founding of the State of Israel.

19. Ludwig Feuerbach, *The Essence of Christianity* (Prometheus Press, 1989); Karl Marx, "Theses on Feuerbach," in Jo Elster (ed.), *Karl Marx: A Reader* (Cambridge University Press, 1986), pp. 20–23; online at http://www.marxists.org/archive/marx/works/1845/theses/theses.htm.

20. While the generative character of ideology is already evident in Marx's "Theses on Feuerbach," for a programmatic account of the role of ideas, religious and otherwise, in shaping social relations, see Louis Althusser, "Ideology and Ideological State Apparatuses" in *Lenin and Philosophy, and Other Essays* (New Left Books, 1972). Toward a materialist study of religion, see Manuel A. Vasquez, *More Than Belief: A Materialist Theory of Religion* (Oxford University Press, 2010).

21. If as a concept the poor man is the child of Karl Marx, the nomenclature is owed to Jacques Rancière, who observed the awkward place allotted the poor man as the paradigmatic *object* of philosophical inquiry. See Jacques Rancière, *The Philosopher and His Poor* (Duke University Press, 2004).

22. Contra the "poor woman" impulse, see R. Marie Griffith, *God's Daughters* (University of California Press, 2000), and Saba Mahmood, *The Politics of Piety* (Princeton University Press, 2005).

23. It is surely a tribute to the Nation of Islam that a man like Charles would associatively couple religion and slavery. See Elijah Muhammad, *Message to the Blackman in America* (Secretarius Memps, 1973). To complicate this picture, see Eugene D. Genovese, *Roll, Jordan, Roll: The World the Slaves Made* (Vintage, 1976), pp. 159–284; Albert Raboteau, *Slave Religion: The "Invisible Institution" in the Antebellum South* (Oxford University Press, 1980); and Curtis J. Evans, *The Burden of Black Religion* (Oxford University Press, 2008), pp. 17–64.

24. This scapegoating function is a dominant feature of the new atheist bestsellers. See, for example, Christopher Hitchens, *God Is Not Great: How Religion Poisons Everything* (Twelve Books, 2007).
25. Listen to Laura Bush's radio address of November 17, 2001, http://www.presidency.ucsb.edu/ws/index.php?pid=24992#axzz1nxwfqpq3. And see Lila Abu-Lughod, "Do Muslim Women Really Need Saving? Anthropological Reflections on Cultural Relativism and Its Others," *American Anthropologist* 104:3, pp. 783–90 (2002).
26. On freedom, see Isaiah Berlin (Henry Hardy, ed.), *Liberty: Incorporating Four Essays on Liberty* (Oxford University Press, 2002), pp. 166–217. On the inextricability of freedom and movement, see Hagar Kotef, *Movement and the Ordering of Freedom: A History of a Political Problem* (Duke University Press, forthcoming). For building an affirmative case for the possibility of achieving freedom in prison, see Boethius, *The Consolation of Philosophy* (Penguin Books, 1999), pp. 116–38; Svetlana Boym, *Another Freedom: The Alternative History of an Idea* (University of Chicago Press, 2010), most especially Boym's discussion of Dostoyevsky's "freer freedom," pp. 108–14; and Jenny Phillips (dir.), *The Dhamma Brothers* (2007).
27. On the prophetic, see Cornel West, *Prophesy Deliverance!* (Westminster John Knox Press, 2002), especially pp. 95–130.
28. John Boorman (dir.), *Deliverance* (1972).
29. Donald Clemmer, *The Prison Community* (Holt, Rinehart, Winston, 1940), p. 236.
30. Rudolph Otto, *Idea of the Holy* (Oxford University Press, 1958), pp. 5–30.
31. See Carrie A. Rentschler, *Second Wounds: Victims' Rights and the Media in the U.S.* (Duke University Press, 2011); and Marie Gottschalk, *The Prison and the Gallows* (Cambridge University Press, 2006), pp. 77–114.
32. On the Truth and Reconciliation Commission, see Desmond Tutu, *No Future Without Forgiveness* (Image Publishing, 2000).
33. Peter Hoffman [pseudonym], "A Path of Penance: A Reflection upon Living St. Francis' Exhortation to Penance" (2005) (unpublished).
34. On restorative justice, see Howard Zehr, *The Little Book of Restorative Justice* (Good Books, 2002), and Barb Toews and Howard Zehr (eds.), *Critical Issues in Restorative Justice* (Criminal Justice Press, 2004). For a critique, see Gregory Shank and Paul Takagi, "Critique of Restorative Justice," *Social Science* Vol. 31, Issue 3 (2004), pp. 147–63.
35. Ephesians 4:22–24.
36. Romans 12:17.
37. Romans 12:21.
38. For Peter's sources see James Meyer, OFM, *The Words of St. Francis* (Franciscan Herald Press, 1982), and Jeffrey Keefe, *Francis of Assisi: Life and Brief Devotions* (Pauline Books, 1993).
39. Romans 12:2.
40. See Genesis 3:19; and Voltaire, *Candide: Or Optimism* (Penguin, 2005), p. 144. For further Christian critique of American criminal justice, see James Samuel Logan, *Good Punishment: Moral Practice and U.S. Imprisonment* (W. B. Eerdmans, 2008) and Mark Lewis Taylor, *The Executed God: The Way of the Cross in Lockdown America* (Fortress Press, 2001).
41. On Inside-Out, see Kerry Dunn, *Re-forming the Social: Neoliberal Voluntarism in the Warehouse Prison* (Ph.D. dissertation, University of Pennsylvania Press, 2009).

42. On the movement from resignation to action, see Søren Kierkegaard, *Fear and Trembling* (Penguin Classics, 1986).

43. To date, no such bill has gotten any traction. For a recent historical reflection and call for reform from a legislative principal, see Senator Stewart Greenleaf: "Prison Reform in the Pennsylvania Legislature," 160 U. PA. L. REV. PENNUMBRA 179 (2011), http://www.pennumbra.com/essays/12-2011/Greenleaf.pdf.

44. Orlando Faulkland Lewis, *The Development of American Prisons and Prison Customs* (Prison Association of New York, 1922), p. 218. On solitary confinement as torture, see Atul Gawande, "Hellhole," *The New Yorker* (March 30, 2009); Matt Stroud, "Why Are Prisoners Committing Suicide in Pennsylvania?" *The Nation* (May 7, 2012); and Shane Baver, "Solitary in Iran Nearly Broke Me. Then I Went Inside America's Prisons," *Mother Jones*, Nov/Dec 2012.

45. The Church's problem did not go away. In March 2011, the Philadelphia Archdiocese placed twenty-one priests on administrative leave for alleged sexual abuse. In June 2012, in a first-of-its-kind ruling nationwide, Monsignor William Lynn was convicted in a Philadelphia County courtroom of endangerment for reassigning priests accused of molesting children. Lynn was sentenced to three to six years in prison.

46. On Mumia, see Mumia Abu-Jamal, *Death Blossoms: Reflections from a Prisoner of Conscience* (Plough Publishing, 1997) and *Live from Death Row* (Harper Perennial, 1996). In 2011, Mumia was removed from Pennsylvania's death row and resentenced to life. Divergent attitudes toward Mumia remain a litmus test of Philadelphia's racial divide. For two recent films that dramatize this fault line, see Tigre Hill (dir.), *The Barrel of a Gun* (2010), and Kouross Esmaeli (dir.), *Justice on Trial: The Case of Mumia Abu-Jamal* (2010).

47. On the roots of crime see Robert J. Sampson and John H. Laub, *Crime in the Making: Pathways and Turning Points through Life* (Harvard University Press, 1995).

48. The simple dualism of innocence and guilt in which the condition of one or the other is thought to be a simple matter of fact obscures the many movements between crime and punishment. Consider, for example, the case of Ephraim of EFM who is serving life for homicide. According to Ephraim's own documentation, prosecutors charged five men with the crime. Ephraim, who was present at the scene, and knew the perpetrators but claims to have had no direct involvement with the crime, was offered a plea deal that would have gotten him out of prison in five years. Largely out of a sense of loyalty to his codefendants, Ephraim refused. The rest of the men took deals and testified against Ephraim. Of the five men originally charged with the crime, Ephraim is the only one still in prison. For critiques of the preoccupation with innocence at the expense of attention to fairness, see Stephen B. Bright, "Is Fairness Irrelevant?: The Evisceration of Federal Habeas Corpus Review and Limits on the Ability of State Courts to Protect Fundamental Rights," 54 *Washington and Lee Law Review* 1 (1997), http://scholarlycommons.law.wlu.edu/wlulr/vol54/iss1/2; and Carol S. Steiker and Jordan M. Steiker, "The Seduction of Innocence: The Attraction and Limitations of the Focus on Innocence in Capital Punishment Law and Advocacy," *Journal of Criminal Law and Criminology*, Vol. 95, No. 2 (Winter 2005), pp. 587–624.

49. For an international perspective on the ascendancy of LWOP sentencing in the United States, see Catherine Appleton and Bent Grover, "The Pros and Cons of Life Without Parole," *British Journal of Criminology* 47 (2007), pp. 597–615.

50. Bennett Miller (dir.), *Capote* (2005).

51. On apocalypticism and millennialism in contemporary American culture, see Kathleen Stewart and Susan Harding, "Bad Endings: American Apocalypsis," *Annual Review of Anthropology* 28 (1999), pp. 285–310. To better understand his own views on such matters, Al lent me his copy of J. Dwight Pentecost, *Things to Come: A Study in Biblical Eschatology* (Academie Books, 1958).
52. On Reginald McFadden, see "Accused Serial Killer And 92 Days of Freedom," *New York Times*, April 4, 1995. On Mudman Simon's history of violence, see "1975 Report: 'Mudman' Is Dangerous," *Philadelphia Inquirer*, May 11, 1995. In 1999, Mudman Simon was beaten to death in New Jersey State Prison.
53. Thomas C. Reeves, *America's Bishop: The Life and Times of Fulton J. Sheen* (Encounter Books, 2001).
54. As Father Gorski explained over dinner, there are three levels of Franciscan brothers: the first level is the cloistered monks; the second level is those who have taken vows of chastity but who work out in the community; the third level is the secular order.
55. On "the event" as an animating concern for ethics, see Alain Badiou, *Ethics* (2000), pp. 40–44 and 67–77. On spiritual exercises, see Pierre Hadot, *Philosophy as a Way of Life* (Wiley-Blackwell, 1995). On spiritual practice and compulsive repetition, see Sigmund Freud, "Obsessive Actions and Religious Practices," in Peter Gay (ed.), *The Freud Reader*, pp. 429–35.

SUNDAY
1. In a still more pointed response to my theses, one Villanova student—himself decidedly not a frequenter of the chapel—employed Nietzsche and Dostoyevsky to assess the chapel's "palliative effect." As R. R. wrote: "A tangential comparison may be made between those seeking solace in the chapel and those who avoid it. I'm thinking specifically of Nietzsche's void—*those who throw themselves into it and perish; those who threw themselves into and return the stronger; or those who see the void, turn, and ignore its presence.* This obviously is redolent of Dostoevsky's Ivan and the three types of men: *fierce and rebellious, rebellious and weak, weak and unhappy.*" R. R. concluded: "You only meet the third type of lifer in the chapel. The second type of lifer you never get to meet as they are all housed—indefinitely—on J or L blocks, while the first type only enter the chapel—in spirit—during their memorial service. The way I see it most are the third type—prayerful and hopeful for the first seven to ten years (the period of time it takes for one's appeals to get shot down). From there many move to the second type. They then age (or tire) and return back to category three, unless they have the strength to step into the void and become the first type" (R. R. Craig, personal correspondence).
2. Isaiah 55:1–5 and 53:1–6.
3. On transsexuality in prisons, see Eric A. Stanley and Nat Smith (eds.), *Captive Genders* (AK Press, 2011).
4. This morning's Sunday Service song list includes, in order: "Thank You, Lord, for Saving Me," "Because of Who You Are," "You Will Surely Drift Away," "He Is Good," "In the Sanctuary," "Ninety Nine and a Half (Won't Do)," "Take It to Jesus," "Think About His Love," "You Ought to Run and Tell That," "God Will Make a Way," and "Happy Birthday."
5. John 3:3.

ACKNOWLEDGMENTS

From first to last, my abiding gratitude to the men and women of Graterford's chapel—chapel workers; chaplains; chapel regulars; correctional officers; and volunteers, from whom I learned so much, and without whose candor and care this book would be nothing. It is impossible to mention you all by name. To the chapel workers especially, please know: I did not take your engagement for granted then, and I do not carry my consequent responsibility lightly now.

Nor would this project have been possible without the trust of the Pennsylvania Department of Corrections' Office of Planning, Research, and Statistics, Graterford's administration, and Princeton University's Institutional Review Board for Human Subjects. Thanks to Todd Clear, Nancy Dubler, Robert Gangi, and Martin Horn for helping me navigate these gatekeepers.

For their support intellectually no less than financially, I'd like to thank Princeton's Department of Religion, the Center for the Study of Religion (CSR), the Whiting Foundation, Columbia's Society of Fellows in the Humanities, and Columbia's University Seminar on Religion in America.

At the dissertation stage, I received extraordinary guidance from my advisors, Marie Griffith, Leigh Schmidt, and Jeffrey Stout. Essential feedback was also provided by Eddie Glaude, Hendrik Hartog, Andrea Jones, and Al Raboteau; the members of CSR's 2005–2006 Religion and Public Life workshop, most notably Heather White and Martin Kavka; the 2007–2008 participants in both the Princeton American Studies workshop, in particular Paul Rauschenbush, and the Princeton Religion Department's American Religions workshop, Anthony Petro and Laura Bennett most especially; and by my Haverford students in 2008's "Religion and Incarceration in the United States," Abby Kromholz especially. Beau Bellenfant assisted with transcription.

In the years since, the book—in part or in sum—has profited from critical readings offered by Jennifer Banks, Courtney Bender, Tina Bennett, Jeremy Brecher, Lisa Cerami, Jill Cutler, Ariela Dubler, Benjamin Fong, Bettina Funcke, Kathleen Holscher, Alonso Indacochea, Erica Levin, Vincent Lloyd, Kathryn Lofton, Greg Lyss, Emily Cone-Miller, Amira Mittermaier, Rachel Price, Cara Rock-Singer, Mark Rosenberg, Mark Rowe, Dan Sofaer, Thomas Tweed, and Matt Weiland. The Columbia students in Courtney Bender's 2012 Field Methods in Religious Studies class and the Syracuse students in Vincent Lloyd's 2012 Theology and Liberation class also gave helpful feedback.

Special gratitude is due to Charles Coley, Walter Dubler, and Stanley Rosenthal, each of whom waded through the manuscript and provided extensive feedback at critical junctures in both stages of the book's inception.

Thanks is also due to those who read my theses and attended my August 8, 2011, Villanova Alumni Association talk in the chapel. For their written feedback I'd especially like to thank R. R. Craig, Andre Davis, Alonzo Garwood, Commer Glass, Rafael Goodman, Jonathan I. Margoles, Makeen McIntyre, Robert Rigler, James White Eagle Robinson, Felix Rosado, Tom Schilk, Aaron Wheeler, and Charles D. Zehring, Jr.

Later-stage bibliographic guidance was furnished by Dan Berger, Joel Blecher, Yaakov Dweck, Chris Garces, Thomas Gibson, Th. Emil Homerin, Suad Khabeer, Johann Kohler, Mike Meneses, and Alex Zakaras.

Generous counsel and aid were also received from Graham Burnett, Joseph Logan, Joshua Prager, and David Rappaport.

Thanks to my agent, Tina Bennett, and her assistant Svetlana Katz, who found in FSG this book's ideal home. At FSG, thanks go to Paul Elie, who dragged the insights out of me, and to Alex Star, who helped me sculpt them so that others might have access to them, too. My appreciation is also due to Ed Cohen, Chris Richards, Dan Gerstle, and to the others involved in the book's production.

Finally, my thanks go to Lisa Cerami, my partner in so many ways. And on behalf of us both, I need to acknowledge all of our family and friends in New York, Yelping Hill, Princeton, Philly, Rochester, and beyond, who give us so much, and whose love and support help shape an extraordinary world for Zahir and Charlie.

INDEX

ABC Bible Studies, 128–30
Abd-al-Wahhab, Muhammad Ibn, 34,
   153, 332n46
Abdul–Jabbar, Kareem, 161
A Block, 4, 36
Abraham (biblical figure), 276, 291
Abraham, Lynne, 51
Abu Bakr (caliph), 178
Abu-Jamal, Mumia, 294, 355n46
acceptance, see contentment; surrender
accommodations, religious, 24–27, 164,
   196–97, 269–70, 310, 332n37, 346n48;
   for Jews, 29, 196; for Moorish Science
   Temple, 211–12; for Muslims, 70–71,
   124, 149, 152, 159, 163, 164–66,
   196–97, 231; for Native Americans,
   188–89, 193, 196
activism by prisoners, see
   accommodations, religious; prisoners'
   rights movement
Adam (biblical figure), 289
addiction to religion, 107
administrative segregation, see
   "hole, the"
Afghanis, 153
Africa, 21, 71–72, 142–43, 207, 209, 247,
   287; "Keita" on, 40, 60–62, 126, 127,
   142–43
afterlife, 59–60, 64, 162, 169, 282,
   345n25; Christians on, 46, 103, 130;
   Jews on, 217, 299–301; Moorish
   Science Temple members on, 207
Agamben, Giorgio, 65

agnostics, 261–62
Ahmad, Mirza Ghulam, 165
Ahmadi Muslims, 162–63, 165–66, 225,
   343n40, 345n17; see also Masjid
   Sajdah
"Ahmed," 231
AIDS, 39, 143
"Al", xi–xiv, xix; activities of, 27, 37, 64,
   66, 206, 243, 311, 325; background of,
   xiii, 13, 15, 99–100, 106, 134, 136–37,
   200; Baraka and, 17–18, 136–37,
   139–40; music and, 170, 173–76,
   188, 199–202, 283, 297; philosophy
   of, vii, 98–122 passim, 128–30, 173,
   210, 215–17, 314, 328n1, 323–24; on
   Ramirez, 79; on reentry, 52–54;
   relationship with author of, 12,
   100–103, 168, 173–76, 217–18,
   299–302
Albani, Muhammad Nasiruddin al-, 153
Albion, 177
al-Bukhari, 232
al-darrur, 348n15
"Alex," 312
Ali, Noble Drew, 207–214 passim;
   background of, 208
Ali, Shamsud-din, 165, 345n26
Alito, Samuel, 51, 302
al-Muslim, 232
al Qaeda, 223, 230
Americans: character of, 22, 330n25;
   culture of, 216; religious history of,
   22, 34, 43–44, 208, 225–26, 268–69

359

"Amos," 313–319 *passim*
"Analytical Concepts of Lakota Beliefs,"
193–94
"Andy," 292, 294–96
animism, 142
anthropology, of religion, 157–58; *see
also* ethnography
Antiterrorism and Effective Death
Penalty Act (AEDPA, 1996), 337*n*32
Arabian Peninsula, 154–55, 226
Arabic language: banning of, 164; study
of, 4, 52, 66, 146–47, 149, 153–55
Arawak Indians, 193
Arendt, Hannah, 40
Aristotle, 132
art, 20–21, 91, 164
atheism, 279, 354*n*24; author and, xiv,
94, 261–262, 264; chapel workers and,
xix, 13; *see also* "Vic"
Aurelius, Marcus, 328*n*8

"bad man of religion," 31–32, 89,
107–108, 191–92, 240, 257, 269,
280, 289
"Ball, Daffy," 93–94, 104; activities of,
104, 315–16, 325; background of, 119,
134; philosophy of, 103–108, 112–18,
122, 280–81
Baptism class, xvii, 39, 249
Baptists, 162
"Baraka," xi–xiv, xix, 8–10, 30, 72,
130–41; activities of, 26, 28–30, 66,
74–75, 170, 172–76, 193, 206, 231, 255,
278, 291, 312; Al and, 17–18, 140,
136–37; background of, xiii, 15, 75–77,
130–31, 134–37, 140, 148, 149–50,
160, 233–34, 295, 296; on death, 58,
59–60, 64; on honor, 36–37, 291;
philosophy of, vii, 8–9, 89, 133–36,
138–41, 210, 229–36, 238–40, 277–78,
289, 310, 328*n*8; on raid, 69, 73, 291;
relationship with author of, 8, 12, 17,
101–102, 136, 139–41, 168, 173–76,
179, 217, 234; on theater, 131–37
"bare life," 340*n*65
"Barkley, Sister," 37, 194
bats, 60–61, 80, 142

Batson v. Kentucky, 338*n*52
Bataille, Georges, 131–32
"Baumgartner, Reverend," xix, 20–21,
119–26, 253; activities of, xvii, 37, 51,
124–25, 131, 188–89, 198, 221–22,
285; on Al, 200; background of, 20,
121–22, 187–88, 301; on blocks, 129;
chaplains and, 61–62, 71, 123–27,
220–21; in DOC hierarchy, 25, 27, 48,
71–72, 125, 188, 221, 294; on
fundamentalism, 112, 120–21,
186–87; hiring by, 11, 13, 123; on
Moorish Science Temple members,
206–207, 211–12, 218–20; on music,
52, 249, 283, 302; on NOI, 167, 168;
on rape, 40–41; on Sayyid, 119,
123–26; at Sunday service, 314,
319–25
Bawa Muhaiyaddeen Fellowship,
343*n*40
B Block, 69, 180, 243, 265, 299
Beard, Jeffrey, 71
beatniks, 162
belief, *see* sincerity
Benedict, Pope, 278
Bentham, Jeremy, 268
"Berkowitz, Lenny," 91, 262, 295;
conversations with, 250–53, 257, 298
Bible: authorship of, xii–xiii, 21, 330*n*24;
and Christian Biblicists, 44, 98–99,
328*n*1; study of, xvi, xvii, 48–50,
103–21, 128–30, 129, 179–87, 207,
243, 246, 248, 299; translations of,
327*n*2
Biblicism 98–99, 328*n*1; *see also* Bible;
Scripture
bikers, 190, 193, 303
"Bilalians," 149
bin Laden, Osama, 223, 230
"Bird, Officer," xix, 37; conversations
with, 65–66, 80–81, 144, 198–99, 202,
285, 295, 297; on Sayyid, 77, 95
"Birdsong, Harry 'Sweets,'" 319
birthdays, 318
bit vs. *bid*, 85
Black Gods of the Metropolis (Fauset),
209
Black Israelites, 60–61, 78–79

Black Judaism, 209
Black Mafia, 76, 160–61, 234
Black Muslims in America (Lincoln),
  168
black nationalism, 9, 26, 61, 78, 161–63,
  226–27, 311, 337n30; vs. Sunni Islam,
  149, 215; see also Moorish Science
  Temple; Nation of Islam
blacks: imprisonment of, xiv, 19, 269,
  282, 327n3, 330n22, 334n5, 339n62;
  incrementalism of, 169; Jews and,
  60–61, 78–79, 86–87, 209, 246–47,
  248, 339n58; popular culture and,
  85–86, 199, 216, 239; religious history
  of, 67–74, 146–53, 158–72, 207–209,
  215, 225–59, 269; skepticism of, 23
Blakey, Art, 162
blocks, 3, 68, 73, 128–30, 224–25, 243,
  248, 338n37; see also cells; specific
  blocks
"blues" (prison grouping), xvi, 5, 48–50,
  95, 129
Board of Pardons, 16, 30, 240, 316–17;
  denials by, 50; see also parole
Bonhoeffer, Dietrich, 187
"Book of Jasher," 21, 330n24
Bourdieu, Pierre, 341n15
BOUT (Brotherhood of United Tribes),
  188–89, 194
boxing, 62
Brady v. Maryland, 75, 249–50
"Brian," xix, 23; activities of, 10, 28–29,
  85–86, 91, 142, 175; on Collins
  ruling, 28–30, 51–52, 249–50;
  philosophy of, 32, 78, 102, 135, 187,
  251–53, 256–64
Brooklyn, 85
Brotherhood Jaycees, 77, 125, 338n54
Brotherhood of United Tribes (BOUT),
  188–89, 194
Brown, Dan, 23, 330n27
"browns" (prison grouping), 4, 11
Buddha, 208
Buddhists, 26, 115, 212, 260, 286
Bureau of Corrections, 152
Bush, George W., 16, 241, 280, 332n39
"busts," 126–27; see also "raid, the";
  "Sayyid"

"Callahan, Mike," xix, 50, 172, 206,
  302–303
Calvinists, 22, 269
Camp Hill, Pennsylvania, 25, 188, 282,
  286
Candide (Voltaire), 185, 289
Candomblé, 207
canonization, xii–xiii, 21–22
"Capote effect," 298
"Carlos," 231
"Carlsby, Gaston," 26–27, 32
Caribbean religions, 207
"Carter, Ruth," 174–75
"Carvel, Reverend," 220, 294
Casey, Bob, 16
Catholics, xii, xvi, xvii, 6, 282–98,
  302–307; becoming Evangelicals, 7;
  beliefs of, 284; Bible translation used
  by, 327n2; black religions and, 207; as
  chapel workers, xi; holidays of, 197;
  Jews and, 91; mass of, xvi, 48,
  302–306; numbers of, 9, 327n3;
  observances of, xvii, 8, 260, 289,
  296–97, 302, 305–306; politics and,
  50–51, 172, 302; in RHU, 291–96;
  sexual abuse and, 293, 355n45
C Block, 5, 47
celibacy, 304–305
cells, 128–30, 137, 178, 242, 257
censorship, 164
ceremonial autonomy, 69, 338n40
certitude, religious, 97–122, 157, 340n1;
  irony vs., 148; pluralism vs., 216; see
  also sincerity
change, 133–36; see also transformation
chapel workers, xix, 5, 11; see also
  specific prisoners
chaplains, xix, 70, 78; on blocks, 128–29;
  conversations among, 60–62, 79–80,
  123–26, 245; role of, xvi–xvii, 61, 69,
  126, 197, 220–21, 231, 293
charity, 197
"Charles," 65, 103, 325–26; activities of,
  108, 110, 193; on Al, 200; philosophy
  of, 104–108, 118–19, 122, 280, 353n23
"Charley," 318
Cherokees, 188, 189, 192
Chicago, 208

Chick, Jack T., 346n34
"Chipmunk," 190, 195, 196
choir, xvi, xvii, 199–200, 248–49, 273
Chomsky, Noam, 329n12, 336n27
Christian Identity movement, 346n31
Christians, 98–122, 242–49, 262, 263,
    272–77, 282–298, 302–307, 311–325;
    bias in favor of, 23–27, 260; certitude
    and, 98–122; conversion of, 26–27;
    freedom and, 22, 330n25;
    fundamentalist, 34, 120–21, 332n45;
    history of American, 22, 34, 330n25;
    Jews and, 79, 95, 202–203, 217–18,
    275–77, 299–301, 323–24; Muslims
    and, xi, 23–24, 79, 84, 149, 162, 163,
    169, 199, 345n25; sects of, 57, 186–87,
    296; self-identification as, xii, 173,
    328n1; see also Bible; Catholics;
    Christian Scientists; Evangelicals;
    Protestants
Christian Scientists, xvii, 7–8, 9, 312
Christmas, 101, 197, 321; gifts for, 47, 77
"Christopher," see "Prophet"
Church of Christ, Scientist, xvii, 7–8, 9,
    312
Church of Latter Day Saints, 330n24
citizenship, 227, 252
"City Slickers principle," 97, 340n1
civil society organizations, 338n54; see
    also specific groups
"Claw," 190, 192–94
clemency hearings, 16
Clemmer, Donald, 254, 285
climate change, 195
Clinton, Bill, 337n32
Clutter murders, 298
CO, see correctional officers
Colbert, Stephen, 340n9
Collective Purchasing Conference
    (CPC), 227, 349n22
Collins ruling, 10, 28–30, 51–52, 249–50
Colson, Charles, 335n12, 349n28
Communion: Catholic, 297, 305–306;
    Episcopal, 47, 54, 98
community, 257; see also neighborhoods;
    specific groups
commutation, 16, 135, 240, 303
concentration camps, 257–58

confession, Catholic, 289, 296–97, 302
confidence, religious, 43–44, 334n
conflict resolution, 225, 235, 349n17
conjugal visits, 88, 245
conscientization, 288–89
conservatism, political, 50–51, 169, 172,
    277–78, 294, 302; theological, 25
conspiracy: charges, 75–76, 113;
    hegemony vs., 89–90, 346n31;
    theories, 71–72, 86, 88, 169
Constitution, U.S. see First Amendment
contentment, 105–106, 262, 281–82, 296
contraband, 71, 123–27, 143, 219–220,
    244, 283; religious objects as, 164, 255
control, methods of, 68, 75, 126–27,
    338n37, 338n49
conversions, 7–8, 26, 100; Jews and,
    78–79, 203, 299–301
convicts, prisoners vs., 309–11
Corbett, Tom, 334n6
Corinthians, 46
Correctional Industries, 11
correctional officers: on blocks, 248;
    boredom of, 28, 73, 95; in chapel, xix,
    24, 117, 252, 304, 307; compensation
    of, 19, 330n21; contraband and, 124;
    effectiveness of, 68, 338n37; humor of,
    4, 198; relationships with prisoners of,
    77, 81, 95, 160, 243, 277, 282, 292;
    during "the raid," 69; see also "Bird,
    Officer"; "Watkins, Officer"
Council of Nicaea, xii
counseling, spiritual: on the blocks,
    128–30; by chaplains, xvii
Craig, R. R., 356n1
"Crews, Chuck," 231
crime: context for, 119, 159, 163, 191,
    213, 269, 295, 349–50n28, 352n11,
    355n48; politicians and, 68–69, 89,
    269, 287–89, 302–303, 332n39,
    337n32, 337n36
"Crocket," see "Sayyid"

"Daffy," see "Ball, Daffy"
Daily News, 16, 51, 70, 283
Dallas (prison), 256
"Damon," 247–49, 313–14

Dark Mischief, 347*n*54
Dar ul-Islam, 342*n*37, 342*n*40
David (biblical figure), 175
"David," xix; activities of, 79, 86, 90–92,
    323; background of, 90, 252, 339*n*63;
    philosophy of, 90–91, 127, 250–52,
    257–64, 277–78
Da Vinci Code, The (Brown), 330*n*27
Day, Dorothy, 89
D Block, 5, 38, 243
deaf people, 285, 304
death, 59–60, 205, 282; in prison,
    127–28, 327*n*4
death penalty: 332*n*39, 337*n*32, 339*n*56
death row, 79, 104, 107, 256, 292–93,
    339*n*56, 356*n*1; transfer from, 104,
    106, 125, 355*n*46
"DeeDee," 318
Department of Corrections (DOC):
    decision-making in, 25, 61; fear of
    Muslims in, 229–30; policy shifts in,
    68–69, 163–64; regulation of religion
    by, *see* accommodations, religious; *see
    also* Bureau of Corrections
Derrida, Jacques, 340*n*12
Descartes, René, 111
Detroit, 208, 209
developmental delays, 199–200, 283,
    297; *see also* "Michael"
Dewey, John, 290
Dickens, Charles, 352*n*8
dinosaurs, 190
disciplinary custody, *see* "hole, the"
discipline, personal, *see* self-mastery
district attorney's office training video,
    338*n*52
"doctrinal dimension," 37–38
Dostoevsky, Fyodor, 53, 347*n*53, 354*n*26,
    356*n*1
"double consciousness," 138
doubt, 112; *see also* sincerity; skepticism
Drew University, 78
Dropsie College, 20, 78, 121–22
drugs, 269; Muslims and, 166, 224;
    post-raid, 73, 338*n*49–50; pre-raid, 68,
    71, 72; street crime and, 20, 89, 91,
    100, 120, 184, 186, 234, 294, 296;
    see also contraband

"dry snitching," 144
dualism, refusal of, 205–206, 210,
    220, 239–40, 249, 253, 279, 289,
    355*n*48
Du Bois, W.E.B., 138, 169
Dungeons and Dragons, 47
Durkheim, Emile, 157

Easter, 197
Eastern State Penitentiary, 268–69,
    292–93, 352*n*8
E Block, 5, 48, 129, 190, 194, 306
ecological devastation, 191, 195–96,
    238
economic empowerment, 227, 349*n*22
ecumenism *see* pluralism
Eddy, Mary Baker, 7
education, in prison, 4–5, 117, 152, 164,
    185, 246, 276, 283, 286; *see also* Bible:
    study of; Education for Ministry;
    Villanova University
Education for Ministry (EFM), xvii, 65,
    100, 103–21, 129–30, 170, 280, 325,
    340*n*6
"Edward," 317
Eid al-Adha, 152, 196–97
Eid ul-Fitr, 152, 177, 196–97
"Eli," 93
Eliade, Mircea, 157, 261
Elijah, 56, 299
Eminem, 290
empiricism, 255
End Violence Program, 49, 335*n*13
Enoch, 299
"Ephraim," 108–110, 355*n*48; activities
    of, 117–18, 314; philosophy of, 116–18,
    121, 122, 129–30
Episcopalians, 9; Bible study of,
    103–121; services of, xvii, 44–47,
    54–55, 98
epoché, 333*n*52
ethics, 239–40, 263, 267, 288, 300;
    groups and, 118, 121, 129–30, 314,
    340*n*12; Jews and, 91, 300;
    revolutionary, 341*n*25
Ethics of War (class), 4–5, 58, 145–46,
    312

ethnography, xiv, 8, 12, 328*n*7; dangers of, 239, 326; debt and, 145, 307–308; design of, 9–10, 78, 253–56, 341*n*19; limits on, 40–41, 83, 168, 173–75, 298–99; methodology of, 93, 128–29, 258, 340*n*67, 341*n*19; perspective and, 175–76, 263, 333*n*52; truth and, 32, 194, 198, 258, 347*n*53
etrog, 92, 323–24
"Eugene," 85, 249–50, 256, 258
Evangelicals: 328*n*1, 332*n*45; Bible study of, 48–50; Catholics vs., 7, 296
"Event, Ethnography, History" (course), 347*n*53
evil, banality of, 40
evolution, 34, 38, 182, 190, 347*n*49
Exodus, 27
"Ezra," 302, 307, 316

Facilities Chaplaincy Program Director (FCPD), *see* "Baumgartner, Reverend"
Facing the Extreme (Todorov), 257–58
faith, 25, 33, 80, 104, 185, 232, 249, 259, 291; *see also* sincerity
Falwell, Jerry, 332*n*45
farming, 26, 164, 190
Farrakhan, Louis, 159, 167, 168
fasting, 104, 149, 166, 169, 210
Father Divine Peace Mission Movement, 209
fatherlessness, 88, 178
Fauset, Arthur Huff, 209
FBI, 230
FCPD (Facilities Chaplaincy Program Director) *see* "Baumgartner, Reverend"
feasts, 196–97, 211–12; *see also specific holidays*
Feuerbach, Ludwig, 278–79, 353*n*20
Final Call, 159
Fiqh, 152
First Amendment, 24–27; religion encouraged by, 164, 228, 257, 269–70, 331*n*33; limiting of, 24, 26, 189, 197, 228, 346*n*48; *see also* accommodations, religious
First Letter of John, 185
fitra, 66, 166

Five Percent Nation of Islam, 26, 331*n*33
Five Pillars of Islam, 223
FOI, *see* Fruit of Islam
food, 15, 26, 60, 81, 104, 169, 186, 244, 273; religion and, 29, 149, 152, 166, 196–97
football, 15
Forster, E. M., 250
fossils, 190
Foucault, Michel, 268, 290
Fowler, Clarence, 165
foxes, 158, 239, 344*n*3
Frackville, Pennsylvania, 286
Franciscans, 286–89, 306, 356*n*54
freedom, spiritual, 105, 184, 220, 258, 289, 310, 330*n*25, 354*n*26; vs. material, 56, 281
free-exercise claims, *see* First Amendment
freethinking, 59
Freire, Paulo, 290
Freud, Sigmund, 132, 139, 347*n*53
"Freud, Nietzsche, Dostoevsky" (course), 347*n*53, 356*n*1
Fruit of Islam (FOI), 77, 104, 159, 160, 165
fundamentalism, 33–36, 332*n*45; appeal of, 33–34, 44, 120–21; *see also* "Education for Ministry"; Salafism
Fundamentals, The (religious tracts), 34
furloughs, 164

"Gabril" ("Sugar"), 62–64, 163, 167
"Galleo, Father," 165–66
"game, the," 213, 339*n*58
gangs: culture of, 119, 159, 183, 205, 233; in prison, 125, 221–22; religions purported to be, 31, 70, 165, 167, 233, 331*n*33, 332*n*40
"Gary," 314, 318
gay rights, 51
GED program, 152
genealogy, 353*n*12
"general economy" theory (Bataille), 131–32
generalization, 253–56
"Georgina, Sister," 188

Germantown (Philadelphia neighborhood), 153
"Gibson, Lucas Sparrowhawk Flying," 188–89, 194, 196
gift exchange, 18–19, 189
Gilligan, Carol, 290
"God Will Make a Way" (Moen), 317, 356n4
Goldstein, Baruch, 251
Goodfellas (movie), 197
"Gorski, Father," xix, 6, 291–98, 303–307; activities of, 172, 278, 286, 356n54; background of, 50, 158, 176–77; chaplains and, 60–62, 79–80, 123–26, 176, 282–83; on Sayyid, 123–26
Gospel bands, 199–202
Gospel Messengers, xvii, 314–16, 317
"Gram," 190–91, 192, 195–98
Graterford Prison: codes of conduct in, 126–27; demographics of, xiii–xiv, 9, 48, 54, 68, 269, 327n3; design of, 3–4, 68, 338n37; era of carceral control in, 72–73, 74, 196, 310–11, 338n49; era of penological progressivism in, 163–64, 196–97; location of, 3; map of, xv; officials of, 123, 237, 241, 293, 301; particularity of, 253–56; raid at, see "raid, the"
Graterford Prison chapel: description of, 10–11; Fridays in, 205–65; location of, 4, 189; Mondays in, 3–41; pluralism of, 9, 23–27, 70–72, 78–79, 164, 188, 216–17, 230–31, 234; porousness of, 123–24; rules of, 48, 69, 90, 338n40; Saturdays in, 267–308; schedule of, xvi–xvii; Sundays in, 309–326; Thursdays in, 157–203; Tuesdays in, 43–95; use of, xiv; Wednesdays in, 97–156; workers in, xix, 5, 11, 24; see also chaplains; specific people and denominations
Graterfriends (newsletter), 78
gratitude, 281–82; of Christians, 93–94, 112, 186, 242, 262, 281, 299, 314; of Muslims, 150–51; of Native Americans, 195
"grays" (prison grouping), 3
Great Awakenings, 22, 34, 269

Great Migration, 208, 209, 269
Great Mystery, 192, 193–94
Green Corn Feast, 196
Grizzly Man (movie), 239

Habashi Muslims, 343n40
hadith, 35, 44, 166, 223, 225, 227, 232, 349n17; specific, 70, 224, 225, 231–32, 240, 350n36
hair exemptions, 193, 196, 347n52
Halalco, 153
halfway houses, 16, 53, 180–81
Ham (biblical figure), 162
Hamas, 241, 250–51
"Hamed," 13, 125
Hanafi Muslims, 161
Hanbali School of Law, 332n46
"Happy Birthday," 318
Happy Days (television show), 321
"Hawk, Bobby," 189, 190, 191
Hebrew language, 91, 248, 261, 277, 286
Hebrews, 185–86
hedgehogs, 239, 344n3
Hegel, Georg Wilhelm Friedrich, 31
hegemony, 89–90; see also ideology
Heller, Joseph, 290
Herzog, Werner, 239
Highway News (religious tract), 346n33
Hillel, 264
hippies, 193
HIV, 39, 143
"hole, the", 54, 196, 282; self-mastery in, 134, 169, 270–71; as protection, 12–13, 52, 307; visitors to, 79, 177–78, 291–93; wives and, 88, 245; see also "Sayyid": detention of
Holiness Christianity, 209
Holmesburg Prison, 159–61, 162–63, 165–66, 230, 344n4
Holy Koran, The (Ali), 207, 208, 210, 212–14; see also Qur'an
Holy Name Society, 197
Homo religiosus (Eliade), 261
homosexuality, 51, 88, 200, 206
honor, 36–37
Hopkins, Bernard, 62
Horn, Martin, 69, 169

hospice program, 91, 104, 113, 281
humanists, 121, 130, 258, 263
hymns *see* music: religious

IAC, *see* ineffective assistance of counsel
I Block, 199–200, 297
ideology, 268–69, 271, 279, 280, 339*n*62, 353*n*12, 353*n*20
idolatry, 161, 227, 228
iftar, 166
illiteracy, 246, 272, 276
"Imam, the (Namir)," xix, 71–72; activities of, 8, 37, 51, 147, 177–78, 206, 235; background of, 60, 62, 71, 178; chaplains and, 60–62, 124–26; *khutbah* of, 178, 231–33, 235–38, 244, 350*n*36–37; Muslim concerns about, 67, 71–72, 207, 223; on recidivism, 240–41; on Sayyid, 124–26, 143, 177
immigration, 209
incarceration rates, 19, 68, 269, 270, 330*n*22, 352*n*11, 377*n*4
incrementalism, 169
Indians, xvii, 9, 65, 188–98
individualism, religious, 22, 43–44, 334*n*1
ineffective assistance of counsel (IAC), 20, 29, 249–50, 338*n*52; *see also* Collins ruling
"Inmate Throne for a Loss" (article in *Philadelphia Daily News*), 70
InnerChange Freedom Initiative, 335*n*12
innocence, 294–96, 355*n*48; presumption of, 220
Inside-Out program, 91, 146, 290–91
Institute for Advanced Study, 59
institutional reproduction, 146, 268–69, 271, 290
intelligent design, *see* evolution
interfaith dialogue group, xvi, 188
interlocutors, 8, 328*n*7
interpretation, 57, 111–12, 121–22, 155, 326
"In the Sanctuary" (Carr), 313
irony, 148
Isaiah, xiii, 182, 316, 331*n*28
Islam *see* Muslims

Islamic Center, 166
Israel, 64, 78, 241, 250–51, 277, 336*n*27, 353*n*18

"Jabaar, Ameen," 68, 69–70, 71, 151
"Jack," xix, 6–8; activities of, 304, 305, 312; philosophy of, 48, 50–51, 172, 302
Jacob (biblical figure), 162, 241
jahaliyya, 178, 235–36
"jailhouse Muslims," 230, 246, 332*n*40, 340*n*9, 349*n*28; reappropriation of, 170; *see also* Muslims
"jailhouse religion," *see* prisoners, religious: public response to
Jakes, T. D., 65
"Jamar," 233
James, William, 9, 261, 270
"Jay," 180–86, 244
J Block, 79, 292–93, 339*n*56, 356*n*1
"Jeff," 302, 305
"Jefferson," 15, 207, 211–15, 216; Baumgartner and, 189, 218–19
Jehovah's Witnesses, xvii, 9, 47–48, 56–58, 212
Jesus, 39, 58, 95, 114; differing beliefs about, xii, 21, 25, 34, 98–99, 121, 130, 187, 274–75, 296; direct relationship with, 92, 98–99, 104, 184; miracles of, 318–23; Moorish Science Temple on, 207, 208; representations of, 20–21
Jews, 9; alcohol and, 55–56; beliefs of, 102, 192, 260–62; biblical, 60–61, 248; blacks and, 60–61, 78–79, 86–87, 209, 246–47, 248, 339*n*58; as chapel workers, xix; Christians and, 79, 95, 202–203, 217–18, 275–77, 299–301, 323–24; ethics and, 91, 300; gatherings of, xvi, 90–92, 249–65, 277; humor of, 176–77, 217; identities of, 259; interpretation and, 57, 111–12; observances of, 29, 78–79, 197, 248, 261–62, 351*n*47; politics and, 250–52, 277; prejudices against, 79, 95, 142–43, 170, 247; reading and, 256
"Jihad," 159, 171
Jihadists, 229–30

"John," 49–50, 313–14
John, Saint, 182, 185, 324
Johnson, Robert, 163
John the Baptist, 319–20
"José," 93, 203
Julius, Doctor, 293
Jum'ah, xvi, 230–33, 235–38; attendance
at, 48, 67–68, 74; other activities
during, 23, 241; preparations for, 124,
152, 166, 215, 217–18, 222–23
"jumpsuits" (new prison inmates), 4
jury selection, 338n52
juvenile lifers, 45, 62, 234, 334n6

Kabbalat Shabbat, 249–65
"Kaduna, Namir," see "Imam, the"
Kapliwatsky, Jochanan, 153–55
"Karl," 225, 226–28, 349n22
"Katie," 146
"Kazi," xix, 12–13, 119–20; activities of,
37, 51, 124, 138–39, 177, 202, 206, 301,
302, 311; background of, 233–34, 295;
conversations with, 244, 298
Keepers of the Faith (prison band), xvii,
170, 188, 199–202
"Keita, Chaplain," xix; activities of, 51,
179, 249, 264–65, 293; on Al, 99;
background of, 40, 60–62, 126, 127,
142; on Brian, 32; on certitude, 112;
chaplains and, 60–62, 79–80, 123–26,
241; NOI and, 176; on rape, 39–41; on
Sayyid, 123–26, 241
Kennedy, Ted, 51
Khaalis, Hamaas Abdul, 161
"Khalifa," 82, 88, 233, 237, 313;
conversations with, 82–90, 242,
244–47, 258
khutbah, 178, 231–33, 235–37
Kierkegaard, Søren, 111, 291
King, Martin Luther, Jr., 290
"Kipling, Richard," 106–121 passim
Knuckles v. Prasse, 164
kufis, 162, 222, 224; legality of, 152, 255

Laban (biblical figure), 162
labor, 11, 13, 235; agricultural, 19, 26, 164

LACEO (Latino Prisoners' Association),
338n54
Lakota Indians, 192, 193–94
Landmark Education, 335n13
language, 248
language barriers, 173–75
"Lap," 284–85, 304
Last Lap, The (Roth), 203
Lateef, Yusef, 162
Latinos, 54, 292, 327n3, 338n54; see also
Puerto Ricans; Spanish language
lawyers, 20, 29, 144, 172–73, 184,
249–50, 338n52, 339n58
L Block, 74, 79, 291–94, 356n1
leadership, 109–10, 113–16
legal remedies, 29, 75, 249–50, 338n52;
Collins ruling and, 10, 28–30, 51–52,
249–50; faith vs., 80
Legion of Mary, xvii, 283–85
Lenape Indians, 189
"Lenny," see "Berkowitz, Lenny"
Lewisburg penitentiary, 189
liberalism, 120–21; political, 78, 263,
279; theological, 25, 34, 78, 228
Liberty Ministries, xvii, 179–87, 199, 244
LIFERS association, 152, 335n11,
338n54
life without parole, xiv, 16, 239–40, 296,
327n4, 329n11, 329–30n17, 356n1;
death and, 127–28; for juveniles, 45,
62, 234, 334n6; legislation
challenging, 292; OSU and, 69;
out-of-state, 65
"Lily," 19–20, 144, 242, 246, 317
Limbaugh, Rush, 91
Lincoln, C. Eric, 168
literalism, 98–99
liturgy, meaning of, 117
"lived religion," 329n10
Lukes, Anthony, 297, 306–307
Lumbees, 188
Lutheran, The (magazine), 187
Lynn, William, 355n45

ma'amin, 261
"Madison, Marcus," 47
"Maggie," 308

"Magical Negro," 239
mail, 164
Maimonides, Moses, 339n55
Malcolm X, 49, 72, 161, 168, 170, 230, 349n27
"Malik," 171–72
"Mamduh," xix; activities of, 4–5, 66–67, 74, 146, 217–18, 240, 349n23; on Imam, 67, 71, 207; philosophy of, 53, 223–24, 226, 227, 246
marriage, 15, 61–62, 88, 154, 235, 245
"Martha," 60
Marx, Karl, 279, 353n20–21
Mary (mother of Jesus), 8, 283–85, 303
masculinity, 263
Masjid An-Nabawiyyah, 153
Masjid Sajdah, 67–74, 84, 151–53, 165–67, 96–97, 223, 227, 233, 342n37; see also Ahmadi Muslims; Salafism
Masjid Taubah, 343n40
Masjid Warith Deen Muhammad, see Muhammad, Warith Deen, brand of Islam of
"Mason," 167–71
masquerade, 133, 138
"Matthew," 93
"matrix, the," 14
Mauss, Marcel, 18
maximum security prisons, 127
McFadden, Reginald, 302–303
Mecca, 72, 223, 237; Moorish Science Temple members and, 208
media, 70, 72, 191–92, 272
medical experimentation, 344n4
memorial services, xvi, 127–28
Mennonites, 180
mental health, 263; biases of, 99, 132; confinement and, 107, 128, 139–40, 269, 352n8, 336n18; meds and, 54–55, 206; parole and, 135; see also contentment; developmental delays; self-mastery
metalheads, 193
"Michael," 283, 285; activities of, 93, 285, 297, 306, 307
Mighty Way, xvii, 247, 312–14, 316–17
"Mike" see "Callahan, Mike"
"Mike, Young," 93

"Mikhael," 231
militarism, 250–52, 280
"ministry of presence," 292–93
miracles, 44, 102–103, 108, 318–23
"missing Muslims," 208–209
mitzvot, 78, 300, 339n55
Moab (biblical tribe), 208, 213
modernity, challenges of, 157–58
"Mohammed," 125, 154–55
Mohammed, Prophet, see Muhammad, Prophet
Mohammedanism, 259, 260
money, in prison, 11, 15, 235
monotheism, 259–61
Moorish Science Temple, xvi, 9, 15, 206–20, 215–220, 226, 259, 337n30; history of, 207–209; oil and, 125–26, 219–20; services of, 206–207, 209–214
"Moose," 113
morality, 40
Mormon Church, 43
Moses (biblical figure), 122
"Mota," 274–77
MOVE, 26
"Mubdi," 146–48; background of, 163, 164–65; class taught by, 52, 146–47, 153–55; philosophy of, 225, 226, 227
Muhammad, Elijah, 43, 161, 169, 171, 196, 209; adulation of, 150, 161, 168, 226; background of, 208, 259; "Jabbar" and, 151; successors of, 36, 148, 167; writings of, 164, 168, 345n25
Muhammad, Prophet, 35, 62–63, 70, 72, 223, 232, 235, 237; Moorish Science Temple on, 208; see also hadith
Muhammad, Wallace Deen, see Muhammad, Warith Deen
Muhammad, Wallace Fard, 148, 161, 168, 172, 209
Muhammad, Warith Deen, 36, 148–50, 225, 226, 349n21
Muhammad, Warith Deen, brand of Islam of, 36, 72, 74, 167, 306; oil and, 124–26; history of, 67–74, 146–53, 255; NOI vs., 169, 215, 226–29; Salafis vs., 33–37, 73–74, 223–30, 233–34; at Jum'ah, 231–32
Muhammad Speaks (newspaper), 164, 226

Muhammad's Temple, xvi, 9, 167, 168, 169–70
Mujaddid, 165, 225
multiculturalism, *see* pluralism
Mural Arts Program, 91
"Musa," 255
music, 170, 194, 347*n*54; Islam and, 224, 225, 348*n*15; religious, xvi, xvii, 52, 54–55, 181–82, 199–202, 247, 248–49, 282–83, 302–306 *passim*, 311–318 *passim*, 356*n*4
Music Behind Bars (television program), 347*n*54
Muslim American Society, 227, 349*n*22
Muslim Brotherhood, 225
Muslim Journal, 226, 227
Muslims, 52, 72, 146–55, 222–41, 263; bias against, 31, 165, 229–30, 252, 332*n*40, 349*n*28; as chapel workers, xix; Christians and, xi, 23–24, 79, 84, 149, 162, 163, 169, 199, 345*n*25; foreign, 71–72, 153, 207, 208–209, 225; Friday service of, xvi, 222–23, 230–33, 235–38; heyday of, 67–68, 148–53, 165, 255, 343*n*40; hierarchy among, 30, 171; history of, 67–74, 146–53, 159–67, 207–209, 223; numbers of, 9, 67, 159, 165, 167, 327*n*3, 337*n*30; observances of, 12, 66–67, 149, 162, 178, 223–25, 348*n*15, 349*n*17; oil and, 124–26, 219–20, 221, 222; politics and, xi–xii, 72; raid on, 67–74; terrorism and, 223, 229–30, 349*n*28; *see also* Moorish Science Temple; Nation of Islam; Salafism; Sunni Islam; Muhammad, Warith Deen, brand of Islam of
"Muti," xix, 206, 217–18, 222
mystics, 267

NAACP, 73, 118, 152, 338*n*54
Nagi, 193
naming, 162, 178, 208, 211, 213
"Namir," *see* "Imam, the"
Nas, 85
"Nashawn," 170
"Nasir," 4, 73

National Origins Act, 209
National Review, 6
Nation of Islam (NOI), xvi, 9, 15, 33, 36, 43, 134, 159–72, 259, 337*n*30, 353*n*23; accommodations won by, 124, 164–65, 196, 270, 285; conservatism of, 169; corruption of, 165, 166–67, 234; history of, 146–53, 159–67, 208, 209, 215–16, 226–29, 342*n*35; mass conversion of, 148–49; paramilitary order of, 7; services of, 167–72, 207; *see also* Muhammad, Warith Deen, brand of Islam of
Native Americans, xvii, 9, 65, 188–198, 262; diversity of, 193, 195
nature/nurture, 134
Nazirites, 193, 347*n*52
Nazis, 193
neighborhoods, 82–85, 232–34, 235; *see also* gangs
"Neil," 47
New Jersey, 78, 90, 183; crimes in, 303; DOC of, 341*n*19; Islam in, 153, 208
New Testament, origins of, xii–xiii; *see also* Bible
New York Times, 62, 191–92
Ni, 193
Nietzsche, Friedrich, 106, 290, 347*n*53, 356*n*1
Nigeria, 60, 62, 71, 178
"Ninety-nine and a Half Won't Do" (Pickett/Cropper/Floyd), 315
Nixon, Richard, 277
NOI, *see* Nation of Islam
North Philadelphia, 4, 93, 100, 163, 225, 233
"Now Is the Time for Decisive Action" (*Watchtower* article) 56

Odinists, 26
oil, 221, 222; as contraband, 124–26, 219–20
"Omar," xix, 50; activism of, 15–16, 32; clemency hearing of, 16, 329–30*n*17; conversations with, 4, 92–93, 226
oppression, internalized, 162, 341*n*25
optimism, 185

Oregon v. Smith, 346n48
orientalism, 154–55, 209
Orthodox Muslims, 161, 162–63,
  165–66, 345n17; *see also* Masjid
  Sajdah
"Oscar," 45, 105; activities of, 49, 52–53,
  283, 313–16
Otto, Rudolph, 286
Outside Service Unit (OSU), 3, 69
Oz (television show), 332n40

pacifism, 145–46
Padilla, José, 349n28
Palestinians, 78, 241, 250–51
panopticon (Bentham), 268, 341n25
"Papa," xix, 17; activities of, 27, 50, 81,
  277; conversations with, 82, 145, 215–17
PAR (People Against Recidivism), 15–16,
  230
"paranoid reading," 339n63
pardons, *see* Board of Pardons;
  commutation
parole: juveniles and, 334–35n6;
  preparation for, 16, 39, 52–54, 135,
  240, 352, 335n12; violation of, 48, 95,
  186, 235–36; *see also* Board of
  Pardons; life without parole;
  recidivism
Passage to India, A (Forster), 250
Passover, 55, 90, 197
"Path of Penance, A" ("Peter"), 286–89
patriotism, 227–28, 251–52
Paul (apostle), 39, 49, 114, 121, 248, 260,
  288, 289; on contentment, 105, 262,
  296; on daily death, 46, 210
"Peanut," 231, 232
penance, 286–89
penitentiary, as concept, 268–69, 273
Pennsylvania: death penalty in, 16, 292,
  339n58; life without parole in, xiv, 16,
  327n4, 329n11, 334–35n6; number of
  prisoners in, 68, 337n36
Pennsylvania Prison Society, 16, 78,
  174–75, 268–69, 346n33, 351n4
Pentecostalism, 34, 92–95, 209
People Against Recidivism (PAR), 15–16,
  230

personal responsibility, *see* self-mastery
Peter (apostle), 318–22
"Peter," 286–89, 291, 295; activities of,
  91, 282, 304, 305, 306
pharmaceutical research, 344n4
Philadelphia: Archdiocese in, 293,
  355n45; Black Mafia in, 76, 160–61,
  234; Catholics in, 293, 355n45;
  demographics of, 159, 344n5, 355n46;
  gangs in, 89, 159, 161, 205, 240;
  Graterford and, 3, 15, 91, 254; history
  of, 268, 351n4, 352n8; new religions
  in, 148, 159–63, 209, 343n40, 345n17;
  North, 4, 93, 100, 163, 225, 233;
  northwest, 153; Pittsburgh and, 47,
  85, 282; politics in, 51, 302, 338n52,
  345n26; prison in, 159–61, 162–63,
  165–66, 230, 344n4; slang from,
  197, 244; South, xiii, 12, 47, 52,
  82–85, 137, 233–34; West, 20, 26,
  100, 149, 162, 163, 225, 233,
  343n40
Philadelphia County Jail, 202
Philadelphia Daily News, 16, 51, 70,
  283
Philadelphia Inquirer, 68
Philadelphia Society for Alleviating the
  Miseries of Public Prisons, 268–69,
  351n4
Philadelphia Tribune, 234
phones, 15, 61, 68, 235, 244, 336n24
Pickett, Wilson, 315
Pink Floyd, 290
pipe rituals, 188–89
Pittsburgh, 47, 85, 167, 177, 282
plea bargaining, 184, 234, 294, 303,
  355n48
pledges of allegiance, 214–15
pluralism: African, 142; American, 9, 97;
  at Graterford, 9, 23–27, 70–72, 78–79,
  164, 188, 216–17, 230–31, 234, 252–53,
  300–301; limits of, 23–27, 31–32, 70,
  120–21, 216–17, 253, 260, 323–24; of
  Moorish Science Temple, 208, 212,
  216;
Poetics (Aristotle), 132
policing, 159–60; *see also* crime
political prisoners, 294, 355n46

politics, *see* black nationalism; conservatism; crime; liberalism; prison industrial complex

Poole, Elijah, *see* Muhammad, Elijah

"poor man of religion," 107–108, 240, 279–81, 289, 353*n*21

Popper, Karl, 290

positive thinking, 209–210

"practice," 351*n*1

pragmatism, 30–37, 65, 74, 164–65, 169, 193, 196–97, 211, 216, 225–29, 256–57, 258–64, 310, 340*n*9; philosophical, 340*n*11

Princeton University, 12, 14, 59, 87, 90, 111, 256, 341*n*19

Prison Community, The (Clemmer), 254

prisoners: activities of, 65, 147–48, 242, 272, 356*n*1; connections between, 82–85, 103, 179, 205, 233–34, 271–73, 312–13; conceptualization of, 31, 61, 89, 119, 191–92, 220, 252, 254, 255–56, 268–69, 288–89, 295, 309–11, 352*n*8, 355*n*48; fascination with, 298

prisoners, religious: motivations of, 65, 256–59, 262–63, 270–73, 309–11, 356*n*1; public response to, xiv, 30–33, 70, 107–108, 220, 229–30, 239–40, 332*n*40, 340*n*9, 349*n*28

prisoners' rights movement, 73, 164, 174–75, 257, 270, 291; Native Americans and, 188–98; *see also* religious accommodations

Prison Fellowship, 335*n*12

prison industrial complex, 68–69, 174, 256, 269, 270, 271, 281, 310–11, 337*n*36

"prisonization," 254

prisons: construction of, 68, 268–69, 337*n*36; early, 268–69, 351*n*4, 352*n*8; labor in, 11; medical research in, 344*n*4; order in, 221; politics of, *see* prison industrial complex

prohibitions: biblical, 248; Islamic, 38, 178, 224–25, 348*n*15

"Prophet" ("Christopher"), 95, 202, 206; activities of, 180, 181, 183, 199–201

Prophet Muhammad, *see* Muhammad, Prophet

proselytizing, 57–58, 113

prosperity gospellers, 92, 183

prostitutes, 68

Protestants: Bible translation used by, 327*n*2; Catholics vs., 7, 296; as chapel workers, xix; as definers of religion, 25, 253, 260; holidays of, 197; liberal, 25, 34, 228; number of, 9, 44, 327*n*3, 328*n*1; Sunday services of, *see* Sunday services; *see also* Bible; Episcopalians; Evangelicals; fundamentalism

pseudoscientism, 168

psychology, *see* mental health

psychopharmacology, 54–55, 73, 141, 206, 283

Puerto Ricans: 202–203, 349*n*28; as Native Americans, 193, 194

punishment, history of, 268–69; transformation vs., 288

Purim, 55

PV, *see* parole: violation of

"Qasim," 84, 144, 152, 298; background of, 234–35; and "the Imam," 223, 232–33, 235; philosophy of, 166–67, 224, 225, 227, 348*n*15

Quakers, 268–69

Qur'an, 223, 224; banning of, 164; on belief, 38; on imams, 70; on spying, 178

Rabah, Bilal ibn, 149

"Rabbi, the," xix, 78–79, 102; activities of, 90–92, 250, 251, 277, 278, 286; office of, 28–29; on Sayyid, 79, 80–81

RAC, *see* Religious Accommodation Committee

"Rafael," 93, 202–203, 273–77

"Rafiq," 76–77

Rahway Prison, 341*n*19

"raid, the," 69–70; context for, 67–69, 302–303; repercussions of, 66–67, 70–74, 84, 90, 123–24, 189, 197, 247–48, 256, 270, 291, 302–303, 338*n*54, 343*n*40

"Ralph," 317

Ramadan, 10; factionalism and, 211–12, 224; fasting for, 149, 223, 237; food during 152, 166, 167, 177
"Ramirez," 79
Rancière, Jacques, 353n21
rape, 39–41, 88, 243, 245, 285, 297, 307, 333n55
Rastafarians, 26, 193, 247, 249
reality, nature of, 13–14, 329n12
rearrest, rate of, 329n17; see also recidivism
rebirth, see transformation
recidivism, 53, 240–41, 303, 306; in PA, 329n16; see also PAR
reconciliation, 39
reentry, see parole: preparation for
Reformation, 98, 260
"Reggie," 317
rehabilitation, 91; punishment vs., 68, 163–64, 257, 268–69, 311; transformation vs., 49, 335n11
religion: as concept, 14–15, 187, 258–64, 267–68; different approaches to, xi–xiii, 102, 169–70, 278–81; legal definition of, 24–26, 228, 331n35; revision of, 225–26; as scapegoat, 280, 354n24; as social control, 14–15, 141, 162, 169, 221, 280, 345n25, 353n23; support for, 270; see also prisoners, religious
"Religion in the Tradition of Social Theory" (course), 347n53
Religious Accommodation Committee (RAC), 25–27, 188, 211–12, 332n37; see also accommodations, religious
Religious Activities Handbook, 152, 338n40
religious diversity, see pluralism
Religious Freedom Restoration Act (RFRA, 1993), 70–71, 189, 197, 346n48
religious groups, xvi–xvii, 9; see also specific groups and denominations
Rendell, Ed, 142
Reno, Janet, 51
resentment, 205–206, 281–82
restorative justice, 286–89
Restricted Housing Unit (RHU), 13, 291–93; see also "hole, the"
revenge, 235–36

revolutionaries, 162; fear of, 72, 230; obsolescence of, 169, 311
RFRA, see Religious Freedom Restoration Act
RHU, see Restricted Housing Unit
"Rico," 194–98, 347n53
Ridge, Tom, 16, 69, 85, 169, 302–303
Rikers Island, 256
riots, 345n27
"Rita," 202, 274
ritual vs. belief, 260–65
Rizzo, Frank, 159, 163
Roman Catholic Church, see Catholics
rosaries, xvii, 283–85, 306
"Rudy," 247–48, 317–18
"Rzonka, Father," 297

"Sabir," 230–31, 232
Sa'di, 52, 336n15
Sadiq, Muhammad al, 162, 345n17
sage, burning of, in Native rites, 188, 189, 190–91, 195–96, 198
Saffat, 162–63
Sahih al-Bukhari, 232, 349n17, 350n36
Sahih Muslim, 232, 349n17
St. Dismas Episcopal services, xvii, 44–47, 54–55, 98, 247, 318; volunteers for, 220, 294
St. Gabe's school, see Saint Gabriel's Hall
Saint Gabriel's Hall, 292
Sajdah, see Masjid Sajdah
"Sal," 56–58
Salafism, 12, 32–37, 38, 63, 73–74, 146–47, 215, 259; history of, 34–35, 44, 332n46; non-Muslims and, 232; Warith Deen Muhammad vs., 33–37, 73–74, 223–230, 233–34; see also Masjid Sajdah
Salat al-Jum'ah, see Jum'ah
Sampson, 193
"Santana," xix, 52; activities of, 66, 93, 172, 206, 277, 306; music of, 52, 248–49, 314–17, 323–24; philosophy of, 52–54, 73, 105, 303
Santería, 193, 207
Satanists, 26
Saudi Arabia, 153

Saul (biblical figure), 175
Saviour's Day, 148, 196, 342n34
"Sayyid" ("Crocket"), xix, 12–13;
    activities of, 27, 37–39, 51–52, 124–26,
    154, 244, 336n15; background of, 234,
    295; conversations with, 19, 129,
    333n52; detention of, xi, 63–64, 77,
    80–81, 95, 123–26, 143, 177, 291, 312;
    speculation about; 74–75, 79, 84, 220,
    241, 293, 298
Schilk, Tom, 341–42n25
Science and Health (Eddy), 7
SCI Graterford, *see* Graterford Prison
Scripture, 261; certitude about, 57, 97–122,
    224; commentary vs., 35, 225; direct
    relationship with God vs., xi–xiii, 21–23,
    34, 43–44, 168, 274–77, 286, 334n1
Second Great Awakening, 22
secrets, 194, 341n15
Secular Franciscans, 286–89, 306, 356n54
secularism, 25, 35, 38, 157, 263, 264; as
    prejudicial, 106–107, 280–81; *see also*
    atheism
Sedgwick, Eve Kosofsky, 339n63
self-defense, 234
selfhood, 133–139, 341n25
self-mastery, 9, 33, 36–37, 134, 168, 169,
    178, 263, 273, 288, 311, 328n8; God's
    will vs., 186–87; Moorish Science
    Temple members and, 209–211,
    213–14; self-sacrifice and, 46
Seneca, 290
Seventh-Day Adventists, xvi, 9, 283
sex, 39, 68, 88, 245, 301–302, 304–305
sexual abuse: 39–41, 243, 285, 297, 307,
    333n55; in childhood, 135, 139–41,
    206, 245; by priests, 293, 355n45
shabbos, 249–65
Shahadah, 147, 163, 236
"Shah, Abdullah," 76, 149, 225
Sharon, Ariel, 241
Sheen, Bishop Fulton, 305
"Sheik, the," 214–15, 218
Shema, 94
"Shepherd," 292
Shiites, 343
Sicun, 193
Sierra Leone, 40, 60–62, 126, 142

Simon, Robert "Mudman," 302–303,
    356n52
"Simpson, Captain," 123–26, 220, 221–22
sin, 279; Christians on, 192, 268, 276, 279,
    288, 289, 305, 316; Moorish Science
    Temple on, 211; Muslims on, 161
sincerity, 30–37, 65, 165–66, 193, 246,
    257, 340n9; certitude and, 97–122,
    340n1; confidence and 43–44; conduct
    and, 32, 50, 77, 116–18, 121, 171, 184,
    224, 232, 249, 274–77, 348n15; in
    "game," 258; presumed centrality of,
    260–64; proof and, 318–23
skepticism, 111–12, 114, 318–23
skinheads, 304
Skippack, Pennsylvania, 180
slavery, 107, 129, 170; Christianity and,
    162, 165, 280, 353n23; legacy of, 148,
    169, 207–208, 213, 215–16, 226, 259;
    naming and, 162, 209, 213
Smart, Ninian, 37
"Smedley," 199
Smith, Joseph, 43
smudging ritual, 188, 189, 190–91,
    195–96, 198
snitching, 294, 303, 355n48; in prison,
    40, 73; *see also* "dry snitching"
Social Gospel, 34
Society of Captives, The (Sykes), 254
solitude, 268–69, 270, 352n8; *see also*
    "hole, the"
Somalia, 334n6
South Africa, 287
South Philadelphia, xiii, 12, 47, 52,
    82–85, 137, 233–34
Sovereign Citizen movement, 346n31
Spanish language: Bible study in, xvi, 7;
    chaplain for speakers of, 79; services
    in, xvi, 48, 188, 198, 202–203, 221–22,
    273–77, 313
Special Needs Unit, 283
Specter, Arlen, 278
State fetishism (Taussig), 339n62
"Steinberg sisters," 248, 250, 252, 256,
    258, 265
"Steve," 181–84
Stewart, John, 340n9
Stop-the-Violence, 152

Stout, Jeffrey, 239*n*10
Street, John, 345*n*26
street culture, 85, 163
strikes, 73
Sufis, 343*n*40
suhoor, 166
suicide, 40, 242, 294; thoughts of, 90,
103, 104
Sukkoth, 92
sunan al-fitra, 66–67
Sunday services, xvi, 48, 273, 311–25;
altar call at, 128, 323–24; music for,
xvi–xvii, 52, 170, 199–202, 247, 249,
312–18, 323–24, 356*n*4; Usher Board
of, xvii, 104, 198, 224, 312, 317, 321
Sunnah, 152
Sunni Islam, 35, 163, 196–97, 207; black
nationalist Islam vs., xi–xii, 10,
147–49, 166, 169, 211–12, 215, 229,
230; distinctions within, 15, 151–53,
231, 342–43*n*37; texts of, 35, 166,
349*n*17; *see also* Jum'ah; Salafism
Supreme Court, 25, 228, 302, 331*n*31; on
juvenile lifers, 334–35*n*6; *see also* First
Amendment
surrender, 45–46, 105, 128, 157
surveillance, 68, 75, 268, 338*n*37
"Swan, Mac," 125–26, 199
sweetgrass, burning of, in Native rites,
190, 195
sweat lodges, 189, 191–92
Sykes, Gresham, 254
"system, the" 89–90, 339*n*62; religion
and, 220, 311

Taino Indians, 193
"Take It to Jesus" (Mann), 315
Talim, xvi, 66–67, 74
tattoos, 144, 179, 221–22, 292, 304
Taussig, Michael, 339*n*62
tawfiq, 166
tea, 18–19, 244–45
"Teddy," xi–xiv, xix, 11; activities of, 51,
77, 99, 123, 139–40, 172–73, 185–86,
195, 206, 238, 242–47, 311, 315, 316;
background of, xiii, 19–20, 88, 120,
233–34, 245, 295, 296, 312–13; on

death, 59–60, 64, 128; marriage of,
15, 242, 246, 317; philosophy of, vii,
21–23, 80–81, 83–89, 102, 107, 112,
129, 130, 258, 314, 317; relationship
with author of, 18–19, 74–75, 86–87,
127, 144–45, 253, 299
tefillin, 261–62, 351*n*47
television shows: about prison, 272,
332*n*40, 339*n*58, 347*n*54; in prison,
73, 147, 278
Temple One, 208, 209
Temple Twelve, 148, 151, 161, 165;
corruption in 160–61
terrorism, 223, 229–30, 349*n*28
testimony, 92, 99, 102, 103, 108, 184;
illiteracy and, 246; to parole board, 50
texts, *see* interpretation; scripture
theater, 131–33
"Think About His Love" (Moen), 316
Third Circuit Court, 25, 26, 51
Third Great Awakening, 34
tikkun olam, 91
Tillich, Paul, 25, 228, 331*n*31
"Tito," 115
tobacco, burning of, in Native rites,
190, 195
Tocqueville, Alexis de, 330*n*25
Todorov, Tzvetan, 257–58
"total institutions," 107, 340*n*9
"tragic, the," 340*n*11
transfers, 63, 69, 73, 177, 189, 196, 310,
343*n*37
transformation, 49, 97, 109, 236, 262,
268, 273, 288–89, 335*n*11–13; names
and, 178
transitional housing, 16, 53, 180–81
translation of Bible, 57, 327*n*2
transsexuals, 318
trauma, 119, 134–35
Traviata, La, 130–31
Treadwell, Timothy, 239
Trenton State, 254
"true vine," in Bible, 49, 323–24
True Vine (musical group), xvii, 283,
302
truth, 111–13, 185, 246, 258; history of,
215; multiplicity of, 114, 130, 216, 249,
263; *see also* certitude; skepticism

Truth and Reconciliation Commission (South Africa), 287
Tucker, Karla Faye, 332*n*39
Turner, Nat, 169

"ultimate concern" (Tillich), 25, 228, 331*n*31
Umar (caliph), 178, 236
Unamuno, Miguel de, 340*n*11
unconditional love, 27–28
uniforms, 70; nomenclature based on, 3–5, 48; supplementation of, 63, 68, 283
universalism, *see* pluralism
urine tests, 196
Uris, Leon, 277, 353*n*18
ushers, xvii, 104, 198, 224, 312, 317, 321

Valentine's Day, 198
Verdi, Giuseppe, 130
veterans, 52, 58, 134, 160, 194, 249, 336*n*16
"Vic," xix, 14, 18–19, 282; activities of, 125, 195, 198, 206, 301–302; philosophy of, 13–15, 58–59, 64, 89, 145–46, 277–82, 287, 290–91, 310, 329*n*12, 336*n*27
victims' families, 286–87
video ministries, xvii, 64–65
Vietnam, 134, 160, 194, 249
Villanova University, 4–5, 37–38, 58, 63, 91, 146–47, 155, 287, 312; alumni of, 75, 341*n*25; author's courses for, 194, 301, 347*n*53, 356*n*1
violence: accidental, 183; cycle of, 119, 134–35; hadith on, 240; rates of, 352*n*11; systemic, 89–90, 119, 339*n*62
violence in prison, 27, 39–41, 64, 243, 307; DOC response to, 13, 88; as religiously motivated, 27, 163, 167, 345*n*27; in youth facilities, 245
Virgin Mary, 8, 283–85, 303
visitors, 44, 68, 75, 152, 242; alerts for, 304, 316, 321; limiting of, 69, 70, 88, 146, 177, 245; from Pennsylvania Prison Society, 174–75, 346*n*31
volunteers, 164, 293, 294; in chapel, 69, 70, 123–24, 165, 166, 180,

188–89, 202, 206–207, 212, 214–15, 248, 274
Voodoo, 207

Wahabbis, 225
Wall Street Journal, 349*n*28
Walzer, Michael, 59
war, *see* Ethics of War; veterans
Warcloud, James Hunt, 188–89
warehousing, 311
Warren Commission Report, 278
Washington, Booker T., 169
WASPs, 87
Watchtower, The, 56–57
"Watkins, Officer," xix; activities of, 23–24, 109, 126, 178–79; philosophy of, 21–23, 27–28; relationship with author of, 5–6, 21
weekends, 17–18, 284, 267–326
"Wendell," 179–86 *passim*, 316
West Philadelphia, 20, 26, 100, 149, 162, 163, 225, 233, 343*n*40
"whitecaps," 123, 237, 241; *see also* "Simpson, Captain"
white flight, 159, 344*n*5
white privilege, 106–107, 242, 252
white supremacists, 287, 346*n*31
Wiccans, 26–27
"Will of God, The" (handout), 92
Wire, The (television show), 339*n*58
women: in Arabian Peninsula, 154–55; poor, in religion, 280
worship, meaning of, 116–17

Yogis, 26
Yokefellows, xvi, 92–95
Yom Kippur, 197
"You Ought to Run and Tell That" (Kelsey), 316
"Yunus," 69, 225, 298, 343*n*40; background of, 163, 165–67; as imam, 151, 152, 343*n*37

Zionism, 64, 78, 241, 250–51, 336*n*27
Zoroastrianism, 260